Emerging and Evolving Business and Management Issues in Vietnam

Research and Practice

ASIA-PACIFIC BUSINESS SERIES **(ISSN: 1793-3137)**

Series Editor
Léo-Paul Dana
Professor
ICD Business School, Paris, France & Dalhousie University, Canada

---

Published

Vol. 15 *Emerging and Evolving Business and Management Issues in Vietnam: Research and Practice*
edited by Hoai Trong Nguyen, Thanh Dinh Su, Toan Luu Duc Huynh & Angelina Nhat-Hanh Le

Vol. 14 *Women Entrepreneurs in the Middle East: Context, Ecosystems, and Future Perspectives for the Region*
edited by Dina Modestus Nziku, Léo-Paul Dana, Helene Balslev Clausen & Aidin Salamzadeh

Vol. 13 *Indian SMEs and Start-Ups: Growth through Innovation and Leadership*
edited by Léo-Paul Dana, Omvir Gautam, Ashish Gupta & Naman Sharma

Vol. 12 *Cooperatives as a Catalyst for Sustainability: Lessons Learned from Asian Models*
edited by Léo-Paul Dana, Naman Sharma, Sneha Kumari, K K Tripathy, B P Pillai & R Jayalakshmi

Vol. 11 *Organising Entrepreneurship and MSMEs Across India*
edited by Léo-Paul Dana, Naman Sharma & Satya Ranjan Acharya

Vol. 10 *Guanxi and Business (Third Edition)*
by Yadong Luo

Vol. 9 *Asian Models of Entrepreneurship: From the Indian Union and Nepal to the Japanese Archipelago: Context, Policy and Practice (Second Edition)*
by Léo-Paul Dana

Vol. 8 *Catalyst for Change: Chinese Business in Asia*
edited by Thomas Menkhoff, Hans-Dieter Evers, Chay Yue Wah & Hoon Chang Yau

Vol. 7 *From Adam Smith to Michael Porter: Evolution of Competitiveness Theory (Extended Edition)*
by Dong-Sung Cho & Hwy-Chang Moon

Vol. 6 *Islamic Banking and Finance in South-East Asia: Its Development and Future (Third Edition)*
by Angelo M. Venardos

The complete list of the published volumes in the series can also be found at
http://www.worldscientific.com/series/apbs

Asia-Pacific Business Series – Vol. 15

Emerging and Evolving Business and Management Issues in Vietnam

Research and Practice

Edited by

Hoai Trong Nguyen
Thanh Dinh Su
Toan Luu Duc Huynh
Angelina Nhat-Hanh Le

University of Economics Ho Chi Minh City, Vietnam

World Scientific

NEW JERSEY • LONDON • SINGAPORE • BEIJING • SHANGHAI • HONG KONG • TAIPEI • CHENNAI • TOKYO

Published by

World Scientific Publishing Co. Pte. Ltd.
5 Toh Tuck Link, Singapore 596224
USA office: 27 Warren Street, Suite 401-402, Hackensack, NJ 07601
UK office: 57 Shelton Street, Covent Garden, London WC2H 9HE

Library of Congress Cataloging-in-Publication Data
Names: Nguyen, Hoai Trong, editor. | Dinh Su, Thanh, editor. | Huynh, Luu Duc Toan, editor. | Nhat-Hanh Le, Angelina, editor.
Title: Emerging and evolving business and management issues in Vietnam : research and practice / edited by Hoai Trong Nguyen, University of Economics Ho Chi Minh City, Vietnam, Thanh Dinh Su, University of Economics Ho Chi Minh City, Vietnam, Toan Luu Duc Huynh, University of Economics Ho Chi Minh City, Vietnam, and Angelina Nhat-Hanh Le, University of Economics Ho Chi Minh City, Vietnam.
Description: New Jersey : World Scientific, [2024] | Series: Asia-Pacific business series, 1793-3137 ; vol. 15 | Includes bibliographical references and index.
Identifiers: LCCN 2023053647 | ISBN 9789811286094 (hardcover) | ISBN 9789811286100 (ebook) | ISBN 9789811286117 (ebook other)
Subjects: LCSH: Vietnam--Economic conditions--21st century. | Management--Vietnam.
Classification: LCC HC444 .E44 2024 | DDC 338.9597--dc23/eng/20231129
LC record available at https://lccn.loc.gov/2023053647

British Library Cataloguing-in-Publication Data
A catalogue record for this book is available from the British Library.

For any available supplementary material, please visit
https://www.worldscientific.com/worldscibooks/10.1142/13673#t=suppl

Desk Editors: Balasubramanian Shanmugam/Catherine Domingo Ong

Typeset by Stallion Press
Email: enquiries@stallionpress.com

https://doi.org/10.1142/9789811286100_fmatter

Preface

The modern world is characterized by rapid changes, technological advancements, globalization, and, above all, uncertainty. Across various disciplines, scholars and practitioners have been grappling with questions related to strategic management, digital marketing, work culture, financial information, tourism, and many more. The chapters included in this specialized book contribute to understanding these complex questions by employing empirical, theoretical, and review-based methodologies.

This specialized book consists of a carefully curated collection of papers from various authors who bring their unique perspectives, methodologies, and insights into the pressing issues of our time. From the landscape of strategic management in uncertain environments to the role of digital literacy in financial behavior, the chapters included here cover a wide range of topics that are both timely and important. They not only provide an analysis of current problems but also suggest pathways for future research.

Kicking off this collection is the paper "Strategic Management under the Context of Environmental Uncertainty" by Thanh Dinh Su, Luc Phan Tan, Thu-Hang Le, and Angelina Nhat Hanh Le. This expansive literature review dissects the complexities of strategic management under environmental uncertainty. The authors sift through 725 publications to highlight key issues and strategies, suggesting that future research should focus on developing more nuanced approaches to managing uncertainty. Their work lays a foundational understanding that is critical for navigating the volatile business landscape.

Following this, we have "Marketing and Advertising: Shifting from Conventional to Digital Marketing" by Tien Minh Dinh, Oanh Le Vu Lan, and Mai Dong Tran. This chapter provides a timely analysis of the transformation in marketing and advertising paradigms, emphasizing the shift from traditional to digital platforms. Utilizing synthetic and descriptive research methodologies, the authors explore the multi-faceted impacts of this shift, both from consumer and business angles. They argue that further studies are needed to fully comprehend the practical implications of this transformation, thereby building upon the foundational understanding laid out in Chapter 1.

Advancing the discourse on workplace dynamics, Chapter 3 "Cultural Intelligence and Job Performance of Employees in FDI Enterprises: The Mediating Role of Work Engagement" is penned by Tan Quoc Phan and Bang Nguyen-Viet. This empirical study probes into the interplay between cultural intelligence and job performance, shedding light on the mediating role of work engagement. The data for this study were gleaned from 307 employees in FDI enterprises in Ho Chi Minh City's industrial zones. The authors reveal that enhancing cultural intelligence can significantly improve work engagement and job performance. This finding adds another layer to our understanding of human resource management, particularly in the context of globalization and cultural diversity, which is an extension of the environmental uncertainties discussed in Chapter 1.

Building upon the theme of quality in decision-making, Chapter 4, "Determinants and Measurement of Financial Information Quality – An Empirical Review," authored by Mai Duc Nghia, delves deep into the nuances of financial information quality. By evaluating various empirical studies, the chapter identifies four categories of quality determinants and critiques different approaches to quality measurement. The author argues that a unified framework for measuring financial information quality is yet to be established, inviting more in-depth research in this area. This chapter complements Chapter 1 by highlighting the role of quality information in strategic management under uncertain conditions.

Next, the chapter "The Impact of Extrinsic Motivation on Prosumption: Digital Service Brands" by Minh T. H. Le and Nhi P. P. Nguyen extends the discussion into the realm of digital marketing. Utilizing self-determination theory, the authors present a model that demonstrates how extrinsic motivations, such as financial incentives and socialization, impact prosumer behaviors. This work provides a nuanced understanding of consumer motivations in the digital space, and it builds upon Chapter 2's exploration of digital marketing trends by focusing on consumer-brand relationships.

Shifting the focus to the tourism sector, the chapter "Tourism Destination Management Model in the Transitional Economy" by Vo Thi Ngoc Thuy and others offers a comprehensive model for managing tourist destinations in transitional economies. The authors meticulously examine various factors within the transitional economy that influence destination management. Their model offers valuable insights for managing tourism destinations, particularly in economies undergoing rapid changes, and extends the conversation on strategic management in uncertain environments started by Chapter 1.

Moving on to technological advances in retail, the chapter "Immersive Technologies: A Critical Success Factor for Modern Retailers" by Dong Phong Nguyen and co-authors, provides a thorough review of the role of immersive technologies like augmented reality, virtual reality, and mixed reality. The authors identify two main categories of immersive technology features and their benefits to retailers and consumers alike. This chapter broadens the scope of our understanding of technology's impact on consumer behavior and business strategies, offering an extension to both the digital marketing and environmental uncertainty themes discussed in previous chapters.

Pivoting to leadership and innovation, the chapter "The Impact of Leaders' Curiosity on the Intention to Introduce IoT-Based Products: The Case of Vietnam" by Manh Phan Dinh and Le Tran Thi Huynh explores the influence of a leader's curiosity on organizational innovation. Employing a survey-based methodology, the authors find that curious leaders are more likely to adopt Internet of Things (IoT) products. This study not only contributes to the literature on leadership and innovation but also draws connections to Chapter 1 by highlighting personal traits as another variable in managing environmental uncertainty.

Next in line is "Market Orientation of Public Organizations in a Transitional Economy" by Thi Thuy Hang Le and Toan Luu Duc Huynh. This chapter discusses the challenges and opportunities of transitioning from a planned economy to a market-oriented economy. The authors emphasize the role of government in encouraging healthy competition among businesses. This chapter complements the earlier chapter on tourism management in transitional economies by addressing the broader economic framework in which businesses operate.

Continuing the theme of technology's impact on business, the chapter "The Role of Social Investment in Information, Communication, Science, and Technology on the Productivity Growth of Enterprises in Vietnam" by Quang Hai Nguyen examines how social investment in technology affects enterprise productivity. Using panel data methods, the author finds different impacts of social investment across sectors, thereby adding nuance to the conversation initiated by papers on digital marketing and immersive technologies.

Adding a financial perspective to the collection, the chapter "Factors Affecting Retail Investors' Intentions to Use Financial Robo-Advisors in the Middle of COVID-19 in Vietnam" by Thuy Chung Phan and co-authors delves into the adoption of fintech solutions during the pandemic. Utilizing structural equation modeling, the authors identify key factors like trust and financial knowledge that influence the adoption of robo-advisors. This chapter ties back to Chapter 4 on financial information quality by discussing another dimension of how technology is shaping financial decisions.

Turning our attention to higher education, the chapter "New Managerialism in Vietnamese Higher Education: Internationalization from Vietnamese University Leaders' Perspective" by Hoai Trong Nguyen and Ba-Linh Tran explores the complexities of internationalization in Vietnamese universities. The authors provide recommendations for budget allocation and FDI attraction, contributing to the ongoing dialog about strategic management in diverse organizational settings.

Rounding off the collection is "Digital Literacy, Financial Literacy, and Financial Management Behavior: Empirical Evidence from Vietnam" by Thuy Chung Phan and co-authors. This study investigates the interplay between digital and financial literacy in financial management behavior. The findings reinforce the critical role of literacy in both the digital and financial realms, tying together themes from several of the earlier chapters, including those on digital marketing, financial information quality, and technology's impact on consumer behavior.

This specialized book is intended for scholars, students, policymakers, and practitioners interested in various facets of management, marketing, finance, and social sciences. Each chapter not only contributes to academic literature but also provides practical implications for businesses, governments, and individuals.

We are immensely grateful to all the authors for their contributions and the reviewers for their insightful comments that greatly improved the quality of the chapters. We would also like to thank the institutions represented by the authors for their support in making this specialized book possible.

Hoai Trong Nguyen
Thanh Dinh Su
Toan Luu Duc Huynh
Angelina Nhat-Hanh Le
University of Economics Ho Chi Minh City
Vietnam

https://doi.org/10.1142/9789811286100_fmatter

About the Editors

Hoai Trong Nguyen is a Professor of Economics at the University of Economics Ho Chi Minh City (UEH). Prof. Dr. Nguyen obtained M.A (1997) and Ph.D (2001) in Economics from the University of Colombo, Sri Lanka. He was the Vice President of UEH between 2011 and 2021, responsible for the areas of international relations and academic research. He was also a member of the Center of Education Accreditation by the Vietnam National University Ho Chi Minh City between 2016 and 2020. In addition, he was the Director of the Vietnam—The Netherlands Programme, the joint program in Development Economics between UEH and the International Institute of Social Study at Erasmus University Rotterdam between 2011 and 2021. Currently, Prof. Dr. Nguyen is the Editor-in-Chief of the *Journal of Asian Business and Economic Studies* (JABES), UEH's own journal published by the Emerald Group Publishing. Since 2021, he has become an advisory member of the *Asia-Pacific Journal of Business Administration* and a member of the scientific consulting committee for the HCMC Vietnam. Prof. Dr. Nguyen's current research interests cover a range of topics, including sustainable development, internationalization of education, green growth, green behavior, public health, regional development, and smart cities.

Thanh Dinh Su has more than 30 years of experience at the University of Economics Ho Chi Minh City (UEH) and currently acts as the University President for the term 2020–2025. Prior to his appointment as President, Professor Su was the Editor-in-Chief of UEH *Journal of Asian Business and Economic Studies* (JABES) and held various roles, including UEH Lecturer, Program Director, and Dean of the School of Public Finance at UEH. He was granted the titles of Associate Professor in 2005 and Professor in 2015.

Toan Luu Duc Huynh is a Lecturer at the University of Economics Ho Chi Minh City (UEH). He currently holds the position of Deputy Editor-in-Chief for the *Journal of Asian Business and Economic Studies*. Specializing in applied economics and financial economics, he has published research articles in leading journals within the fields of economics and management. These include but are not limited to *Nature Communications*, *Economics Letters*, *Journal of Economic Behavior and Organization*, and *Energy Economics*.

Angelina Nhat-Hanh Le is an Associate Professor of Marketing, College of Business, University of Economics HCM City, Vietnam, where she teaches strategic marketing, marketing management, and consumer behavior. Her research interests include marketing channels, Internet marketing, brand management, green marketing, and meta-analysis. Her research has been published in the *Journal of the Academy of Marketing Science*, *Journal of International Marketing*, *International Journal of Advertising*, *Journal of Business Research*, *Journal of Consumer Behaviour*, *Management Decision*, *Asia Pacific Journal of Marketing and Logistics*, and so on.

https://doi.org/10.1142/9789811286100_fmatter

Acknowledgement

This book was funded by University of Economics Ho Chi Minh City (UEH). The editors also acknowledge the significant contribution of Binh Quang Nguyen, whose assistance with professional and administrative tasks was essential to completing this book. We cannot imagine publishing it without his involvement. Furthermore, we are grateful to all colleagues who served as language editors and academic advisors, ensuring the highest quality for our audience.

https://doi.org/10.1142/9789811286100_fmatter

List of Reviewers

Ha Quang An
University of Economics Ho Chi Minh City, Vietnam
anhq@ueh.edu.vn

Md. Abul Kalam Azad
Islamic University of Technology, Pakistan
kalam@iut-dhaka.edu

Nguyen Hoai Bao
Australian National University, Australia
bao.nguyen@anu.edu.au

Tran Mai Dong
University of Economics Ho Chi Minh City, Vietnam
tmdong@ueh.edu.vn

Tran Kim Dung
University of Economics Ho Chi Minh City, Vietnam
tkd@ueh.edu.vn

Luong Vinh Quoc Duy
University of Economics Ho Chi Minh City, Vietnam
quocduy@ueh.edu.vn

Truong Nu To Giang
University of Economics Ho Chi Minh City, Vietnam
giangtnt@ueh.edu.vn

Huynh Viet Khai
Can Tho University, Vietnam
hvkhai@ctu.edu.vn

Nguyen Thi Tuyet Mai
National Economics University, Vietnam
mainguyen@ktpt.edu.vn

Nguyen Phong Nguyen
University of Economics Ho Chi Minh City, Vietnam
nguyenphongnguyen@ueh.edu.vn

Mia Hang Pham
Massey University, New Zealand
M.H.Pham@massey.ac.nz

Nguyen Ngoc Duy Phuong
International University, Vietnam
nndphuong@hcmiu.edu.vn

Kim Huong Trang
Foreign Trade University, Vietnam
kimhuongtrang@ftu.edu.vn

Le Dinh Minh Tri
International University, Vietnam
ldmtri@hcmiu.edu.vn

https://doi.org/10.1142/9789811286100_fmatter

Contents

Preface v

About the Editors xi

Acknowledgement xiii

List of Reviewers xv

Chapter 1 Strategic Management under the Context of Environmental Uncertainty 1
Thanh Dinh Su, Luc Phan Tan, Thu-Hang Le and Angelina Nhat Hanh Le

Chapter 2 Marketing and Advertising: Shifting from Conventional to Digital Marketing 43
Tien Minh Dinh, Oanh Le Vu Lan and Mai Dong Tran

Chapter 3 Cultural Intelligence and Job Performance of Employees in FDI Enterprises: The Mediating Role of Work Engagement 87
Tan Quoc Phan and Bang Nguyen-Viet

Chapter 4 Determinants and Measurement of Financial Information Quality — An Empirical Review 113
Mai Duc Nghia

Chapter 5 The Impact of Extrinsic Motivation on Prosumption: Digital Service Brands 137

Minh T. H. Le and Nhi P. P. Nguyen

Chapter 6 Tourism Destination Management Model in the Transitional Economy 159

Vo Thi Ngọc Thuy, Ho Thi My Linh, Truong Thi Hong Minh and Thanh-Binh Phung

Chapter 7 Immersive Technologies: A Critical Success Factor for Modern Retailers 193

Dong Phong Nguyen, Huong Ho Xuan, Truong Thi Hoang Oanh, Vo Kim Nhan and Angelina Nhat Hanh Le

Chapter 8 The Impact of Leaders' Curiosity on the Intention to Introduce IoT-Based Products: The Case of Vietnam 241

Manh Phan Dinh and Le Tran Thi Huynh

Chapter 9 Market Orientation of Public Organizations in a Transitional Economy 283

Thi Thuy Hang Le and Toan Luu Duc Huynh

Chapter 10 The Role of Social Investment in Information, Communication, Science, and Technology on the Productivity Growth of Enterprises in Vietnam 315

Quang Hai Nguyen

Chapter 11 Factors Affecting Retail Investors' Intentions to Use Financial Robo-Advisors in the Middle of COVID-19 in Vietnam 335

Thuy Chung Phan, Dao Quynh Dam Nguyen, Lam Van Le and Kurniawan Saefullah

Chapter 12 New Managerialism in Vietnamese Higher Education: Internationalization from Vietnamese University Leaders' Perspective 369

Hoai Trong Nguyen and Ba-Linh Tran

Chapter 13 Digital Literacy, Financial Literacy, and Financial Management Behavior: Empirical Evidence from Vietnam 399

Thuy Chung Phan, Thai Thi Van Anh, Hien Thu Phan, Lam Van Le and Trang Minh Thai Phung

Index 433

https://doi.org/10.1142/9789811286100_0001

Chapter 1

Strategic Management under the Context of Environmental Uncertainty

Thanh Dinh Su[*,¶], Luc Phan Tan[†,||], Thu-Hang Le[‡,§,**] and Angelina Nhat Hanh Le[*,††]

[*]*School of Public Finance, School of Management, University of Economics Ho Chi Minh City, Vietnam*

[†]*Faculty of Economics, Thu Dau Mot University, Vietnam*

[‡]*Becamex Business School, Eastern International University, Vietnam*

[§]*School of Business, International University, Hochiminh National University, Ho Chi Minh City, Vietnam*

[¶]*dinhthanh@ueh.edu.vn*

[||]*lucpt@tdmu.edu.vn*

[**]*hang.le@eiu.edu.vn*

[††]*hanhln@ueh.edu.vn*

Abstract

Uncertainty is an inevitable aspect of business strategy. This chapter aims to provide a systematic literature review of strategic management under the context of environmental uncertainty by compiling some of the most important problems and difficulties in its strategic management. A total of 725 publications from the Web of Science databases were analyzed in an effort to compile some of the

Received on March 14, 2023; accepted on May 19, 2023

most important problems and difficulties in the strategic management of this issue. Research has explored the dimensions of environmental uncertainty, factors affecting perceived environmental uncertainty, relationships in the context of environmental uncertainty, methods and new approaches to environmental uncertainty, strategies for different types of environmental uncertainty, theoretical problems in strategic management under the context of environmental uncertainty, aspects of strategic management (strategic planning, strategy formulation, and strategy implementation) and environmental uncertainty, and environmental uncertainty management. The results provide an overall picture of strategic management issues within the context of environmental uncertainty in order to suggest possibilities for future research into the problems and solutions, as well as identify more sophisticated approaches to managing uncertainty.

Keywords: Strategic Management, Environmental Uncertainty, Uncertainty, Systematic Literature Review.

1. Introduction

There is always a certain level of risk and uncertainty involved in doing business (Mascarenhas, 1982). As a result, the academic community devotes a great deal of attention to the nature of risks and various uncertainties, their impact on business operations, and business strategies for identifying, forecasting, mitigating, and managing these risks in their day-to-day operations (Sniazhko, 2019). Uncertainty is defined as the lack of knowledge about the probabilities of future events that may affect the company (Knight, 1921). Uncertainty studies are diverse. Early attempts to conceptualize uncertainty refer to early management scholars, such as Knight (1921) and March (1991). For decades, researchers in the field of strategic management have conducted studies and investigations on the concept of uncertainty, especially environmental uncertainty (Milliken, 1987). Environmental uncertainty has been discussed from a variety of angles, and psychologists and economists frequently address the matter. These concepts basically characterize environmental uncertainty as the inability to assess the probability of future events, the lack of knowledge regarding cause-and-effect linkages, and the incapacity to precisely forecast the consequences of an action. Milliken (1987) defines uncertainty as an individual's perception of not being able to predict accurately. It is caused by either the lack of sufficient data to make an accurate prediction or the inability to distinguish between relevant and irrelevant data (Milliken, 1987). The literature on both strategic management (Miles *et al.*, 1978; Teece, 2007) and organization theory (Thompson, 2017) has long emphasized the role of the environment as a major source of uncertainty for strategic planners responsible for responding to emerging opportunities and threats.

Previous studies have identified different types of uncertainty in international business contexts based on its origin (environmental, industry, or company characteristics) or its nature (exogenous versus endogenous) (Certo *et al.*, 2008). Traditional strategic theories like industrial organization, evolutionary theory, and resource-based theory have been studied in depth (Barney *et al.*, 2001; Freeman *et al.*, 2021); however, non-strategic theories like transaction cost economics, agency theory, and the dynamic capabilities view have also offered valuable insights into the functioning and adaptability of firms in an uncertain environment (Barney *et al.*, 2012; Teece, 2019). Transaction cost economics focuses on minimizing transaction costs in governance choices, while agency theory addresses the challenges of aligning the interests of principals and agents. The dynamic capabilities view emphasizes the importance of sensing and shaping opportunities and threats for long-term company performance and innovation. Understanding these theories is crucial for firms to develop effective strategies to succeed in dynamic and uncertain environments. However, research on strategic management under the context of environmental uncertainties remains fragmentary and elusive (Etemad, 2020; Sharma *et al.*, 2020). Therefore, a systematic literature review is necessary for researchers to understand the current research and avoid duplicating previous studies. In addition, there is a scarcity of analysis of the classification and categorization of the precursors of environmental uncertainties (Haarhaus and Liening, 2020). Furthermore, the quantity and quality of research on strategic management under the context of environmental uncertainties are unclear and unsystematic. These challenges underscore the need for this literature review study. This chapter aims to compile and classify some of the most significant problems and difficulties in strategic management within the context of environmental uncertainty and further analyze them to suggest possibilities for future research into problems and solutions while outlining more sophisticated approaches to managing uncertainty.

2. Strategic Management

Strategic management has a rich history that spans thousands of years and has evolved over time to become a formal discipline taught in business schools and practiced in corporations worldwide (Rumelt *et al.*, 1991). Strategic management is the process of analyzing an organization's situation to formulate strategies to achieve a competitive advantage. Strategy is defined as the decision-making process undertaken to achieve a long-term, sustainable competitive advantage over one's competitors (Eisenhardt and Martin, 2000). Strategists such as Michael Porter believe that competitive strategy is about being different by choosing a different set of activities to deliver a unique mix of value to customers (Porter and Donthu, 2008). An organization must analyze its internal resources and capabilities, as well as the macro-environment and competitive environment, to determine the best way to configure these resources and capabilities to meet the needs of the environment and achieve a competitive advantage to outperform its competitors in the industry (David, 2011; Porter, 1980).

Strategic management can be defined from several different perspectives such as the resource-based view (RBV) (Barney, 2001), the environmental view (Aragón-Correa and Sharma, 2003), the industry view (Porter, 1980), and the stakeholder view (Freeman and McVea, 2005). The RBV focuses on the internal resources and capabilities of an organization and how they can be leveraged to achieve a competitive advantage. It emphasizes the role of intangible assets such as brand reputation in creating a sustainable competitive advantage. The environmental view takes into account the external environment in which the organization operates, including economic, political, and technological factors. It emphasizes the importance of adapting to the external environment to achieve success. The industry view focuses on the competitive environment in which the organization operates. It emphasizes the importance of understanding the industry structure, the behavior of competitors, and the sources of competitive advantage. The stakeholder view recognizes the importance of considering the interests of stakeholders, including shareholders, employees, customers, suppliers, and communities. It emphasizes the importance of balancing the interests of different stakeholders to achieve sustainable success. Each of these perspectives provides a different lens for viewing the strategic management process and can offer valuable insights and considerations for organizations looking to achieve a competitive advantage.

2.1. *Development of strategic management: An overview*

Strategic management is one of the most rapidly expanding social science disciplines. As a multidisciplinary field at the convergence of economics, sociology, and organization theory, it exists within a vibrant and substantial scholarly community (Durand *et al.*, 2017). Strategic management was largely regarded as a scientific topic by the 1980s, when economists dominated the field. Strategic management is viewed as a basic factor that explains the success or failure of businesses (Prahalad and Hamel, 1994).

This field originated in the early 1960s with the major works of Chandler (1962), Ansoff (1991), and Andrews (1971). The focus of these investigations was normative prescription rather than analysis. The research paradigm evolved from a deterministic, one-best-way perspective to a more contingent one in which businesses must adapt to their external environment. In the 1970s, in response to the challenge of generalizability, two distinct lines of research founded on radically divergent ontological and epistemological orientations emerged. The "process approach" consisted mostly of descriptive research into how strategies were formulated and implemented. The environment and its link to a company were an additional focus of strategic management during this era. Deductive and extensive statistical research established and tested hypotheses based on models derived from the structure–conduct–performance (S–C–P) paradigm (Bain, 1968; Mason, 1939). Porter (1980) provides a framework for comprehending industry structure. This paradigm is useful for evaluating the attractiveness of an industry and facilitating competition analysis.

Since the 1980s, studies have shifted their attention from industry structure to the internal structure, resources, and capabilities of firms. Due to their emphasis on the internal structure of organizations, two lines of study in organizational economics have caught the interest of strategic management researchers: transaction cost economics (TCE) (Jones and Hill, 1988) and agency theory (Eisenhardt, 1989). TCE provides a theoretical basis for large, diversified enterprises to adopt a multi-divisional structure. Agency theory illustrates how managers may aim to maximize their own interests at the expense of the interests of shareholders. It has been used to address a wide range of strategic management issues, including innovation, corporate governance, and diversification. The possession of strategically significant resources and capabilities is a key source of a company's competitive advantage. In the early 1990s, approaches closely related to the resource-based paradigm emerged, but at a lower level of analysis. From the mid-1990s forward, perspectives emerged that sought to investigate the simple possession of resources and emphasize the relevance of their generation and management.

In the 2000s, a perspective that was more grounded in Austrian economics-based conceptions of entrepreneurship gained traction (Pacheco *et al.*, 2010). According to this view, businesses must engage in entrepreneurial behavior aimed at discovering a priori unknown profit prospects. These advances form the basis for the concept of strategic entrepreneurship, which blends opportunity searching with strategic management. Recent studies in the field of micro-foundations and behavioral strategy focus on the individual level to examine the behaviors that influence strategy (Felin and Foss, 2005; Olson *et al.*, 2005). The objective is to use knowledge from the behavioral sciences, namely psychology and organizational behavior, to address strategic management concerns. The general objective is to examine and criticize strategy using plausible assumptions about human cognition, emotions, and social behavior (Powell *et al.*, 2011). Therefore, this strategy emphasizes the internal components of a company while highlighting the impact of the individual level on business success.

2.2. *Strategic management in an uncertain environment (Dynamic capability view)*

In recent years, strategic management has become increasingly important as organizations face numerous geopolitical and economic uncertainties. The ongoing war in Ukraine, escalating tensions between the United States and China, and high inflation in many countries are just a few examples of the challenges that organizations must navigate. In such a complex and dynamic environment, organizations must be nimble and adaptive in order to maintain their competitive advantage. The field of strategic management has been shaped by several theoretical perspectives, including the RBV, the dynamic capability view, and the transaction cost economics view. The dynamic capability view, in particular, is well suited to help organizations navigate uncertain environments (Ambrosini and Bowman, 2009). According to this view, organizations must have the capability to continuously learn, reconfigure their resources, and develop new competencies in order to stay ahead of their competitors. Dynamic capability refers to the firm's ability to integrate, build, and reconfigure internal and external competencies to address rapidly changing environments. It is a continuous and ongoing process of learning, renewal, and evolution that enables organizations to create and capture new opportunities, even in highly uncertain environments (Teece *et al.*, 2016). In a world characterized by constant change and disruption, dynamic capabilities are crucial for organizations to remain resilient and competitive. This perspective recognizes that an organization's resources and capabilities are not fixed, but can be developed and improved over time (Schilke, 2014). For example, an organization may acquire new technology, develop new products, or improve its supply chain processes to better meet the needs of its customers. By continuously improving its internal processes and resources, an organization can stay ahead of its competitors and maintain a sustainable competitive advantage.

In today's rapidly changing business landscape, characterized by uncertainty and unpredictability, companies are facing the challenge of balancing exploration and exploitation activities in their pursuit of growth and competitiveness (O'Reilly and Tushman, 2004). Exploration refers to the process of pursuing new opportunities and ventures that may lead to innovation and breakthroughs, while exploitation involves leveraging existing resources, capabilities, and knowledge to achieve efficiencies and improve performance. The concept of exploration and exploitation has been widely recognized in the field of strategic management as a crucial factor in determining a firm's ability to navigate uncertainty and thrive in dynamic environments (Teece, 2007). In an uncertain environment, companies that focus exclusively on exploitation may struggle to adapt to new market trends and challenges, leading to declining performance and competitiveness over time. On the other hand, organizations that focus excessively on exploration may face challenges in effectively commercializing their innovations and may divert resources away from established core businesses (O'Reilly and Tushman, 2004). In uncertain circumstances, firms must strike a balance between exploration and exploitation to maintain their competitive edge and achieve continuous growth. To balance exploration and exploitation, organizations must adopt an ambidextrous approach, wherein they can switch between exploration and exploitation as needed (Jansen, 2005). This requires organizations to have the flexibility and adaptability to shift their focus as the external environment changes.

2.3. *Strategic process*

The strategic process is a management approach that involves setting objectives and analyzing the situation facing an organization to formulate multiple strategies for dealing with challenges and achieving a competitive advantage. The purpose of the strategic process is to align the organization's internal resources and capabilities with the needs of the external environment to maximize opportunities and minimize threats (McGrath *et al.*, 1995). The strategic process involves a series of interrelated steps, including analyzing the organization's internal and external environment, defining the organization's objectives, developing alternative strategies, selecting a preferred strategy, implementing the chosen strategy, and evaluating the results (Kaplan and Norton, 1996). The internal environment includes the organization's resources, capabilities, and culture, while the external environment encompasses the macro-economic, political, technological, and competitive factors that influence the organization's performance. To be effective, the strategic process must be integrated with the organization's overall planning and decision-making processes, and it must be supported by strong leadership and a clear commitment to continuous improvement. The strategic process also requires a deep understanding of the organization's strengths, weaknesses, opportunities, and threats (SWOT), as well as a clear understanding of the competitive landscape and the forces driving change in the external environment (Kaplan and Norton, 1996). A well-designed and properly executed strategic process can help an organization achieve its goals, maximize its potential, and stay ahead of the competition. However, the strategic process is always ongoing and must be regularly reviewed and updated to ensure that it remains relevant and effective in the face of changing conditions (Helfat and Martin, 2015).

Strategic process refers to the overall process of developing and implementing a company's strategy. It includes all the steps involved in strategic planning, formulation, and implementation (Alkhafaji, 2011; Clarke and Fuller, 2010). Strategic planning, strategic formulation, and strategic implementation are interrelated stages within the strategic management process. Each stage builds on the previous one and lays the foundation for the next (Mintzberg *et al.*, 2020). In other words, the strategic planning, formulation, and implementation stages are interrelated and dependent on each other for success in achieving the company's desired outcomes.

2.3.1. *Strategic planning*

Strategic planning is a methodical process for determining an organization's direction and allocating its resources to pursue this path. It involves creating a long-term plan for an organization that defines how it will fulfill its vision and mission, set goals and objectives, and address obstacles and opportunities. The process of strategic planning begins with an analysis of the organization's existing position, including its SWOT, followed by the development of a strategic plan (Mintzberg *et al.*, 2020). Strategic planning is a crucial instrument for businesses to navigate a complicated and uncertain business environment and make informed decisions. In a rapidly changing market, firms must anticipate trends, opportunities, and difficulties to remain competitive (Ambrosini and Bowman, 2009). A well-designed and executed strategic plan assists firms in aligning their resources and skills with their aims and objectives while preserving their competitive edge.

In a volatile, uncertain, complex, and ambiguous environment, it is particularly important for organizations to have a well-designed and well-executed strategic plan. Such a plan enables organizations to respond quickly and effectively to changing circumstances and maintain their competitive advantage. It helps organizations allocate their resources in a way that maximizes their impact and ensures that they are well positioned to take advantage of new opportunities (Ranjan, 2008; Schraeder, 2002). Effective strategic planning requires the participation of all stakeholders, including employees, customers, suppliers, and shareholders. This enables enterprises to gather diverse viewpoints and insights and develop a strategy plan that aligns with the requirements and expectations of all stakeholders (Freeman and McVea, 2005).

2.3.2. *Strategic formulation*

Strategic formulation is a vital stage in the strategic management process that involves the creation of a comprehensive strategy to achieve an organization's long-term goals and objectives (Mintzberg, 1977). The process of strategic formulation encompasses running a SWOT analysis for the organization, a thorough examination of the external and internal environments, and the determination of the best course of action to achieve the organization's desired future state (Dyson, 2004). The strategic formulation process starts with gaining a clear understanding of the organization's mission and vision. The next step involves the collection of data and information about the external and internal environments, including an analysis of market trends, competition, and customer preferences. The organization's strengths, weaknesses, opportunities, and threats are then identified through a SWOT analysis. This analysis provides the basis for the identification of the organization's strategic objectives and the formulation of strategies to achieve these objectives.

Once the objectives have been established, the organization must then determine the best course of action to achieve them. This involves the selection of the most appropriate strategies, including market penetration, market development, product development, and diversification. The chosen strategies must be integrated into a cohesive plan that addresses the organization's overall goals and objectives while taking into consideration the external and internal environments.

In today's rapidly changing and uncertain business environment, organizations must be flexible and able to adapt to new challenges and opportunities. A well-designed and properly executed strategic formulation process enables organizations to respond to these changes and remain competitive (Bowen and Bowen, 2014; Harrington *et al.*, 2004). As such, organizations must ensure that their strategic formulation process is thorough, systematic, and continuously reviewed and updated.

2.3.3. *Strategic implementation*

Strategic implementation refers to the process of putting into action plans and decisions made during the strategy formulation stage (Mintzberg, 1977; Mišanková and Kočišová, 2014). This stage of the strategic management process involves translating the broader, abstract plans developed in the strategy formulation stage into concrete actions and initiatives that can be executed by the organization. The goal of strategic implementation is to ensure that the organization's resources are aligned in support of the strategy and that the desired changes are actually brought about. Strategic implementation requires a high level of coordination and collaboration among different functions and departments within the organization, as well as a commitment to the strategy on the part of employees at all levels. Key components of effective strategic implementation include clear communication of the strategy, effective resource allocation, the development of policies and processes to support the strategy, and the establishment of performance metrics to track progress (Brenes *et al.*, 2008; Rajasekar, 2014).

One of the key challenges of strategic implementation is balancing the need for consistency and stability with the need for flexibility and adaptation. Organizations must find a way to maintain their core values and capabilities while adapting to new circumstances and opportunities. This requires a culture of innovation and a willingness to take calculated risks (Atkinson, 2006). The role of top management is critical in the strategic implementation process. Top managers must provide leadership, direction, and support to ensure that the organization is aligned with the strategy and that all members of the organization understand their roles in its implementation (Steiss, 2019). The development of a clear and comprehensive implementation plan which outlines specific actions and initiatives is essential to ensure that the strategy is executed effectively. The effectiveness of the implementation of a strategic plan can be evaluated based on the attainment of tangible, quantifiable targets and an improvement in the organization's overall performance and competitiveness

(Elbanna *et al.*, 2016). A successful implementation process, characterized by thorough planning and efficient execution, can enable organizations to attain their strategic goals, establish a lasting advantage over competitors, and foster long-term development and achievement (Bryson, 2018).

3. Uncertainty and Environmental Uncertainty

3.1. *Uncertainty and its levels*

Uncertainty is a significant feature of strategic management (Vecchiato, 2012). It is the inability to make accurate predictions, causing challenges for managers (March, 1991). Previous research has identified various types of uncertainty, such as environmental uncertainty, industry uncertainty, and uncertainty regarding firm-specific factors. However, disagreement persists regarding how to differentiate between the various types (Certo *et al.*, 2008), resulting in inconsistency, making it difficult for managers to make decisions. The exact definition of uncertainty remains elusive, with debates surrounding whether it is an objective description of a firm's environment or the perceived subjectivity of an individual manager or decision-maker (Milliken, 1987). Environmental sources of uncertainty include rivals, consumers, suppliers, sociopolitical variables, and technical advancements (Sniazhko, 2019), while demand, supply, and technology are seen as the elements of environmental uncertainty that directly interact and influence business capacity to achieve objectives (Huo *et al.*, 2018).

There are four levels of uncertainty identified in strategic planning research (Courtney *et al.*, 1997). The first level involves an adequately clear future where managers can develop a single forecast based on accurate predictions for their strategies. The second level involves alternate futures, where a few alternative outcomes are possible, but their likelihood can be determined to some extent. At level three, a range of potential futures can be identified, but no specific scenario is available. Finally, level four involves true ambiguity, where the factors of the future are unknown, and no potential consequences can be identified, making it impossible to determine scenarios and even potential scope consequences.

These degrees of unpredictability are associated with these levels of uncertainty, and managers must adapt their strategies accordingly.

3.2. *Environmental uncertainty*

In strategic management research, the external environment refers to the physical and social factors that influence the decision-making behavior of individuals in organizations (Duncan, 1972). Such factors include customers, competitors, government laws, and labor unions. Researchers have different perspectives on the environment and its elements, but they all agree that various forces within the environment render things unpredictable for companies. Barnard (1938) was one of the first scholars to explore the relationship between firms and their external environment. He argued that the physical environment is inherently unpredictable, giving rise to strategic uncertainty for businesses. This uncertainty results from the failure of managers to make sense of all the available information in a given environmental condition. Therefore, companies should carefully consider the possibilities and hazards of operating in a particular environment before making any decision.

Furthermore, Simon (1957) as well as Cyert and March (1963) expanded on Barnard's study and emphasized that managers must make decisions within the context of "bounded rationality", meaning that they have limited knowledge and resources to fully understand a complex environment. Consequently, companies cannot completely understand their strategic choices but must nevertheless make decisions with incomplete information. In summary, the unpredictability of the environment poses serious challenges for managers in making strategic decisions. To overcome this, it is essential for companies to identify key strategic factors and match them with their current capacities to create advantageous opportunities for the organization.

4. Method

A systematic literature review was performed to synthesize and classify knowledge, identify main categories and themes, as well as suggest possibilities for future research (Xia *et al.*, 2018). This three-stage review process was carried out as suggested by Tan *et al.* (2019).

4.1. *Stage 1. Data collection*

All English publications related to strategic management under the context of environmental uncertainties (articles, books, editorial material, book chapters, notes, and letters) were searched in the Web of Science database. The following keywords were used to locate relevant articles: ("Environmental uncertain*" OR "Economic uncertainty" OR "Political uncertain*" OR "Government uncertain*" OR "Cultural uncertain*" and "Discontinuous uncertain*") AND ("strategy*" OR "plan*" OR "formulate*" OR "implement*"). This study examined publications that were published before January 2022. The preliminary searches within the databases using the above-mentioned keywords identified 1,148 articles.

4.2. *Stage 2. Screening*

Titles and abstracts of all publications were carefully considered for relevance to strategic management under the context of environmental uncertainties. Publications that were not related to the topic were excluded from the sample. As a result, a total of 725 publications were retained for the next stage.

4.3. *Stage 3. Analyzing the data*

The technique of content analysis was used to analyze 725 publications, as this technique has the potential to identify the main areas of the research topic (Krippendorff, 2004). The authors analyzed and synthesized the main issues related to strategic management under the context of environmental uncertainty; these issues will be summarized in this section, namely the dimensions of environmental uncertainty, perceived environmental uncertainty, relationships in the context of environmental uncertainty, methods and new approaches to environmental uncertainty, strategies for different types of environmental uncertainty, and theoretical problems in strategic management uncertainty under the context of environmental uncertainty. The authors then consider environmental uncertainty within the process of strategic management, including planning, formulation, implementation, and environmental uncertainty management.

5. Results

5.1. *Dimensions of environmental uncertainty*

Dess and Beard (1984) used the three environmental dimensions of dynamism, complexity, and munificence to measure environmental uncertainty. The first dimension, dynamism, measures how quickly an industry is changing and innovating, as well as how unpredictable or predictable rivals' and consumers' behavior is (Miller and Friesen, 1983). The second aspect of the measure is complexity, which refers to the level of knowledge complexity required for an understanding of the environment (Sharfman and Dean Jr, 1991). This aspect concerns the total number of factors that a company needs to analyze in its external environment. The last aspect is munificence, also known as hostility. Munificence describes "the extent to which resources are available to firms from a variety of environmental sources" (Tan, 1996). Covin and Slevin (1989) argue that "hostile environments are characterized by precarious industry".

In extending the multidimensional concept of uncertainty, Milliken (1987) builds on the work of Lawrence and Lorsch (1967) to develop a measure that distinguishes between the three types of uncertainty that exist in the environment outside of a company. The three types that Milliken (1987) includes are state uncertainty, effect uncertainty, and response uncertainty. State uncertainty refers to the environment's overall unpredictable nature and its different elements. Components of the environment and their relationships with each other change in ways that are not understood (Vecchiato, 2012). The inability of businesses to foresee the effects of upcoming environmental changes on their operations is known as effect uncertainty, the incapability of management to foresee the type, scope, and duration of the change's consequences on the organization. Uncertainty of this kind relates to a lack of comprehension of cause-and-effect connections. Response uncertainty refers to the difficulties businesses have in foreseeing how rivals will respond to a certain approach. This kind of uncertainty is derived from ignorance of the options or an inability to foresee the effects of a selected course of action.

5.2. *Perceived environmental uncertainty*

Environmental uncertainty has long been a central concept in the study of organizations. Some researchers view this uncertainty as an objective attribute of the environment, while others see it as a cognitive phenomenon, suggesting that uncertainty is in the eye of the beholder (Afshar Jahanshahi and Brem, 2020). Perceived environmental uncertainty is fundamental to entrepreneurs (Westhead *et al.*, 2004), as strategic actions are based on their perceptions (Xu *et al.*, 2012). When environmental uncertainty is regarded as an objective property of the environment, it is often evaluated using constructs related to environment-specific properties such as instability, speed of change, richness, and complexity (Bourgeois III, 1985). Many researchers consider managers' perceptions of environmental uncertainty to be more relevant than any objective reality, as they can change quite rapidly (Ashill and Jobber, 2001). Studies that explore the impact of perceived environmental uncertainty on various factors are presented in Table 1.

Table 1. Factors affecting perceived environmental uncertainty.

Variable	Source
Organizational predisposition	Sia *et al.* (2004)
Strategic planning	Huang and O'Brien (2015)
Supply chain flexibility	Merschmann and Thonemann (2011)
Supplier alliances	Lee *et al.* (2009)
Strategic choice	Ondersteijn *et al.* (2006)
Competitive advantage	Oyewo (2022)
The mortality problem of learning and mimetic practice	Miller (2012)
Strategy formulation and perceived internal change	Huang *et al.* (2005)
Performance	Bergeron *et al.* (2001), Kallmuenzer *et al.* (2019)
Value chain flexibility	Zhang *et al.* (2002)
Emergent marketing strategies	Chari *et al.* (2014)
Organizational structure	Plugge and Brook (2011)

Table 1. (*Continued*)

Variable	Source
Patterns of network change	Huang *et al.* (2011)
Strategic decision making	Elbanna *et al.* (2011)
Growth-orientation	Lahnamäki-Kivelä (2022)
The level of strategic management	Svandova and Jirásek (2016)
Strategic management accounting usage	Ojra *et al.* (2021)
Strategic management accounting techniques	Petera and Šoljaková (2020)
Organizational effectiveness in the retail pharmacy industry	Harrison (2009)
Strategic management accounting	Pavlatos (2015)
Strategic business unit (SBU) strategy	Chong and Chong (1997)
Strategic involvement	Oswald *et al.* (1997)
Innovation capability	Grabner *et al.* (2018)
Experiential market learning and vicarious market learning	Bao *et al.* (2020)

5.3. *Relationships in the context of environmental uncertainty*

Corporate relationships can be influenced by environmental factors in which a company operates and competes (Kafetzopoulos *et al.*, 2020). Constant changes in the economic and market environment have created an environment of uncertainty, affecting various aspects of businesses (Tsai and Yang, 2013). Environmental factors present opportunities, constraints, and threats; as such, the relationships between those factors in the enterprise are deeply influenced by uncertain environmental conditions (Kafetzopoulos *et al.*, 2020). Factors and relationships considered in the context of environmental uncertainty are all important considerations, such as strategic leadership, strategic change, and innovativeness (Aslan *et al.*, 2011); firms' entrepreneurial orientations and the adoption of quality management practices (Bello-Pintado *et al.*, 2018); organizational capacity for change and strategic ambidexterity (Judge and Blocker, 2008); robust capabilities and firm performance (Swan *et al.*, 2005); strategic entrepreneurship and sustaining innovation performance

(Swan *et al.*, 2005); stakeholder orientation's contribution and firm performance (Vaitoonkiat and Charoensukmongkol, 2020); intellectual capital and firm performance (Nhon *et al.*, 2020); use of management accounting systems and managerial performance (Agbejule, 2005); green innovation strategies, dynamic capabilities, and sustainable competitive advantages (Ge *et al.*, 2018); effects of network and managerial capabilities on the performance of entrepreneurial firms (Srećković, 2018); the relationship between organizational strategy, HR strategy, and HR operational strategy (McMackin and Heffernan, 2021); influence of managers' time orientation on strategic practices (Abu-Rahma and Jaleel, 2017); and the effect of alliance proactiveness on market-based firm performance (Sarkar *et al.*, 2001).

5.4. *Methods and new approaches to environmental uncertainty*

Scholars have presented a variety of methods and techniques for dealing with different types and levels of uncertainty in various environments (Bowen and Bowen, 2014; Sharma *et al.*, 2020; Sniazhko, 2019) (See Figure 1). These methods are divided into two approaches: methods based on strategic flexibility and strategic foresight. Strategic flexibility refers to an organization's ability to adjust its strategies and actions in response to changes in the business environment (Brozovic, 2018). This flexibility enables organizations to take advantage of new opportunities, respond to new threats, and adapt to changing circumstances (Xin, 2020). Strategic foresight, on the other hand, is the ability of an organization to anticipate and plan for future changes in the business environment (Haarhaus and Liening, 2020). This involves gathering and analyzing data and trends, identifying potential future scenarios, and developing strategies to address those scenarios (Pinto and Medina, 2020). While strategic flexibility and strategic foresight are distinct concepts, they are closely related. Strategic foresight provides the information and insights necessary for an organization to make informed decisions and adapt its strategies as needed. Strategic flexibility, in turn, enables an organization to quickly and effectively implement those strategies while responding to changes in the business environment.

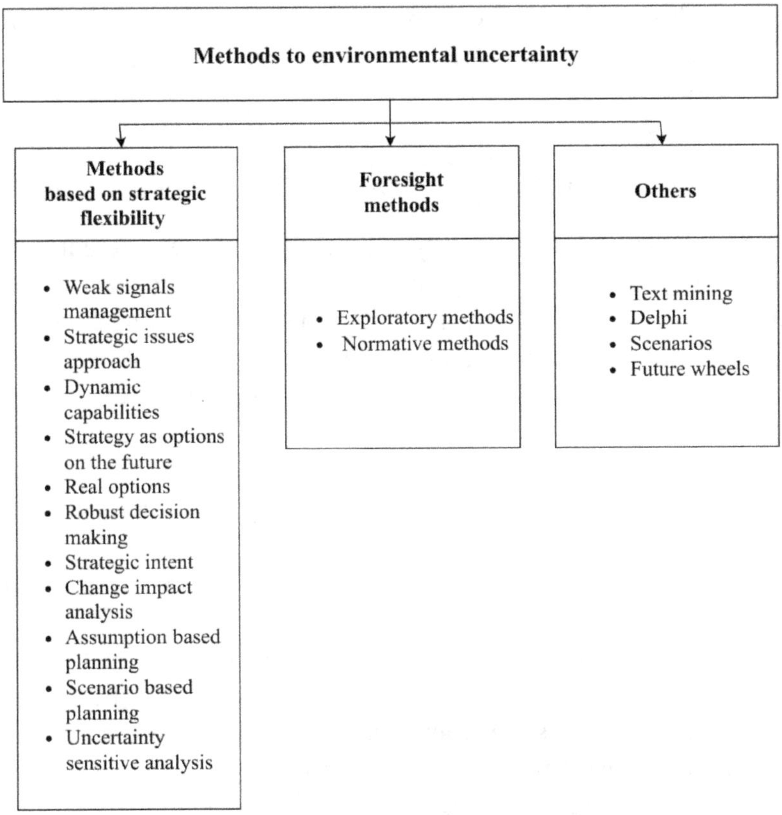

Figure 1. Methods to address environmental uncertainty.

Methods based on strategic flexibility enable changing strategies when dealing with various future states. Approaches for predicting the future fall into two broad categories: normative methods and a wide range of quantitative and qualitative techniques. In addition, several new approaches have been introduced by scholars, including text mining, Delphi, scenarios, future wheels, embedding real options in scenario planning (Favato and Vecchiato, 2017), the Rasch model (Oreja-Rodríguez and Yanes-Estévez, 2007), storytelling theory and the scenario process (Bowman *et al.*, 2013), cognitive models (Weiss and Wittmann, 2018), the Strategic Management of Organizational Resilience (SMOR) framework

(Moura and Tomei, 2021), the corporate governance perspective (Oyewo *et al.*, 2022), and the strategic IT management perspective (Raymond *et al.*, 2019).

5.5. *Strategies for different types of environmental uncertainty*

Types of environmental uncertainty will inevitably have different impacts on a company's strategic management process. With state environmental uncertainties, managers may spend more time understanding the environment, but due to their lack of complete understanding and ability to evaluate available options, they may use broad strategies to shield the organization's core operations from unexpected environmental changes. Additionally, some organizations may employ defensive tactics to reduce their exposure to the outside world. The study of opportunities and risks from the external environment is where the impact of environmental uncertainty is most prominent. As a result, managers may spend a lot of time in the opportunity and threat analysis phase when faced with environmental uncertainty. An evaluation of the implications of environmental changes for the organization is necessary. Some argue that strategic planning is hindered by a significant amount of uncertainty, while others believe that contingency plans can be modified. With regard to the response to environmental uncertainty, managers have different responses. Some may mimic the strategic responses of others. If an incorrect response is costly, strategy implementation may be postponed until suitable alternatives are available and an assessment of accuracy is made (Milliken, 1987).

5.6. *Theoretical problems in strategic management under the context of environmental uncertainty*

The study of the strategic management of environmental uncertainty has developed around two fundamental theoretical problems: "prediction" and "control". Regarding prediction, two main approaches exist: the "planning school" and the "adaptive school". The planning school states that companies will pay more attention to and concentrate more on forecasts about environmental change as uncertainty rises. Consequently, this strategy places a strong emphasis on the value of methodical analysis, planning, forecasting, logical interpretation of information, and integration into the company's current activities. The adaptive school encourages responding to environmental changes as they happen and encourages quick adaptability to environmental change. Avoidance is encouraged as much as possible. Both the planning school and the adaptive school view the fundamental components of the business environment as exogenous to the organization's own efforts. However, recent studies highlight the positive ability of organizations to shape the development of some of their environmental factors. Under this assumption (endogeneity), the company can do something more than simply position itself within its environment in an attempt to drive its development toward a favorable structure. In order to properly comprehend an organization's potential reactions to environmental uncertainty, some researchers contend that a new dimension beyond simple prediction must be taken into account: the dimension of control (Wiltbank *et al.*, 2006). Control quantifies the extent to which an organization can control the elements of its environment and, consequently, the extent to which those elements may be endogenous to that organization's own efforts. Thus, two subsequent approaches to the strategic management of environmental uncertainty have been identified: "visionary" and "transformative". The essence of the visionary approach is to set inspiring goals to create and occupy new spaces within the environment, imagine future possibilities, and actively work to make them a reality. In contrast, the transformational approach suggests that companies should focus their efforts not on prediction, but on co-creating goals with other business ecosystem participants in different processes of mutual support (Kim, 2005). Figure 2 summarizes the main strategic management approaches to dealing with uncertainty (Vecchiato, 2012; Wiltbank *et al.*, 2006).

5.7. *Strategic planning and environmental uncertainty*

The concept of strategic planning emerged in the 1950s when organizations became interested in "maintaining a productive and viable relationship between themselves and the environment". This was later referred to as the "strategic issue" (Ansoff *et al.*, 1976). Strategic planning may be done in an uncertain context, according to several writers. Swamidass and

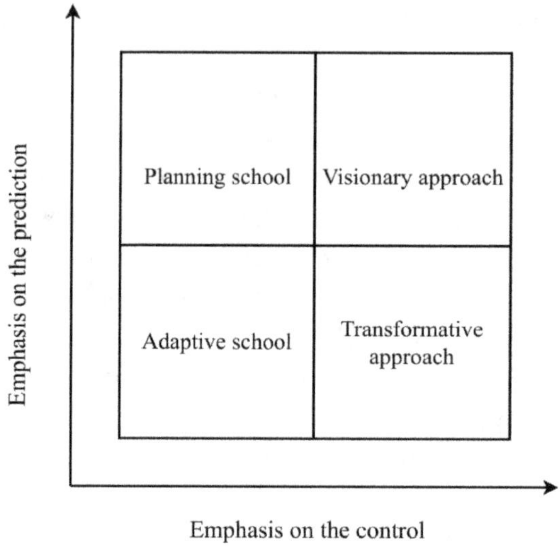

Figure 2. Strategic management of environmental uncertainty: framework of prediction and control.

Source: Vecchiato (2012).

Newell (1987) support the idea of information uncertainty, suggesting that environmental stresses enhance the necessity for information gathering and, hence, the significance of strategic planning. This idea illustrates the findings of Ansoff *et al.* (1976) and Miller and Friesen (1983), who demonstrate that businesses must constantly adapt to changes in their environment and use strategic planning as a tool to deal with the unpredictable nature of results. Numerous studies have suggested that in order for businesses to manage changing, unexpected, and volatile environments, extensive strategic planning is required (Hopkins and Hopkins, 1997; Miller and Cardinal, 1994). This view considers the reduction of uncertainty through access to high-quality information as one of the main goals of strategic planning (Fuller, 1996). However, it has also been suggested that changes in the environment make the information necessary for strategic planning rapidly obsolete (Eisenhardt and Bourgeois III, 1988). Heene (1997) found that when faced with ambiguity or complexity, companies are more likely to adjust their products or operations than to adjust their strategy. Their findings suggest that due to ongoing environmental pressures, organizations tend to be preoccupied with operational adjustments, and long-term strategic issues tend to be overlooked. In a similar vein, Matthews and Scott (1995) contend that in dangerous circumstances, future orientation might give way to an obsession with present survival. In other words, businesses must be more concerned with maintaining the status quo than with obtaining a desirable future state.

Environmental uncertainty can make strategic planning more challenging, as it is difficult to predict how these external factors will evolve over time (Cohen, 2001). However, by acknowledging and accounting for environmental uncertainty in their planning process, organizations can develop more robust and flexible strategies that can adapt to changing conditions (Chaib Lababidi *et al.*, 2020). One approach to addressing environmental uncertainty in strategic planning is to conduct a SWOT analysis. Another approach is scenario planning, which involves developing multiple scenarios for how the future may unfold based on different assumptions about key environmental factors. By exploring a range of potential scenarios, organizations can identify strategies that are robust across a variety of potential future environments. Overall, while environmental uncertainty can pose challenges to strategic planning, it also presents opportunities for organizations to develop more resilient and adaptable strategies that can thrive in a rapidly changing business environment.

5.8. *Strategy formulation and environmental uncertainty*

The idea of strategic planning first appeared in the 1950s, when businesses began to focus on "maintaining an effective and viable connection" with their surroundings, known as the "strategic issue" (Ansoff *et al.*, 1976). As traditional management approaches proved insufficient, new management strategies were necessary to address this issue (Ansoff *et al.*, 1976). Controlling a company's finances to steer a company towards success became no longer adequate (Gray, 1986), and long-term planning has also proven ineffective (Tregoe and Tobia, 1991). Design and planning schools have emerged as the leading proponents of strategic planning as a logical method of formulating strategy (Mintzberg, 1990).

According to these schools, a plan must be developed beforehand. The value of strategic planning is determined by how much it can raise the chance of success and how much it aids key decision-makers in thinking and acting strategically to accomplish the company's goals (Bryson, 2018). The creation of a logical, analytical, and purposeful strategy built on the idea of strategic planning has evolved into the new doctrine for managers worldwide and the standard method of management strategy instruction.

Miller (1988) suggests that the relationship between perceived environmental uncertainty and strategy is more important than other factors (Gerloff *et al.*, 1991). Strategic choices heavily rely on the perceptions of managers, as their viewpoints form the foundation of strategy formulation (Priem *et al.*, 2002). Firms that perceive distinct strategic issues respond differently, according to Litschert and Bonham (1979), while those that see the same strategic challenges may not always have the same strategy response. This suggests that perceived environmental uncertainty is more important than other characteristics (Child, 1972). In addition, differences in psychological characteristics, the ability to obtain resources, and organizational structures, capacities, and goals can determine the degree of influence of values and ideology in the choice of strategic responses (Litschert and Bonham, 1979).

A manager's perception and cognitive style are crucial in detecting problems and finding solutions throughout the stage of strategy formulation. Managers working in the same setting may see environmental uncertainty differently, so they must communicate their knowledge, viewpoints, and views (Gerloff *et al.*, 1991). Additionally, as events in the organizational environment change, managers' perceptions of environmental uncertainty may change as well (Buchko, 1994). In short, strategy formulation is a response to environmental uncertainty. The success of a strategy depends more on the ability of the manager than on resources and competition (Parnell *et al.*, 2000). The purpose of strategy formulation is to link internal capabilities to the external environment. However, it is not possible to predict the future performance of the environment, especially when it is uncertain, and managers need to make appropriate strategic decisions. This will require methods of limiting uncertainty (Bowen and Bowen, 2014).

When formulating a strategy in the face of environmental uncertainty, it is important for organizations to adopt a flexible and adaptive approach that can respond to changing conditions. This may involve incorporating contingency plans into the strategy to address potential risks and challenges, as well as regularly monitoring and adjusting the strategy in response to changing external factors. There are several key factors that organizations should consider when formulating a strategy in the face of environmental uncertainty, such as scenario planning, risk management, flexibility, and innovation. In addition, there are several other important considerations for strategy formulation in the face of environmental uncertainty such as competitive analysis, resource allocation, stakeholder engagement, long-term perspective, monitoring, and evaluation.

Overall, strategy formulation in the face of environmental uncertainty requires a comprehensive and dynamic approach that takes into account a wide range of factors and stakeholders. By adopting a flexible and adaptive strategy, organizations can position themselves to thrive in a rapidly changing business environment.

5.9. *Strategy implementation and environmental uncertainty*

Strategy implementation is a very complex process, as it depends on many factors that directly or indirectly affect its progress. To improve implementation efficiency and effectiveness, it is necessary to balance the management of impacts from inside and outside the enterprise. Almost every business has a strategy; however, not all strategies are good strategies, meaning that strategic plans by themselves are not enough to achieve the desired results. Although it is clear that combining good strategy formulation with good implementation results in better performance (Cespedes and Piercy, 1996), some authors, such as Kaplan and Norton (2005) and Hrebiniak (2006) have pointed out that it is better to have a poorly defined but well-executed strategy than a very good but only partially implemented strategy. The implementation phase seems to be the most important stage of the strategic management process, given that the success of a business depends first and foremost on what it can achieve in practice (Guerras-Martín *et al.*, 2014). Hrebiniak (2006) argues that an inadequate strategy can hinder implementation; conversely, good implementation can overcome the presence of a poor strategy.

Running a strategic plan is essential for the success of every business. The "who, where, when, and how" questions related to achieving corporate goals and objectives are important aspects of the process. Before the strategy execution stage, an environmental scan, SWOT analysis, and determination of strategic goals are conducted. According to Hrebiniak (2006), implementing organizational strategy is the most challenging management task. Formulating a strategy can be a science because it follows a set method, according to Noble (1999). This is why issues can still arise during the strategy execution stage, despite a careful formulation process. According to Gottschalk and Gudmundsen (2009), companies are slow to adapt to environmental changes and often end up having to clean up the mess left behind by their failure to do so. The leadership, control, and coordination systems of the organizations within these corporations are just a few of the many factors that seem to affect the process of implementing strategies effectively. Even though strategy design involves creative and intellectual effort that requires the study and synthesis of several factors, implementation is the most challenging and time-consuming aspect for management units. Although contextual uncertainty affects the implementation process and potentially reduces its success, studies have shown insufficient evidence to explain why different firms in the same industry execute their strategies more successfully than other firms (Whipp and Pettigrew, 1992). The degree of uncertainty can be objective and measurable or subjective and perceived. However, what matters is how the business behaves under specific environmental conditions. Environmental uncertainty increases information processing in the enterprise, as managers must identify opportunities, detect and interpret problems, and implement strategic or structural adaptations (Tushman *et al.*, 1986). To effectively implement a strategy in the face of environmental uncertainty, organizations should focus on the following key factors: communication and alignment, organizational structure and design, resource allocation, risk management, and performance management. Overall, strategy implementation in the face of environmental uncertainty requires a flexible and adaptive approach that takes into account the changing external environment. By focusing on effective communication and alignment, organizational structure and design, resource allocation, risk management, and performance management, organizations can successfully implement their strategies and achieve their long-term objectives.

5.10. *Environmental uncertainty management*

Managing environmental uncertainty involves strategies that help companies reduce or deal with environmental uncertainty. While minimizing environmental uncertainty is a natural driver that shapes the behavior of companies, dealing with environmental uncertainty allows companies to adjust their strategies to deal with the uncertainty they face (Sniazhko, 2019). The reduction of environmental uncertainty can be achieved through information gathering, proactive collaboration or cooperation, and networking. On the other hand, dealing with uncertainty involves flexibility (diversification and operational adaptation), imitation (copying competitors and forerunners), reactive collaboration and/or cooperation, control, and avoidance (Simangunsong *et al.*, 2012).

5.10.1. *Environmental uncertainty reduction*

The three approaches to reducing environmental uncertainty are information gathering, proactive collaboration/cooperation, and networking. The information-gathering approach refers to the process of gathering information up to the point of decision-making when the analytical comprehensiveness of the environment is achieved (Ji and Dimitratos, 2013). Information gathering is the most frequently deployed approach used to reduce uncertainty and is mainly used to reduce demand, competition, and cultural uncertainty (Grunert *et al.*, 2010). Another strategy to improve the predictability of situations in the external environment is proactive collaboration and cooperation. This involves working with local subsidiaries to lessen risks pertaining to the overall environment, industry, and firm. According to studies, working with local partners can help minimize environmental uncertainty as well as factors of industrial uncertainty like demand and competitiveness (Brouthers *et al.*, 2008; Slangen and Van Tulder, 2009). The reduction of uncertainty through networking occurs when collecting data through social relationships and strengthening existing networks (Luo, 2003). The network is mainly used to reduce the uncertainty of inputs, demand, and competition (Beckman *et al.*, 2004).

5.10.2. *Environmental uncertainty coping*

Five approaches to dealing with environmental uncertainty are defined as flexibility, imitation, reactive collaboration/cooperation, control, and avoidance. Flexibility is expressed in the form of diversification and adaptation of activities. Flexibility helps organizations cope with industry uncertainties by entering different markets or diversifying their products (Chiao *et al.*, 2010; Liu *et al.*, 2012). Organizations believe that imitating competitors' actions, paired with learning, will help them avoid the pitfalls of early movers (Gaba *et al.*, 2002). Political, governmental, cultural, demand, and competitive uncertainties can be managed through the imitation of competitors' actions (Gaba *et al.*, 2002). Reactive collaboration/cooperation is the most common approach taken to deal with environmental uncertainties (Brouthers and Brouthers, 2003; López-Duarte and Vidal-Suárez, 2010; Tseng and Lee, 2010). As the environment of uncertainty increases, organizations tend to choose strategies that transfer or produce uncertainty and risk for their counterparts. Control input modes include vertical integration and horizontal integration. The use of vertical integration with suppliers is an attempt to manage the unpredictability of input and demand. Especially during times of economic change, horizontal integration (such as mergers and acquisitions) is utilized to address competition-related uncertainty.

6. Discussion, Conclusions, and Limitations

A total of 725 publications from the Web of Science databases were analyzed in an effort to compile some of the most important problems and difficulties in strategic management within the context of environmental uncertainty. Research has explored the dimensions of environmental uncertainty, factors affecting perceived environmental uncertainty, relationships in the context of environmental uncertainty, methods and new approaches to environmental uncertainty, strategies for different types of environmental uncertainty, theoretical problems in strategic management under the context of environmental uncertainty, aspects of strategic management (strategic planning, strategy formulation, strategy implementation) and environmental uncertainty, and environmental uncertainty management.

The results provide an overall picture of strategic management issues under the context of environmental uncertainty. Environmental uncertainty coping is a crucial concept in organizational management, and researchers have identified five primary approaches to addressing this issue. The gap between theory and practice must be bridged in order for managers to make strategic decisions in uncertain environments using these approaches. To accomplish this, managers must conduct a comprehensive analysis of their organization's internal and external environment in order to gain insight into the nature and degree of the uncertainty they face. Based on this analysis, managers can implement strategies that align with the five identified scholarly approaches: flexibility, imitation, reactive collaboration/cooperation, control, and avoidance. For example, if the organization is facing industry uncertainties, managers can implement the flexibility approach by diversifying their products or entering different markets. They can also consider imitating competitors' strategies to avoid the mistakes of early movers. If the organization is facing political, governmental, cultural, demand, or competitive uncertainties, the imitation approach can also be useful. Reactive collaboration/cooperation is another approach that can be used to deal with environmental uncertainty. Managers respond to uncertainty as it arises, often by transferring or sharing risk with their counterparts. This can help reduce the overall level of uncertainty and risk for both parties involved. Control input modes, such as vertical and horizontal integration, can also be used to manage unpredictability and address competition-related uncertainty. To be specific, vertical integration with suppliers can help manage input/demand unpredictability, while horizontal integration such as mergers and acquisitions can address competition-related uncertainty. By taking a proactive approach to environmental uncertainty, managers can identify and capitalize on growth and sustainability opportunities while mitigating risks. These methods can be utilized by managers to reduce their organization's overall level of uncertainty and risk, and thus ensure its long-term success. Therefore, a better understanding of environmental uncertainty and its effect on strategic leadership, entrepreneurial orientation, and innovation performance can assist managers in transforming potential threats into organizational success opportunities.

The research has several limitations. To begin with, the review only searched the Web of Science database for publications; this search may not include all relevant articles in the field of strategic management with regard to environmental uncertainty. Future studies should look into additional databases and sources to include a broader range of publications. Second, the inclusion criteria were solely based on the titles and abstracts of the publications, and may not provide a thorough understanding of their content. To address this limitation, future studies should include a full-text screening stage in which the entire publication is reviewed to ensure that it meets the inclusion criteria. Finally, the study's content analysis technique may be subjective and may not capture all relevant information. Additional methods, such as meta-analysis, should be considered in future studies to provide a more objective synthesis of the findings.

Acknowledgements

This research is funded by the University of Economics Ho Chi Minh City, Vietnam.

References

Abu-Rahma, A. & Jaleel, B. (2017). Influence of managers' time orientation on strategic practices in the UAE: The moderating role of environmental uncertainty. *International Journal of Emerging Markets*, *12*(2), 219–237.

Afshar Jahanshahi, A. & Brem, A. (2020). Entrepreneurs in post-sanctions Iran: Innovation or imitation under conditions of perceived environmental uncertainty? *Asia Pacific Journal of Management*, *37*(2), 531–551.

Agbejule, A. (2005). The relationship between management accounting systems and perceived environmental uncertainty on managerial performance: A research note. *Accounting and Business Research*, *35*(4), 295–305.

Alkhafaji, A. F. (2011). Strategic management: Formulation, implementation, and control in a dynamic environment. *Development and Learning in Organizations: An International Journal*, *25*(2).

Ambrosini, V. & Bowman, C. (2009). What are dynamic capabilities and are they a useful construct in strategic management? *International Journal of Management Reviews*, *11*(1), 29–49.

Andrews, K. R. (1971). *The Concept of Corporate Strategy*. Homewood, Illinois: Dow Jones-Irwin.

Ansoff, H. I. (1991). Critique of Henry Mintzberg's 'The design school: Reconsidering the basic premises of strategic management'. *Strategic Management Journal*, *12*(6), 449–461.

Ansoff, H. I., Declerck, R. P., & Hayes, R. L. (1976). From strategic planning to strategic management. In *International Conference on Strategic Management 1973*, Vanderbilt University.

Aragón-Correa, J. A. & Sharma, S. (2003). A contingent resource-based view of proactive corporate environmental strategy. *Academy of Management Review*, *28*(1), 71–88.

Ashill, N. J. & Jobber, D. (2001). Defining the domain of perceived environmental uncertainty: An exploratory study of senior marketing executives. *Journal of Marketing Management*, *17*(5-6), 543–558.

Aslan, Ş., Diken, A., & Şendoğdu, A. A. (2011). Investigation of the effects of strategic leadership on strategic change and innovativeness of SMEs in a perceived environmental uncertainity. *Procedia-Social and Behavioral Sciences*, *24*, 627–642.

Atkinson, H. (2006). Strategy implementation: A role for the balanced scorecard? *Management Decision*.

Bain, J. S. (1968). *Industrial Organization*. New York: Wiley.

Bao, Y., Wei, Z., & Di Benedetto, A. (2020). Identifying the tacit entrepreneurial opportunity of latent customer needs in an emerging economy: The effects of experiential market learning versus vicarious market learning. *Strategic Entrepreneurship Journal*, *14*(3), 444–469.

Barnard, C. I. (1938). The economy of incentives. *Classics of Organization Theory*, 93–102.

Barney, J., Wright, M., & Ketchen Jr, D. J. (2001). The resource-based view of the firm: Ten years after 1991. *Journal of Management*, *27*(6), 625–641.

Barney, J. B. (2001). Is the resource-based "view" a useful perspective for strategic management research? Yes. *Academy of Management Review*, *26*(1), 41–56.

Barney, J. B., Della Corte, V., Sciarelli, M., & Arikan, A. (2012). The role of resource-based theory in strategic management studies: Managerial implications and hints for research. *Handbook of Research on Competitive Strategy*, 109–146.

Beckman, C. M., Haunschild, P. R., & Phillips, D. J. (2004). Friends or strangers? Firm-specific uncertainty, market uncertainty, and network partner selection. *Organization Science*, *15*(3), 259–275.

Bello-Pintado, A., Kaufmann, R., & de Cerio, J. M. D. (2018). Firms' entrepreneurial orientation and the adoption of quality management practices: Empirical evidence from a Latin American context. *International Journal of Quality & Reliability Management*, *35*(9), 1734–1754.

Bergeron, F., Raymond, L., & Rivard, S. (2001). Fit in strategic information technology management research: An empirical comparison of perspectives. *Omega*, *29*(2), 125–142.

Bourgeois III, L. J. (1985). Strategic goals, perceived uncertainty, and economic performance in volatile environments. *Academy of Management Journal*, *28*(3), 548–573.

Bowen, G. & Bowen, D. (2014). Strategy formulation and uncertainty in environments. *Journal of Business and Economics*, *5*(12), 2315–2326.

Bowman, G., MacKay, R. B., Masrani, S., & McKiernan, P. (2013). Storytelling and the scenario process: Understanding success and failure. *Technological Forecasting and Social Change*, *80*(4), 735–748.

Brenes, E. R., Mena, M., & Molina, G. E. (2008). Key success factors for strategy implementation in Latin America. *Journal of Business Research*, *61*(6), 590–598.

Brouthers, K. D. & Brouthers, L. E. (2003). Why service and manufacturing entry mode choices differ: The influence of transaction cost factors, risk and trust. *Journal of Management Studies*, *40*(5), 1179–1204.

Brouthers, K. D., Brouthers, L. E., & Werner, S. (2008). Real options, international entry mode choice and performance. *Journal of Management Studies*, *45*(5), 936–960.

Brozovic, D. (2018). Strategic flexibility: A review of the literature. *International Journal of Management Reviews*, *20*(1), 3–31.

Bryson, J. M. (2018). *Strategic Planning for Public and Nonprofit Organizations: A Guide to Strengthening and Sustaining Organizational Achievement*. John Wiley & Sons.

Buchko, A. A. (1994). Conceptualization and measurement of environmental uncertainty: An assessment of the Miles and Snow perceived environmental uncertainty scale. *Academy of Management Journal*, *37*(2), 410–425.

Certo, S. T., Connelly, B. L., & Tihanyi, L. (2008). Managers and their not-so rational decisions. *Business Horizons*, *51*(2), 113–119.

Cespedes, F. V. & Piercy, N. F. (1996). Implementing marketing strategy. *Journal of Marketing Management*, *12*(1-3), 135–160.

Chaib Lababidi, H., Lababidi, R., Colak, M., & Dayan, M. (2020). Contingency effects of firm structure and environmental uncertainty on strategic planning process and firm performance: Evidence from UAE enterprises. *Strategic Change*, *29*(2), 241–252.

Chandler, A. D. (1962). *Strategy and Structure: Chapters in the History of the Industrial Empire*. Cambridge Mass.

Chari, S., Katsikeas, C. S., Balabanis, G., & Robson, M. J. (2014). Emergent marketing strategies and performance: The effects of market uncertainty and strategic feedback systems. *British Journal of Management*, *25*(2), 145–165.

Chiao, Y. C., Lo, F. Y., & Yu, C. M. (2010). Choosing between wholly-owned subsidiaries and joint ventures of MNCs from an emerging market. *International Marketing Review*, *27*(3), 338–365.

Child, J. (1972). Organizational structure, environment and performance: The role of strategic choice. *Sociology*, *6*(1), 1–22.

Chong, V. K. & Chong, K. M. (1997). Strategic choices, environmental uncertainty and SBU performance: A note on the intervening role of management accounting systems. *Accounting and Business Research*, *27*(4), 268–276.

Clarke, A. & Fuller, M. (2010). Collaborative strategic management: Strategy formulation and implementation by multi-organizational cross-sector social partnerships. *Journal of Business Ethics*, *94*, 85–101.

Cohen, J. (2001). Environmental uncertainty and managerial attitude: Effects on strategic planning, non-strategic decision-making and organisational performance. *South African Journal of Business Management*, *32*(3), 17–31.

Courtney, H., Kirkland, J., & Viguerie, P. (1997). Strategy under uncertainty. *Harvard Business Review*, *75*(6), 67–79.

Covin, J. G. & Slevin, D. P. (1989). Strategic management of small firms in hostile and benign environments. *Strategic Management Journal*, *10*(1), 75–87.

Cyert, R. M. & March, J. G. (1963). A behavioral theory of the firm. *Englewood Cliffs, NJ*, *2*(4), 169–187.

David, F. R. (2011). *Strategic Management Concepts and Cases*. Prentice Hall.

Dess, G. G. & Beard, D. W. (1984). Dimensions of organizational task environments. *Administrative Science Quarterly*, *29*(7), 52–73.

Duncan, R. B. (1972). Characteristics of organizational environments and perceived environmental uncertainty. *Administrative Science Quarterly*, 313–327.

Durand, R., Grant, R. M., & Madsen, T. L. (2017). The expanding domain of strategic management research and the quest for integration. *Strategic Management Journal*, *38*(1), 4–16.

Dyson, R. G. (2004). Strategic development and SWOT analysis at the University of Warwick. *European Journal of Operational Research*, *152*(3), 631–640.

Eisenhardt, K. M. (1989). Agency theory: An assessment and review. *Academy of Management Review*, *14*(1), 57–74.

Eisenhardt, K. M. & Bourgeois III, L. J. (1988). Politics of strategic decision making in high-velocity environments: Toward a midrange theory. *Academy of Management Journal*, *31*(4), 737–770.

Eisenhardt, K. M. & Martin, J. A. (2000). Dynamic capabilities: What are they? *Strategic Management Journal*, *21*(10–11), 1105–1121.

Elbanna, S., Ali, A. J., & Dayan, M. (2011). Conflict in strategic decision making: Do the setting and environment matter? *International Journal of Conflict Management*, *22*(3), 278–299.

Elbanna, S., Andrews, R., & Pollanen, R. (2016). Strategic planning and implementation success in public service organizations: Evidence from Canada. *Public Management Review*, *18*(7), 1017–1042.

Etemad, H. (2020). Managing uncertain consequences of a global crisis: SMEs encountering adversities, losses, and new opportunities. *Journal of International Entrepreneurship*, *18*, 125–144.

Favato, G. & Vecchiato, R. (2017). Embedding real options in scenario planning: A new methodological approach. *Technological Forecasting and Social Change*, *124*, 135–149.

Felin, T. & Foss, N. J. (2005). *Strategic Organization: A Field in Search of Microfoundations* (Vol. 3, pp. 441–455). London, Thousand Oaks, CA and New Delhi: Sage Publications.

Freeman, R. E. & McVea, J. (2005). A stakeholder approach to strategic management. *The Blackwell Handbook of Strategic Management*, 183–201.

Freeman, R. E., Dmytriyev, S. D., & Phillips, R. A. (2021). Stakeholder theory and the resource-based view of the firm. *Journal of Management*, *47*(7), 1757–1770.

Fuller, M. (1996). Strategic planning in an era of total competition. *Strategy & Leadership*, *24*(3), 22–27.

Gaba, V., Pan, Y., & Ungson, G. R. (2002). Timing of entry in international market: An empirical study of US Fortune 500 firms in China. *Journal of International Business Studies*, 39–55.

Ge, B., Yang, Y., Jiang, D., Gao, Y., Du, X., & Zhou, T. (2018). An empirical study on green innovation strategy and sustainable competitive advantages: Path and boundary. *Sustainability*, *10*(10), 1–18.

Gerloff, E. A., Muir, N. K., & Bodensteiner, W. D. (1991). Three components of perceived environmental uncertainty: An exploratory analysis of the effects of aggregation. *Journal of Management*, *17*(4), 749–768.

Gottschalk, P. & Gudmundsen, Y. S. (2009). Police culture as a determinant of intelligence strategy implementation. *International Journal of Police Science & Management*, *11*(2), 170–182.

Grabner, I., Posch, A., & Wabnegg, M. (2018). Materializing innovation capability: A management control perspective. *Journal of Management Accounting Research*, *30*(2), 163–185.

Grunert, K. G., Trondsen, T., Campos, E. G., & Young, J. A. (2010). Market orientation in the mental models of decision makers: Two cross-border value chains. *International Marketing Review*, *27*(1), 7–27.

Guerras-Martín, L. Á., Madhok, A., & Montoro-Sánchez, Á. (2014). The evolution of strategic management research: Recent trends and current directions. *BRQ Business Research Quarterly*, *17*(2), 69–76.

Haarhaus, T. & Liening, A. (2020). Building dynamic capabilities to cope with environmental uncertainty: The role of strategic foresight. *Technological Forecasting and Social Change*, *155*(1), 1–15.

Harrington, R. J., Lemak, D. J., Reed, R., & Kendall, K. W. (2004). A question of fit: The links among environment, strategy formulation, and performance. *Journal of Business & Management*, *10*(1), 15–38.

Harrison, J. L. (2009). Untangling the value of information scope: An investigation in retail pharmacies. *Journal of Management & Organization*, *15*(4), 470–485.

Heene, A. (1997). The nature of strategic management. *Long Range Planning*, *30*(6), 933–938.

Helfat, C. E. & Martin, J. A. (2015). Dynamic managerial capabilities: Review and assessment of managerial impact on strategic change. *Journal of Management*, *41*(5), 1281–1312.

Hopkins, W. E. & Hopkins, S. A. (1997). Strategic planning–financial performance relationships in banks: A causal examination. *Strategic Management Journal*, *18*(8), 635–652.

Hrebiniak, L. G. (2006). Obstacles to effective strategy implementation. *Organizational Dynamics*.

Huang, C. & O'Brien, K. M. (2015). The impacts of perceived environmental uncertainty, outlook, and size on strategic planning in private clubs. *Journal of Hospitality Marketing & Management*, *24*(5), 554–571.

Huang, H.-C., Shih, H.-Y., & Liu, P.-Y. (2011). Environment effects on patterns of network change: The flat panel display industry network evolution. In *2011 Proceedings of PICMET'11: Technology Management in the Energy Smart World (PICMET)*.

Huang, L. K., Lin, Y., & Lin, T. (2005). The nexus between information technology and competitive strategy: A conceptual framework and its hypotheses. In *IEEE International Conference on e-Business Engineering (ICEBE'05)*.

Huo, B., Ye, Y., Zhao, X., Wei, J., & Hua, Z. (2018). Environmental uncertainty, specific assets, and opportunism in 3PL relationships: A transaction cost economics perspective. *International Journal of Production Economics*, *203*, 154–163.

Jansen, J. (2005). Ambidextrous organizations: A multiple-level study of absorptive capacity. *Exploratory and Exploitative Innovation and Performance*, *1*(1), 1–19.

Ji, J. & Dimitratos, P. (2013). An empirical investigation into international entry mode decision-making effectiveness. *International Business Review*, *22*(6), 994–1007.

Jones, G. R. & Hill, C. W. (1988). Transaction cost analysis of strategy-structure choice. *Strategic Management Journal*, *9*(2), 159–172.

Judge, W. Q. & Blocker, C. P. (2008). Organizational capacity for change and strategic ambidexterity: Flying the plane while rewiring it. *European Journal of Marketing*, *42*(9), 915–926.

Kafetzopoulos, D., Psomas, E., & Skalkos, D. (2020). Innovation dimensions and business performance under environmental uncertainty. *European Journal of Innovation Management*, *23*(5), 856–876.

Kallmuenzer, A., Kraus, S., Peters, M., Steiner, J., & Cheng, C.-F. (2019). Entrepreneurship in tourism firms: A mixed-methods analysis of performance driver configurations. *Tourism Management*, *74*, 319–330.

Kaplan, R. S. & Norton, D. P. (1996). *The Balanced Scorecard: Translating Strategy into Action*. Harvard Business School Press.

Kaplan, R. S. & Norton, D. P. (2005). The office of strategy management. *Harvard Business Review*, *83*(10), 72.

Kim, W. C. (2005). Blue ocean strategy: From theory to practice. *California Management Review*, *47*(3), 105–121.

Knight, F. H. (1921). *Risk, Uncertainty and Profit* (Vol. 31). Houghton Mifflin.

Krippendorff, K. (2004). *Content Analysis: An Introduction to its Methodology.* Thousand Oaks: Sage Publications.

Lahnamäki-Kivelä, S. (2022). Coping with uncertainty: Exploring the foresight actions' role in supporting growth-orientation among Finnish dairy farmers. *Futures*, *135*, 102870.

Lawrence, P. R. & Lorsch, J. W. (1967). Differentiation and integration in complex organizations. *Administrative Science Quarterly*, 1–47.

Lee, P. K., Yeung, A. C., & Cheng, T. E. (2009). Supplier alliances and environmental uncertainty: An empirical study. *International Journal of Production Economics*, *120*(1), 190–204.

Litschert, R. J. & Bonham, T. (1979). Strategic responses to different perceived strategic challenges. *Journal of Management*, *5*(1), 91–105.

Liu, G., Shah, R., & Babakus, E. (2012). When to mass customize: The impact of environmental uncertainty. *Decision Sciences*, *43*(5), 851–887.

López-Duarte, C. & Vidal-Suárez, M. M. (2010). External uncertainty and entry mode choice: Cultural distance, political risk and language diversity. *International Business Review*, *19*(6), 575–588.

Luo, Y. (2003). Industrial dynamics and managerial networking in an emerging market: The case of China. *Strategic Management Journal*, *24*(13), 1315–1327.

March, J. G. (1991). Simon. HA (1958). *Organizations*. New York.

Mascarenhas, B. (1982). Coping with uncertainty in international business. *Journal of International Business Studies*, *13*, 87–98.

Mason, E. S. (1939). Price and production policies of large-scale enterprise. *The American Economic Review*, *29*(1), 61–74.

Matthews, C. H. & Scott, S. G. (1995). Uncertainty and planning in small and entrepreneurial firms: An empirical assessment. *Journal of Small Business Management*, *33*(4), 34–52.

McGrath, R. G., MacMillan, I. C., & Venkataraman, S. (1995). Defining and developing competence: A strategic process paradigm. *Strategic Management Journal*, *16*(4), 251–275.

McMackin, J. & Heffernan, M. (2021). Agile for HR: Fine in practice, but will it work in theory? *Human Resource Management Review*, *31*(4), 1–14.

Merschmann, U. & Thonemann, U. W. (2011). Supply chain flexibility, uncertainty and firm performance: An empirical analysis of German manufacturing firms. *International Journal of Production Economics*, *130*(1), 43–53.

Miles, R. E., Snow, C. C., Meyer, A. D., & Coleman Jr, H. J. (1978). Organizational strategy, structure, and process. *Academy of Management Review*, *3*(3), 546–562.

Miller, C. C. & Cardinal, L. B. (1994). Strategic planning and firm performance: A synthesis of more than two decades of research. *Academy of Management Journal*, *37*(6), 1649–1665.

Miller, D. (1988). Relating Porter's business strategies to environment and structure: Analysis and performance implications. *Academy of Management Journal*, *31*(2), 280–308.

Miller, D. & Friesen, P. H. (1983). Strategy-making and environment: The third link. *Strategic Management Journal*, *4*(3), 221–235.

Miller, J. I. (2012). The mortality problem of learning and mimetic practice in emerging industries: Dying to be legitimate. *Strategic Entrepreneurship Journal*, *6*(1), 59–88.

Milliken, F. J. (1987). Three types of perceived uncertainty about the environment: State, effect, and response uncertainty. *Academy of Management Review*, *12*(1), 133–143.

Mintzberg, H. (1977). Strategy formulation as a historical process. *International Studies of Management & Organization*, *7*(2), 28–40.

Mintzberg, H. (1990). The design school: Reconsidering the basic premises of strategic management. *Strategic Management Journal*, *11*(3), 171–195.

Mintzberg, H., Ahlstrand, B., & Lampel, J. B. (2020). *Strategy Safari*. UK: Pearson.

Mišanková, M. & Kočišová, K. (2014). Strategic implementation as a part of strategic management. *Procedia-Social and Behavioral Sciences*, *110*, 861–870.

Moura, D. D. & Tomei, P. A. (2021). Strategic management of organizational resilience (SMOR): A framework proposition. *Revista Brasileira de Gestão de Negócios*, *23*, 536–556.

Nhon, H. T., Thong, B. Q., & Trung, N. Q. (2020). The effects of intellectual capital on information communication technology firm performance: A moderated mediation analysis of environmental uncertainty. *Cogent Business & Management*, *7*(1), 1–18.

Noble, C. H. (1999). The eclectic roots of strategy implementation research. *Journal of Business Research*, *45*(2), 119–134.

O'Reilly, C. A. & Tushman, M. L. (2004). The ambidextrous organization. *Harvard Business Review*, *82*(4), 74–83.

Ojra, J., Opute, A. P., & Alsolmi, M. M. (2021). Strategic management accounting and performance implications: A literature review and research agenda. *Future Business Journal*, *7*(1), 1–17.

Olson, E. M., Slater, S. F., & Hult, G. T. M. (2005). The performance implications of fit among business strategy, marketing organization structure, and strategic behavior. *Journal of Marketing*, *69*(3), 49–65.

Ondersteijn, C., Giesen, G., & Huirne, R. (2006). Perceived environmental uncertainty in Dutch dairy farming: The effect of external farm context on strategic choice. *Agricultural Systems*, *88*(2–3), 205–226.

Oreja-Rodríguez, J. R. & Yanes-Estévez, V. (2007). Perceived environmental uncertainty in tourism: A new approach using the Rasch model. *Tourism Management*, *28*(6), 1450–1463.

Oswald, S. L., Mossholder, K. W., & Harris, S. G. (1997). Relations between strategic involvement and managers' perceptions of environment and competitive strengths: The effect of vision salience. *Group & Organization Management*, *22*(3), 343–365.

Oyewo, B. (2022). Contextual factors moderating the impact of strategic management accounting on competitive advantage. *Journal of Applied Accounting Research*, *23*(5), 921–949.

Oyewo, B., Tawiah, V., & Hussain, S. T. (2022). Drivers of environmental and social sustainability accounting practices in Nigeria: A corporate governance perspective. *Corporate Governance: The International Journal of Business in Society*, *23*(2), 397–421.

Pacheco, D. F., York, J. G., Dean, T. J., & Sarasvathy, S. D. (2010). The coevolution of institutional entrepreneurship: A tale of two theories. *Journal of Management*, *36*(4), 974–1010.

Parnell, J. A., Lester, D. L., & Menefee, M. L. (2000). Strategy as a response to organizational uncertainty: An alternative perspective on the strategy-performance relationship. *Management Decision*, *38*(8), 520–530.

Pavlatos, O. (2015). An empirical investigation of strategic management accounting in hotels. *International Journal of Contemporary Hospitality Management*, *27*(8), 756–767.

Petera, P. & Šoljaková, L. (2020). Use of strategic management accounting techniques by companies in the Czech Republic. *Economic Research-Ekonomska Istraživanja*, *33*(1), 46–67.

Pinto, J. P. & Medina, J. (2020). Hybrid processes for a new era of strategic foresight. *Foresight*, *22*(3), 287–307.

Plugge, A. & Brook, J. (2011). Examining the implications of organizational structure changes from a transaction cost perspective. International Workshop on Global Sourcing of Information Technology and Business Processes, Courchevel, France.

Porter, C. E. & Donthu, N. (2008). Cultivating trust and harvesting value in virtual communities. *Management Science*, *54*(1), 113–128.

Porter, M. E. (1980). Industry structure and competitive strategy: Keys to profitability. *Financial Analysts Journal*, *36*(4), 30–41.

Powell, T. C., Lovallo, D., & Fox, C. R. (2011). Behavioral strategy. *Strategic Management Journal*, *32*(13), 1369–1386.

Prahalad, C. K. & Hamel, G. (1994). Strategy as a field of study: Why search for a new paradigm? *Strategic Management Journal*, *15*(S2), 5–16.

Priem, R. L., Love, L. G., & Shaffer, M. A. (2002). Executives' perceptions of uncertainty sources: A numerical taxonomy and underlying dimensions. *Journal of Management*, *28*(6), 725–746.

Rajasekar, J. (2014). Factors affecting effective strategy implementation in a service industry: A study of electricity distribution companies in the Sultanate of Oman. *International Journal of Business and Social Science*, *5*(9), 169–183.

Ranjan, J. (2008). Business justification with business intelligence. *Vine*, *38*(4), 461–475.

Raymond, L., Bergeron, F., Croteau, A.-M., & Uwizeyemungu, S. (2019). Determinants and outcomes of IT governance in manufacturing SMEs: A strategic IT management perspective. *International Journal of Accounting Information Systems*, *35*(1), 1–22.

Rumelt, R. P., Schendel, D., & Teece, D. J. (1991). Strategic management and economics. *Strategic Management Journal*, *12*(S2), 5–29.

Sarkar, M. B., Echambadi, R., & Harrison, J. S. (2001). Alliance entrepreneurship and firm market performance. *Strategic Management Journal*, *22*(6–7), 701–711.

Schilke, O. (2014). On the contingent value of dynamic capabilities for competitive advantage: The nonlinear moderating effect of environmental dynamism. *Strategic Management Journal*, *35*(2), 179–203.

Schraeder, M. (2002). A simplified approach to strategic planning: Practical considerations and an illustrated example. *Business Process Management Journal*, *8*(1), 8–18.

Sharfman, M. P. & Dean Jr, J. W. (1991). Conceptualizing and measuring the organizational environment: A multidimensional approach. *Journal of Management*, *17*(4), 681–700.

Sharma, P., Leung, T. Y., Kingshott, R. P., Davcik, N. S., & Cardinali, S. (2020). Managing uncertainty during a global pandemic: An international business perspective. *Journal of Business Research*, *116*, 188–192.

Sia, C.-L., Teo, H.-H., Tan, B. C., & Wei, K.-K. (2004). Effects of environmental uncertainty on organizational intention to adopt distributed work arrangements. *IEEE Transactions on Engineering Management*, *51*(3), 253–267.

Simangunsong, E., Hendry, L. C., & Stevenson, M. (2012). Supply-chain uncertainty: A review and theoretical foundation for future research. *International journal of production research*, *50*(16), 4493–4523.

Simon, H. A. (1957). *Models of Man; Social and Rational*. Wiley.

Slangen, A. H. & Van Tulder, R. J. (2009). Cultural distance, political risk, or governance quality? Towards a more accurate conceptualization and measurement of external uncertainty in foreign entry mode research. *International Business Review*, *18*(3), 276–291.

Sniazhko, S. (2019). Uncertainty in decision-making: A review of the international business literature. *Cogent Business & Management*, *6*(1), 1–32.

Srećković, M. (2018). The performance effect of network and managerial capabilities of entrepreneurial firms. *Small Business Economics*, *50*(4), 807–824.

Steiss, A. W. (2019). *Strategic Management for Public and Nonprofit Organizations*. Routledge.

Svandova, E. & Jirásek, M. (2016). The analysis of perceived environmental uncertainty as a dependant variable. In *3rd International Multidisciplinary Scientific Conference on Social Sciences and Arts SGEM 2016*.

Swamidass, P. M. & Newell, W. T. (1987). Manufacturing strategy, environmental uncertainty and performance: A path analytic model. *Management Science*, *33*(4), 509–524.

Swan, K. S., Kotabe, M., & Allred, B. B. (2005). Exploring robust design capabilities, their role in creating global products, and their relationship to firm performance. *Journal of Product Innovation Management*, *22*(2), 144–164.

Tan, J. (1996). Regulatory environment and strategic orientations in a transitional economy: A study of Chinese private enterprise. *Entrepreneurship Theory and Practice*, *21*(1), 31–46.

Tan, L. P., Le, A. N. H., & Xuan, L. P. (2019). A systematic literature review on social entrepreneurial intention. *Journal of Social Entrepreneurship*, *3*(1), 1–16.

Teece, D., Peteraf, M., & Leih, S. (2016). Dynamic capabilities and organizational agility: Risk, uncertainty, and strategy in the innovation economy. *California Management Review*, *58*(4), 13–35.

Teece, D. J. (2007). Explicating dynamic capabilities: The nature and microfoundations of (sustainable) enterprise performance. *Strategic Management Journal*, *28*(13), 1319–1350.

Teece, D. J. (2019). A capability theory of the firm: An economics and (strategic) management perspective. *New Zealand Economic Papers*, *53*(1), 1–43.

Thompson, J. D. (2017). *Organizations in Action: Social Science Bases of Administrative Theory*. Routledge.

Tregoe, B. B. & Tobia, P. M. (1991). Strategy versus planning: Bridging the gap. *Journal of Business Strategy*, *12*(6), 14–19.

Tsai, K.-H. & Yang, S.-Y. (2013). Firm innovativeness and business performance: The joint moderating effects of market turbulence and competition. *Industrial Marketing Management*, *42*(8), 1279–1294.

Tseng, C.-H. & Lee, R. P. (2010). Host environmental uncertainty and equity-based entry mode dilemma: The role of market linking capability. *International Business Review*, *19*(4), 407–418.

Tushman, M. L., Newman, W. H., & Romanelli, E. (1986). Convergence and upheaval: Managing the unsteady pace of organizational evolution. *California Management Review*, *29*(1), 29–44.

Vaitoonkiat, E. & Charoensukmongkol, P. (2020). Stakeholder orientation's contribution to firm performance: The moderating effect of perceived market uncertainty. *Management Research Review*, *43*(7), 863–883.

Vecchiato, R. (2012). Strategic foresight and environmental uncertainty: A research agenda. *Foresight*, *14*(5), 387–400.

Weiss, M. & Wittmann, C. (2018). Objective environmental conditions and perceived environmental uncertainty: Cognitive models as explanation for a perceptual gap. *Journal of Accounting & Organizational Change*, *14*(1), 33–60.

Westhead, P., Wright, M., & Ucbasaran, D. (2004). Internationalization of private firms: Environmental turbulence and organizational strategies and resources. *Entrepreneurship & Regional Development*, *16*(6), 501–522.

Whipp, R. & Pettigrew, A. (1992). Managing change for competitive success: Bridging the strategic and the operational. *Industrial and Corporate Change*, *1*(1), 205–233.

Wiltbank, R., Dew, N., Read, S., & Sarasvathy, S. D. (2006). What to do next? The case for non-predictive strategy. *Strategic Management Journal*, *27*(10), 981–998.

Xia, N., Zou, P. X., Griffin, M. A., Wang, X., & Zhong, R. (2018). Towards integrating construction risk management and stakeholder management: A systematic literature review and future research agendas. *International Journal of Project Management*, *36*(5), 701–715.

Xin, W. (2020). Exploring the impact of strategic flexibility on business model innovation under the open innovation activity: The moderating roles of multiple factors with competitive ties and cooperative ties. *International Business Research*, *13*(7), 1–80.

Xu, K., Huang, K.-F., & Gao, S. (2012). The effect of institutional ties on knowledge acquisition in uncertain environments. *Asia Pacific Journal of Management*, *29*(2), 387–408.

Zhang, Q., Vonderembse, M. A., & Lim, J.-S. (2002). Value chain flexibility: A dichotomy of competence and capability. *International Journal of Production Research*, *40*(3), 561–583.

https://doi.org/10.1142/9789811286100_0002

Chapter 2

Marketing and Advertising: Shifting from Conventional to Digital Marketing

Tien Minh Dinh[*,‡], Oanh Le Vu Lan[*,†,§]
and Mai Dong Tran[*,¶]

[*]*School of International Business and Marketing, College of Business, University of Economics Ho Chi Minh City, Vietnam*

[†]*Van Lang University, Ho Chi Minh City, Vietnam*

[‡]*dinhtienminh@ueh.edu.vn*

[§]*oanhlvl@ueh.edu.vn; oanh.lvl@vlu.edu.vn.*

[¶]*tmdong@ueh.edu.vn*

Abstract

With the advent of technology, marketing and advertising have undergone constant development and refinement. This chapter aims to provide an illustration of how marketing and advertising techniques have changed from conventional to digital marketing. Synthetic and descriptive research methodologies were employed. The findings address two distinct subjects: (1) consumer and business perspectives on the impact of technology and (2) the development of digital marketing over time. Finally, some directions for further research as well as practical commercial solutions are suggested.

Received on March 3, 2023; accepted on May 13, 2023

Keywords: Digital Marketing, Marketing and Digital Shift, Conventional to Digital.

1. Introduction

The transformation toward digital media has resulted in new opportunities for businesses to engage with their customers in more meaningful, personalized ways and to track and measure the effectiveness of their marketing campaigns in real time. The world is witnessing the emergence, development, and rapid diffusion of information and communications technologies (ICTs) and digital media such as email, search engines, websites, and social media platforms (Kulkarni *et al.*, 2020). As of January 2021, the number of internet users worldwide reached 4.66 billion, of which 92% accessed the internet from their mobile phones. Meanwhile, the number of real social media users recorded was 4.33 billion, which represents about 55% of the global population (Meltwater and WeAreSocial, 2023). Instead of passively receiving product information through conventional channels such as radio, television, and newspapers, consumers can switch to actively using digital communication channels to search for information about products and services. Social media has progressed drastically in building successful consumer engagement both in brand building and sustainable consumption (Bryła *et al.*, 2022). It has become a part of everyone's daily lives (Lamberton and Stephen, 2016). The dramatic increase in reach over time and geography has also empowered consumers to influence brands, products, and services (Plume *et al.*, 2016). Technological advancements and digital media have made it easier for businesses to reach and interact with consumers (Alghizzawi *et al.*, 2018). Responding to the changes in technology and consumers, marketers have increased the use of digital marketing channels such as email marketing, social media marketing, and mobile marketing. These marketers are relying on ICTs such as big data, artificial intelligence (AI), GPS, Bluetooth, and other internet and mobile connectivity technologies to deliver messages that have been fine-tuned to best suit different customer segments in many different locations and countries (Singh and Keating, 2018). Digital marketing and advertising are therefore the future of business. They enable businesses to create personalized content and offers that resonate with their target audiences, leading to higher conversion rates (Kapoor *et al.*,

2016). Furthermore, digital marketing is generally more cost-effective than traditional marketing; for instance, running an ad campaign on social media or search engines is less expensive than running a TV or radio ad. With digital marketing, it is easier to track and measure the success of marketing campaigns. Businesses can see how many people clicked on an ad, how long they spent on a website, and whether they made a purchase. These data can be used to optimize future marketing efforts. In terms of reach and engagement, digital marketing allows businesses to reach larger audiences and engage with customers in real time. Social media, email marketing, and content marketing are all effective ways to build relationships with customers and increase brand loyalty (Habes *et al.*, 2018).

The advent and advancement of digital technology have dramatically changed consumer behavior as innovative technology and the widespread adoption of electronic devices directly contribute to how users interact to make decisions and shop online. The increasing use of digital marketing and social media has positively influenced consumer attitudes toward online shopping, and the growing number of shopping channels has also influenced consumer behavior. The trend of personalized, targeted advertising has led to an increase in consumer privacy concerns, and research has shown that factors such as invasiveness, privacy control, and consumer innovation consumption can directly affect consumers' behavioral intentions regarding privacy concerns (Gironda, 2018). However, it is worth noting that these findings have primarily been based on studies of consumers in developed countries. Another study by Abou-Elgheit (2018) highlights the importance of considering cognitive, emotional, experiential, and personality aspects that can influence consumer decision-making around privacy concerns. This suggests that a one-size-fits-all approach to addressing consumer privacy concerns may not be effective and that companies should take a more nuanced approach that considers individual differences in consumer behavior and decision-making.

Since the voice of consumers has become more substantial due to the advancement of social media and is now heard by more people, researchers have focused on analyzing user interactions through factors such as brand interaction, brand image, brand image relevance, motivation, and the significant impact of electronic word of mouth (eWOM) communication on information reception, consumer attitudes, purchase intention, and brand loyalty intention. If, in the past, businesses were the factors that influenced users' decisions, now the influence of the people around them, both online and offline, is the basis for promoting shopping behavior. With the increasing use of the internet and social media, people are spending more time online looking for information about products and services and interacting with businesses and other consumers. This change in consumer behavior has prompted businesses to incorporate social and digital media into their marketing strategies to reach their target audiences more effectively. Social and digital media have become integral components of business marketing plans, allowing companies to engage with their customers in real time, build relationships, and gather valuable insights into consumer behavior and preferences (Stephen, 2016). By leveraging social and digital media platforms, businesses can create more targeted and personalized marketing campaigns that resonate with their target audiences, ultimately leading to increased customer loyalty and revenue.

In this chapter, we implemented a synthetic and descriptive method that involves analyzing, synthesizing, and examining a large body of research from Web of Science data to identify common themes, patterns, and trends in the emergence and growth of digital marketing from different viewpoints. The chapter depicts the synthetic and descriptive analysis of research approaches to broadly characterize the emergence and growth of digital marketing from two viewpoints that help to provide a comprehensive understanding of the emergence and growth of digital marketing and the ways in which it has transformed the marketing landscape. The first viewpoint involves understanding insights in connection with the impacts of digital marketing, while the second focuses on the phases of growth of digital marketing from a research standpoint.

To begin with, we illustrate the attributes of digital technologies that have a significant impact on the marketing process and strategy based on our reading of multiple papers that focus on development in the digital marketing context from the Web of Science data. The result shows four themes: (a) a move toward digitalizing the customer, (b) a shift in marketing tactics to account for altered consumer behavior, (c) a business transformation to better meet reality, and (d) a screenshot of expected outcomes.

- "A move toward digitalizing the customer" begins with considering the five *C*s — customers, collaborators, competitors, context, and company — which are significantly affected by the advent of digital technological advances and significantly reduce information asymmetries between customers and sellers (Kannan and Li, 2017). Environmental factor analysis focuses on analyzing changes in consumer behavior through access to online media, online reviews and ratings, and interactions on social networks; reviewing search engine studies and interactions between customers, search engines, and businesses; and examining the interactions between digital technology in different geo-cultural contexts, security and privacy, and regulation and piracy (Dwivedi *et al.*, 2021).

- "A shift in marketing tactics" occurs based on the information gathered from research and analysis and marketing mix elements. Research topics include the influence of social media and digital technology on customer value, from which stem marketing strategies related to brand management and customer value. Another topic also studies the interaction between digital marketing strategies, such as the communication strategies of brands on social networks (Kusumasondjaja, 2018), information strategies (Tafesse and Wien, 2018), and digital social viewing strategies (Ang *et al.*, 2018), and consumer behavior and feedback to choose the right platform and tools for a business's marketing.
- Within "a business transformation to better meet the reality", the transformation of a business's quality is a topic of discussion, marked by changes in customer approach and the application of new marketing techniques. Recent research has shown that the values, vision, and mission of a company have become more important factors than the products or services that the company provides. Nowadays, consumers are interested in the values and vision of a company, such as its ethics, diversity, and inclusiveness. Businesses can use digital marketing to demonstrate their commitment to social responsibility by, for example, sponsoring charity programs or sharing stories about diverse employees. Data analysis technology can also be used to understand customer behavior and preferences, helping to create personalized marketing strategies and increase effective commercial connections.
- "A screenshot of expected outcomes" reflects how users are currently expecting a seamless and analytics-driven experience across all touch points, including digital marketing. They want to quickly navigate the web, receive prompt answers to their requests, and have a consistent experience across different channels. Businesses are placing emphasis

on user experience to enhance satisfaction and retain customers. In addition, consumers expect businesses to provide value beyond transactions, such as useful content or educational resources. Businesses can offer valuable content to enhance engagement and build long-term relationships with their customers.

The next step is to continue outlining the overview of the research across different periods of time using the Web of Science data. The world has seen a tremendous increase in digital marketing research activities, particularly after the year 2000, and especially in digital marketing theory and application. The five key stages are as follows:

- **Stage 1: Time to start digital marketing (before the 2000s)**: The period before the year 2000 was the period that laid the foundation for the transition from conventional marketing to digital marketing. The advent of the internet was the driving force behind research during this time, mainly focused on its effects and related issues, as well as the first step into understanding the application of the internet in marketing. Research during this period revolved around issues such as social and corporate interests in digital marketing (Bush *et al.*, 2000) or advertising through online websites (Berthon *et al.*, 1996).
- **Stage 2: How to build customer satisfaction and loyalty (2001–2005)**: Along with the development of the internet, new opportunities and problems arose that affected a customer's experience in cyberspace. Examples included the massive growth of e-commerce and related security issues such as spamming and network hijacking (Stead and Gilbert, 2001) or security issues related to customer acceptance of e-commerce and online transactions (Palmer, 2005). The growing risk gave rise to the need for businesses to ensure customer satisfaction and security digitally.
- **Stage 3: Deeper concept of customer loyalty and social network development (2006–2010)**: After nearly a decade since the internet appeared, consumers gradually became more adaptive and active on online platforms, so there was an increase in the network of groups and online communities. Simultaneously, an increasing number of businesses began using multiple platforms for their operation activities, and the trend of the multichannel approach was gradually becoming

popular. The research in this period focused on keywords such as *social network* and *multichannel*, and notable research relating to the use of social cognitive theory to analyze the knowledge shared in online communities came from Chiu *et al.* (2006).

- **Stage 4: Co-creation and customer engagement activities (2011–2015)**: Following the development of digital marketing, businesses were then interested in taking advantage of cyberspace to connect with customers and encourage them to participate in the value-creation process in business, so there were many related studies on co-creation in marketing communication (Bacile *et al.*, 2014) or the customer engagement (CE) concept (van Doorn *et al.*, 2010b).
- **Stage 5: Prosperous times of machine intelligence and IoT-based virtual reality (2016 up to now)**: This is a time of technology explosion with the advent of smartphones, AI, and virtual reality (VR) technology. These are the technological innovations of the century with a profound impact on all aspects of life. Along with the flow of the digital era, businesses have an increasing need to apply AI or VR to digital marketing.

Digital marketing has had a significant impact on the marketing landscape, and its growth can be broadly characterized in several stages. By taking a deeper and more specific look at these insights, we can gain a comprehensive understanding of the evolution of digital marketing and its impact on businesses and consumers.

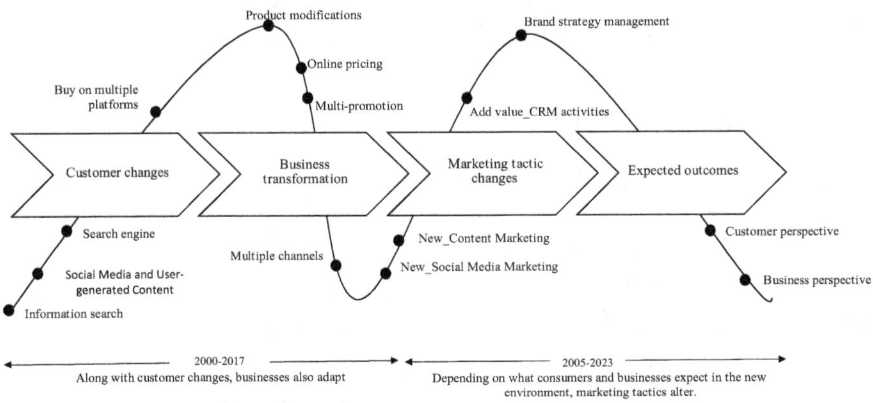

Figure 1. Insights in connection with the impacts of technology development.
Source: Adapted from Kannan, P. K. (2017) and Dwivedi, Y. K. *et al.* (2021).

2. Insights in Connection with the Impacts of Technology Development

2.1. *Theme 1: A look at digitalizing the customer*

In a typical offline environment, the customer process can be quite lengthy, especially during the product review and evaluation phase, but in a digital environment, the stages can be compressed or eliminated (Edelman and Singer, 2015). Customers are attracted by modern and fast processes: automation, which ensures a smooth online experience; personalization, which makes shopping recommendations based on individual preferences; contextual interaction, which engages customers and arranges for them to take the appropriate steps; and innovation in the journey, which drives customer loyalty. In the online environment, customers can access an extremely large number of products, so it will be difficult for them to compare substitute products (Häubl and Trifts, 2000). Research has been conducted on the impact that interactive decision-support tools can have on consumer decision-making in the online shopping environment. The first tool is the recommendation agent, which assists the consumer in the initial screening of alternatives. The second is a comparison matrix, designed to help consumers make in-depth comparisons between selected alternatives. A comparison matrix facilitates an in-depth comparison of any selected alternatives that are seriously being considered for purchase. These two tools make it easier for customers to choose products with less time and effort, improving their ability to identify the right products for themselves and reap significant benefits.

2.1.1. *How customers are impacted*

Consumer behavior is also influenced by the characteristics of mobile devices. Shankar *et al.* (2010) indicate that mobile devices are increasingly important in the internet retail industry. These devices have the ability to change the retail model from a model based on consumers participating in the retail environment to a retail model that penetrates the environment of consumers through mobile devices anytime, anywhere. Customers can access a retailer's programs instantly through a mobile device. However, in a store, customers can only interact with a brick-and-mortar retailer when they are near the store. The evolution of consumer behavior in the online shopping environment is due to consumers' previous experience with the various interactive decision-support tools available in stores (Shi and Zhang, 2014). Retailers can use various tools and decision aids to track and infer customer behavior by, for example, analyzing patterns in their purchasing history, browsing behavior, and studying interactions with a retailer's online and offline channels. Information search is a critical component of a customer's decision journey, and the availability of online search engines, social media, and other digital channels has made it easier for customers to access and evaluate information about products and services. These tools assist customers in the initial screening process and have a strong and positive impact on purchasing decisions (Häubl and Trifts, 2000). Shoppers can make better decisions with less effort. In the digital environment, customers can influence other potential buyers both before and after purchasing a product through online reviews, social media, and more (Court *et al.*, 2009). Customers choose how much information they want to collect, trading the benefits of a purchase for the cost of searching. The cost of searching is quite high for a product that is not purchased often, and the effort of checking the price each time you shop can outweigh the benefits of spending less. If search costs were halved, the elasticity of demand could triple (Seiler, 2013). Trust is a key factor influencing customers' selective search and information-sourcing behavior in the digital environment. From the point of view of customers, they want their retail websites to be trustworthy and their transactions and personal information to be safe (Mandal *et al.*, 2019). However, such customer requirements may not be fully aligned with a supplier's performance perspective. The emerging trend of personalized, targeted advertising has led to an increase in consumer privacy concerns, supporting research into theories about online trust (Shankar *et al.*, 2002).

2.1.2. *Customers take advantage of social media, user-generated content, and search engines*

In the digital environment, customers can easily share word-of-mouth information with acquaintances or even strangers on social networks

(Watts, 2007). A key feature that distinguishes the digital environment from traditional marketing environments is the ability for customers to share eWOM with a few close friends as well as strangers. In the digital environment, customers can post reviews of products, services, brands, and businesses on a company's website as well as third-party websites and social networks. One widely studied form of online customer interaction is online reviews (e.g., user-generated content and eWOM). In particular, eWOM can have richer content and volume than traditional word of mouth and can be much more accessible and widely disseminated in the digital environment. This type of communication can have a significant impact on information reception, consumer attitudes, purchase intention, loyalty, and trust toward a brand (Filieri and McLeay, 2014). However, even though eWOM is directly proportional to sales, the effect varies across platform, product, and metric factors (Babić Rosario *et al.*, 2016). Other research has concluded that showing subjectivity in online reviews can increase consumer purchase intention (Babić Rosario *et al.*, 2016; Ismagilova *et al.*, 2020); consumers' online product ratings reflect both the customer's experience with the product and the influence of other people's ratings, so eWOM communication can bring significant benefits to organizations while also presenting challenges (Liu *et al.*, 2018). Negative eWOM communication can have serious consequences for businesses, leading to a damaged reputation, negative consumer attitudes, and reduced sales. Search engines allow customers to obtain free information about products and services and identify businesses and brands that match their search criteria. Search engines such as Google, Bing, and Yahoo provide both organic and paid search listings in response to users' search queries. Moe and Trusov (2011) have shown that customers acquired through paid searches tend to spend more and generate higher lifetime value compared to customers from other online or offline channels. This is because paid search ads allow advertisers to target specific keywords and demographics, which increases the likelihood of reaching their desired audiences and generating conversions. Search engines provide businesses with keyword performance reports to help them understand the effectiveness of their paid search ads. An empirical study of search engines found that the monetary value of a click is not uniform across all positions since conversion rates are highest at the top and decrease in rank as a person descends the search engine results page (Moe and Trusov, 2011). At the same time, the analysis also shows that keywords with more prominent positions on the search engine results page have higher click-through or conversion rates and that keywords in the middle of the page bring more profit than keywords at the top and bottom of the page.

2.1.3. *Customers have more choices regarding different platforms and two-sided markets with contextual interactions*

In a digital environment, multiple platforms and platform markets exist, such as those that connect individual customers to other individual sellers (eBay), those that connect customers to multiple businesses or sellers (Alibaba, Amazon, media sites, etc.), those that connect businesses to businesses (business-to-business platforms), and those that connect businesses to crowds (provisioning platforms) for community service and innovation (such as Kickstarter). Trustworthy platforms generate revenue through various means, such as commissions, performance-based fees, and impression-based fees. A community sourcing platform is another type of platform that helps to connect businesses with their customers (crowds) and generate ideas for new products and services. The platform creates a network effect where more users and buyers attract more sellers and advertisers to the two-sided marketplace. Research on indirect networks shows that a seller may prefer a market with many other sellers because it is more attractive to buyers (Ghose and Yang, 2009). In addition, the platform and two-sided marketplace generate active income for service providers by charging commissions or service fees from transactions made on their systems. However, they can also lead to an unequal distribution of profits among the participants, depending on the decisions of the platform and the evolution of the two-sided market. Dual platforms and marketplaces allow businesses to continuously gather ideas from dispersed groups of customers and select the best ideas for future growth. The platforms should customize their task structures based on each customer's domain-specific knowledge to increase the quality of ideas (Tucker and Zhang, 2010). In addition, businesses also need to use these platforms to create interactions with their customers and enhance their marketing and advertising activities. Although the digital landscape transcends geographic boundaries, online consumer preferences and choices are still highly geography dependent. Differences between interactions in different contexts lead to different behaviors; for instance, the fact that customers choose between several book formats that are made available by publishers demonstrates that geographical disparities can have unobserved impacts due to differences in location and price sensitivity. (Luo and Toubia, 2015). Meanwhile, researchers studying customer trials at Netgrocer.com found that spatial exposure to people nearby (either through observation or direct social interaction) influenced the judgments of those who had not tried the service (Jank and Kannan, 2005). Online businesses are increasingly committed to leveraging valuable personal information about their customers' search behavior, online reviews, social media activity, and everything else they interact with online. In the United States, a customer's personally identifiable information may be shared between businesses if a company clearly states its intent in its privacy policy. Detailed data collected from businesses help marketers better understand when, where, and how they meet customer needs. However, customers' concerns about their privacy are worth noting (Bell and Song, 2007); even in the absence of network effects, piracy can increase a company's profits because weaker copyright protection can allow businesses to reduce price competition by copying products for price-sensitive consumers (Pingitore *et al.*, 2013).

2.2. *Theme 2: A business transformation to better meet the reality*

The development trend of technology has made digital media an indispensable consideration, and digital media has a significant impact on the marketing activities of businesses related to elements such as product, price, promotion, and distribution. In addition, the interaction between digital media and a business is also manifested through the reshaping of information-gathering activities through marketing research and analysis to form the marketing strategy of the company.

Regarding products, digital technology is gradually changing the concept of products in three ways. First, businesses can enhance the core values of products with digital services where the core value of a product is increased by the value derived from digital improvements such as cars with GPS systems and self-driving technology based on sensors. Second, digital technology unlocks the inherent values of products as seen with, for example, renting through the use of technology and digital networks in the business models of rental services such as Airbnb, Uber, and Lyft (Jain, 2008). Third, products and services are evolving into digital services. This modification significantly lowers the cost of producing and distributing digital content. In addition, the concept of *economies of aggregation* can result in the bundling of content on a massive scale (Sundararajan, 2017). These trends create customization and personalization of customer services. The term "customerization" refers to a business's product approach that integrates mass customization and personalized marketing by utilizing online menus to personalize modular products (Bakos and Brynjolfsson, 2000).

The development of technology has brought about many changes in the pricing of products. Digital products and services have production and distribution costs that are very low or close to zero. One study shows that optimal pricing for online and offline content can lead to higher profits by serving as a tool for price differentiation (Wind and Rangaswamy, 2001). Pricing for online products and services is more dynamic than for traditional businesses for several reasons: (a) low search costs for consumers, (b) low menu costs for retailers, (c) rapid changes in shopping environments, and (d) the fact that retailers can respond to customer searches more quickly.

In terms of promotion, in addition to traditional media, the digital environment provides new means of reaching customers and promoting products and services through email, display advertising, and social media (promotions). The more creative the advertising method, the more effect the business gets. Many businesses are faced with how to extract useful and relevant information from large volumes of data, known as *big data*. Another challenge is *real-time* execution, which requires the use of large datasets with the help of automation. The emergence of mobile devices, their features, and how consumers use them are of significant importance to place activities. Nowadays, some customers may choose to search and purchase through online channels, while others may use the internet to collect information but will ultimately purchase from a traditional store (Venkatesh and Chatterjee, 2006), thus creating a challenge in channel management. A big question that should be considered is which channels businesses need to build, but regardless, developing and distributing products through multiple channels is essential in today's digital environment (Verhoef *et al.*, 2007).

In marketing research activities, the digital environment creates a range of different data from customer reviews and ratings to mouse-click data, social interaction data, and data from competing opponents. These data are very useful for a company to understand online customer behavior and develop or measure marketing strategies and their effectiveness. In addition, other studies have used social media tagging data and developed activity-tagged metrics as measures representing customer-based brand equity to explain abnormal profits (Li and Kannan, 2014). This line of research suggests that digital environment data can contain very useful information for tracking a company's operations. Moe (2003) employed clickstream information to experimentally evaluate a classification of store visits that differed based on shoppers' intentions, including purchasing, browsing, searching, or knowledge acquisition. By using this behavioral data to classify visits, businesses can recognize and target potential buyers and develop more efficient and personalized promotional messages. Moreover, data generated in digital environments can produce performance-related metrics for a company. Finally, Nam and Kannan (2014) utilized data from social tagging and created metrics that served as approximate indicators for customer-based brand valuations and accounted for abnormal returns. This line of inquiry demonstrates that information obtained from digital environments can be highly beneficial for monitoring a company's progress.

2.3. *Theme 3: A shift in marketing tactics to account for altered consumer behavior*

2.3.1. *Social media marketing*

The use of social media and digital marketing is now becoming a strategic tool for building brand awareness and marketing campaigns. These shape-shifting promotional activities focus on interactive communication with customers rather than sending one-way messages to the mass population through traditional media (Nam and Kannan, 2014). Social media and the semantic web offer businesses important opportunities to manage personalized behavioral advertising campaigns (Jara *et al.*, 2012). Businesses today use different social media platforms for marketing, such as Facebook, Instagram, TikTok, and Twitter. Some research shows that a firm's brand positioning strategy can be impacted by its search engine marketing (SEM) and search engine optimization (SEO) strategies (Li and Du, 2012); social media websites have resonated with brand communications, forming complex feedback loops between firm communications, news media, and user-generated social media (Dou *et al.*, 2010). Interactive branded posts drive more engagement than generic informational posts (Hewett *et al.*, 2016). However, in order to utilize this opportunity, businesses need to research and choose the right marketing activities or platforms based on their target customers and marketing strategies.

2.3.2. *Content marketing*

Today, content advertising and marketing have emerged as important considerations in online advertising and marketing campaigns, and are considered to be a vital device in virtual advertising and marketing. Nowadays, content advertising and marketing are not always best finished with the aid of big businesses (specifically businesses within the discipline of facts generation including Microsoft, Facebook, Apple, and Google) and may instead benefit from the aid of small and medium businesses. The number one goal of content advertising and marketing is to give and teach audiences information, to shape and expand relationships with them, and to outline logo loyalty. This strategy becomes more authentic in the eyes of consumers if it is oriented toward live streaming instead of prerecorded videos (Kusumasondjaja, 2018); the inclusion of humor and emotion can lead to more consumer engagement (Tyson Ang *et al.*, 2018). Looking at the content advertising and marketing techniques of eleven business-to-business corporations, we realize that the usage of feelings in content advertising and marketing can aggressively grow benefits and logo price (Lee *et al.*, 2018). By growing treasured content, businesses can construct targeted interests and develop them into long-term client relationships.

We can see that content advertising and marketing bring lots of advantages to corporations, including commercial value and loyalty.

2.3.3. *Customer relationship management*

Presenting modern channels and items and collaborating with modern clients require businesses to upgrade and learn all about client administration and brand administration and require businesses to rethink promoting measurements and their customer relationship management (CRM) measurements. Social media has reshaped *social CRM* procedures. It highlights the fact that customer esteem encompasses more than just fair purchase-based esteem items and also includes the esteem of their social influence (Hutchins and Rodriguez, 2018). With the rise of tremendous social organizing platforms, customers are not restricted to an inactive part in their relationship with a company. Nowadays, social media and other unused avenues have enabled buyers. Innovation has empowered buyers to filter through publicity and CRM messages, compare costs with competitors from any place by employing a versatile gadget, and recognize positive or negative brand messages to a worldwide group of onlookers. CRM must advance if it is to outlive today's advanced commercial center by creating touch points that lock in shoppers and convey esteem to both the company and the shopper instead of only centering on company esteem.

2.3.4. *Brand strategy management*

At the center of brand administration is understanding how brands are made, adjusted, and fortified within the advanced scene. A firm's brand positioning strategy can be impacted by its SEM and SEO strategies (Malthouse *et al.*, 2013). Businesses can thus take advantage of the opportunity to leverage these tools in the process of developing a branding strategy. Creating brand mindfulness is the primary and most vital arrangement when showcasing communications. Different types of communication tools have been utilized to achieve this within trade preparation, and SEM and SEO techniques can have an impact on a company's brand positioning strategy. More aspects and metrics must be considered when building a branding strategy as SEM and SEO are adapted and utilized for mobile, voice search, in-app search, and chat room commerce. Hanssens and Pauwels (2016) offer a thorough examination of the metrics and indicators required to assess strategy implementation and determine the value of marketing to a firm. Finally, this strategy needs to work together with other strategies to get better results.

2.4. *Theme 4: A screenshot of expected outcomes*

The transition from traditional marketing to digital marketing (using digital tools and channels to attract and build customer profiles, promote brand awareness, retain customers, and increase revenue) has impacted factors such as customer behavior, contextual communication, social media, search tools, and two-way markets. It has opened up new opportunities for us to gain a deeper understanding of consumers and the market. We can recognize its value for customers and businesses. It includes the aspects of fair value (the objective value a customer receives), brand value, relationship value, customer satisfaction, customer value and its factors, and company value and its factors (Dou *et al.*, 2010).

Regarding the value of customers, there have been studies conducted using online research tools to analyze customer content posted on social media platforms, search keywords, eWOM (Rust *et al.*, 2005), and online communities (Habibi *et al.*, 2014; Liu and Karahanna, 2017). Issues regarding the quality of information, reliability, usefulness, and authenticity have been raised. Online evaluations can lead to changes in consumer attitudes and purchasing behaviors, affecting the operations of a company. Studies have found that digital marketing based on social media has a positive impact on customer retention (Liu *et al.*, 2018) and purchase intentions in the context of hotels (Hanaysha, 2018), luxury fashion brands (Alansari *et al.*, 2018), and universities (Morra *et al.*, 2018). At the same time, it also affects customers' perceptions of the company's brand. This can take the form of aspects such as brand meaning (Wong *et al.*, 2018), brand assets (Stojanovic *et al.*, 2018; Tarnovskaya and Biedenbach, 2018), brand loyalty, and brand sustainability (Mishra, 2019). Social media platforms, such as Instagram and Facebook, allow customers to interact regularly with a company and with other customers, allowing them to exchange opinions and share their experiences. They can act in groups, gather users together with a common interest, and follow a specific brand, meaning they co-create the image of the company that owns that brand. In addition, many studies on the effects of the digital environment reveal that while customer satisfaction remained constant, customer loyalty to a service provider increased when the service was selected online (Ahmed *et al.*, 2019). Daily online word-of-mouth or eWOM has a significant impact on sales performance (Shankar *et al.*, 2003), and online chat has a significant impact on firm value when excluding all plausible alternative explanations (Sonnier *et al.*, 2011). Company-generated content can impact social media pages and affect individual customers' purchase behavior (Kumar and Reinartz, 2016).

Regarding the value of a business, digital technology plays a crucial role in increasing competitiveness, particularly in the digital transformation process involving new technology models. Organizations supported by digital tools, such as content marketing, SEO, SEM, social media marketing, email marketing, pay-per-click, and mobile marketing, can build foundational capabilities to create value for their customers and themselves. Processes activated by digital technology generate value through new customer experiences, interactions with customers, customer-to-customer interactions, and other means. Digital technology and marketing strategies can support businesses in monitoring customer behavior, analyzing requested content, and more, both on organizational platforms and on social media. Businesses can manage their budgets more effectively and have full control over the real-time execution of their tasks. In addition, an advantage of digital marketing over traditional marketing is the optimization of costs for collecting, storing, and analyzing customer data (McAlister *et al.*, 2012). This can help reduce costs such as search costs, replication costs, shipping costs, tracking costs, and desired customer analysis costs. Compared to geographically limited traditional marketing, digital marketing can reach an endless number of targeted customers and be adjusted to specific criteria for each campaign. Thanks to these advantages, numerous studies demonstrate the impact of digital marketing tools on sales revenue (Dubé and Misra, 2023; James, 2020; Onyango, 2016). Digital marketing is not limited by national and territorial borders. It can react quickly, at any time, anywhere, and

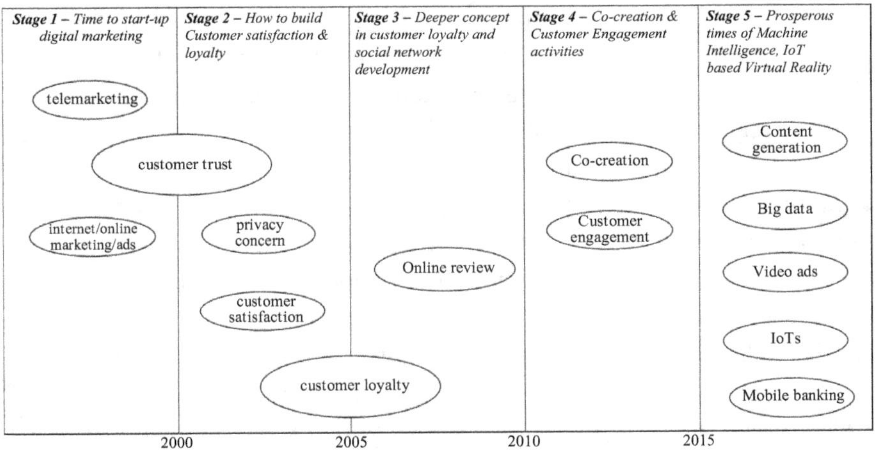

Figure 2. The development of digital marketing over time.

Source: Adapted from Herhausen, D. *et al.* (2020) and Krishen, A. S. *et al.* (2021).

disseminate information quickly on a large scale. It can choose target customers and personalize contact with them. Businesses can store customer information more easily and contact each individual customer more quickly.

3. The Development of Digital Marketing Over Time

3.1. *Stage 1: Time to start digital marketing (Before 2000s)*

The term *digital marketing* first appeared in the 1990s in conjunction with the introduction of the internet and the development of the Web 1.0 platform. Users could search for information on the Web 1.0 platform, but they could not share it. Up until then, marketers had no assurance that they would be able to enter digital platforms. Since the internet was not widely available at the time, they had no reason to believe that their strategies would be effective. By the 2000s, when the internet was experiencing rapid growth, traditional marketing had gradually transitioned to digital marketing. This transition to a digital model opened up many profitable opportunities for organizations and businesses, but it also raised many concerns about trust and the security of personal information. During this time, the main digital marketing studies focused on topics such as telemarketing, customer trust, and internet or online marketing and advertising. The growth rate of the research results in these areas was relatively slow, which is regarded as a sign of the first transition stage, the start-up stage.

At the beginning of this period, there was the development of digital marketing methods, and users were gradually becoming interested in indirect marketing forms rather than traditional direct marketing and advertising. One of the very first publications about direct marketing on the internet and assessments of consumer attitude came from Mehta and Sivadas (1995), who reported on the results of attitudes toward direct internet marketing and then assessed the strengths and weaknesses of using the internet as a direct marketing medium. An interesting finding from another study indicates that the respondents who reacted negatively to "cyber junk" had no goals but were more sympathetic to targeted marketing communications efforts on the internet (Yasmin *et al.*, 2015). This period saw how the development of information technology revolutionized the way businesses operate and interact with their customers. The availability of powerful computing systems and storage devices, combined with the increasing sophistication of software applications, made it possible for businesses to collect, process, and analyze vast amounts of data about their customers and their transactions. The ability to capture and analyze customer data in real time enabled businesses to develop more personalized marketing programs that could target individual customers with products and services that match their preferences and buying behavior (Mehta and Sivadas, 1995). However, the same information practices that provide value to organizations also raise privacy concerns for individuals. Many people became concerned about the collection, use, and sharing of their personal data by businesses and other organizations and worried that their information may be used for purposes that they had not authorized or that could be harmful to them.

Thanks to the development of telecommunications technologies, individuals were able to shop without leaving the house, and businesses were able to develop telemarketing. Teleshopping options gave individuals a choice between shopping at home and in-store. This involves trade-offs between the costs (in terms of time and money) and the benefits of taking a trip or communicating with vendors. Studies have focused on analyzing consumers' choices between physical mobility and e-mobility (Salomon, 1992). Furthermore, customer trust is considered a survival factor in an increasingly competitive global economy because businesses need huge amounts of information to build strong relationships with existing customers and attract new ones. The attributes of a salesperson, such as expertise, intent, the ability to influence customer trust in the salesperson, and trust in the organization represented by the salespeople, also have a significant impact on customer trust (Mehta and Sivadas, 1995). The development revolution dramatically changed the traditional view of advertising and media as a new marketing medium capable of completely changing the way businesses conduct themselves with their customers. This period saw the emergence of the World Wide Web. From a commercial perspective, the web includes locations or websites that businesses erect on servers and consumers on the web. Meanwhile, consumer-oriented network navigation includes visiting a variety of websites in search of information or advertisements about consumer products and services or content (which may be home support ads) or placing an order for a product. The huge number of visitors led to the success of internet marketing and online advertisements (Andaleeb and Anwar, 1996).

From that base, internet or online marketing and advertising gradually became accepted by users and became popular. There are many studies about the intermediate roles of internet channels in providing categorization systems that elucidate the possible influence of the internet on various products and services, situating the internet in relation to retail channels. There is no obvious reason why the internet, or any internet-based business, should cost users money on its own or make them spend more money. Rather, utilizing the internet to promote products or services to customers will most likely result in income redistribution across channels or between members within a channel (Hoffman and Novak, 1996). Customers are clearly informed about the fair practices regarding the information used, and privacy concerns do not distinguish consumers who are willing to be profiled from those who do not want their personal information used in this way (Peterson *et al.*, 1997). However, some issues related to the accurate measurement of gross rating point, reach, and the frequency of online advertising are often included in the discussion when compared to traditional media, such as advertising and print (Culnan and Armstrong, 1999).

On the trend of global digitization, to compete and develop in the digital era, the application of digital marketing is considered an effective solution, helping businesses increase their competitiveness, easily reach potential customers, and bring higher business efficiency because digital marketing is changing the role of marketing communication by becoming the trend of the times and opening up many new opportunities for society. In terms of business, sales and profits are the ultimate goals. Customer data are the most valuable asset to a marketer. How to collect user data and make customers no longer worry about their privacy is an issue that businesses and organizations must handle carefully because customer trust is essential. The evolution of the internet and its associated forms, such as digital marketing, telemarketing, and internet forums, is the foundation for the growth of the digital marketing industry, and with it, the development of customer trust is more important than ever.

3.2. *Stage 2: How to build customer satisfaction and loyalty (2001–2005)*

Since 2000, the internet has become more popular globally with the strong development of Yahoo and Google. The rapid growth of online transactions in service industries has raised important research questions about how satisfied customers are with digital marketing compared to the previous type of marketing. Compared to conventional marketing, digital marketing offers more opportunities for interactive and personalized marketing. This phase has many articles on topics related to optimizing customer trust, addressing privacy concerns, and building customer satisfaction and loyalty.

In this stage, with the rise of e-commerce, user information being collected by businesses created anxiety for users. Many surveys before the 2000s show that users were interested in what a company knew about them and how the company collected and used their information (Dreze and Zufryden, 1998). Many consumers also supported privacy protection. Therefore, in the post-2000 period, privacy issues received much attention and research. For instance, research looked at whether customers were willing to share their personal information with online marketers and other retailers, as well as their beliefs about the benefits of providing personal information in the workplace (Miller and Weckert, 2000; Phelps *et al.*, 2000); another study explored how consumers perceive and react to privacy concerns regarding digital privacy and the implementation of a number of regulations aimed at both businesses and regulators based on user responses to violated privacy (Phelps *et al.*, 2000). Moreover, trust continues to be an important factor that affects customers participating in e-commerce (Ashworth and Free, 2006), with online trust considerations including the belief that a supplier achieves nothing by cheating and the belief that safety mechanisms are built into websites with a featured interface or an easy-to-use interface (McKnight and Chervany, 2000).

The growing e-commerce system, which included CRM and e-CRM, was greatly improved and developed between 2001 and 2005. Some websites have multiple component items with detailed information. Therefore, customer service satisfaction is positively related to the level of information available at the site. In the process of service consumption, consumers can determine the quality of service and their level of satisfaction. Perceived value will have a direct positive impact on customer satisfaction and indirectly affect customer post-purchase behavior. Therefore, in this stage, businesses were very focused on customer satisfaction, and digital marketing helped many businesses grow customer satisfaction by approaching and connecting with customers easily through a website. Customer satisfaction is a key objective for every firm since customers are the most precious assets. In the current market economy, there is increasing rivalry between firms not only for customers' business but also for the quality of their products and the adoption of comprehensive total quality management. Customer satisfaction is acknowledged as a gauge of consumer-perceived quality (Disney, 1999). Consequently, a direct and intimate link should be established between customer pleasure, customer loyalty, and consumer's impression of quality. Also, the Customer Satisfaction Index, which assesses a customer's perception of quality and delivers the findings for its evaluation of customer satisfaction, plays a crucial part in the relational model. The use of CRM applications is positively associated with improving customer knowledge and customer satisfaction (Gefen *et al.*, 2003). Furthermore, for the same level of access and use of information, customers will only need to spend a very small amount of effort in the online environment, which leads to greater customer satisfaction with the online environment than the in-person environment (Mithas *et al.*, 2005).

With the rapid growth of e-commerce, a question arises as to what retains customers and makes them come back to an e-vendor or an online brand (Meuter *et al.*, 2000), which is the premise for loyalty development. Some studies have shown, interestingly, that while customer satisfaction is the same whether a service is selected online or offline, loyalty to the service provider is higher when the selected service is online rather than offline (Phelps *et al.*, 2000). In addition, among consumer-level factors, convenience motivation and purchase size were discovered to highlight the impact of electronic satisfaction on electronic loyalty, whereas inertia suppressed the effect of electronic satisfaction on electronic loyalty. When it comes to business-level factors, a company's trust and perceived value highlight the impact of e-satisfaction on e-loyalty significantly (Shankar *et al.*, 2003). Finally, in this stage, the online community is considered a bright spot in research, and discussions exist about how online communities affect business and how to come up with methods and solutions to attract customers, improve customer loyalty toward a brand, and enhance brand value in online communities (Anderson and Srinivasan, 2003; Muniz Jr and O'guinn, 2001).

In general, no one can deny the potential of digital marketing development in the near future, so the number of research papers recorded in this period steadily increased compared to the previous period. This work focused on consumer satisfaction and trust in the online platform, how businesses can modify and develop themselves to attract customers and increase sales, how online communities affect businesses, and how to come up with ways and solutions to attract customers and improve customer loyalty toward a brand. The second stage is still quite new and has not yet reached the level of widespread popularity among the masses, so it is necessary to conduct more research to understand the concerns and worries (e.g., about privacy and confidentiality) of users who are participating in the online environment to understand and find remedial measures.

3.3. *Stage 3: The deeper concept of customer loyalty and social network development (2006–2010)*

The period from 2006 to 2010 is called the digital era of *business transformation*. This stage highlights how the business model grew with the social networking and multichannel marketing boom. This period helps to go deeper into the topics of customer loyalty and online reviews in the context of social networks. Online social networking usage significantly increased after 2005. Social networks have become the most popular online communication tools. They allow people to build a network to interact with others over the internet through, for example, Facebook, Twitter, and Pinterest (McWilliam, 2000). Social networks can be used for customer research, engagement, and marketing. They provide a channel that connects businesses and clients directly. Brands can create a community around themselves. Social networks collect information about users' likes and dislikes, allowing for extremely targeted advertising. Social networks also offer an affordable way to expand the reach of digital marketing, which has sparked the development of the social media marketing model and analytics-related marketing. Social networks offer a practical way to broaden contacts at a reasonable price. As a result, digital marketing research was expanded to include new angles such as social marketing, online banking, model and network optimization, and mining to forecast demand. The loyalty of customers operating on social networking platforms also became a topic of interest. The studies in stage 3 focused on explaining the factors that influence customer loyalty. They show that attitudes and satisfaction can influence the next purchase (Boyd and Ellison, 2007). Attitudinal considerations such as intent to repurchase, willingness to recommend, and other probable market actions have been included to provide the basis for developing indicators of customer loyalty, and behavioral measures such as purchasing, volume or frequency of purchasing, returns, debt, complaints and interactions, and customer retention and longevity have been included as lagging indicators of customer loyalty.

As a signal that appeared at the end of stage 2, online reviews became the next development after the appearance of the online community. Online reviews play an important and highly regarded role. This was also a time when information interchange was enhanced and provided another way for customers to defend each other. The review function was established as an information channel to collect customer comments and reactions regarding a service or product obtained. Reviews of lodging, attractions, goods, and services were made publicly available. Users were able to objectively reach more and more users. Concerns with online reviews, eWOM, and e-travel were the main topics of marketing research from this time. Studies that looked into online reviews, or eWOM, tended to concentrate mostly on topics such as the social motivations of and interactions between users and reviewers of websites (Donio' *et al.*, 2006), customers are reading more online reviews or considering experts as more knowledgeable and reliable (Hennig-Thurau *et al.*, 2004), the effect of media coverage on business image (Senecal and Nantel, 2004), how exposure to online reviews impacts consumers' attitudes and purchase choices or the effect of internet reviews on consumer decision-making (Meijer and Kleinnijenhuis, 2006), and how online hotel reviews impact attitude and hotel rating (Chevalier and Mayzlin, 2006).

In conclusion, some primary marketing trends of this era are (a) concentrating on creating online social networking communities, (b) building clientele, (c) utilizing information found from searching blogs and messages on social networks to locate clients, (d) forecasting demand for guidance in making decisions, and (e) creating online e-tourism. At this point, marketing research became necessary, and social media marketing began its initial rise.

3.4. *Stage 4: Co-creation and customer engagement activities (2011–2015)*

This stage comes up with the evolution of technology and the internet, and the widespread adoption of social media for advertising and digital marketing are the main factors that have had a strong impact on the field of marketing. The spread of the internet and mobile devices has changed the way customers find information and interact with brands. Therefore, instead of focusing on reaching customers through traditional channels, businesses began stepping up to reach customers through online channels such as email, social networks, online advertising, websites, and mobile devices (Vermeulen and Seegers, 2009). During this time, research topics in the field of marketing changed from those mainly focusing on social networks and the trend of multichannel marketing to forming a deeper understanding of co-creation between customers and business and CE activities.

At this stage, virtual communities were of greater interest to researchers and administrators. To understand this issue, social capital theories and social cognitive theories were developed. According to them, individuals visit online communities not only to look for information and find solutions to issues but also to make new acquaintances and feel more at home. CE has been highlighted as a key element influencing the degree of sharing and participation in online communities. Moreover, the CE behavior management model for enterprises consists of three steps: identifying customer objects and interactive behavior types (e.g., word of mouth, online reviews, and recommendations), evaluating interactive expressions, and taking action based on customer interaction behavior (Hofacker and Belanche, 2016). Researchers such as Van Doorn also focused on CE concepts, while Brodie *et al.* (2011) had a different approach based on service-dominant logic and its relationship with marketing theory, using it to analyze the theoretical foundations of CE and to propose five basic postulates to develop a common definition of CE (Van Doorn *et al.*, 2010a). Another approach was to consider both CE and co-creation simultaneously in a mutually reinforcing relationship such as the role of social media and the relationship between seller and buyer. There are four types of connections that result from this: transactional customers, satisfied customers, loyal customers, and fans (Brodie *et al.*, 2011).

Co-creating content and developing interactive customer-facing strategies are crucial marketing directions. Recently, the phrase *social CRM* has come to be used to describe this innovative method of establishing and maintaining customer relationships (Sashi, 2012). To improve their consumer relationships, marketing managers began making strong combinations of existing process systems and developing technologies. Businesses made large investments in this technology as they recognized the potential of social CRM. Spending on social CRM technology increased by more than 40% in 2010 and was anticipated to reach 1 billion USD by 2013 (Greenberg, 2010). Marketing managers are being challenged by this change in expectations to encourage more customer–business connections by utilizing new technologies and capabilities (Andzulis *et al.*, 2012; Sarner, 2011). Researchers and practitioners are being forced to reconsider what it means to manage customer interactions as a result of the rise of the "social consumer" (Trainor, 2012). Therefore, the idea of CRM is giving way to a broader viewpoint that takes into account new capabilities made possible by technology and society. In addition, many studies have focused on consumer co-creation in the new product development process, the impact of co-creation at each stage of this process, and the different outcomes associated with businesses and consumers (Greenberg, 2010). Co-creation in marketing communication suggests that businesses should perceive personal media as a process of interacting with customers instead of pursuing a traditional one-way marketing method (Hoyer *et al.*, 2010), while another study concluded that the brands that use a lot of social media channels are the ones with more followers and higher engagement scores (Bacile *et al.*, 2014).

As can be seen, the opportunities offered by social media to help build close relationships with customers seem to have caused excitement among businesses and economic scholars of various industries worldwide. However, academic scholarship on co-creation and CE prior to this period was still in its infancy, lagged in practice, and had a relatively underdeveloped theoretical foundation. A better understanding of these concepts was therefore essential to developing strategies for CE, interaction, and co-creation. This urgent need for practice explains why researchers around the world during this period devoted so much attention to the issues surrounding CE and co-creation.

3.5. *Stage 5: Prosperous times of machine intelligence and IoT-based VR (2016 up to now)*

The fifth phase, which began in 2016, is a significant transformation that is expected to reach maturity between 2025 and 2030 (Ashley and Tuten, 2015). Key trends during this period include content generation, big data analytics, video advertising, Internet of Things (IoT) applications, and mobile banking.

At the beginning of the period in 2016, customer-generated content for marketing and advertising became a trend and a big development of the year. Utilizing user-generated content is a marketing approach that relies on user-generated content to promote a company's brands and products. Product reviews, videos, podcasts, social media posts, articles, blogs, photo tagging, and other activities are included. Sponsored content on blogs, wikis, forums, social networking platforms, and personal websites is referred to as consumer-generated advertising (Krishen *et al.*, 2021).

This shows that the network effect of customer-generated content for marketing and advertising is highly influential.

In 2017, research focused on video advertising and big data analytics. Big data analytics is important for business and social purposes. Data come from anywhere such as sensors used to gather climate information, data posted or shared on social networking sites, videos, movies, and audio. Big data have the potential to help businesses improve operations and make faster, smarter decisions. The main goals of big data analytics are to help organizations make better business decisions, predict the future, analyze the large number of transactions made within an organization, and update the type of data the organization uses (Kumar *et al.*, 2016). Big data have sparked a lot of interest in academics and industries at the moment. The focus of big data research is on technological concerns; data are not only a subject of technology but also involve a variety of stakeholders. Current research is focused on the security and privacy challenges that affect both data suppliers and users. In addition, new analytical methods for decision support in corporate management have been investigated. The effects of message format and advertising comprehension on media effectiveness and the effectiveness of consumers sharing media-based advertising are moderated by social affinity through the internet. Businesses can also use promotional videos to market their products or services by making video content. To get closer to customers, promotional videos are shared on social media platforms, websites, and other digital channels. The interaction between the customer and the brand is referred to as CE. This entails establishing interactions with clients via multiple channels such as social media, email, and chatbots.

Next is the question of when to deploy IoT applications. Social networking apps during this period are being driven by user-generated content and are highly influential in a myriad of settings, from buying and selling behavior to entrepreneurship, political issues, and venture capitalism. Facebook has a high position as the market leader of the social media world, with 1.97 billion monthly users (Verma *et al.*, 2016). In addition to posts, social networking sites are inundated with photo and video uploads, and according to recent figures, about 400 million snapshots per day have been recorded on Snapchat, with about 9,000 photos shared every second. While 50 million businesses are active on Facebook, two million are using

Facebook ads. Moreover, 88% of businesses are using Twitter for marketing purposes (Kapoor *et al.*, 2018). Another study by Kapoor shows that the trends emerging during this period center on pay-per-click; the use of pay-per-click advertising on websites or applications, digital marketing, affiliate marketing, email marketing, and other forms of marketing are all examples of forms of advertising that advertisers may employ. These ways of digital marketing are being widely used to effectively market products and services in order to achieve increased sales and higher revenue (Kapoor *et al.*, 2018).

Mobile banking, the sharing economy (SE), and the application of VR, particularly in e-tourism and e-learning, are new major topics that were added to the digital marketing field around 2019. The Internet of Everything (IoE) incorporates IoT, including radio-frequency identification, sensors added to everyday objects, and applications that allow consumers to check the statuses of household devices from their smartphones, monitor their homes, or check their vital signs. The main difference between IoE and IoT is intelligent connectivity as IoT refers to physical objects and concepts that communicate with each other. In contrast, IoE brings network intelligence to manage all these concepts in one cohesive system. IoE includes not only machine-to-machine communication (from IoT) but also human-to-machine and human-to-human communication through technology, following the input and output framework (Kapoor *et al.*, 2016). At the same time, eWOM via the internet during this period has been frequently studied and findings indicate that eWOM has an effect on purchase intention and consumer loyalty and commitment (Petrescu *et al.*, 2020). The SE emphasizes the sharing of underutilized assets in a way that enhances efficiency and sustainability. The SE phenomenon offers opportunities for new businesses, such as Airbnb and Uber, to become household names for travelers around the world. Sharing may be an old practice, but SEs driven by the internet and other supporting tools and features are a phenomenon in this period (Ismagilova *et al.*, 2021).

Opinion mining, content generation, big data analytics, video advertising, IoT applications, and mobile banking are new key areas brought to the field of digital research around 2019. This stage places a greater emphasis on social media marketing. People are interacting more online, in part because of the COVID-19 pandemic. In the context of the time, social media has presented users with an unparalleled level of convenience for developing and sharing ideas, opinions, and experiences. Although social media is very popular and has received a lot of attention from academia, the number of studies linking big data and social media is still limited. Mobile banking is one of the most promising technologies to emerge in recent years and could prove to be of great value to both businesses and their customers. Research on m-banking shows that we need to look at the key factors that predict mobile banking use or influence customer satisfaction and loyalty.

4. Conclusion and Future Research

4.1. *Conclusion*

Digital marketing strategies are collections of controllable e-marketing variables that firms use to fulfill their marketing objectives and meet the needs of their customers. They are the most essential criteria that electronic-marketing managers consider when determining the optimal plan to accomplish their goals for sales and profitability (Hossain, 2020). Digital marketing has been considered the trend of the world for many years, ever since it became one of the guiding principles in the communication activities of most businesses (Forghani *et al.*, 2022). This type of marketing helps brands cover and get closer to more customers through the internet network connected to the globe. A large amount of academic research has been done on various aspects such as SEO, social media marketing, affiliate marketing, content marketing, and video marketing. This paper provides a comprehensive systematic review of the transition from conventional marketing to digital marketing through two main contributions on four insights in the context of the impact of digital marketing and the five growth stages of digital marketing from a research perspective.

In terms of insights in connection with the impacts of digital marketing, the strong development of digital marketing has created a shift from traditional channels to digital, which has had a strong impact on the business environment, creating new values for customers and increasing sales (Kulkarni *et al.*, 2020). A company's performance is demonstrated through changes in customer behavior, media, business–customer platforms, search engines, and interactions with technology. Young people today are growing up in a social environment where digital technology and social media are pervasive (Stephen, 2016), so a marketing strategy is a long-term plan to achieve business goals by creating value for customers and increasing sales. In today's reality, consumer behavior is constantly changing, and this requires a company to adapt and have a strategy in accordance with the social and market contexts. Companies have adopted different digital and social media strategies to promote their products and services to consumers. Among them are businesses that actively support social media strategies and actively use these tools to enhance interaction and communication with their customers. Finally, outcomes in digital marketing have a great influence on customers' consumption behavior as well as customers' purchasing decisions in the future. Digital marketing helps to create a buyback effect, and introduces people to it, thereby spreading the positive word about a brand. Outcomes also play a significant role in building trust and creating customer loyalty to the brand.

In terms of the five growth stages of digital marketing, we presented a generalized view through related studies that will inform later studies and digital marketers about the development, trends, and history of digital marketing, thus allowing researchers to identify research gaps that need to be filled with further research in the future. Our analysis showed that digital marketing is the most used keyword in most studies. Other related keywords that should also be studied include consumer behavior, social networking, machine learning, big data, advertising, mobile marketing, Web 2.0, and branding. The summary also shows that research on digital marketing has received much focus since 2010 due to the development of the internet and social media. As social media continues to encourage customers to talk about brands, global businesses are increasingly focusing on digital marketing as an effective brand communication tool (Habito *et al.*, 2022). By understanding the research on the five stages of transition from conventional marketing to digital marketing, businesses will have a more comprehensive view of each specific step when they want to transition to digital marketing with the aim of attracting customers, building and promoting brands and products effectively online, and offering marketing strategies that spread meaningful messages quickly but at low cost to easily reach potential customer segments.

4.2. *Limitations and future research*

This chapter provides a unique overview of the breadth of digital marketing research articles from a multidisciplinary perspective to broadly categorize prominent research topics. The data details of digital marketing research were studied from 1990 up to 2023. The primary themes and key growth stages of digital marketing were studied chronologically, providing an overview of the evolution of research topics in the discipline. The rise in the number of articles published during the last two decades implies that digital marketing is still in its early stages of development and that its popularity has not yet attained maturity. However, the research paper still has some limitations. First, the paper focuses on presenting a series of research reports on the main topic at different stages, leading to an overload of knowledge and information while being unable to dig deeply into the insights in each stage. Second, the research prioritizes and selects highly cited papers from each period or theme, so interesting and novel concepts may be missed. Third, it focuses on using documents written in English from Web of Science data, so the findings may not be fully generalizable for the development of digital marketing worldwide.

Technology is undeniably influential because it facilitates communication with clients, the management of operations, the enhancement of output, and so forth. However, many problems are spawned by this lightning-fast progress, which opens avenues for future study.

From the themes of insight, researchers may consider growing research directions as mentioned in the following. Starting off theme 1, we could focus on finding new digital platforms and changing consumer behavior by studying, for example, (a) mobile devices and technologies including wearable technologies (e.g., smartwatches and smart glasses), VR technologies, augmented reality technologies, extended reality technologies, and mobile apps; (b) computing technologies and analytical methodologies such as cloud computing, AI, cognitive computing and deep learning, machine learning techniques, and big data analytics; (c) search technologies for images, videos, voice-recognition-based searches, eye-tracking technologies, and search technologies for the dark web; and (d) as the digital world is evolving at an incredible speed and technology has empowered us, whether there could be a chance that the excessive use of ICTs and the internet will have a negative impact on our mental and physical health or, in other words, the possibility of wariness toward high technology. Based on theme 2, researchers could move on to updating the trend of online business forms such as auctions, content distribution, sharing, and social networking (Plume *et al.*, 2016). Based on theme 3, researchers could predict innovations in developing digitalized products, future trending channels and pricing, and unbelievable promotions. Finally, researchers can provide some findings on whether there will be any changes in the future expectations for the online shopping behavior of consumers and businesses. The idea would be to focus on how and why those elements affect consumers' behavior and the decision-making process as well as the interaction between them based on the four themes of digital marketing: environment, marketing strategy, company, and outcomes.

From the point of view of the development of digital marketing over time, researchers can readily influence the future direction of research as follows. It is suggested that in addition to stage 1, researchers can continue to think about the innovative features of entrepreneurship on digital platforms, particularly in light of the introduction of brand-new AI applications. The scope of research is expanding more and more in the direction of reducing friction in the exchange of information between buyers and sellers. Future trends are anticipated to favor the improvement of already-existing platforms while exploring the possibility of generating new platforms with novel ideas (e.g., since 2020, the concept of key opinion leaders has become more popular because this model can hit the buying insights of the majority of young people). Stages 2 and 3 show that much work has been done in studies on loyalty, satisfaction, and the growth of social networks, but there is still room for growth in this area. The relationship between consumer experience, the demands of technical development, and electronic devices can be examined in a combined scene. Along with the explosion of technology, we can fully expect the inclusion of VR experiences and further research into the trend of using AI in marketing in the distant future. Businesses must hire the best digital marketing personnel and foster an environment where everyone can freely innovate and express their ideas if they are to stay on top of current and future marketing trends. Consequently, finding the best management strategy that fosters an environment that encourages innovation and productivity will be a challenge that any company must overcome if it hopes to develop a long-lasting team. Furthermore, by relying on pre-existing platforms and inheriting research in the field of digital marketing, firms have the ability to swiftly identify current trends, which can then be used as a basis for learning and production. Since a significant portion of the research reveals the motivations and psychology of consumers before, after, and during the usage of various services and products, it is simpler to gain customer insights. Such research findings will give organizations a thorough enough understanding of the digital world in which they operate (including counterparts, clients, etc.) as well as a more expansive view of the future with any anticipated problems. Businesses can then develop a long-term, efficient marketing strategy from which their future directions will also become clearer. The power that digital marketing brings to business is undeniable: it has the ability to convert simple content into powerful brand messages, and the cost is low while the reach to consumers is high. However, the rapid development of technology also creates many challenges for marketers. Digital marketers are constantly faced with customer privacy regulations. As they continue to attract more and more visitors from all over the world to a website, agencies must ensure they remain compliant with any laws covering the population in whatever country they are targeting. This research direction will help businesses and consumers better understand the privacy rights of each individual and the safety of customer information when using social networks. At stage 4, there is no denying that customers play a part in helping to build corporate ideas or advertising on digital platforms; as a result, future research guidelines should support the strengthening of co-creation in developing marketing trends. Last but not least, stage 5, the stage that offers the most potential directions for research, saw a notable development with the introduction of ChatGPT. Businesses should exploit this as an opportunity for research due to the unanticipated development of AI. For instance, researchers could consider how to employ AI to quickly get consumer insights or what will happen to consumer behavior if AI is used too much.

Acknowledgement

This research is funded by University of Economics Ho Chi Minh City, Vietnam.

References

Ahmed, R. R., Streimikiene, D., Berchtold, G., Vveinhardt, J., Channar, Z. A., & Soomro, R. H. (2019). Effectiveness of Online Digital Media Advertising as A Strategic Tool for Building Brand Sustainability: Evidence from FMCGs and Services Sectors of Pakistan. *Sustainability*, *11*(12), 3436. Available at: https://www.mdpi.com/2071-1050/11/12/3436.

Alansari, M. T., Velikova, N., & Jai, T.-M. C. (2018). Marketing effectiveness of hotel Twitter accounts: The case of Saudi Arabia. *Journal of Hospitality and Tourism Technology*, *9*(1), 65–79.

Alghizzawi, M., Salloum, S. A., & Habes, M. (2018). The role of social media in tourism marketing in Jordan. *International Journal of Information Technology and Language Studies*, *2*(3), 59–70.

Andaleeb, S. S. & Anwar, S. F. (1996). Factors influencing customer trust in salespersons in a developing country. *Journal of International Marketing*, *4*(4), 35–52.

Anderson, R. E. & Srinivasan, S. S. (2003). E-satisfaction and e-loyalty: A contingency framework. *Psychology & Marketing*, *20*(2), 123–138.

Andzulis, J. M., Panagopoulos, N. G., & Rapp, A. (2012). A review of social media and implications for the sales process. *Journal of Personal Selling & Sales Management*, *32*(3), 305–316.

Ang, T., Wei, S., & Anaza, N. A. (2018). Livestreaming vs pre-recorded: How social viewing strategies impact consumers' viewing experiences and behavioral intentions. *European Journal of Marketing*, *52*(9-10), 2075–2104.

Ashley, C. & Tuten, T. (2015). Creative strategies in social media marketing: An exploratory study of branded social content and consumer engagement. *Psychology and Marketing*, *32*(1), 15–27.

Ashworth, L. & Free, C. (2006). Marketing dataveillance and digital privacy: Using theories of justice to understand consumers' online privacy concerns. *Journal of Business Ethics*, *67*, 107–123.

Babić Rosario, A., Sotgiu, F., De Valck, K., & Bijmolt, T. H. (2016). The effect of electronic word of mouth on sales: A meta-analytic review of platform, product, and metric factors. *Journal of Marketing Research*, *53*(3), 297–318.

Bacile, T. J., Ye, C., & Swilley, E. (2014). From firm-controlled to consumer-contributed: Consumer co-production of personal media marketing communication. *Journal of Direct Marketing*, *28*(2), 117–133.

Bakos, Y. & Brynjolfsson, E. (2000). Bundling and competition on the internet. *Marketing Science*, *19*(1), 63–82.

Bell, D. R. & Song, S. (2007). Neighborhood effects and trial on the Internet: Evidence from online grocery retailing. *Quantitative Marketing and Economics*, *5*, 361–400.

Berthon, P., Pitt, L. F., & Watson, R. T. (1996). The world wide web as an advertising medium. *Journal of Advertising Research*, *36*(1), 43–54.

Boyd, D. M. & Ellison, N. B. (2007). Social network sites: Definition, history, and scholarship. *Journal of Computer-Mediated Communication*, *13*(1), 210–230.

Brodie, R. J., Hollebeek, L. D., Jurić, B., & Ilić, A. (2011). Customer engagement: Conceptual domain, fundamental propositions, and implications for research. *Journal of Service Research*, *14*(3), 252–271.

Bryła, P., Chatterjee, S., & Ciabiada-Bryła, B. (2022). The impact of social media marketing on consumer engagement in sustainable consumption: A Systematic literature review. *International Journal of Environmental Research and Public Health*, *19*(24), 16637.

Bush, V. D., Venable, B. T., & Bush, A. J. (2000). Ethics and marketing on this internet: Practitioners' perceptions of societal, industry and company concerns. *Journal of Business Ethics*, *23*, 237–248.

Chevalier, J. A. & Mayzlin, D. (2006). The effect of word of mouth on sales: Online book reviews. *Journal of Marketing Research, 43*(3), 345–354.

Court, C., Elzinga, D., Mulder, S., Vetvik, O., & Journey, C. D. (2009). *McKinsey Quarterly*. In.

Culnan, M. J. & Armstrong, P. K. (1999). Information privacy concerns, procedural fairness, and impersonal trust: An empirical investigation. *Organization Science*, *10*(1), 104–115.

Donio', J., Massari, P., & Passiante, G. (2006). Customer satisfaction and loyalty in a digital environment: An empirical test. *Journal of Consumer Marketing*, *23*(7), 445–457.

Dou, W., Lim, K. H., Su, C., Zhou, N., & Cui, N. (2010). Brand positioning strategy using search engine marketing. *MIS Quarterly*, 261–279.

Dreze, X. & Zufryden, F. (1998). Is Internet advertising ready for prime time? *Journal of Advertising Research*, *38*, 7–18.

Dubé, J.-P. & Misra, S. (2023). Personalized pricing and consumer welfare. *Journal of Political Economy*, *131*(1), 131–189.

Dwivedi, Y. K., Ismagilova, E., Hughes, D. L., Carlson, J., Filieri, R., Jacobson, J., . . . Jarri Salo, G. A. T., Wang. Y., (2021). Setting the future of digital and social media marketing research: Perspectives and research propositions. *International Journal of Information Management*, *59*, 102168.

Edelman, D. C. & Singer, M. (2015). Competing on customer journeys. *Harvard Business Review*, *93*(11), 88–100.

Filieri, R. & McLeay, F. (2014). E-WOM and accommodation: An analysis of the factors that influence travelers' adoption of information from online reviews. *Journal of Travel Research*, *53*(1), 44–57.

Forghani, E., Sheikh, R., Hosseini, S. M. H., & Sana, S. S. (2022). The impact of digital marketing strategies on customer's buying behavior in online shopping using the rough set theory. *International Journal of System Assurance Engineering and Management*, 1–16.

Gefen, D., Karahanna, E., & Straub, D. W. (2003). Trust and TAM in online shopping: An integrated model. *MIS Quarterly*, 51–90.

Ghose, A. & Yang, S. (2009). An empirical analysis of search engine advertising: Sponsored search in electronic markets. *Management Science*, *55*(10), 1605–1622.

Gironda, J. T. & Korgaonkar, P. K. (2018). Tailored versus invasive ads and consumers' perceptions of personalized advertising. *Electronic Commerce Research and Applications*, 64–77.

Greenberg. (2010). *CRM at the Speed of Light: Social CRM Strategies, Tools, and Techniques*. Available at:

Habes, M., Alghizzawi, M., Khalaf, R., Salloum, S. A., & Ghani, M. A. (2018). The relationship between social media and academic performance: Facebook perspective. *International Journal of Information Technology and Language Studies*, *2*(1), 12–18.

Habibi, M. R., Laroche, M., & Richard, M.-O. (2014). The roles of brand community and community engagement in building brand trust on social media. *Computers in Human Behavior*, *37*, 152–161.

Habito, C. M., Morgan, A., & Vaughan, C. (2022). 'Direct' and 'instant': The role of digital technology and social media in young Filipinos' intimate relationships. *Culture, Health & Sexuality, 24*(5), 657–672.

Hanaysha, J. R. (2018). An examination of the factors affecting consumer's purchase decision in the Malaysian retail market. *PSU Research Review*, *2*(1), 7–23.

Häubl, G. & Trifts, V. (2000). Consumer decision making in online shopping environments: The effects of interactive decision aids. *Marketing Science*, *19*(1), 4–21.

Hennig-Thurau, T., Gwinner, K. P., Walsh, G., & Gremler, D. D. (2004). Electronic word-of-mouth via consumer-opinion platforms: What motivates consumers to articulate themselves on the internet? *Journal of Interactive Marketing*, *18*(1), 38–52.

Hewett, K., Rand, W., Rust, R., & van Heerde, H. (2016). Ads by category.

Hofacker, C. F. & Belanche, D. (2016). Eight social media challenges for marketing managers. *Spanish Journal of Marketing-ESIC, 20*(2), 73–80.

Hoffman, D. L. & Novak, T. P. (1996). Marketing in hypermedia computer-mediated environments: Conceptual foundations. *Journal of Marketing*, *60*(3), 50–68.

Hossain, M. (2020). Sharing economy: A comprehensive literature review. *International Journal of Hospitality Management*, *87*, 102470.

Hoyer, W. D., Chandy, R., Dorotic, M., Krafft, M., & Singh, S. S. (2010). Consumer cocreation in new product development. *Journal of Service Research*, *13*(3), 283–296.

Hutchins, J. & Rodriguez, D. X. (2018). The soft side of branding: Leveraging emotional intelligence. *Journal of Business & Industrial Marketing*.

Ismagilova, E., Rana, N. P., Slade, E. L., & Dwivedi, Y. K. (2021). A meta-analysis of the factors affecting eWOM providing behaviour. *European Journal of Marketing*, *55*(4), 1067–1102.

Ismagilova, E., Slade, E., Rana, N. P., & Dwivedi, Y. K. (2020). The effect of characteristics of source credibility on consumer behaviour: A meta-analysis. *Journal of Retailing and Consumer Services*, *53*, 101736.

Jain, S. (2008). Digital piracy: A competitive analysis. *Marketing Science*, *27*(4), 610–626.

James, L. (2020). Identifying the effect of Digital marketing channels on the growth of SME in South Asia: A case study on Faheem Haydar Dealzmag.

Jank, W. & Kannan, P. (2005). Understanding geographical markets of online firms using spatial models of customer choice. *Marketing Science*, *24*(4), 623–634.

Jara, A. J., Parra, M. C., & Skarmeta, A. F. (2012). Marketing 4.0: A new value added to the Marketing through the Internet of Things. In Paper presented at the 2012 *Sixth International Conference on Innovative Mobile and Internet Services in Ubiquitous Computing*.

Kannan, P. K. & Li, H. A. (2017). Digital marketing: A framework, review and research agenda. *International Journal of Research in Marketing*, *34*(1), 22–45.

Kapoor, K. K., Dwivedi, Y. K., & Piercy, N. C. (2016). Pay-per-click advertising: A literature review. *The Marketing Review*, *16*(2), 183–202.

Kapoor, K. K., Tamilmani, K., Rana, N. P., Patil, P., Dwivedi, Y. K., & Nerur, S. (2018). Advances in social media research: Past, present and future. *Information Systems Frontiers*, *20*, 531–558.

Krishen, A. S., Dwivedi, Y. K., Bindu, N., & Kumar, K. S. (2021). A broad overview of interactive digital marketing: A bibliometric network analysis. *Journal of Business Research*, *131*, 183–195.

Kulkarni, K. K., Kalro, A. D., Sharma, D., & Sharma, P. (2020). A typology of viral ad sharers using sentiment analysis. *Journal of Retailing and Consumer Services*, *53*, 101739.

Kumar, A., Bezawada, R., Rishika, R., Janakiraman, R., & Kannan, P. (2016). From social to sale: The effects of firm-generated content in social media on customer behavior. *Journal of Marketing*, *80*(1), 7–25.

Kusumasondjaja, S. (2018). The roles of message appeals and orientation on social media brand communication effectiveness: An evidence from Indonesia. *Asia Pacific Journal of Marketing and Logistics*, 30(4), 1135–1158.

Lamberton, C. & Stephen, A. T. (2016). A thematic exploration of digital, social media, and mobile marketing: Research evolution from 2000 to 2015 and an agenda for future inquiry. *Journal of Marketing*, *80*(6), 146–172.

Lee, D., Hosanagar, K., & Nair, H. S. (2018). Advertising content and consumer engagement on social media: Evidence from Facebook. *Management Science*, *64*(11), 5105–5131.

Li, H. & Kannan, P. (2014). Attributing conversions in a multichannel online marketing environment: An empirical model and a field experiment. *Journal of Marketing Research*, *51*(1), 40–56.

Li, K. & Du, T. C. (2012). Building a targeted mobile advertising system for location-based services. *Decision Support Systems*, *54*(1), 1–8.

Liu, Q. B. & Karahanna, E. (2017). The dark side of reviews. *MIS Quarterly*, *41*(2), 427–448.

Liu, S. Q., Ozanne, M., & Mattila, A. S. (2018). Does expressing subjectivity in online reviews enhance persuasion? *Journal of Consumer Marketing*, *35*(4), 403–413.

Luo, L. & Toubia, O. (2015). Improving online idea generation platforms and customizing the task structure on the basis of consumers' domain-specific knowledge. *Journal of Marketing*, *79*(5), 100–114.

Malthouse, E. C., Haenlein, M., Skiera, B., Wege, E., & Zhang, M. (2013). Managing customer relationships in the social media era: Introducing the social CRM house. *Journal of Interactive Marketing*, *27*(4), 270–280.

Mandal, R., Samstein, R. M., Lee, K.-W., Havel, J. J., Wang, H., Krishna, C., . . . Blecua, P. (2019). Genetic diversity of tumors with mismatch repair deficiency influences anti–PD-1 immunotherapy response. *Science*, *364*(6439), 485–491.

McAlister, L., Sonnier, G., & Shively, T. (2012). The relationship between online chatter and firm value. *Marketing Letters*, *23*, 1–12.

McKnight, D. H. & Chervany, N. L. (2000). What is trust? A conceptual analysis and an interdisciplinary model. *AMCIS 2000 Proceedings*. 382. https://aisel.aisnet.org/amcis2000/382.

McWilliam, G. (2000). Building stronger brands through online communities. *MIT Sloan Management Review*, *41*(3), 43.

Mehta, R. & Sivadas, E. (1995). Comparing response rates and response content in mail versus electronic mail surveys. *Market Research Society Journal*, *37*(4), 1–12.

Meijer & Kleinnijenhuis. (2006). Issue news and corporate reputation: Applying the theories of agenda setting and issue ownership in the field of business communication. Available at:

Meltwater, & WeAreSocial. (2023). Digital 2023 global overview report. Available at: https://datareportal.com/reports/digital-2023-global-overview-report?utm_source=SlideShare&utm_medium=PDF&utm_campaign=Digital_2023&utm_content=QR_Code_Page.

Meuter, M. L., Ostrom, A. L., Roundtree, R. I., & Bitner, M. J. (2000). Self-service technologies: Understanding customer satisfaction with technology-based service encounters. *Journal of Marketing*, *64*(3), 50–64.

Miller, S. & Weckert, J. (2000). Privacy, the workplace and the internet. *Journal of Business Ethics*, *28*, 255–265.

Mishra, A. S. (2019). Antecedents of consumers' engagement with brand-related content on social media. *Marketing Intelligence & Planning*, *37*(4), 386–400.

Mithas, S., Krishnan, M. S., & Fornell, C. (2005). Why do customer relationship management applications affect customer satisfaction? *Journal of Marketing*, *69*(4), 201–209.

Moe, W. W. & Trusov, M. (2011). The value of social dynamics in online product ratings forums. *Journal of Marketing Research*, *48*(3), 444–456.

Morra, M. C., Gelosa, V., Ceruti, F., & Mazzucchelli, A. (2018). Original or counterfeit luxury fashion brands? The effect of social media on purchase intention. *Journal of Global Fashion Marketing*, *9*(1), 24–39.

Muniz Jr, A. M. & O'guinn, T. C. (2001). Brand community. *Journal of Consumer Research*, *27*(4), 412–432.

Nam, H. & Kannan, P. K. (2014). The informational value of social tagging networks. *Journal of Marketing*, *78*(4), 21–40.

Onyango, K. (2016). Influence of digital marketing strategies on performance of cutflowers exporting firms in Kenya.

Palmer, D. E. (2005). Pop-ups, cookies, and spam: Toward a deeper analysis of the ethical significance of internet marketing practices. *Journal of Business Ethics*, *58*, 271–280.

Peterson, R. A., Balasubramanian, S., & Bronnenberg, B. J. (1997). Exploring the implications of the Internet for consumer marketing. *Journal of the Academy of Marketing Science*, *25*, 329–346.

Petrescu, M., Krishen, A., & Bui, M. (2020). The internet of everything: Implications of marketing analytics from a consumer policy perspective. *Journal of Consumer Marketing*, *37*(6), 675–686.

Phelps, J., Nowak, G., & Ferrell, E. (2000). Privacy concerns and consumer willingness to provide personal information. *Journal of Public Policy & Marketing*, *19*(1), 27–41.

Pingitore, G., Meyers, J., Clancy, M., & Cavallaro, K. (2013). Consumer concerns about data privacy rising: What can business do. Retrieved October 29, 2014.

Plume, C. J., Dwivedi, Y. K., & Slade, E. L. (2016). Social media in the marketing context: A state of the art analysis and future directions.

Rust, R. T., Lemon, K. N., & Narayandas, D. (2005). *Customer Equity Management*. Pearson: Prentice Hall.

Sarner. (2011). *Magic Quadrant for Social CRM*. Available at:

Sashi, C. M. (2012). Customer engagement, buyer-seller relationships, and social media. *Management Decision*, *50*, 253–272.

Seiler, S. (2013). The impact of search costs on consumer behavior: A dynamic approach. *Quantitative Marketing and Economics*, *11*, 155–203.

Senecal & Nantel. (2004). The influence of online product recommendations on consumers' online choices. Available at:

Shankar, V., Smith, A. K., & Rangaswamy, A. (2003). Customer satisfaction and loyalty in online and offline environments. *International Journal of Research in Marketing*, *20*(2), 153–175.

Shankar, V., Urban, G. L., & Sultan, F. (2002). Online trust: A stakeholder perspective, concepts, implications, and future directions. *The Journal of Strategic Information Systems*, *11*(3–4), 325–344.

Shi, S. W. & Zhang, J. (2014). Usage experience with decision aids and evolution of online purchase behavior. *Marketing Science*, *33*(6), 871–882.

Singh, N. & Keating, B. M. (2018). Hyper-localizing e-commerce strategy: An emerging market perspective. *Emerging Markets from a Multidisciplinary Perspective: Challenges, Opportunities and Research Agenda*, 89–94.

Sonnier, G. P., McAlister, L., & Rutz, O. J. (2011). A Dynamic model of the effect of online communications on firm sales. *Marketing Science, 30*, 702–716.

Stead, B. A. & Gilbert, J. (2001). Ethical Issues in electronic commerce. *Journal of Business Ethics*, *34*(2), 75–85.

Stephen, A. T. (2016). The role of digital and social media marketing in consumer behavior. *Current Opinión in Psychology*, *10*, 17–21.

Stojanovic, I., Andreu, L., & Curras-Perez, R. (2018). Effects of the intensity of use of social media on brand equity: An empirical study in a tourist destination. *European Journal of Management and Business Economics*, *27*(1), 83–100.

Sundararajan, A. (2017). *The Sharing Economy: The End of Employment and the Rise of Crowd-Based Capitalism*: MIT Press.

Tafesse, W. & Wien, A. (2018). Using message strategy to drive consumer behavioral engagement on social media. *The Journal of Consumer Marketing*, *35*(3), 241–253.

Tarnovskaya, V. & Biedenbach, G. (2018). Corporate rebranding failure and brand meanings in the digital environment. *Marketing Intelligence & Planning*, *36*(4), 455–469.

Trainor, K. J. (2012). Relating social media technologies to performance: A capabilities-based perspective. *Journal of Personal Selling & Sales Management*, *32*(3), 317–331.

Tucker, C. & Zhang, J. (2010). Growing two-sided networks by advertising the user base: A field experiment. *Marketing Science*, *29*(5), 805–814.

Van Doorn, J., Lemon, K. N., Mittal, V., Nass, S., Pick, D., Pirner, P., & Verhoef, P. C. (2010a). Customer engagement behavior: Theoretical foundations and research directions. *Journal of Service Research*, *13*(3), 253–266.

van Doorn, J., Lemon, K. N., Mittal, V., Nass, S., Pick, D. N., Pirner, P., & Verhoef, P. C. (2010b). Customer engagement behavior: Theoretical foundations and research directions. *Journal of Service Research*, *13*(3), 253–266.

Venkatesh, R. & Chatterjee, R. (2006). Bundling, unbundling, and pricing of multiform products: The case of magazine content. *Journal of Interactive Marketing*, *20*(2), 21–40.

Verhoef, P. C., Neslin, S. A., & Vroomen, B. (2007). Multichannel customer management: Understanding the research-shopper phenomenon. *International Journal of Research in Marketing*, *24*(2), 129–148.

Verma, J. P., Agrawal, S., Patel, B., & Patel, A. (2016). Big data analytics: Challenges and applications for text, audio, video, and social media data. *International Journal on Soft Computing, Artificial Intelligence and Applications (IJSCAI)*, *5*(1), 41–51.

Vermeulen, I. E. & Seegers, D. (2009). Tried and tested: The impact of online hotel reviews on consumer consideration. Available at:

Watts, D. J. (2007). A twenty-first century science. *Nature, 445*(7127), 489–489.

Wind, J. & Rangaswamy, A. (2001). Customerization: The next revolution in mass customization. *Journal of Interactive Marketing*, *15*(1), 13–32.

Wong, P., Lee, D., & ML Ng, P. (2018). Online search for information about universities: A Hong Kong study. *International Journal of Educational Management*, *32*(3), 511–524.

Yasmin, A., Tasneem, S., & Fatema, K. (2015). Effectiveness of digital marketing in the challenging age: An empirical study. *International Journal of Management Science and Business Administration*, *1*(5), 69–80.

https://doi.org/10.1142/9789811286100_0003

Chapter 3

Cultural Intelligence and Job Performance of Employees in FDI Enterprises: The Mediating Role of Work Engagement

Tan Quoc Phan* and Bang Nguyen-Viet†

School of Management,
University of Economics Ho Chi Minh City, Vietnam

*tanpq@ueh.edu.vn

†bangnv@ueh.edu.vn

Abstract

This study aims to test the direct impact of cultural intelligence on employee performance and examine the mediating role of work engagement. Data were collected from 307 provincial employees who were working in foreign direct investment (FDI) enterprises located within the Industrial Zones of Ho Chi Minh (IZHCM) City. The results reveal that cultural intelligence has a significant positive effect on work engagement and job performance with work engagement acting as a mediating influence mechanism. The study also found the role of demographic variables (gender, professional qualifications, and seniority) in the relationship between cultural intelligence, work engagement, and job performance. The research offers valuable insights for managers of FDI enterprises seeking to enhance job performance by improving human resource policies and fostering cultural intelligence and work engagement among their employees.

Received on January 31, 2023; accepted on March 29, 2023

Keywords: Cultural Intelligence, Work Engagement, Performance, Industrial Zone.

1. Introduction

With more extended and intensive globalization, employees need to possess appropriate communication skills and function in a multicultural environment at foreign direct investment (FDI) enterprises. People from a region are influenced by the culture of that region (Jyoti and Kour, 2015).

Till December 31, 2021, there were 502 FDI projects (in a total of 1,326 valid investment projects) in IZHCM, accounting for 37.78% of the total investment projects in the Industrial Zones of Ho Chi Minh City with a registered investment capital of 5.052 billion USD, according to the Ho Chi Minh City (HCMC) Export Processing Zones and Industrial Parks Authority (Hepza). Total export turnover reached 6.36 billion USD/year, while total import turnover reached 5.33 billion USD/year. The number of employees working in FDI enterprises was 185,347 (72%). A majority of enterprises in the IZHCM are FDI enterprises (Decree 192/CP of the Government); about 69% of the employees come from the provinces, of which more than 72% work for FDI enterprises. The board of directors and technical experts in such enterprises are mostly foreigners. Therefore, employees working in FDI enterprises in IZHCM are a collection of people with different professional qualifications, cultural levels and ideas, awareness levels, social relations, and coming from diverse geographical regions. These differences have created a varied and complex working environment, which often causes conflicts between workers, superiors, and subordinates due to different backgrounds in different regions and countries (Farndale and Murrer, 2015). A characteristic of the FDI enterprises in the Industrial Park of HCMC is that up to 5–7% of the total number of employees are foreign workers (from the parent company). They include key managers, such as directors, department heads, and technical experts, working directly with Vietnamese engineers, technicians, and office staff.

Employees working in any company, especially FDI enterprises, mostly come from different regions and countries, so they demonstrate different kinds of cultural awareness and thinking (Trefry, 2006), thereby creating a complex working environment that easily leads to conflicts

(Farndale and Murrer, 2015). To survive and develop in a culturally diverse environment, FDI enterprises require employees to practice and develop cultural intelligence (Earley and Ang, 2003; Karma and Vedina, 2009). Earley and Ang (2003) argue that cultural intelligence is a person's ability to adapt well to a new cultural environment. People with high cultural intelligence are observant, empathetic, understand people and situations, are able to draw inferences, make informed decisions, and take conscious actions in response to cultural differences. They try to first understand why people act in a certain manner, instead of making quick judgments or relying on stereotypes. Thereafter, they adapt their own behavior, which in turn enhances their work performance (Earley and Ang, 2003).

Re-studies mean Jyoti and Kour, 2015; Ng *et al.*, 2012; Ott and Michailova, 2016). In addition, the studies of Mahboobeh Davaei *et al.* (2022), GabelShemueli *et al.* (2019), Van Dyne *et al.* (2010), and Halbesleben *et al.* (2014) show that the more cultural intelligence individuals possess, the more engaged they are in working for multinational companies (MNCs) in different industrial sectors. Thus, the higher employees' work engagement, the better their job performance (Karatepe and Karadas, 2015; Anitha, 2014).

From the above issues, the authors realize that it is necessary to simultaneously study the influence of cultural intelligence on employees' job performance, through the mediating role of work engagement, and lay the basis for proposing managerial implications of cultural intelligence and work engagement to improve employee work results, thereby contributing to the efficiency of production activities for FDI enterprises in the HCMC industrial zones. Moreover, this relationship has not been studied much in Vietnam, in general, and in HCMC industrial zones, in particular. Therefore, to supplement the theory of cultural intelligence, this study aims to achieve the following objectives: (1) identify the components of cultural intelligence; (2) build and test a model of the relationship between cultural intelligence and employee performance through the role of work engagement in FDI enterprises in the HCMC industrial zones; and (3) propose some implications for employees' cultural intelligence, drawn from research results, to increase work engagement and performance, thereby contributing to improving the efficiency of the production activities of FDI enterprises in the HCMC industrial zones.

The subjects of the survey were provincial workers (engineers, technicians, and office workers) working at FDI enterprises in HCMC's industrial parks. The three regions (North, Central, and South) in Vietnam have diverse cultures; therefore, workers belonging to a particular region are influenced by its culture. Thus, workers from different provinces (especially the Northern and Central provinces) will initially not be familiar with the culture at HCMC. As they enter it, they come into contact with the Southern culture and work in a foreign environment.

2. Literature Review

2.1. *Cultural intelligence*

Cultural intelligence (CQ) is a theoretical extension of contemporary approaches to understanding intelligence (Earley and Ang, 2003). Earley and Ang (2003) defined cultural intelligence as a person's ability to function and manage themselves effectively in a multicultural work environment; it is an important asset for job performance in MNCs. Meanwhile, Jyoti and Kour (2015) argued that cultural intelligence is an adaptive state of expression that can be developed over time. People with high cultural intelligence can think about what is happening (or not happening) and adjust according to their understanding in the context of different cultures.

Unlike traditional forms of intelligence, CQ is a supplementary type of intelligence that helps explain an individual's ability to adapt to cross-cultural interactions and diversity. CQ is unique because it focuses on settings and interactions that are characterized by cultural diversity (Van Dyne *et al.*, 2010).

Therefore, cultural intelligence is understood as a person's ability to function and manage themselves effectively in a multicultural working environment — a state of expression of adaptability that can be developed over time.

Earley and Ang (2003) identified three key areas of individual intelligence that have significant implications for human interaction: mental (which includes metacognition and cognition), motivational, and behavioral. Ang *et al.* (2007) argued that cultural intelligence is a multidimensional construct composed of four dimensions:

(1) **Motivational cultural intelligence**: Motivational CQ is the basis for learning and adapting to a new culture; it reflects an individual's ability to direct their attention and energy toward learning about new cultures and operating in situations characterized by cultural differences (Van Dyne *et al.*, 2010). This component reflects a person's tendency to perform adaptive behaviors when thrust into a culturally unfamiliar environment (Earley and Peterson, 2004). This includes a natural inclination towards communicating with individuals from diverse cultures, confidence in engaging in culturally varied interactions, and effective stress management when adapting to new and unfamiliar situations. People with cultural intelligence are highly motivated and direct energy towards cross-cultural situations based on intrinsic interests (Deci and Ryan, 1985), and are confident in their cross-cultural effectiveness (Bandura, 2002). Therefore, Motivational CQ can be understood as the foundation of learning, adapting, and communicating with people from different cultures.

(2) **Cognitive cultural intelligence**: Cognitive CQ, according to Van Dyne *et al.* (2010), refers to an individual's awareness of the norms and conventions in different cultural environments. It is related to how an individual perceives similarities and differences across cultures (Ang *et al.*, 2007), and includes knowledge of economic and legal systems, religious beliefs, marriage systems, arts and crafts, languages (Triandis, 2006), and the basic framework of cultural values (Hofstede, 2001). In general, cognitive cultural intelligence encompasses an individual's perception of cultures, norms, and conventions in culturally diverse settings.

(3) **Megacognitive cultural intelligence**: Megacognitive CQ can be understood as planning cross-cultural interactions in advance and adjusting cultural knowledge when interacting with people from different cultures (Ang *et al.*, 2007). This component refers to the mental processes that individuals use to acquire and understand cultural knowledge, including the knowledge and control of culturally related personal thought processes (Flavell, 1979).

(4) **Behavioral cultural intelligence**: Behavioral CQ refers to the ability to express appropriate verbal and nonverbal expressions when dealing with people from different countries (Van Dyne *et al.*, 2010).

It includes a sense of flexibility for behavioral responses appropriate to a wide range of culturally diverse situations, and the ability to adapt to both verbal and nonverbal behavior when coherence is required (Ang *et al.*, 2004).

Van Dyne *et al.* (2010) tested the scale of four components of cultural intelligence outlined by Earley and Ang (2003) in two countries: the US and Singapore. The studies by Ng *et al.* (2012), Ott and Michailova (2016), Jyoti and Kour (2015), and Gabel-Shemueli *et al.* (2019) also use the scale of Van Dyne *et al.* (2010).

Work engagement is a positive state that manifests as energy, total dedication, and enthusiasm toward work (Macey and Schneider, 2008). Karatepe and Karadas (2015) argue that work engagement is a positive state of an individual, with a high degree of work energy, involvement, and commitment invested in work, to perform a job effectively. The authors use the definition and scale of Karatepe and Karadas (2015) to study work engagement in this chapter.

The relationship between cultural intelligence and employee work engagement: Previous studies have found that cultural intelligence can help meet the needs of workers, which, in turn, enables them to engage in their jobs in culturally diverse environments (Gabel-Shemueli *et al.*, 2019), causing them to be bolder in communication (Bücker *et al.*, 2014), cooperation (Imai and Gelfand, 2010), and negotiation (Groves *et al.*, 2015).

Employees with high cultural intelligence will be more confident in their ability to effectively interact with colleagues and superiors in a multicultural environment and may feel more comfortable at work (Temler *et al.*, 2006). High cultural intelligence can also lead to a greater sense of autonomy, as employees feel more influence and control over their environment; this allows them to better monitor, analyze, and adjust their behavior (Tay *et al.*, 2008), thereby overcoming negative reactions and misunderstandings that arise during their interactions with other members of the organization (Rockstuhl and Ng, 2008; Triandis, 2006). Therefore, the proposed hypothesis is as follows:

H1: Cultural intelligence positively affects employee work engagement.

Job performance is defined by Avey *et al.* (2010) as achievements in the workplace. Performance involves planning for results. Evaluating an individual's performance is highly dependent on organizational policies and strategies. Motowidlo (2003) defines job performance as the total expected value an organization achieves from the set of activities performed by individuals in a certain period of time. Rotundo and Sackett (2002) argue that job performance includes the quantity, quality, working skills, and professional knowledge of employees. Hosmani *et al.* (2014) define job performance as the level of task completion of each individual in the organization. In this article, job performance is understood according to Nguyen and Nguyen's (2011) approach, as the assessment of superiors, colleagues, and the evaluation by the employee himself wherein he/she is satisfied with the quality and efficiency of work accomplished.

The relationship between cultural intelligence and job performance: Individuals with high cultural intelligence can gather and manage information, draw inferences, and perform cognitive and emotional actions in response to regional cultural differences in the work environment, which improves their job performance (Earley and Ang, 2003). In contrast, individuals often perform poorly when they do not understand the cultural differences in line with the requirements and expectations of company leadership (Stone *et al.*, 2003). Most subsequent studies have had the same opinion (Ang *et al.*, 2004 and 2007; Lee and Sukoco, 2010). Thus, we propose the following hypothesis:

H2: Cultural intelligence has a positive effect on job performance.

The relationship between work engagement and job performance: Studies by Fleming and Asplund (2007), Macey and Schineider (2008), and Rich *et al.* (2010) suggest that the higher the level of employee work engagement, the better the job performance, work productivity, positive employee behavior, organizational commitment, and customer service. Anitha (2014) showed that an important way to improve job performance is to focus on work engagement. Thus, a positive relationship exists between work engagement and job performance.

H3: Work engagement has a positive effect on job performance.

Conservation of resources (COR) theory suggests that individuals who experience stress often rely on their personal resources, both existing and new, as a form of motivation (Halbesleben *et al.*, 2014; Hobfoll, 2001) to reduce the negative impact of stress and achieve their goals (Bakker and Demerouti, 2007; Gorgievsky and Hobfoll, 2008; Halbesleben *et al.*, 2014). A resource is anything perceived as helping an individual achieve a goal, including objects, personal characteristics, conditions, or energies.

COR theory proposes that employees experience stress when they perceive a threat to their resources (Hobfoll, 2012). To mitigate the impact of this stressor, individuals must invest more resources. Therefore, those with more resources are less likely to lose them and more likely to accumulate more (Hobfoll, 2001; 2012). Employees with fewer resources may attempt to access additional resources through social support (Hobfoll, 1989).

This study uses COR theory to explain the mediating mechanism of job engagement in the relationship between cultural intelligence and employee job performance. Cultural intelligence is a meaningful personal resource for specific challenges faced by employees in MNCs (Gabel-Shemueli *et al.*, 2019). Employees focus on resources (cultural intelligence) to minimize the pressures of a culturally diverse work environment perceived by an individual as helping achieve goals (performance). The available resources (cultural intelligence) facilitate motivational processes that cause employees to become more engaged (Bakker and Demerouti, 2007). Therefore, when individuals have more resources (cultural intelligence and work engagement), they are less pressured and stressed in their work and have the ability to achieve higher work performance (Hobfoll, 2001; 2012). Therefore, the following hypothesis is proposed:

H4: Work engagement mediates the relationship between cultural intelligence and job performance.

From the above-mentioned research overview, the authors propose the research model as shown in Figure 1.

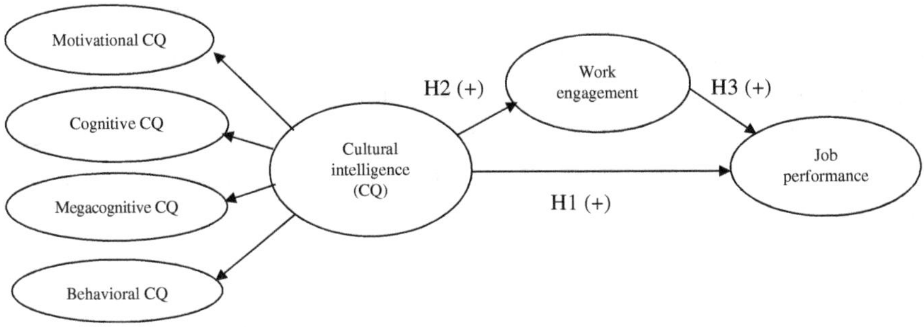

Figure 1. Expected research model.

3. Methodology

3.1. *Preliminary research*

This was conducted using the focus group discussion technique to correct the draft scale and measure the research concepts of cultural intelligence, work engagement, and job performance.

To obtain a draft scale for the components of cultural intelligence, the authors have used the study of Van Dyne *et al.* (2010), which, in turn, is based on the study of Karatepe and Karadas (2015); the job performance scale is based on the study of Nguyen and Nguyen (2011).

Participants in the group discussion included five experts from the Labor Department of Hepza and 10 provincial employees, currently working at FDI enterprises in the HCMC Industrial Parks. In the focus group discussion, the authors explained the concepts in the research model to the members and clarified the definition and nature of the components of cultural intelligence, work engagement, and job performance, through which the members exchanged and expressed their views to calibrate the scales.

The results were adjusted with 28 observed variables, measured using a 5-level Likert scale (1 = completely disagree to 5 = completely agree) to conduct preliminary quantitative research.

Preliminary quantitative research was conducted to test the reliability of the scale and analyze EFA through the data collected from 150 provincial employees (engineers, technicians, office staff) at FDI enterprises in the HCMC industrial zone, by convenient sampling. The authors collected 142 questionnaires, of which six were invalid because the responses lacked information. Based on the test results (see Table 1), three variables were excluded owing to the total variable correlation coefficient <0.3 in the first test (NT3 = 0.213; KT4 = 0.191; HD2 = 0.272).

From the above-mentioned results, the scale of Cultural Intelligence, Work Engagement, and Job performance included 25 observed variables as the official research basis.

3.2. *Formal research*

According to Hoelter (1983), the minimum sample size for the linear structural analysis method should be 200. On the other hand, Bollen (1989) suggested that the minimum sample size for the parameter to be estimated is five. Thus, the authors decided that the expected sample size of this study was 300.

The authors collected data from provincial employees, including engineers, technicians, and office staff, at FDI enterprises in the HCMC industrial zone using a convenient sampling method. With the permission of Hepza leaders, the authors scheduled an appointment to survey 21 FDI enterprises in Tan Thuan and Linh Trung export processing zones, Vinh Loc, and Tan Binh Industrial Park. In response, 15 enterprises agreed to allow the survey, including 9 Japanese enterprises, 3 Taiwanese enterprises, 2 Korean enterprises, and 1 Hong Kong enterprise. Among these

Table 1. Preliminary research results.

			Number of observed variables		
Scales	**Original scale**	**Code**	**Draft scale**	**Results of focus group discussions**	**Preliminary quantitative results**
Motivational CQ	Van Dyne *et al.* (2010)	NT	5	5	4
Cognitive CQ	Van Dyne *et al.* (2010)	KT	6	5	4
Megacognitive CQ	Van Dyne *et al.* (2010)	CL	4	4	4
Behavioral CQ	Van Dyne *et al.* (2010)	HD	5	5	4
Work engagement	Karatepe and Karadas (2015)	CK	5	5	5
Job performance	Nguyen and Nguyen (2011)	KQ	4	4	4

enterprises, as well as FDI enterprises in the HCMC Industrial Park in general, foreign workers (from the parent company) account for approximately 5–7% of the total number of employees in the company and constitute key managers such as directors, department heads, technical experts, working directly with Vietnamese engineers, technicians, and office staff.

Before conducting the survey at each enterprise, the authors explained the research model, the statements contained in the questionnaire, and the manner in which to answer them to the representatives of the staff; the authors also asked these representatives to re-instruct others in the company and made an appointment to receive the survey responses a week later. Of the 350 questionnaires distributed, 307 were used for the study. Incomplete questionnaires were excluded from the study. Overall, a response rate of 87.71% was observed. The results demonstrated that a majority of respondents (Table 2) were male (70.4%), graduate level and above (64.5%), technicians and office staff (78.8%), and under 30 years of age (65.8%).

Table 2. Information about the study sample.

Criteria		**Frequency**	**Percentage (%)**
Gender	Male	216	70.4
	Female	91	29.6
Age	Under 30	202	65.8
	From 30 to 45	94	30.6
	Over 45	11	3.6
Academic level	College, Vocational High School	109	35.5
	Graduate-level	193	62.9
	Above graduate-level	5	1.6
Position	Head/Deputy Head of Department	26	8.5
	Engineer	39	12.7
	Office staff	180	58.6
	Technicians	62	20.2
Seniority	Under 2 years	88	28.7
	From 2 to 5 years	120	39.1
	From 5 to 10 years	64	20.8
	Over 10 years	35	11.4
Total		307	100.0

Data collected from the survey were analyzed using Smart PLS software. Hair *et al.* (2014) indicated two steps to be taken for PLS-SEM: measurement model evaluation and structural model evaluation. The evaluation of the measurement model indicated the reliability, convergence value, and discriminant value of the scales in the research model. Next, the results of the Bootstrapping analysis were used to test the SEM structural model, thereby accepting or rejecting the hypotheses of the research model.

4. Results

4.1. *Evaluation of measurement model*

It is necessary to use Cronbach's Alpha index and Composite Reliability (CR) to evaluate the reliability of the SmartPLS scale. If the coefficients of Cronbach's Alpha (Robert and Carolyn, 2012) and CR (Bagozzi & Youjae, 1988) are greater than or equal to 0.7, the scale is reliable. To test the convergence value of the scale, it is necessary to check the quality of the observed variables through the outer loading coefficient which is an indicator of the degree of association between the observed and latent variables with the average extracted variance (AVE). According to Hair (2016), an observed variable with an outer loading coefficient >0.708 indicates that the observed variable possesses the desired quality. For an AVE greater than or equal to 0.5, the scale will achieve convergence (Joseph, 2021).

Fornell and Larcker (1981) used the square root index of the AVE coefficient to test discriminant validity; if this index is greater than the correlation of the latent variables, it is passed. However, Henseler and Sarstedt (2015) demonstrated that the discriminant value is better evaluated by the Heterotrait–Monotrait Ratio (HTMT), and this value <0.9 is warranted.

We used the variance inflation factor (VIF) of the collinearity statistics to evaluate the multicollinearity of the variables in the model. Inner and Outer VIF values were used to evaluate latent and observed variables, respectively. Multicollinearity may not occur (Hair *et al.*, 2019).

Table 3 shows that the scale of measuring concepts in the research model demonstrates Cronbach's alpha values >0.7, rho_A >0.7, CR >0.7, and AVE >0.5, which meet the requirements. The Fornell–Larcker matrix

Table 3. Results of the reliability analysis, the convergent value of the scale, and the outer loading coefficients of the observed variables.

Code	Observed variables	Outer loading coefficients
Motivational CQ (Alpha = 0.881; rho_A = 0.883; CR = 0.918; AVE = 0.737)		
MoC1	I enjoy interacting with people from different cultures	0.839
MoC2	I am confident that I can communicate with the locals where I come from	0.877
MoC3	I enjoy living in cultures different from my own	0.861
MoC4	I am confident that I can get accustomed to the shopping conditions where I come from	0.857
Cognitive CQ (Alpha = 0.823; rho_A = 0.825; CR = 0.883; AVE = 0.654)		
CoC1	I know the legal and economic system where I come from	0.791
CoC2	I know the language where I come from	0.836
CoC3	I know the cultural values and religious beliefs of the culture where I come from	0.817
CoC4	I know the rules of expressing nonverbal behavior where I go	0.789
Megacognitive CQ (Alpha = 0.868; rho_A = 0.869; CR = 0.910; AVE = 0.717)		
MeC1	I am aware of the cultural knowledge I use when I interact with people from different cultural backgrounds	0.859
MeC2	I adjust my cultural knowledge when I interact with people whose background is different from mine	0.832
MeC3	I am aware of the cultural knowledge I apply to cross-cultural interactions	0.847
MeC4	I test the accuracy of my cultural knowledge when interacting with people from different cultures	0.848
Behavioral CQ (Alpha = 0.842; rho_A = 0.844; CR = 0.894; AVE = 0.678)		
BeC1	I change my verbal behavior (e.g., accent, tone) as needed to communicate in a cross-cultural environment	0.808
BeC2	I change my speaking speed as needed to communicate in a cross-cultural environment	0.856
BeC3	I change my body language as needed to communicate in a cross-cultural environment	0.827
BeC4	I change my facial expression as needed to communicate in a cross-cultural environment	0.803

(*Continued*)

Table 3. (*Continued*)

Code	Observed variables	Outer loading coefficients
Work engagement (Alpha = 0.884; rho_A = 0.894; CR = 0.915; AVE = 0.683)		
WE1	At my work, I feel like I am bursting with energy	0.853
WE2	At my job, I feel strong and vigorous	0.856
WE3	I am enthusiastic about my job	0.811
WE4	I feel happy doing my job	0.842
WE5	I am proud of the work that I do	0.768
Job performance (Alpha = 0.858; rho_A = 0.859; CR = 0.904; AVE = 0.701)		
JP1	I believe I am an effective employee	0.827
JP2	I am happy with the quality of my work output	0.866
JP3	My superiors believe I am an efficient employee	0.836
JP4	My colleagues believe I am a very productive employee	0.820

Note: CR — composite reliability; AVE — average variance extracted.

coefficients are all larger than the coefficients in the same column; at the same time, the VIF values of the observed variables are all <5.0 (see Tables 4–7). Therefore, the model fits the market data.

4.2. *Evaluation of structural model*

The authors tested the linear structural model through the Bootstrapping procedure with the recommended Bootstrapping sample size of $n = 5000$ (Henseler *et al.*, 2015). From the results of Table 8, it can be concluded that the estimates in the model are reliable.

Therefore, hypotheses H1, H2, and H3 are accepted, showing that cultural intelligence has the strongest positive impact on work engagement ($\beta = 0.615$; $p = 0.000$), followed by job performance ($\beta = 0.584$; $p = 0.000$), and work engagement affects job performance ($\beta = 0.273$; $p = 0.000$). The scale of the concepts in the research model reached the theoretical value. Thus, all the hypotheses are supported.

Table 4. Fornell–Larcker criterion.

	BeC	CQ	CoC	JP	MeC	MoQ	WE
BeC	**0.824**						
CQ	0.767	0.615					
CoC	0.390	0.727	**0.809**				
JP	0.594	0.753	0.533	**0.838**			
MeC	0.450	0.786	0.512	0.658	**0.847**		
MoQ	0.401	0.666	0.287	0.418	0.303	**0.859**	
WE	0.516	0.615	0.315	0.633	0.417	0.56	**0.827**

Table 5. Heterotrait–Monotrait (HTMT) ratio.

	BeC	CQ	CoC	JP	MeC	MoQ	WE
BeC							
CQ	0.875						
CoC	0.468	0.86					
JP	0.699	0.854	0.631				
MeC	0.525	0.875	0.606	0.761			
MoQ	0.463	0.77	0.334	0.48	0.346		
WE	0.582	0.681	0.359	0.718	0.465	0.632	

Table 6. Outer VIF values of observed variables.

MoQ1	2.080	MeC1	2.169	WE1	2.278
MoQ1	2.307	MeC1	2.501	WE2	2.358
MoQ2	2.411	MeC2	1.969	WE3	1.952
MoQ2	2.623	MeC2	2.149	WE4	2.210
MoQ3	2.274	MeC3	2.104	WE5	1.860
MoQ3	2.358	MeC3	2.182	JP1	1.888
MoQ4	2.220	MeC4	2.070	JP2	2.261
MoQ4	2.332	MeC4	2.169	JP3	1.953
CoC1	1.701	BeC1	1.771	JP4	1.897
CoC1	1.882	BeC1	1.872		
CoC2	1.918	BeC2	2.057		
CoC2	1.997	BeC2	2.280		
CoC3	1.743	BeC3	1.922		
CoC3	1.952	BeC3	2.056		
CoC4	1.640	BeC4	1.766		
CoC4	1.755	BeC4	1.877		

Table 7. Inner VIF values of latent variables.

	BeC	**CQ**	**CoC**	**JP**	**MeC**	**MoQ**	**WE**
BeC							
CQ	1		1	1.609	1	1	1
CoC							
JP							
MeC							
MoQ							
WE				1.609			

Table 8. Bootstrapping results of structural model and hypothesis testing.

Path	**Original sample (β)**	**Sample mean bootstrapping**	**Standard Deviation (STDEV)**	***t*-statistics**	***p*-values**	**Results**
CQ –> JP	0.584	0.587	0.041	14.347	0.000(*)	Supported
CQ –> WE	0.615	0.617	0.040	15.249	0.000(*)	Supported
WE –> JP	0.273	0.271	0.046	5.953	0.000(*)	Supported

The results of the structural model estimation and hypothesis testing are shown in Figure 2.

Testing hypothesis H4

From Table 9, it is found that cultural intelligence has an indirect impact on job performance through work engagement, with an impact level of $\beta = 0.168$.

Thus, it can be concluded that work engagement mediates the relationship between cultural intelligence and job performance. This means that H4 is accepted.

4.3. *Testing for differences*

According to David Garson (2016), for the Smart_PLS tool, in multi-group analysis (MGA) if *p*-value <5%, 10% or *p*-value >95%, 90%, the

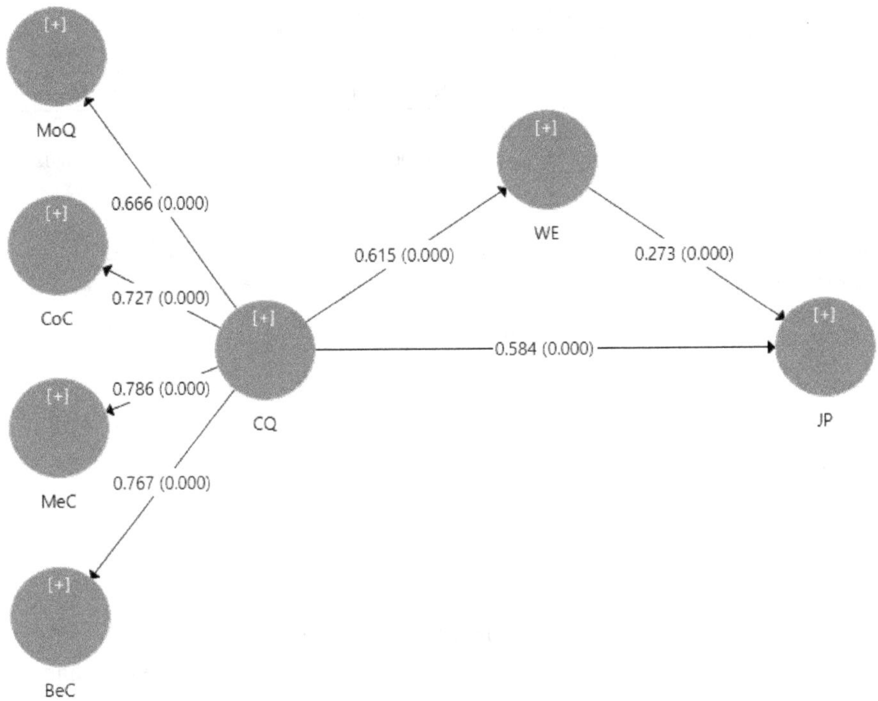

Figure 2. PLS_SEM structural model (normalized).

Table 9. Degree of impact (β) of the relationships.

Relationship	Path coefficients	Indirect effects	Total effects
CQ –> WE	0.615		0.615
CQ –> JP	0.584	0.168	0.753
WE –> JP	0.273		0.273

difference between groups is statistically significant at 5% and 10%. Table 10 shows the following:

- There is a difference between males and females in the relationship between cultural intelligence and work engagement (at 90%) and employee job performance (at 95%) in FDI enterprises in HCMC industrial zones.

Table 10. Testing for differences.

	Gender		Age		Education		Working year	
Relationship	***p*-value**	**Results**	***p*-value**	**Results**	***p*-value**	**Results**	***p*-value**	**Results**
Work engagement –> Job performance	0.458	Meaningless	0.643	Meaningless	0.013	(*)	0.836	Meaningless
Cultural intelligence –> Work engagement	0.930	(**)	0.851			Meaningless	0.792	
Cultural intelligence –> Job performance	0.047	(*)	0.942	(**)	0.000	(*)	0.693	

Note: *Significant at the 95% level; **significant at the 90% level.

- There is a difference in age (under 30 years old and over 30 years old) in the relationship between cultural intelligence and job performance (at 90%).
- There is a difference in professional qualifications (College, Vocational College, and graduate level) in the relationship between work engagement and cultural intelligence, and job performance (at 95%).

5. Discussion and Managerial Implications

This study examined the influence of cultural intelligence on job performance and the mediating role of work engagement in FDI enterprises in HCMC industrial zones. The results show that cultural intelligence has a positive impact on job performance and work engagement; the factor of work engagement plays an intermediary role in the relationship between cultural intelligence and job performance. This result is consistent with those of Jyoti and Kour (2015, 2017), Ramalu *et al.* (2012), Konanahalli *et al.* (2014), Anitha (2014), and Gabel-Shemueli *et al.* (2019). The results show that there are differences between men and women, levels of education, and age groups in the relationship between cultural intelligence and job performance, a difference between the levels of education in the relationship between work engagement and job performance, and a difference between men and women in the relationship between cultural intelligence and work engagement in FDI enterprises in the HCMC industrial zones.

Explaining this result, the previous group interview participants stated that a majority of workers working in HCMC industrial zones, in general, are young, so they adapt easily to the new living and working environment, and quickly integrate with the cultural diversity in FDI enterprises. The characteristics of enterprises in HCMC industrial parks are that they employ mostly young, unskilled workers coming from remote provinces. Therefore, in the initial stage of being employed, they are often overwhelmed and intimidated in a working environment with foreign experts. They face many difficulties and obstacles because they have to adapt to the culture of HCMC and integrate it with the culture of FDI companies and foreigners. Therefore, many employees, especially female workers, are unable to perform well and quit in the first few days of work. This finding is significant in developing the implications of human resource management policy for enterprises to improve employees' job performance by enhancing the cultural intelligence of college-educated employees with vocational intermediate-level training, and young female employees. Some policies that increase work engagement among high-skilled workers and new female employees are as follows:

- **For cultural intelligence**: For employees, especially those with college and vocational qualifications and young female employees, the key characteristics of enterprises in the HCMC Industrial Parks are that a majority are FDI enterprises; 69% of the employees come from the provinces, of which more than 71% work for FDI enterprises; and the board of directors is constituted mostly by foreigners. When workers in the province have just been recruited to work in industrial parks, they are unfamiliar with both the way of life in big cities like HCMC and working in a corporate environment with foreign managers. Therefore, they are limited by a lack of knowledge of foreign languages, the culture of the region they come to (in particular, HCMC), and corporate culture, which affects their job performance. So:
    - The Human Resources Department of FDI enterprises must add additional selection criteria for employees with high cultural intelligence in their recruitment process.

- The Human Resources Department of FDI enterprises should organize training courses for new employees on foreign languages and corporate culture, especially the culture of the origin country of the business owner and the customs of the place of work (specifically, HCMC); these should especially be targeted at female workers from the provinces, to help them integrate into the new living and working environment.
- The company needs to coordinate with the Trade Union to support recently recruited employees, or newly arrived in HCMC, in terms of finding hostels or having a dormitory regime for provincial employees and providing guidance on living in the city.
- Furthermore, the Human Resources Department should establish and refine a system of key performance indicators (KPIs) to serve as the foundation for evaluations. Additionally, implementing an objective and equitable reward policy is essential. This approach aims to motivate employees to exert greater effort and foster commitment, ultimately contributing to improved performance outcomes.

- **For work engagement**: Companies' Human Resources Departments are very interested in developing policies to increase employee work engagement, especially for highly qualified people as well as new female employees. Human resources experts explained that employees with high qualifications often tend to work in the short term to gain experience and then move to other companies with better working environments and promotion opportunities. Due to the characteristics of FDI enterprises in industrial zones, most of them are into production, so all activities of the company only focus on producing the orders from the parent company in foreign countries; therefore, the company's strategy and development orientation are rarely shared with workers. So, workers are unaware and unclear about the company's future. Therefore, FDI enterprises must consider the following:
  - The board of directors needs to share the vision and development orientation of the company with employees and indicate the importance of the work they are undertaking to them. This will help communicate to them that their contribution to the company

is meaningful and will make them feel proud of their work. This motivates employees and enhances their work engagement, helping them achieve better performance.

- A company needs to improve its employee performance management. The Human Resources Department needs to develop and complete the KPIs clearly and specifically. The Management should regularly discuss and eliminate difficulties and encourage employees to perform well.
- Today's young generation is interested in career development and asserting themselves in the workplace, besides the reasonable salary policy. Therefore, if employees want to engage in their jobs for a long time, it is necessary for businesses to develop a career path for them and clearly inform them about the total rewards in the company.

5.1. *Limitations and future directions*

This study makes the following contributions: (1) simultaneously testing the relationship between cultural intelligence and employee job performance as well as the mediating role of work engagement in FDI enterprises in the HCMC industrial zones; and (2) considering demographic characteristics such as gender, age, and education level of employees in FDI enterprises in the HCMC industrial zones in the relationship between cultural intelligence, work engagement, and job performance. However, this study has some limitations that should be addressed in future studies. The authors collected data using convenience sampling, with a sample size of 307 in industrial zones in HCMC. Therefore, to increase the generalizability of the proposed research model, future studies need to use the method of probability sampling with a larger sample size, and the research scope needs to be expanded to make research frameworks more general and valid in different contexts.

Acknowledgment

This research is funded by University of Economics Ho Chi Minh City (Vietnam).

References

Ang, S., van Dyne, L., Koh, C., & Ng, K. Y. (2004). *The Measure of Cultural Intelligence*. New Orleans: Academy of Management.

Ang, S., van Dyne, L., Koh, C., Ng, K. Y., Templer, K. J., Tay, C., & Chandrasekar, N. A. (2007). Cultural intelligence: Its measurement and effects on cultural judgment and decision making, cultural adaptation and task performance. *Management and Organization Review*, *3*(3), 335–371.

Anitha, J. (2014). Determinants of employee engagement and their impact on job performance. *International Journal of Productivity and Performance Management*, *63*(3), 308–323.

Bagozzi, R. P. & Youjae, Y. (1988). On the evaluation of structural equation models. *Journal of the Academy of Marketing Science.* Available at: https://link.springer.com/article/10.1007/BF02723327.

Bakker, A. B. & Demerouti, E. (2007). The job demands-resources model: State of the art. *Journal of Managerial Psychology*, *22*(3), 309–328.

Bandura, A. (2002). Social cognitive theory in cultural context. *Applied Psychology*, *51*(2), 269–290.

Bollen, K. A. (1989). *Structural Equations with Latent Variable*. New York: John Wiley & Sons.

Bücker, J. J., Furrer, O., Poutsma, E., & Buyens, D. (2014). The impact of cultural intelligence on communication effectiveness, job satisfaction and anxiety for Chinese host country managers working for foreign multinationals. *The International Journal of Human Resource Management*, *25*(14), 2068–2087.

David Garson, G. (2016). *Partial Least Squares: Regression & Structural Equation Models.* Asheboro, NC, USA: Statistical Associates Publishing.

Deci, E. L. & Ryan, R. M. (1985). *Intrinsic Motivation and Self-determination in Human Behavior.* New York: Plenum.

Earley, P. C. & Ang, S. (2003). *Cultural Intelligence: Individual Interactions Across Cultures.* Stanford, CA: Stanford University Press.

Earley, P. C. & Peterson, R. S. (2004). The elusive cultural chameleon: Cultural intelligence as a new approach to intercultural training for the global manager, *Academy of Management Learning and Education*, *3*(1), 100–115.

Farndale, E. & Murrer, I. (2015). Job resources and employee engagement: A cross-national study. *Journal of Managerial Psychology*, *30*(5), 610–626.

Flavell, J. H. (1979). Meta-cognitive and Cognitive monitoring: A new area of cognitive inquiry. *American Psychologist*, *34*(10), 906–911.

Fleming, J. H. & Asplund, J. (2007). *Human Sigma*. New York, NY: Gallup Press.

Fornell, C. & Larcker, D. F. (1981). Structural equation model with unobservable variables and measurement error: Algebra and statistics. *Journal of Marketing Research*, Available at: https://journals.sagepub.com/doi/abs/10.1177/002224378101800313.

Gabel-Shemueli, R., Westman, M., Chen, S., & Bahamonde, D. (2019). Does cultural intelligence increase work engagement? The role of idiocentrism-allocentrism and organizational culture in MNCs. *Cross Cultural & Strategic Management*, *26*(1), 46–66.

Gorgievsky, M. J. & Hobfoll, S. E. (2008). Work can burn us out and fire us up: Conservation of resources in burnout and engagement. In Halbesleben, J. R. B. (ed.), *Handbook of Stress and Burnout in Health Care* (pp. 7–22). Hauppauge, NY: Nova Science Publishers.

Groves, K. S., Feyerherm, A., & Gu, M. (2015). Examining cultural intelligence and cross-cultural negotiation effectiveness. *Journal of Management Education*, *39*(2), 209–243.

Hair, J. G. (2016). *Partial Least Squares Structural Equation Modeling (PLS_SEM) Using R*. Classroom Companion: Business.

Hair, J. F. (2021). Reflections on SEM: An introspective, idiosyncratic journey to composite-based structural equation modeling. *ACM SIGMIS Database: The DATABASE for Advances in Information Systems*, *52*(SI), 101–113.

Hair, J. F., Anderson, R. E., Tatham, R. L., & William, C. B. (2006). *Multivariate Data Analysis*. UK: Pearson Education.

Hair, J. F., Sarstedt, M., Pieper, T. M., & Ringle, C. M. (2012). The use of partial least squares structural equation modeling in strategic management research: A review of past practices and recommendations for future applications. *Long Range Planning*, *45*(5–6), 320–340.

Hair, J. F., Risher, J. J., Sarstedt, M., & Ringle, C. M. (2019). When to use and how to report the results of PLS_SEM. *European Business Review*, *31*, 1. Available at: https://www.emerald.com/insight/content/doi/10.1108/EJM-10-2018-0665/full/html.

Halbesleben, J. R. B., Neveu, J. P., Paustian-Underdahl, S. C., & Westman, M. (2014). Getting to the 'COR': Understanding the role of resources in conservation of resources theory. *Journal of Management*, *40*(5), 1334–1364.

Henseler, J. & Sarstedt, C. M. (2015). A new criterion for assessing discriminant validity in variance-based structural equation modeling. *Journal of the Academy of Marketing Science*. Available at: https://links.springer.com/artical/10.1007/s11747-014-0403-8.

Henseler, J., Fassott, G., & Coelho, P. (2016). Testing moderating effects in PLS path models with composite variables. *Industrial Management & Data Systems*, *116*(9), 1887–1900.

Henseler, J. F., Raz, Y., Kolk, A., Riaz, M., van der Zwaal, P., Nagels, J., …, & Raz, V. (2015). Patterns of age-associated degeneration differ in shoulder muscles. *Frontiers in Aging Neuroscience*, *7*, 236.

Hepza. (2015). General introduction. Accessed October 19, 2019, from http://www.hepza.hochiminhcity.gov.vn/web/guest/kcn_kcx-tphcm/gioi-thieu-chung.

Hobfoll, S. E. (1989). Conservation of resources: A new attempt at conceptualizing stress. *American Psychologist*, *44*(3), 513–524.

Hobfoll, S. E. (2001). The influence of culture, community, and the nested self in the stress process: Advancing conservation of resources theory. *Applied Psychology*, *50*(3), 337–421.

Hobfoll, S. E. (2012). Conservation of resources and disaster in cultural context: The caravans and passageways for resources. *Psychiatry: Interpersonal and Biological Processes*, *75*(3), 227–232.

Hoelter, J. W. (1983). The analysis of covariance structures. *Sociological Methods & Research*, *11*(3), 325–344.

Hofstede, G. (2001). *Culture's Consequences: Comparing Values, Behaviors, Institutions, and Organizations Across Nations*. Thousand Oaks, CA: Sage.

Imai, L. & Gelfand, M. J. (2010). The culturally intelligent negotiator: The impact of cultural intelligence (CQ) on negotiation sequences and outcomes. *Organizational Behavior and Human Decision Processes*, *112*(2), 83–98.

Jyoti, J. & Kour, S. (2015). Assessing the cultural intelligence and task performance equation: Mediating role of cultural adjustment. *Cross-cultural Management: An International Journal*, *22*(2), 236–258.

Jyoti, J. & Kour, S. (2017). Factors affecting cultural intelligence and its impact on job performance: Role of cross-cultural adjustment, experience and perceived social support. *Personnel Review*, *46*(4), 767–791.

Karatepe, O. M. & Karadas, G. (2015). Do psychological capital and work engagement foster frontline employees' satisfaction? *International Journal of Contemporary Hospitality Management*, *27*(6), 1254–1278.

Karma, K. & Vedina, R. (2009). Cultural intelligence as a prism between workforce diversity and performance in a modern organization. *Review of International Comparative Management*, *10*(3), 527–542.

Konanahalli, A., Oyedele, L., Spillane, J., Coates, R., von Meding, J., & Ebohon, J. (2014). Cross-cultural intelligence (CQ). *International Journal of Managing Projects in Business*, *7*(3), 423–448.

Lee, L. Y. & Sukoco, B. M. (2010). The effects of cultural intelligence on expatriate performance: The moderating effects of international experience. *The International Journal of Human Resource Management*, *21*(7), 963–981.

Macey, W. H. & Schneider, B. (2008). The meaning of employee engagement. *Industrial and Organizational Psychology*, *1*(1), 3–30.

Mahboobeh, D., Gunkel, M., Veglio, V., & Taras, V. (2022). The influence of cultural intelligence and emotional intelligence on conflict occurrence and performance in global virtual teams. *Journal of International Management*, *28*(4).

Ng, K. Y., van Dyne, L., & Ang, S. (2009). From experience to experiential learning: Cultural intelligence as a learning capability for global leader development. *Academy of Management Learning and Education*, *8*(4), 511–526.

Ng, K. Y., van Dyne, L., & Ang, S. (2012). Cultural intelligence: A review, reflections, and recommendations for future research, in Ryan, A. M., Leong, F. T. L., & Oswald, F. L. (eds.), *Conducting Multinational Research: Applying Organizational Psychology in the Workplace* (pp. 29–58). Washington, DC: American Psychological Association.

Nguyen, T. D. & Nguyen, T. T. M. (2011). Psychological capital, quality of work life, and quality of life of marketers: Evidence from Vietnam. *Journal of Macromarketing*, *32*(1), 87–95.

Nicholson, N. (1984). A theory of work role transitions. *Administrative Science Quarterly*, *29*(2), 172–191.

Ott, D. L. & Michailova, S. (2016). Cultural intelligence: A review and new research avenues. *International Journal of Management Reviews*, *20*(1), 99–119.

Ramalu, S., Rose, R. C., Kumar, N., & Uli, J. (2010). Doing business in global arena: An examination of the relationship between cultural intelligence and cross-cultural adjustment. *Asian Academy of Management Journal*, *15*(1), 79–97.

Rich, B. L., Lepine, J. A., & Crawford, E. R. (2010). Job engagement: Antecedents and effects on job performance. *Academy of Management Journal*, *53*(3), 617–635.

Robert, F. DeVellis, & Carolyn, T. Thorpe. (2012). *Scale Development.* SAGE Publications Ltd.

Rockstuhl, T. & Ng, K. Y. (2008). The effects of cultural intelligence on interpersonal trust in multicultural teams. In Ang, S., & van Dyne, L. (eds.), *Handbook of Cultural Intelligence: Theory, Measurement, and Applications* (pp. 206–220). Armonk, NY: M. E. Sharpe.

Stone-Romero, E., Stone D. L., & Salas E. (2003). The influence of culture on role conceptions and role behavior in organizations. *Applied Psychology: An International Review*, *52*(3), 328–362.

Tay, C., Westman, M., & Chia, A. (2008). Antecedents and consequences of cultural intelligence among short-term business travelers. In Ang, S., & van Dyne, L. (eds.), *Handbook of Cultural Intelligence: Theory, Measurement, and Applications* (pp. 126–144). Armonk, NY: M. E. Sharpe.

Templer, K. J., Tay, C., & Chandrasekar, N. A. (2006). Motivational cultural intelligence, realistic job previews and realistic living conditions preview and cross-cultural adjustment. *Group Organization Management*, *31*(1), 154–173.

Trefry, M. G. (2006). A double-edged sword: Organizational culture in multicultural organizations. *International Journal of Management*, *23*(3), 563–575.

Triandis, H. C. (2006). Cultural intelligence in organizations. *Group Organization Management*, *3*(1), 20–26.

Van Dyne, L., Ang, S., & Livermore, D. (2010). Cultural intelligence: A pathway for leading in a rapidly globalizing world, in Hannum, K. M., McFeeters, B. & Booysen, L. (eds.), *Leadership Across Differences* (pp. 131–138). San Francisco, CA: Pfeiffer.

https://doi.org/10.1142/9789811286100_0004

Chapter 4

Determinants and Measurement of Financial Information Quality — An Empirical Review

Mai Duc Nghia

School of Accounting,
University of Economics Ho Chi Minh City, Vietnam

ducnghia@ueh.edu.vn

Abstract

This research aims to evaluate the commonality among numerous empirical studies on the determinants and measurement of financial information quality. It also attempts to examine the research results through the lens of governing bodies such as the International Federation of Accountants (IFAC) and the International Organization for Economic Co-operation and Development (OECD). Thus, this chapter provides a comprehensive review of the determinants and measurement of financial information quality. As a result, four categories of quality determinants (corporate governance, the financial reporting process, the audit of financial statements, and the usefulness of financial statements) have been identified and two approaches to quality measurement with their own weaknesses have been critically analyzed. However, quality measurement is still fertile ground for future research because the best way to quantify such quality has not been developed yet.

Keywords: Quality of Financial Information, Quality Measurement, Corporate Governance, Audit Committee, Quality Determinant, IFRS.

Received on December 9, 2022; accepted on May 19, 2023

1. Introduction

The quality of financial information plays a central role in any capital market, and the benefits of this quality have been extensively proven in empirical research. These include increased efficiency of investment (Hilary *et al.*, 2009; Chen *et al.*, 2011), improved performance of peer-based valuation models (Young and Zeng, 2015), and lower costs of acquiring information (De Franco *et al.*, 2011).

Many researchers have focused on understanding factors that affect financial information quality and seeking ways to measure such quality (Brown and Tarca, 2007; Barth *et al.*, 2008; Debreceny *et al.*, 2010; Chandar *et al.*, 2012; Chen *et al.*, 2014; Karthik and Ertan, 2018; Arniati *et al.*, 2019; Hashim *et al.*, 2019; Castillo-Merino *et al.*, 2019; Garcia-Blandon *et al.*, 2020; Key and Kim, 2020).

Considering the above-mentioned research, it is logical to raise the following questions: Do these empirical studies examine the same factor or use the same measurement of quality construct? If not, is there any commonality among these studies? In other words, this study seeks to answer these questions.

This study had two objectives: (1) to analyze different ways of measuring the quality of financial information, and (2) to identify and synthesize quality determinants. To this end, a review of empirical research on the subject matter was conducted.

The main findings of this study identify two approaches to quality measurement and four groups of determinants of financial information quality. Multiple measures of financial information quality have been deployed in various empirical research studies with direct and indirect ways of measurement. Each approach to measurement has its own weakness, and none of them appeared to be superior to the rest. Rather, the results of these empirical studies seemed to complement each other. In addition, there was a commonality among these studies in that whatever factor they employed belonged to one of the four groups of quality factors, namely corporate governance, the process of financial reporting, the audit of financial statements, or the usefulness of financial statements. Each empirical study examined only one or two dimensions of each quality factor. Therefore, this study aimed at a comprehensive review, seeking to help potential authors make informed decisions on two key aspects: how to select the method of quality measurement (be it direct or indirect) and how to select the quality determinants for research. I mean that my paper will help future authors save their effort and quickly get the right focus regarding the quality of financial information.

This chapter is organized into three main parts: (1) an overview of financial information quality, (2) an analysis of quality measurement, and (3) a comprehensive examination of empirical research on the quality determinants. In addition, the study includes other sections such as results, discussion, and conclusion.

2. Literature Review

2.1. *Qualitative characteristics of financial information*

The qualitative characteristics of financial information stated in the *Conceptual Framework for Financial Reporting* by the International Federation of Accountants (IFAC) have been the most popular and widely accepted. These characteristics include relevance, faithful representation, comparability, verifiability, timeliness, and understandability (International Accounting Standards Board [IASB], 2018). Financial information having these qualitative features is considered to be of quality and useful for decision-making.

2.1.1. *Relevance*

Capital market participants need different information that is relevant to their decision-making. Wang and Hussainey (2013) argued that disclosures of forward-looking information on corporate governance helped stock markets better forecast a firm's future earnings, and Tahat and Alhadab (2017) found the information on operation cash flows the most relevant to users of financial reports.

2.1.2. *Faithful representation*

To be a faithful representation, a piece of financial information must depict an economic phenomenon in a complete, neutral, and error-free manner. Research has indicated that disclosures of financial statements contributed to the faithful representation of financial information (Caramanolis-Cotelli and Birgul, 1999; Daske and Gebhardt, 2006). Maintaining the neutrality of financial information requires the absence of bias in the presentation of such information.

Comparability: Investors need comparable information to make informed decisions. Thus, the comparability of financial information is crucial as it allows for identifying the similarities and differences between pieces of information. Chen and Gong (2019) proved that the comparability of financial information improved the ability of management to predict the future performance of a firm. Further, De Franco *et al.* (2011) found that financial report comparability decreased the cost of acquiring information and increased the forecasting ability of analysts concerning the firm.

Verifiability: Verifiability allows users of financial reports to ensure that a piece of information faithfully represents an economic phenomenon. In other words, the verifiability of financial information refers to the degree of consensus among different users regarding its faithful representation. Beretta and Bozzolan (2007) demonstrated that analysts' forecast accuracy had improved with verifiable disclosures and that the dispersion of forecasts had decreased as well.

Timeliness: Financial information must be accessible for users' decision-making in a timely manner. Barth *et al.* (2008) found that firms applying International Accounting Standards (IAS) were more timely in recognizing losses overall and presented more relevant financial information compared with non-IAS applicating firms. Ball *et al.* (2000) revealed that firms in common law countries were more timely in recognizing bad news than those in code law regimes (and vice versa for good news).

Understandability: For users of financial reports to easily comprehend and interpret financial information, it must be organized and presented clearly and concisely (IASB, 2018).

In summary, financial information having the above-mentioned qualitative characteristics is considered to be of quality. In the US, the

Conceptual Framework of the Financial Accounting Standards Board (FASB) has the same definitions as the Framework of the IFAC.

2.2. *Empirical measurement of financial information quality*

Empirical studies indicate that financial information quality could be measured in different ways (be it direct or indirect).

Regarding direct measurement of quality, authors have concentrated on gauging the qualitative characteristics of financial information. For example, some directly measured the comparability of financial information (Krisement, 1997; De Franco *et al.*, 2011), while others focused on the timeliness of loss recognition (Leuz *et al.*, 2003; Barth *et al.*, 2008; Ball *et al.*, 2005). Smith and Jones (2014) measured the understandability of financial information using the meaning identification test (MIT) and the sentence verification technique (SVT). With the logical reasoning that users of financial reports must read them before they can interpret financial information for their understanding, some authors consider "how readable the financial statements are". For example, Li (2008), Loughran and McDonald (2014), and Bonsall *et al.* (2017) defined and measured the readability of financial reports diversely. While Jonas *et al.* (2000) considered the completeness of financial statement disclosures, Anderson *et al.* (2009) showed that investors seemingly valued the disclosure quality component more than the market scrutiny factor. The problem hindering the direct measurement of quality was the lack of consistent and specific scales. For example, for measuring the comparability of financial information, Krisement (1997) used an input approach, while De Franco *et al.* (2011) deployed output metrics.

Research incorporating indirect ways of quality measurement focused on observing proxies of financial reports such as reported earnings or non-earnings or responses of stock exchanges. For example, Martínez-Ferrero *et al.* (2015) found that firms implemented earnings management practices to a lesser extent and provided higher quality of financial information. Burgstahler and Dichev (1997) found that firms' reported earnings were managed to avoid reporting earnings declines and losses. Wang *et al.* (2011) used restatements of financial statements to measure the quality of past financial information reported in China's capital market and concluded that the accounting credibility in China was lower than that in the

US. However, the frequency of restatements decreased over the period 1999–2005 due to regulators' efforts to enhance the quality of financial information and increase the disclosure of listed firms.

Barth *et al.* (2001), Nichols and Wahlen (2004), and Schipper and Vincent (2003) examined the relationship between reported earnings and stock exchange responses. They assumed that the stock prices in capital markets would accordingly reflect changes in reported earnings on financial statements. However, the big issues affecting this measurement were the effect on prices by elements other than reported earnings and the limited use of only one element of the financial statement as proxy instead of comprehensive lists.

In summary, multiple measures of financial information quality have been employed in empirical research. However, each way of measuring has its own weakness, and none of them appeared to be superior to the rest. Rather, the results of these empirical studies complement each other.

The next section presents the results of empirical research on the determinants of financial information quality.

2.3. *Empirical research on quality determinants*

Authors examined the effects of various elements on the quality of financial information. For example, Arniati *et al.* (2019), Hashim *et al.* (2019), Kusnadi *et al.* (2014), and Chandar *et al.* (2012) explored whether the board of directors or audit committees affect the quality of financial reports, while Gunz and Thorne (2019), Chen *et al.* (2014), and Harris (2012) considered the possible effects of compliance to the Sarbanes–Oxley (SOX) Act. From other perspectives, Morais *et al.* (2018), Liu *et al.* (2011), Chua *et al.* (2012), and Ismail *et al.* (2013) compared the impact of applying IFRS and domestic accounting standards on financial information quality. In addition, the potential impacts of auditors' tenures and independence on the quality of financial information were examined by Garcia-Blandon *et al.* (2020), Castillo-Merino *et al.* (2019), Sumiadji and Subiyantoro (2019), Achyarsyah and Molina (2014), and Abdel-Meguid *et al.* (2013).

The various elements of empirical research need to be sorted and synthesized in a more concise and systematic order. Based on the OECD's *Principles of Corporate Governance* (OECD, 2015) and some IFAC-commissioned publications such as *Rebuilding Public Confidence in Financial Reporting* (2004) and *Financial Reporting Supply Chain — Current Perspectives and Directions* (2008), the quality determinants used in empirical studies can be classified into four groups of quality factors: corporate governance, the process of financial reporting, the audit of financial statements, and the usefulness of financial statements. Each of these factors reflects the concerns of different stakeholders about financial reporting quality and can include various dimensions. For example, the factor of corporate governance consists of elements such as compositions or sizes of the board of directors and audit committees or the roles of the CEO, while the factor of financial reporting process includes the application of IFRS and domestic accounting standards or the debate of principles vs rules. The factor of financial statement audit concerns the types of auditing standards applied, auditors' independence, and mandatory rotation. Finally, the usefulness of financial statements pertains to the contents, formats, and frequencies of financial reports. The following is a summary of empirical studies on quality determinants.

Impacts of Corporate Governance Factor: Corporate governance impacts the following aspects.

- *Roles of Audit Committees and Board of Directors*: This seems to be the most popular research subject related to corporate governance, with studies conducted by Arniati *et al.* (2019), Hashim *et al.* (2019), Kusnadi *et al.* (2014), Almaqtari *et al.* (2018), Pucheta-Martínez and De Fuentes (2007), Klein (2002), Goerge (2003), Chandar *et al.* (2012), and Chalaki and Didar (2012). For example, corporate governance components including board structure, internal audit function, and internal control activities (Arniati *et al.*, 2019) or the board's nationality and ethnicity diversity (Hashim *et al.*, 2019) were proved to significantly impact earnings quality, while gender and age variance did not (Hashim *et al.*, 2019). Kusnadi *et al.* (2014) showed that the quality of financial reporting would be higher if audit committees contain members with a combination of accounting, finance, and/or supervisory skills; however, the independence of audit committees does not affect the quality. Almaqtari *et al.* (2018) concluded that the size, composition, and diligence of the board of directors and audit committees do not impact the quality of financial reporting. Further, Pucheta-Martínez and De Fuentes (2007) found that the existence of an audit committee and its composition were not associated with the receipt of qualified audit opinion, whereas the audit committee's smaller size or higher percentage of independent members reduced the company's likelihood of receiving qualified audit opinions due to error or non-compliance. Goerge (2003) revealed that most audit committee members at 50 companies listed on New York Stock Exchange companies rely on the management and independent auditors for information to fulfill their supervisory responsibilities; thus, the failure of an audit committee to question the management's choice of accounting methods might result in poor financial reporting. Chandar *et al.* (2012) proved that financial reporting quality is higher among companies with an overlapping membership of audit and compensation committees. The presence of these overlapping members will mitigate the effects of earnings management behaviours displayed by company executives. Klein (2002) identified a negative relation between audit committee independence and earnings management. In addition, the more independent the CEO of the board of directors is, the more effective the overseeing process of financial reporting. However, Chalaki and Didar (2012) did not find any association between board size, board independence, and the quality of financial information.

In summary, there are mixed results on the effects of audit committees and the board of directors on financial information quality, although the positive association seems more prevalent.

- *Roles of Compliance with SOX Act*: Nagy (2010) demonstrated that companies compliant with Section 404 of SOX had a significant negative association with the issuance of materially misstated financial reports. This suggests that compliance improves the quality of financial information. Meanwhile, Hirschey *et al.* (2012) found that SOX reforms have had a substantial impact in improving investors' perceptions of a company's reporting reliability. Verleun *et al.* (2011) found significant improvements in earnings management and in value relevance measures of financial reports over the 4-year period after SOX application. Li *et al.* (2008) observed a positive relation between SOX event stock returns and the level of earnings management. Specifically, SOX constrained earnings management and improved the quality of financial information.

Turner and Weirich (2006) and Chen *et al.* (2014) demonstrated that the number of financial restatements rose considerably at the beginning of SOX implementation, but this trend had reversed by 2005 (Harris, 2012).

Gunz and Thorne (2019) revealed that 15 years after the introduction of SOX, there was an increase in the number of restatements of companies' financial reports, a decrease in lawsuits for deficiencies in audit quality, and a substantial rise in audit fees. As a result, the debate is still open: "Is the cost increase due to SOX worth the improvement in the quality of financial information?"

In conclusion, compliance with SOX has a non-monotonic effect on financial information quality. The relationship has changed over time with the implementation of SOX practices.

Impacts of the Financial Reporting Process: The financial reporting process affects the following aspects:

- *Roles of IFRS/IAS Application*: Many empirical studies examine the effects of IFRS/IAS application on financial reporting quality at both national and global levels, e.g., Key and Kim (2020) in South Korea; Morais *et al.* (2018), Chen *et al.* (2010), and Narktabtee and Patpanichchot (2011) in the EU; Liu *et al.* (2011) in China; Chua *et al.* (2012) and Brown and Tarca (2007) in Australia; Bartov and Goldberg (2002) in Germany; and Ismail *et al.* (2013) in Malaysia. At the international level, there have been empirical studies by Wong (2004), Barth *et al.* (2008), and Jacob and Madu (2009). A majority of these studies show positive impacts of IFRS/IAS implementation on the quality of financial reports as well as the challenges to this application. For example, Key and Kim (2020) found an increase in the accounting quality of listed firms' financial reports when South Korea adopted IFRS. Morais *et al.* (2018) found that IFRS adoption led to different effects on accounting quality among EU countries, and the differences were explained by the ways whereby each country integrated IFRS into its national accounting system. Narktabtee and Patpanichchot (2011) revealed that the implementation of IFRS improves the value relevance of financial information at both national and firm levels. In addition, in countries with weak investor protection, the adoption of IFRS does not lead to much improvement in value relevance of financial reports (Narktabtee and Patpanichchot, 2011). Barth *et al.* (2008) found that financial reports of firms implementing IFRS/IAS from 21 nations exhibit more timely loss recognition and more value relevance of information than those using domestic accounting regulations.

To sum up, most empirical studies support the positive effects of IFRS application on the quality of financial information.

- *Roles of Principles Versus Rules in Accounting Regulations*: There has been a long debate on which base (the rule base or principle base) to develop accounting regulations on and their advantages. Rule-based accounting standards include many specific regulations, allow many exceptions, and provide detailed guidelines for application (US GAAP is a typical rule-based system). On the other hand, a principle-based accounting framework sets many principles instead of specific regulations, requires more judgment of application, and allows fewer exceptions. The IFRS and IAS are clearly principle-based regimes. A study of the US Securities and Exchange Commission (SEC, 2003) submitted to the Committee on Financial Services of the US House of Representatives mentioned three disadvantages of the US GAAP (a rule-based system), as follows: the excessive amount of detail provided by the standards, the overly wide scope of exceptions, and lack of permission for a true and fair override. This study also suggested a new model (objectives-oriented) for building the future US GAAP. An objectives-oriented regime is a combination of the current principle and rule bases. The SEC believed that this regime would improve by clearly stating the objectives of accounting standards, providing adequate implementation guidance, and permitting fewer exceptions.

Cunningham (2007) identified a promiscuous use of the concepts of rules and principles bases. Although these concepts were valuable for classifying particular provisions of laws, their application was not suitable for the whole regulatory system. Kohlbeck and Warfield (2005) studied four US accounting standards (SFAS 87, 106, 109, and 115) that included important components of a principles-based accounting system and found that the application of these standards had improved accounting quality by providing better valuation models for financial analysts. Webster and Thornton (2004) indicated that the accrual quality of the Canadian GAAP is higher than that of the US GAAP, although the former is believed to be relatively principles-based.

In conclusion, the trend toward a principles-based framework has been prevalent globally; thus, accounting standard setters have shown a preference for principles-base that come with more comprehensive explanations or guidance.

Impacts of the Audit of Financial Reports. Financial reports' audit affects the following aspects:

- *Roles of Auditor's Tenures and Switches*: Some empirical studies have considered the relationship between auditor's tenures and restatements of financial reports or the quality of reported earnings. Johnson *et al.* (2002) found that the length of auditor's tenures from short (2–3 years) to medium (4–8 years) terms had an association with lower quality of financial information. However, the authors did not find evidence of lower financial reporting quality for audit tenures of 9 years or more. Meanwhile, Myers *et al.* (2003) found that higher quality was associated with longer tenure. They elaborated that with longer tenure, auditors could take stronger deterrent actions on earnings management. On the other hand, they also proved that there were no significant associations between auditor tenure and the probability of restatement of annual reports.

Carcello and Nagy (2004) found that in the first three years of an auditor's tenure, the quality of financial information was lower, but they did not find evidence for financial reporting fraud with longer tenure. As a result, audit-mandated rotations might not function as intended. Gipper *et al.* (2020) found minimal support for the "fresh-look" benefits offered by the new audit partner and no indication that audit quality declines across the tenure cycle.

Chen *et al.* (2009) showed that clients with high earnings management behaviors were more likely to follow their former audit partners to a new audit firm, and that their financial reports were less likely to have abnormal earnings items in the first post-switch year and more likely to become significantly more aggressive in the next two years.

Chi and Huang (2005) used signed abnormal accruals as a proxy for the quality of financial information and found higher quality at an earlier period of audit tenures, which started decreasing after five years. It was explained that auditors' incremental learning experience had been traded off for excessive familiarity with clients.

Siregar *et al.* (2012) and Achyarsyah and Molina (2014) did not find evidence to support the regulation on the limit of audit firm tenures in Indonesia, and Garcia-Blandon *et al.* (2020) found that EU companies with more than 10 years of tenure with the same audit firm did not exhibit lower information quality, as opposed to the expectations of EU regulators who set 10-year tenure limits. In contrast, Sumiadji and Subiyantoro (2019) found that auditor sizes and audit tenures significantly and positively impacted earning quality, while audit specialization did not. Specifically, these authors documented that audit firms of larger size and with longer tenure allowed the acquisition of more insights into the client's conditions and resulted in better information quality.

Ultimately, the effects of auditors' tenures and mandatory rotation on financial information quality have been controversial and need more empirical research.

- *Roles of Auditor's Independence*: Abdel-Meguid *et al.* (2013) proved that a higher dependence of auditors on their clients led to greater abnormal accruals in financial statements, while Hodge (2003) reported that the perceived quality of earnings for US-listed firms had deteriorated over time, as had the perceived independence of auditors. In addition, Castillo-Merino *et al.* (2019) revealed that auditors' independence could be impaired by the potential purchase of other non-audit services in the EU market.

Overall, external auditors are required to maintain their independence, and this attribute positively impacts financial information quality.

Impacts of Financial Statement Usefulness: The usefulness of financial statements was mostly considered in terms of their content, frequency, and format. For example, annual reports were viewed as the most useful source of information, followed by interim reports, and media statements were the least (Lyle, 2008). Miller (2002), ex-chief accountant of SEC and officer of FASB, stated that providing quality financial reports demands firms' voluntary improvement in terms of the content, format, and frequency of their statements (out of requirement of US GAAP).

Karthik and Ertan (2018) found that banks' quarterly reporting improved their loan portfolio quality, brought about lower deposit interest rates, and spread credit default swaps.

Gigler and Hemmer (1998) proved that mandated financial reports did not contain new information and firms should thus voluntarily disclose other information anticipated by the market. Lyle (2008) reported investors' complaints about the decrease in the usefulness of financial reports due to the complexity of accounting regulations.

Financial statements published in XBRL format could be a useful tool (Lyle, 2008). Tienshih and Bedard (2018) found that XBRL has not benefited all voluntary adopting firms; rather, only those with stronger corporate governance have obtained measurable gains. Debreceny *et al.* (2010) concluded that the data quality of filings in XBRL format is still a big challenge. At the first time of submissions, one-quarter of the filings by the 400 big firms contained errors, with mathematical inaccuracies in the taxonomy and the instance documents.

To sum up, the usefulness of financial information was increased if firms made more voluntary disclosures, issued reports more frequently, and packed the reports in easy-to-use formats.

3. Methodology

This chapter analyzes ways of measuring the quality of financial information by reviewing empirical research. The key phrase "quality of financial information" was deployed to choose relevant research papers and related publications by the IFAC and OECD. With the focus on two aspects (the determinants and measurement of financial information), the most important criterion to select or screen articles was their relevance to the focus.

The next step involved identifying different quality determinants and synthesizing them into four groups of factors in a concise order. As a result, 76 research articles and five publications officially issued by the IFAC and OECD over the period 2000–2021 were reviewed or summarized. Most of them were from journals in the ABCD list and FT50 rankings. Ultimately, this chapter serves as an empirical review of financial information quality in terms of determinants and measurement.

4. Results

The main results of this study show two approaches to measuring financial information quality and four group determinants of financial information. Measuring the quality of financial information has been a complex issue with different approaches as well as specific scales. However, there are two main ways to conduct such quantification: direct and indirect. With regard to the direct way, researchers have focused on gauging the qualitative characteristics of financial information such as the comparability of information (Krisement, 1997; De Franco *et al.*, 2011), timeliness of loss recognition (Leuz *et al.*, 2003; Barth *et al.*, 2008; Ball *et al.*, 2005), or understandability (Smith and Jones, 2014). Meanwhile, using indirect methods, other researchers concentrated on observing proxies of financial reports such as reported earnings, disclosures, restatements, or responses of stock exchanges (Nichols and Wahlen, 2004, Schipper and Vincent, 2003, Wang *et al.*, 2011, Martínez-Ferrero *et al.*, 2015).

In addition, four groups of quality determinants were identified and synthesized in a concise manner. They include corporate governance, the process of financial reporting, the audit of financial statements, and the usefulness of financial statements. These four groups provide a framework for systematically arranging various empirical research studies on quality determinants.

5. Discussion

The question of how to measure the quality of financial information continues to be an unresolved issue. For example, for measuring the comparability of financial information, Krisement (1997) used an input approach, while De Franco *et al.* (2011) deployed output metrics. Further, members of audit committees have different viewpoints on quality measurement. Pomeroy and Thornton (2008) noted that members of audit committees used different measures to assess the quality of financial reports. Consequently, the assessment results were biased by these members.

Furthermore, the effects of auditors' tenures on the quality of financial information were proven to be non-monotonic (Chi and Huang, 2005, Carey and Simnett, 2006, Bell *et al.*, 2015, Sengers, 2017). This meant that over time, the quality of financial information gradually increased, reaching its peak before starting to decline. The cut-off time could be five years (Chi and Huang, 2005) or seven years (Carey and Simnett, 2006). It was explained by the authors that client-specific knowledge (or auditors' incremental learning experience) had been traded off for excessive familiarity with the client. Thus, it is reasonable to do more related research to find out the optimum number of years for audit tenures.

In addition, compliance to SOX is still a controversy: Is the cost increase due to SOX worth the improvement in the quality of financial information (Gunz and Thorne, 2019)? Thus, more empirical studies are required to find out to what extent SOX compliance will balance its costs and benefits.

Moreover, Srivastava (2014) found that the average earnings quality of listed firms declined over 40 years due to the higher ratio of intangible assets and the inclusion of newly listed firms in the original sample. However, this finding needs more evidence for its acceptance or rejection.

Finally, there are various dimensions of each quality determinant that demand examination. Out of those that have been mentioned in preceding sections, the roles of blockchain techniques or even artificial intelligence on the quality of financial information are appealing to explore.

6. Conclusion

To sum up, this study provides a comprehensive review of the determinants and measures of financial information quality by reviewing empirical research. Thus, it serves as a bridge to further explore the effects of different factors on the quality of financial information. Specifically, this chapter helps potential authors make informed decisions on two key issues: how to measure the quality of financial information (direct or indirect approach) and how to select the quality determinants for exploring (regardless of the determinant selected, it will fall into one of the four groups of determinants). Multiple measures of financial information quality have been deployed through empirical research. Each measuring approach has its own weakness, and none of them appeared to be superior to the rest. Rather, the results of these empirical studies seemed to complement each other. In addition, with four groups of quality determinants identified in this study, it is expected to save future researchers effort and help them navigate better through numerous empirical studies on the subject matter.

6.1. *Limitations and further research direction*

Although this study has depicted the big picture of financial information quality in terms of determinants and measurement, the number of empirical studies that have been reviewed is still limited. Indeed, conclusions cannot consider all elements of quality factors. Still, there have been other ways of measuring information quality and other determinants to explore. For example, in terms of quality determinants, potential research can examine the effects of financial reporting frameworks outside of accounting standards, explore the roles of blockchain techniques, or aggregate the effects of multiple elements on financial information quality. Furthermore, the effects of auditors' tenures or mandatory rotation on the quality of financial information need more empirical research in different contexts (such as developed countries, emerging countries, or the EU) to understand the effectiveness of such regulations. For example, some studies with data from Indonesia did not find evidence to support the regulation on the limit of audit firm tenures (Siregar *et al.*, 2012; Achyarsyah and Molina, 2014), while Garcia-Blandon *et al.* (2020) found that companies with more than 10 years of tenure with the same audit firm did not exhibit lower audit quality. In other words, the EU limit of a 10-year audit term may not be as good as expected by EU regulators. At the same time, in other developing countries (Egypt), Fathi and Rashed (2021) revealed that the effects of regulation on mandatory audit firm rotation were negative on client-specific knowledge but positive the auditors' independence and skepticism; thus, the net effect of such regulation was still controversial. In terms of quality measurement, future research can use new metric scales or even a continuous measuring approach with data mining or artificial intelligence to gauge and report the results.

Acknowledgement

I would like to express my profound gratitude to the editors of the *Journal of Asian Business and Economic Studies* (JABES) and its reviewers for their valuable contributions and suggestions to my work. I am thankful for the opportunity to write this book chapter, as it has significantly enriched my knowledge in various aspects. Furthermore, I am deeply grateful to the University of Economics Ho Chi Minh City for its support.

This research is funded by University of Economics Ho Chi Minh City, Vietnam.

References

Abdel-Meguid, A. M., Ahmed, A. S., & Duellman, S. (2013). Auditor independence, corporate governance and aggressive financial reporting: An empirical analysis. *Journal of Management and Governance*, *17*, 283–307. Available at: https://doi.org/10.1007/s10997-011-9176-3.

Achyarsyah P. & Molina. (2014). Audit firm tenure, audit firm size and audit quality. *Global Journal of Business and Social Science Review*, *2*(4), 69–76. Available at: https://ssrn.com/abstract=3001689.

Almaqtari, F., Al-Homaidi, E., & Ahmad, A. (2018). Impact of corporate governance mechanisms on financial reporting quality: Evidence from India. *Asian Journal of Management Applications and Research*, *8*(1), 96–110.

Anderson, R. C., Duru, A., & Reeb, D. M. (2009). Founders, heirs, and corporate opacity in the United States. *Journal of Financial Economics*, *92*(2), 205–222.

Arniati, T., Puspita, D. A., Amin, A., & Pirzada, K. (2019). The implementation of good corporate governance model and auditor independence in earnings' quality improvement. *Entrepreneurship and Sustainability Issues*. Available at: https://doi.org/10.9770/jesi.2019.7.1(15).

Ball, R. & Shivakumar, L. (2005). Earnings quality in U.K. private firms: Comparative loss recognition timeliness. *Journal of Accounting and Economics*, *39*(1), 83–128.

Ball, R., Kothari, S. P., & Robin, A. (2000). The effect of international institutional factors on properties of accounting earnings. *Journal of Accounting and Economics*, *29*(1), 1–51.

Barth, M. E., Beaver, W. H., & Landsman, W. R. (2001). The relevance of the value relevance literature for financial accounting standard setting: Another view. *Journal of Accounting and Economics*, *31*(77), 104.

Barth, M. E., Landsman, W. R., & Lang, M. H. (2008). International accounting standards and accounting quality. *Journal of Accounting Research*, *46*(3), 467–498. Available at: http://www.jstor.org/stable/40058143.

Bartov, E. L. I. & Goldberg, S. R. (2002). Comparative value relevance among German, U.S., and international accounting standards: A German stock market perspective. *Accounting, Auditing & Finance*, *20*(2), 95–119.

Bell, T. B., Causholli, M., & Knechel, W. R. (2015). Audit firm tenure, non-audit services, and internal assessments of audit quality. *Journal of Accounting Research*, *53*(3), 461–509. Available at: https://doi.org/10.1111/1475-679X.12078.

Beretta, S. & Bozzolan, S. (2007). Quality versus quantity: The case of forward-looking disclosure. *Journal of Accounting, Auditing and Finance*, *23*(3), 333–376. Available at: https://doi.org/10.1177/0148558X0802300304.

Bonsall, S. B., Leone, A. J., Miller, B. P., & Rennekamp, K. (2017). A plain English measure of financial reporting readability. *Journal of Accounting and Economics*, *63*(2–3), 329–357.

Brown, P. R. & Tarca, A. (2007). Achieving high quality, comparable financial reporting: A review of independent enforcement bodies in Australia and the United Kingdom. *Abacus*, *43*(4), 438–473. Available at: https://ssrn.com/abstract=1031774 or http://dx.doi.org/10.1111/j.1467-6281.2007.00241.x.

Burgstahler, D. & Dichev, I. (1997). Earnings management to avoid earnings decreases and losses. *Journal of Accounting and Economics*, *24*(1), 99–126.

Caramanolis-Çötelli, B., Gardiol, L., Gibson-Asner, R., & Tuchschmid, N. S. (1999). Are investors sensitive to the quality and the disclosure of financial statements. *Review of Finance*, *3*(2), 131–159.

Carcello, J. V. & Nagy, A. L. (2004). Audit firm tenure and fraudulent financial reporting. *Auditing: A Journal of Practice & Theory*, *23*(2), 55–69. Available at: https://doi.org/10.2308/aud.2004.23.2.55.

Carey, P. & Simnett, R. (2006). Audit partner tenure and audit quality. *The Accounting Review*, *81*(3), 653–676.

Castillo-Merino, D., Garcia-Blandon, J., & Martinez-Blasco, M. (2019). Auditor independence, current and future NAS fees and audit quality: Were European regulators right? *European Accounting Review*, *29*(2). Available at: https://doi.org/10.1080/09638180.2019.1577151.

Chalaki, P. & Didar, H. (2012). Corporate governance attributes and financial reporting quality: Empirical evidence from Iran. *International Journal of Business and Social Science*, *3*(15), 223–229.

Chandar, N., Chang, H., & Zheng, X. (2012). Does overlapping membership on audit and compensation committees improve a firm's financial reporting quality? *Review of Accounting and Finance*, *11*(2), 141–165. Available at: https://doi.org/10.1108/14757701211228192.

Chen, A. & Gong, J. J. (2019). Accounting comparability, financial reporting quality, and the pricing of accruals. *Advances in Accounting*, *45*(C), 100415.

Chen, C., Su, X., & Wu, X. (2009). Forced audit firm change, continued partner-client relationship, and financial reporting quality. *Auditing: A Journal of Practice & Theory*, *28*(2), 227–246. Available at: https://doi.org/10.2308/aud.2009.28.2.227.

Chen, F., Hope, O.-K., Li, Q., & Wang, X. (2011). Financial reporting quality and investment efficiency of private firms in emerging markets. *The Accounting Review*, *86*(4), 1255–1288. Available at: https://doi.org/10.2308/accr-10040.

Chen, K. Y., Elder, R. J., & Hung, S. (2014). Do post-restatement firms care about financial credibility? Evidence from the pre- and post-SOX eras. *Journal of Accounting and Public Policy*, *33*(2), 107–126.

Chi, W. & Huang, H. (2005). Discretionary accruals, audit-firm tenure and auditor tenure: An empirical case in Taiwan. *Journal of Contemporary Accounting and Economics*, *1*(1), 65–92.

Chua, Y. L., Cheong, C. S., & Gould, G. (2012). The impact of mandatory IFRS adoption on accounting quality: Evidence from Australia. *Journal of International Accounting Research*, *11*(1), 119–146. Available at: https://doi.org/10.2308/jiar-10212.

Cunningham, L. A. (2007). A prescription to retire the rhetoric of 'principles-based systems' in corporate law, securities regulation and accounting. *Vanderbilt Law Review*, *60*, 1409. Available at: https://ssrn.com/abstract=970646.

Daske, H. & Gebhardt, G. (2006). International financial reporting standards and experts' perceptions of disclosure quality. *Abacus*, *42*(3–4), 461–498. Available at: https://doi.org/10.1111/j.1467-6281.2006.00211.x.

De Franco, G., Kothari, S. P., & Verdi, R. S. (2011). The benefits of financial statement comparability. *Journal of Accounting Research*, *49*(4), 895–931. Available at: https://ssrn.com/abstract=1266659 or Available at: http://dx.doi.org/10.2139/ssrn.1266659.

Debreceny, R., Farewell, S., Piechocki, M., Felden, C., & Gräning, A. (2010). Does it add up? Early evidence on the data quality of XBRL filings to the SEC. *Journal of Accounting and Public Policy*, *29*(3), 296–306. doi: 10.1016/j.jaccpubpol.2010.04.001.

Fathi, E. & Rashed, A. (2021). Exploring the impact of mandatory audit firm rotation on audit quality: An empirical study. *Academy of Accounting and Financial Studies Journal*, *25*(6), 1–18.

Garcia-Blandon, J., Argilés, J., & Ravenda, D. (2020). Audit firm tenure and audit quality: A cross-European study. *Journal of International Financial Management & Accounting*, *31*(1), 35–64. Available at: https://doi.org/10.1111/jifm.12098.

Gigler, F. & Hemmer, T. (1998). On the frequency, quality, and informational role of mandatory financial reports. *Journal of Accounting Research*, *36*, 117–147.

Gipper, B., Hail, L., & Leuz, C. (2020). On the economics of mandatory audit partner rotation and tenure: Evidence from PCAOB data. *The Accounting Review*, *96*(2), 303–331. Available at: https://doi.org/10.2308/tar-2018-0347.

Goerge, N. (2003). Audit committees: The solution to quality financial reporting. *The CPA Journal*, *73*(12), 6–10.

Gunz, S. & Thorne, L. (2019). Thematic symposium: Accounting ethics and regulation: SOX 15 years later. *Journal of Business Ethics*, *158*, 293–296. Available at: https://doi.org/10.1007/s10551-018-3845-y.

Harris, S. B. (2012, September 24). *Remarks on the Sarbanes–Oxley Act of 2002: Ten years later* [Speech transcript]. The Public Company Accounting Oversight Board. Available at: https://pcaobus.org/news-events/speeches/speech-detail/remarks-on-the-sarbanes-oxley-act-of-2002-ten-years-later_438.

Hashim, F., Ahmed, E. R., & Huey, Y. M. (2019). Board diversity and earning quality: Examining the role of internal audit as a moderator. *Australasian Accounting, Business and Finance Journal*, *13*(4), 73–91.

Hilary, G., Verdi, R. S., & Biddle, G. C. (2009). How does financial reporting quality relate to investment efficiency? *Journal of Accounting and Economics*, *48*(2–3), 112–131.

Hirschey, M., Smith, K., & Wilson, W. (2010). Financial reporting credibility after SOX: Evidence from earnings restatements. *SSRN Electronic Journal*. Available at: https://doi.org/10.2139/ssrn.1652982.

Hodge, F. D. (2003). Investors' perceptions of earnings quality, auditor independence, and the usefulness of audited financial information. *Accounting Horizons*, *17*(s-1), 37–48. Available at: https://doi.org/10.2308/acch.2003.17.s-1.37.

IASB (2018). Conceptual framework for financial reporting. Available at: https://www.ifrs.org/content/dam/ifrs/publications/pdf-standards/english/2021/issued/part-a/conceptual-framework-for-financial-reporting.pdf.

IFAC (2004). Rebuilding public confidence in financial reporting. Available at: https://www.ifac.org/system/files/publications/files/rebuilding-public-confidenc.pdf.

IFAC (2008). Financial reporting supply chain — Current perspectives and directions. Available at: https://www.ifac.org/system/files/publications/files/financial-reporting-supply.pdf.

Ismail, W. A. W., Kamarudin, K. A., Van Zijl, T., & Dunstan, K. (2013). Earnings quality and the adoption of IFRS-based accounting standards: Evidence from an emerging market. *Asian Review of Accounting*, *21*(1), 53–73. Available at: https://doi.org/10.1108/13217341311316940.

Jacob, R. A. & Madu, C. N. (2009). International financial reporting standards: An indicator of high quality? *International Journal of Quality & Reliability Management*, *26*(7), 712–722. Available at: https://doi.org/0.1108/02656710910975778.

Jonas, G. J., Blanche, J., & Blanchet, J. (2000). Assessing quality of financial reporting. *Accounting Horizons*, *14*(3), 353–363.

Johnson, V. E., Khurana, I. K., & Reynolds, J. K. (2002). Audit-firm tenure and the quality of financial reports. *Contemporary Accounting Research*, *19*(4), 637–660. Available at: https://doi.org/10.1506/LLTH-JXQV-8CEW-8MXD.

Karthik, B. & Ertan, A. (2018). Banks' financial reporting frequency and asset quality. *The Accounting Review*, *93*(3), 1–24. Available at: https://doi.org/10.2308/accr-51936.

Key, K. G. & Kim, J. Y. (2020). IFRS and accounting quality: Additional evidence from Korea. *Journal of International Accounting, Auditing and Taxation*, *39*, 100306.

Klein, A. (2002). Audit committee, board of director characteristics, and earnings management. *Accounting and Economics*, *33*(8), 365–400.

Krisement, V. M. (1997). An approach for measuring the degree of comparability of financial accounting information. *European Accounting Review*, *6*(3), 465–485.

Kusnadi, Y., Leong, K., Suwardy, T., & Wang, J. (2014). Audit committees and financial reporting quality in Singapore. *SSRN Electronic Journal*, *139*(1). doi: 10.2139/ssrn.2467456.

Leuz, C., Nanda, D., & Wysocki, P. D. (2003). Earnings management and investor protection: An international comparison. *Journal of Financial Economics*,

69(3), 505–527. Available at: http://dx.doi.org/10.1016/S0304-405X(03)00121-1.

Li, F. (2008). Annual report readability, current earnings, and earnings persistence. *Journal of Accounting and Economics*, *45*(2–3), 221–247.

Liu, C., Yao, L. J., Hu, N., & Liu, L. (2011). The impact of IFRS on accounting quality in a regulated market: An empirical study of China. *Journal of Accounting, Auditing & Finance*, *26*(4), 659–676. Available at: https://doi.org/10.1177/0148558X11409164.

Loughran, T. & McDonald, B. (2014). Measuring readability in financial disclosures. *The Journal of Finance*, *69*(4), 1643–1671.

Lyle, N. (2008). *Financial Reporting Supply Chain: Current Perspectives and Directions* (pp. 1–60). New York, USA: International Federation of Accountants.

Martínez-Ferrero, J., Sánchez, I., & Cuadrado-Ballesteros, B. (2015). Effect of financial reporting quality on sustainability information disclosure. *Corporate Social Responsibility and Environmental Management*, *22*(1), 45–64. Available at: https://doi.org/10.1002/csr.1330.

Miller, B. W. (2002). Quality financial reporting. *Journal of Accountancy*, *April*, 70–75.

Morais, A. I., Fialho, A., & Dionísio, A. (2018). Is the accounting quality after the mandatory adoption of IFRS a random walk? Evidence from Europe. *Journal of Applied Accounting Research*, *19*(3), 334–350. Available at: https://doi.org/10.1108/JAAR-07-2016-0073.

Myers, J. N., Myers, L. A., & Omer, T. C. (2003). Exploring the term of the auditor-client relationship and the quality of earnings: A case for mandatory auditor rotation?. *The Accounting Review*, *78*(3), 779–799.

Myers, J. N., Myers, L. A., & Scholz, S. (2003). *Mandatory Auditor Rotation: Evidence from Restatements*. In *Proceedings of the Mid-Year Meeting of the Auditing Section of the American Accounting Association*, Clearwater, FL.

Nagy, A. L. (2010). Section 404 compliance and financial reporting quality. *Accounting Horizons*, *24*(3), 441–454. Available at: https://doi.org/10.2308/acch.2010.24.3.441.

Narktabtee, K. & Patpanichchot, S. (2011). The impact of country-level vs firm-level factors on the effectiveness of IFRS adoption: The case of European Union. *The International Business & Economics Research Journal*, *10*(10), 79–92. Available at: https://doi.org/10.19030/iber.v10i10.5985.

Nichols, D. C. & Wahlen, J. M. (2004). How do earnings numbers relate to stock returns? A review of classic accounting research with updated evidence. *Accounting Horizons*, *18*(4), 263–286.

OECD. (2015). *G20/OECD principles of Corporate Governance*. OECD Publishing. Available at: http://dx.doi.org/10.1787/9789264236882-en.

Pomeroy, B. & Thornton, D. B. (2008). Meta-analysis and the accounting literature: The case of audit committee independence and financial reporting quality. *European Accounting Review*, *17*(2), 305–330. Available at: https://doi.org/10.1080/09638180701819832.

Pucheta-martínez, M. C. & De Fuentes, C. (2007). The impact of audit committee characteristics on the enhancement of the quality of financial reporting: An empirical study in the Spanish context. *Corporate Governance: An International Review*, *15*(6), 1394–1413. Available at: https://doi.org/10.1111/j.1467-8683.2007.00653.x.

Schipper, K. & Vincent, L. (2003). Earnings quality. *Journal of Accounting Horizons*, *17*, 97–110.

SEC. (2003). Study pursuant to Section 108(d) of the Sarbanes–Oxley Act of 2002 on the adoption by the United States Financial Reporting System of a principles-based accounting system. Available at: http://www.sec.gov/news/studies/principlesbasedstand.htm.

Sengers, T. (2017). The effect of audit partner and firm tenure on audit quality. Master Thesis, Radboud University.

Siregar, S., Amarullah, F., Wibowo, A., & Anggraita, V. (2012). Audit tenure, auditor rotation, and audit quality: The case of Indonesia. *Asian Journal of Business and Accounting*, *5*, 55–74.

Smith, M. & Jones, M. (2014). Traditional and alternative methods of measuring the understandability of accounting narratives. *Accounting, Auditing & Accountability Journal*, *27*(1), 183–208.

Srivastava, A. (2014). Why have measures of earnings quality changed over time? *Journal of Accounting and Economics*, *57*(2–3), 196–217. Available at: https://doi.org/10.1016/j.jacceco.2014.04.001.

Sumiadji, G. C. & Subiyantoro, E. (2019). Effect of audit quality on earnings quality: Evidence from Indonesia stock exchange. *International Journal of Financial Research*, *10*(1), 86–97.

Tahat, Y. A. & Alhadab, M. (2017). Have accounting numbers lost their value relevance during the recent financial credit crisis? *The Quarterly Review of Economics and Finance*, *66*, 182–191.

Tienshih, H. & Bedard, J. C. (2018). Impact of XBRL on voluntary adopters' financial reporting quality and cost of equity capital. *Journal of Emerging Technologies in Accounting*, *15*(2), 45–65. Available at: https://doi.org/10.2308/jeta-52235.

Turner, L. E. & Weirich, T. R. (2006). A closer look at financial statement restatements analyzing the reasons behind the trend. *CPA Journal*, *76*(12), 12.

Verleun, M., Georgakopoulos, G., Sotiropoulos, I., & Vasileiou, K. Z. (2011). The Sarbanes-Oxley Act and accounting quality: A comprehensive examination. *International Journal of Economics and Finance*, *3*(5), 49–64. Available at: https://doi.org/10.5539/ijef.v3n5p49.

Wang, M. & Hussainey, K. (2013). Voluntary forward-looking statements driven by corporate governance and their value relevance. *Journal of Accounting and Public Policy*, *32*(3), 26–49.

Wang, X. & Wu, M. (2011). The quality of financial reporting in China: An examination from an accounting restatement perspective. *China Journal of Accounting Research*, *4*, 167–196. Available at: https://doi.org/10.1016/j.cjar.2011.09.001.

Webster, E. & Thornton, D. (2004). Earnings quality under rules vs. principles-based accounting standards: A rest of the Skinner hypothesis. *SSRN Electronic Journal*, *4*(2). Available at: https://doi.org/10.2139/ssrn.557983.

Wong, P. (2004). *Challenges and Successes in Implementing International Standards: Achieving Convergence to IFRS and IASs* (pp. 1–27). IFAC.

Young, S. & Zeng, Y. (2015). Accounting comparability and the accuracy of peer-based valuation models. *The Accounting Review*, *90*(6), 2571–2601.

https://doi.org/10.1142/9789811286100_0005

Chapter 5

The Impact of Extrinsic Motivation on Prosumption: Digital Service Brands

Minh T. H. Le* and Nhi P. P. Nguyen†

School of International Business and Marketing, College of Business, University of Economics Ho Chi Minh City, Vietnam

**minhlth@ueh.edu.vn*

†*nhinpp@ueh.edu.vn*

Abstract

Prosumption is a proactive way of enhancing consumer–brand relationships and better meeting consumer needs. Although the prosumer concept has received considerable research attention, the number of empirical research studies on this topic is still significantly low. Based on the self-determination theory, this study developed and proposed a model exhibiting how extrinsic motivations affect prosumer behaviors. Data were collected online, and we used a structural equation model to predict the research model. Sample analysis revealed that three typical components of extrinsic motivations — a desire for financial incentives, a desire for socialization, and a sense of belonging — have significant positive effects on prosumption. Additionally, the evidence from this study emphasized the causal associations between prosumer behaviors. We also discussed the implications of the study findings for practice and research, along with limitations and future research directions. The chapter contributes to the prosumption

Received on December 7, 2022; accepted on April 6, 2023

literature and provides comprehensive insights to brand managers who desire to improve their digital service strategies.

Keywords: Prosumer, Prosumption, Extrinsic Motivations, Digital Brands.

1. Introduction

The prosumer concept was first introduced by Toffler (1980), and has been gradually explored by other researchers (Kotler, 1986; Tapscott, 1997; Wei *et al.*, 2021). Prosumers were initially described as individuals who produce products and services for their own consumption (e.g., do-it-yourself projects, home-cooking, house painting) (Toffler, 1980). More recently, the development of advanced technology and higher levels of education have enabled people to more easily participate in production tasks and personalize market offerings (Piller and Müller, 2004). Prosumers now behave as co-creators of value by actively providing user-generated content via digital platforms and contributing to service improvement and product innovation (Chandler and Chen, 2015). This phenomenon presents new challenges to the traditional consumer–firm lens which assumes consumers only play a passive role in consumption.

A company that uses digital branding can raise awareness of its brand across many online platforms, such as social networking sites, mobile apps, and news media websites (Wang, 2021). Making a personal connection between a company's brand and the people it intends to sell to has become a necessity for a business to build a reputation for itself on the internet. Digital services include games, e-books, software hosted in the cloud, website hosting, and music streaming. In this research, we focus on banking technology products, specifically banking apps such as Techcombank, ACB, OCB bank, Grab, Bee, and Go Jek. In the year 2020, the IT services industry in Vietnam brought in a total revenue of 7.32 million USD, representing an increase of over one million dollars compared to the previous year. The income generated by this sector has been showing a consistent upward trend over the past few years. These brands can benefit from enhancing their interactions with consumers (Statista, 2022) (see Figure 1). The term *ridesharing* has tremendously influenced the international mobility industry during the past decade. Southeast Asia's growing population and fast rate of digitization have led to the fast growth

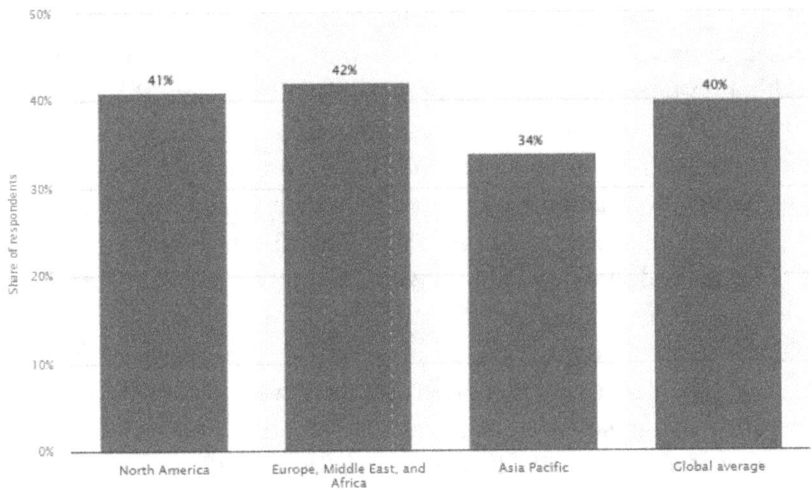

Figure 1. Percentage of brands creating more ways for customers to interact with them in 2022, by global region.

Source: Statista (2022).

of the online ride-hailing industry, which is expected to be worth 42 billion USD by 2025 (Statista, 2021).

Nowadays, consumers are able to interact with various entities, such as a company, via a business construct known as digital services. Digital services encompass processes and flows that come together in such a manner as to make this interaction possible. Online shopping is a digital service and the use of this type of service is known as the *digital experience* (Ibáñez *et al.*, 2022). Digital gadgets may be used for entertainment as well as activities like online banking, shopping, and controlling home appliances. This has allowed people to avoid having to travel as frequently, which has freed up a significant amount of time to spend on other aspects of our personal lives. The advent of value co-creation as an alternative to long-term client relationships, customer loyalty, and bottom-line earnings is yet another factor affecting businesses' branding methods. At various points in product development, cooperative efforts are made between the firms and the customers. In this way, the relationship is strengthened, and consumer loyalty and engagement increase (Teng and Tsai, 2020). A sense of cohabitation among market rivals may be achieved through active interaction between enterprises and their business intermediaries, leading to beneficial cooperation and promotion as well as inventive redesign.

Although prosumers have gained scholarly attention, the number of empirical research studies on prosumption is still significantly low. Previous research has shown the efficiency of prosumption in generating new ideas for goods and services, connecting consumers and brands, and, consequently, enhancing customer satisfaction by boosting competitiveness (Lucyna and Hanna, 2016; Ritzer and Jurgenson, 2010). However, the motives that encourage prosumption among a large number of clients and allow them to enjoy and commit to the concept have not been described. Wei *et al.* (2021) reported that there was no explicit discussion of the underlying motives enhancing prosumption and its related outcomes. Our study aims to address this gap. Specifically, our purpose is to clarify extrinsic motivations, including a desire for financial incentives, a desire for socialization, and a sense of belonging, which lead to more prosumptive behaviors. In doing so, we seek answers to the following research question:

> To what extent do extrinsic motivations significantly affect prosumption behaviors in digital service brands?

Our research aligns with the self-determination theory (Deci and Ryan, 2008), which suggests that external motivations explicitly shape human behaviors, including that of prosumers. By focusing on the main drivers and related outcomes of prosumer behaviors, this study contributes to the current literature. Moreover, understanding the critical components of our proposed model will help firms develop online digital service brands, foster customer satisfaction, and achieve higher customer engagement.

The core principles of prosumption and the notion of external agent motivation, which encourages involvement, are used to comprehend the logic of factors and construct our study models accordingly. Following this, we describe our research methodology and present the results of our analysis. Next, relevant insights are mentioned in a detailed discussion. Finally, the article concludes with the implications of the findings, limitations of the study, and recommendations for future research.

2. The Self-Determination Theory

Our study refers to the self-determination theory to develop the essential factors driving prosumption behaviors. This theory was developed by Deci and Ryan (2008) and has been applied widely in different contexts (e.g., education, healthcare, sports). Recently, this theory has been used to explain the underlying forces that promote emerging services in the sharing economy (Tussyadiah, 2016). Self-determination theory places human motivations that shape consumer behaviors on a spectrum (Deci and Ryan, 2008). On one extreme, it represents extrinsic motivations aiming to attain external outcomes such as rewards or punishments. On the other, it identifies intrinsic motivations that are entirely self-determined and highly related to the internal locus of control. While some academics emphasize internal motivations, others argue that external factors are the primary causes of co-production involvement (Lindenberg, 2001). According to Hamari *et al.* (2016), prosumers are extrinsically motivated by economic rewards (e.g., financial incentives, earning, or conserving money) and/or social requirements (e.g., meeting people, making new friends, being a community member). Therefore, in this research, extrinsic reasons, such as a desire for financial rewards, socializing, and a feeling of belonging, will be investigated (Lindenberg, 2001).

3. The Concept of Prosumption

The term 'prosumer' was coined by Alvin Toffler in 1980, combining 'producer' and 'consumer' to signify individuals who both produce and consume goods and services for personal use/actively engage in generating products and services for their own personal use (Strähle and Grünewald, 2017). Shen *et al.* (2019) further argued that prosumers have become an integrated part of production by contributing their ideas to product improvement and innovation. Wei *et al.* (2021) additionally argued that the notion of prosumerism could be applied to understand the nature of collaborative consumption business models (e.g., Airbnb or bike-sharing). Table 1 shows the history of the word prosumption since 1980 with important milestones. Figure 2 shows the frequency of occurrence of terms related to prosumption downloaded

Table 1. The evolution of prosumption.

The evolution of prosumption	Authors	Concepts
Prosumption	Toffler (1980, p. 1)	The interrelated process of production and consumption.
Do-it-yourself (DIY)	Watson and Shove (2008, p. 1)	"Do-it-yourself" ("DIY") is the method of building, modifying, or repairing things by oneself without the direct aid of professionals or certified experts.
Craft consumption	Campbell (2005, p. 2, p. 1)	The term "craft" is used to refer to a consumption activity in which the "product" concerned is essentially both "made and designed by the same person" and to which the consumer typically brings skill, knowledge, judgment, and passion while being motivated by a desire for self-expression.
Co-creation	Prahalad and Ramaswamy (2004, p. 4)	Armed with new tools and dissatisfied with available choices, consumers want to interact with firms and thereby co-create value.
Service-dominant logic	Lusch *et al.* (2007, p. 2)	Marketing inherited a model of exchange from economics, which had a dominant logic based on the exchange of "goods" which usually are manufactured output. The dominant logic focused on tangible resources, embedded value, and transactions.
Commons-based peer production	Benkler (2006, p. 2)	This is a socio-economic system of production that is emerging in the digitally networked environment.
Collaborative capitalism involving both value co-creation and service-dominant logic	Bernard Cova (2011, p. 3)	Service-dominant (S-D) logic is a service-centered orientation that reframes the purpose and process of economic exchange.
Crowd- and open-sourcing	Howe (2008, p. 6)	Crowdsourcing is the combination of efforts from various sets of individuals who are either volunteering or working part-time for socio-economic production, basically in the cyber world.

Table 1. (*Continued*)

The evolution of prosumption	Authors	Concepts
Putting customers to work	Ritzer and Miles (2019, p. 8)	Instead of sitting passively at a table in a traditional restaurant, having one's order taken, being served by waitpersons, and having employees clear the debris after the meal was done, McDonald's customers do all of this work, and unlike employees, they do it for no pay. As a result, McDonald's needs far fewer paid employees than comparable full-service restaurants.

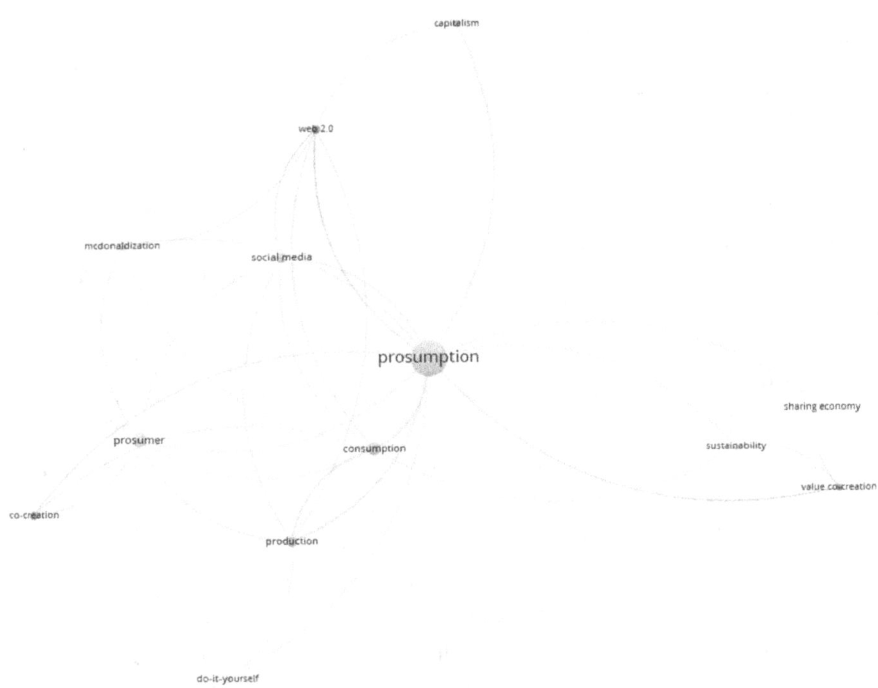

Figure 2. Co-occurrence of related prosumption terms in Scopus.

from the list of articles to date containing a title, abstract, or keywords on this topic on the Scopus database.

According to Toffler (1980), the prosumer concept was developed through three historical stages (as shown in Table 2). The initial stage had

Table 2. Prosumers in different industries.

Items	First stage	Second stage	Third stage
Focal sector	Farming	Manufacturing	Home-based
Number of prosumers and consumers	Many prosumers Few consumers	Few prosumers Many consumers	More prosumers Fewer consumers
Mechanism	Self-production	Mass production	Deindustrialization
Dominant characteristics	Existence	Indulgence efficiency	Personalization and customization
Applications	Household; neighborhood	Workplace; transaction	Family; friends; community

Source: Adapted from Toffler (1980) and Kotler (1986).

its origins in farming. In the past, most people were hunting and growing food for their own use. They were responsible for their own production and consumption; hence, they were so-called prosumers. The second stage was fostered by industrialization and marketization (Strähle and Grünewald, 2017). Individuals now had the opportunity to experience various offerings from different suppliers. In this period, consumption was characterized by indulgence while production was noted for its efficiency. The third stage was triggered by individualization and de-marketization (Kotler, 2010). More people now spend their time engaging in prosumption. As people take ownership of the production and consumption process, markets become less crucial, and society focuses on personalization and customization rather than mass distribution.

Inspired by the promises of the third stage, more people are currently interested in prosumption activities, and many researchers have turned their attention to exploring this emerging phenomenon. Watson and Shove (2008) used the expression *do-it-yourself* to highlight a state where individuals play coincident roles as designers, makers, and consumers. Leadbeater and Miller (2004) also suggested the term "pro-am" (i.e., professional amateur) to define persons who are highly concerned with professional standards and engage in production activities as amateurs. Some researchers have made an effort to explore prominent drivers fostering prosumption activities. Technological advances, the desire for customized products/services, higher demand for better-quality goods, higher unemployment rate, and increasing cost of labor are strongly believed to be the main reasons for promoting prosumer behaviors (Strähle and Grünewald, 2017). Despite the growing interest in prosumption, the number of empirical research studies on this phenomenon is still significantly low. Hence, it merits further investigation.

4. Hypotheses Development

4.1. *Desire for financial incentives*

Regarding co-production studies, economic incentives are believed to be an extrinsic motivation facilitating consumers' participation in the sharing economy. Based on the social exchange theory, Hajibaba *et al.* (2016) argued that prosumers in tourism industries are strongly motivated by financial values (e.g., obtained income). Similarly, employing the transaction cost analysis theory, Nagel *et al.* (2018) identified perceived economic benefits as a primary factor explaining why people engage in a higher (or lower) co-production or co-creation of value. These finding are consistent with many past studies (Prahalad and Ramaswamy, 2004; Teng and Tsai, 2020).

Limited budgets drive people to find efficient practices like prosumption as a way to save money (Nagel *et al.*, 2018). This effect was found to be present at all income levels (Wolf and McQuitty, 2013). It is also parallel to the concept of service-dominant logic (Vargo and Lusch, 2004) which states that prosumption is a kind of value-creating act (Xie *et al.*, 2008). Vargo and Lusch (2004) questioned the passive role of consumers and argued that consumers are actively involved in value creation (e.g., individuals might prefer cooking at home as they desire nutrition, enjoyment, and saving money). Shen *et al.* (2019) further pointed out that prosumers not only cooperate with business organizations to actively create value but they also generate value independently (e.g., people can create their own content, express their preferences, and share information via digital technology 4.0). As discussed, we believe that financial incentives directly impact prosumption. Thus, the following hypothesis is proposed:

H1: Financial incentives positively influence prosumptive behaviors toward online digital service brands.

4.2. *Desire for socialization*

Besides economic incentives, consumer social needs, including a desire for socialization, have been seen as extrinsic motivations enhancing collaborative consumption (Tussyadiah, 2016). The concept of *consumer socialization* has been seen as "the process by which young people develop consumer-related skills, knowledge, and attitudes" (Moschis and Churchill Jr, 1978, p. 599). This suggests that consumer buying behaviors and experiences are motivated by their related knowledge and attitudes, which are collectively shaped through the consumption environment, information seeking, advertisement observation, and interaction with others. Sabermajidi *et al.* (2020) suggest three key elements relevant to consumer socialization: individual characteristics, social agents, and behavioral outcomes. Social agents such as parents, relatives, friends, public sources, social media, and the Internet directly affect consumers' opinions and attitudes, ultimately leading to their buying or re-buying decisions (i.e., the socialization process). The chosen individual will be honored for providing ideas, improvements, etc., for a product or on a website or public channel while engaging in consumption-related activities. Those who get such acknowledgment feel proud of themselves and appreciated by others. Companies may get exposure through popups on websites or applications for a certain time. Recent studies in the sharing economy reported that co-consumption and co-production potentially satisfy consumer desire to establish and enhance social relationships. Chandler and Chen (2015) contend that people participating in prosumption activities are highly motivated by extrinsic reasons such as developing social networks or building a community. Kim *et al.* (2015) have additionally argued that other participants socially influence high or low levels of prosumers' engagement in value co-creation. In our context, we also believe prosumers seek co-production to satisfy their aspirations for socialization. Thus, we propose the following:

H2: The desire for socialization positively influences prosumptive behaviors toward online digital service brands.

4.3. *Sense of belonging*

A sense of belonging is defined as "a sense of emotional involvement with the group" (Cheung and Lee, 2012, p. 220). Fine *et al.* (2017) stated that a sense of belonging refers to the extrinsic state that influences consumer behavioral intention. Albinsson *et al.* (2012) further found that the motivation to be part of a group or community has been seen as a prominent antecedent of collaborative consumption activities. Parallel to past research, Möhlmann (2015) emphasized that community membership or the sense of belonging to the group increases the likelihood of participation in sharing activities. For example, people might desire to associate with like-minded persons through social media such as Facebook, encouraging them to interact confidently with others, show their hobbies, and share information and knowledge (Cheung and Lee, 2012). Users of digital applications may give recommendations for services using the contact or customer support features. Consumers may also contact a company directly through a toll-free number or website to exchange further pertinent information. Additionally, companies sometimes establish fan pages with an enthusiastic admin staff that actively responds to posts, allowing users to experience a sense of belonging to the community. The fact that companies listen to constructive input to improve the efficiency of their tools is crucial for fostering a feeling of belonging. From there, it is

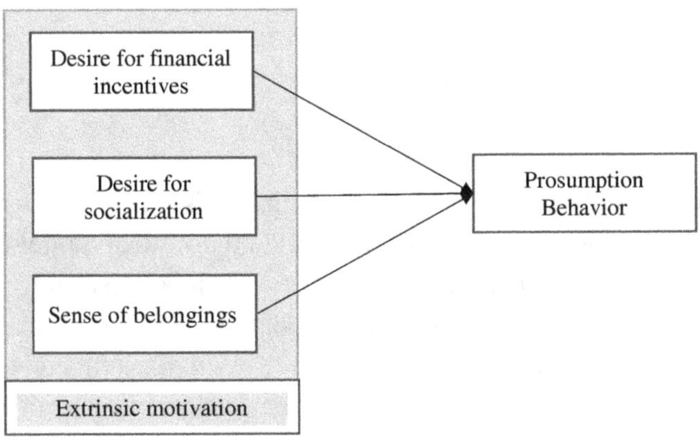

Figure 3. Research model.

feasible for companies and consumers to develop a solid connection. As discussed, it is reasonable to infer that a higher sense of belonging to co-production activities leads to more prosumption behaviors related to online digital service brands. Hence, we propose the following hypothesis:

H3: The sense of belonging positively influences prosumptive behaviors toward online digital service brands.

The research model that combined all proposed hypotheses is represented in Figure 3. The next sections will discuss the methodology and empirical findings.

5. Methodology

5.1. *Data collection*

The survey was administrated in Vietnam. A pilot test of the questionnaire was also conducted using a convenience sample of 10 respondents to assess the questionnaire's length, readability of instructions, and the design and sequence of questions. The questionnaire was distributed to 333 participants over a month-long period in 2021 using Google Forms and was shared with communities as well as with friends, bankers, and related businesses. We used the snowball sampling method because it is based on associations of relationships. However, due to inaccurate brand name submissions, ten of the 333 participants who completed the survey were removed, leaving 323 questionnaires for data analysis (see Table 3).

5.2. *Measurement*

The questionnaire was developed to test the study's research hypotheses. Scales from the literature were used to test the theoretical model. All measures used five-point Likert scales with the same labels (strongly disagree/somewhat disagree/neither disagree nor agree/somewhat agree/strongly agree). Prosumption behavior was measured with six items adapted from Baruk (2019) and Casaló *et al.* (2010), e.g., "I actively participate in the virtual community activities related to OSB". The desire for financial incentives was measured with four items adapted from Tussyadiah (2016),

Table 3. Demographic descriptive.

Variable	Responses	Total number	Percentage (%)
Gender	**Total**	**321**	**100**
	Masculine	236	73.5
	Feminine	85	26.5
Age group	**Total**	**321**	**100**
	18–24	294	91.6
	25–35	19	5.9
	36–45	7	2.2
	Over 45	1	0.3
Education	**Total**	**321**	**100**
	High School	4	1.2
	Bachelor	308	96.0
	Post-graduate	9	2.8
Job	**Total**	**321**	**100**
		278	86.6
		31	9.7
		4	1.2
		8	2.5
Household incomes	**Total**	**321**	**100**
		249	77.6
		36	11.2
		25	7.8
		9	2.8
		2	0.6

e.g., “Prosumption benefits me financially”. The desire for socialization was measured with four items adapted from Sabermajidi *et al.* (2020), e.g., “It will convey my beliefs”. The sense of belonging was measured using five items adapted from Hsieh *et al.* (2005), e.g., “I am pleased to participate in Brand X’s manufacturing processes” (see Table 4).

Table 4. Measurement model.

Constructs	Items	Loading
Desire for socialization (DS), Cronbach's alpha = 0.889; CR = 0.923; AVE = 0.751		
DS1	It will convey my beliefs.	0.837
DS2	It will make the other person aware of my own values.	0.902
DS3	That will help the other individual comprehend my priorities.	0.872
DS4	It will prompt me to consider good aspects of myself.	0.853
Desire for financial incentives (DFI), Cronbach's alpha = 0.865; CR = 0.908; AVE = 0.771		
Carrying out collaborative behavior toward OSB…		
DFI1	Prosumption benefits me financially.	0.856
DFI2	Prosumption provides a better price than most people.	0.822
DFI3	I save money compared to people who don't join co-creation.	0.887
DFI4	I will get commission.	0.807
Sense of belonging (SB), Cronbach's alpha = 0.960; CR = 0.930; AVE = 0.726		
SB1	I am pleased to participate in Brand X's manufacturing processes.	0.873
SB2	I feel a feeling of kinship to Brand X's manufacturing processes.	0.849
SB3	I care about the long-term success of Brand X's marketing strategy; I am a devoted supporter of Brand X's consumer activities.	0.832
SB4	I want to maintain a lasting engagement with Brand X's consumer activities.	0.834
SB5	I am pleased to participate in Brand X's manufacturing processes.	0.872
Collaborative behavior toward OSB (PRB), Cronbach's alpha = 0.912; CR = 0.931; AVE = 0.694		
PRB1	I regularly engage in OSB-related virtual community activities.	0.840
PRB2	I often supply people with important OSB-related knowledge.	0.824
PRB3	I often and enthusiastically publish comments and replies to OSB (like, share, and comment on OSB or user-generated digital material).	0.837

Table 4. (*Continued*)

Constructs	Items	Loading
PRB4	I contribute actively to the enhancement of OSB.	0.833
PRB5	I actively contribute to making OSB's advertising efforts more engaging and effective.	0.845

Notes: All values are significant at the 0.05 level. α = Cronbach's alpha; CR = composite reliability, AVE = average variance extracted, SB = Sense of belonging, DS = desire for socialization, DFI = desire for financial incentives, PRB = collaborative behavior.

6. Data Analysis and Results

First, the raw data were checked and filtered for inappropriate answers, such as mentioning different brands that are not digital. We then tested the demographics and checked the reliability and validity of the scale before testing the SEM model using SPSS and Smart PLS software (Hair *et al.*, 2020). After verifying the measures' reliability and validity, the research hypothesis was tested using a bootstrapping procedure with 5000 subsamples. We used structural equation modeling to test our latent construct measurement model (AMOS, 26). We started by testing models and found that all of them had loadings greater than 0.50. Structural equation modeling (SEM) was then used to assess the structural model's fit (Anderson and Gerbing, 1988). The data were well suited to the model (Chi-square/df = 2.041, CFI = 0.897, TLI = 0.889, RMSEA = 0.046, SRMR = 0.0498). Constructs were checked using the correlation matrix to ensure reliability and validity before assessing the measurement model. The findings indicated that all requirements were satisfied (see Tables 4–6).

In terms of extrinsic motivations, our findings showed that the relationships between the desire for financial incentives, desire for socialization, sense of belonging, and prosumption behavior were statistically significant (H1 = 0.895, p-value < 0.0001; H2 = 0.829, p-value < 0.0001; and H3 = 0.937, p-value < 0.0001, respectively); thus, H1, H2, and H3 are supported (see Table 7).

Table 5. Fornell–Larcker Criterion.

	DFI	DS	PRB	SB
DFI	**0.843**			
DS	0.571	**0.867**		
PRB	0.506	0.609	**0.833**	
SB	0.521	0.635	0.576	**0.794**

Notes: The diagonal scores (in bold) indicate the square root of AVE; SB: sense of belonging, DS: desire for socialization, DFI: desire for financial incentives, PRB: prosumptive behavior.

Table 6. Correlations matrix.

	PRB	DS	DFI	SB
PRB	1			
DS	0.607**	1		
DFI	0.499**	0.563**	1	
SB	0.593**	0.700**	0.641**	1
TCE	0.620**	0.683**	0.563**	0.684**

Notes: SB: Sense of belonging, DS: desire for socialization, DFI: desire for financial incentives, PRB: prosumptive behavior. ***$p<0.001$; **$p<0.01$; *$p<0.05$.

Table 7. Results of the hypotheses testing.

Hypotheses	SPC	Support
H1: Desire for financial incentives → Prosumption behavior	0.859***	Supported
H2: Desire for socialization → Prosumption behavior	0.829***	Supported
H3: Sense of belonging → Prosumption behavior	0.937***	Supported

Notes: SPC: Standardized path coefficient. ***$p < 0.0001$.

7. Conclusion and Future Research

This study makes a salient contribution to our knowledge of the prosumption literature regarding online service experiences. Based on the empirical analysis, our findings confirmed the positive effect of extrinsic motivations on prosumption. Most notably, three typical extrinsic motivators — the desire for financial incentives, desire for socialization, and sense of belonging — explain the underlying factors driving the increasing prosumptive behaviors in online digital service brands.

The sensation of belonging to an organization or having strong brand recognition is the most motivating of the three external variables. This feeling of belonging must be fostered via initiatives such as brand community development and fanzone events. It is the link between the brand's personality and the customer's personality and this overlap generates brand engagement. To increase brand engagement, brand managers should emphasize the brand's attributes during the launch of new items or those created from prosumption activities. Marketing directors must accentuate the special characteristics of their brand, highlighting them as a source of pride. Thereafter, the sense of affiliation will reverberate and serve as a powerful incentive for further prosumption behaviors.

The influence of the desire for financial incentives is somewhat greater than the impact of the desire for sociability. This demonstrates that financial incentives also push consumers to engage in prosumption-related activities. Calls for prosumption-related activities should be supported with financial incentives, such as presents, monetary awards, and in-kind benefits. Equally crucial, though, is the need for social recognition. The acknowledgment of the idea's creator demonstrates the brand's appreciation of client contributions. This award also demonstrates that the brand constantly considers consumer feedback, develops its value from the customer's viewpoint, and thus grows its brand value. This view offers a helpful starting point for brand managers who desire to engage consumers in co-production and the co-creation of value.

Despite its significant contributions, this study also has limitations which will open new avenues for future research. In particular, many possible consequences of prosumption have remained unexplored, such as brand engagement, brand attachment, and brand trust. While current research articles concentrate on the positive performance outcomes of prosumption, academics should explore its underlying drawbacks. Anti-prosumption groups favor using regulations to discourage people from doing things for themselves. For example, doctors have repeatedly warned patients not to buy medicine without a prescription for self-treatment. Beyond those concerns, future researchers could develop a proposed framework to investigate the antecedents and consequences of prosumption in different contexts and cultures (our study only applied to digital service brands in Vietnam). Additionally, scholars could look into longitudinal data to observe prosumer behaviors, which may affect the stability of study results.

Acknowledgement

We sincerely thank the reviewers for their valuable comments and Editors for their support in completing this book chapter.

Conflict of interest: The author states that there is no conflict of interest.

Funding sources: This research is funded by University of Economics Ho Chi Minh City (UEH), Vietnam.

References

Albinsson, P. A., & Yasanthi Perera, B. (2012). Alternative marketplaces in the 21st century: Building community through sharing events. *Journal of Consumer Behaviour, 11*(4), 303–315. https://doi.org/10.1002/cb.1389.

Anderson, J. C., & Gerbing, D. W. (1988). Structural equation modeling in practice: A review and recommended two-step approach. *Psychological bulletin, 103*(3), 411.

Baruk, A. I. (2019). The effect of consumers' ethnocentric attitudes on their willingness for prosumption. *Heliyon, 5*(7), e02015. https://doi.org/10.1016/j.heliyon.2019.e02015.

Bellotti, V., Ambard, A., Turner, D., Gossmann, C., Demkova, K., & Carroll, J. M. (2015). A muddle of models of motivation for using peer-to-peer economy systems. *Paper presented at the Proceedings of the 33rd Annual ACM Conference on Human Factors in Computing Systems.*

Benkler. (2006). Commons-based peer production and virtue. *Journal of Political Philosophy, 14*(4), 26. Available at: https://doi.org/ssrn.com/abstract=2567434.

Bernard Cova. (2011). Critical perspectives on consumers' role as 'producers': Broadening the debate on value co-creation in marketing processes. *Marketing Theory, 11*, 231–241. Available at: https://doi.org/10.1177/1470593111408171.

Campbell. (2005). The craft consumer: Culture, craft and consumption in a post-modern society. *Journal of Consumer Culture*, *5*(1), 23–42. Available at: https://doi.org/10.1177/1469540505049843.

Casaló, L. V., Flavián, C., & Guinalíu, M. (2010). Antecedents and Consequences of Consumer Participation in On-Line Communities: The Case of the Travel Sector. *International Journal of Electronic Commerce, 15*(2), 137–167. doi:10.2753/JEC1086-4415150205.

Chandler, J., & Chen, S. (2015). Prosumer motivations in service experiences. *Journal of Service Theory and Practice, 25*(2), 220–239. doi:10.1108/JSTP-09-2013-0195.

Cheung, C. M. K., & Lee, M. K. O. (2012). What drives consumers to spread electronic word of mouth in online consumer-opinion platforms. *Decision Support Systems, 53*(1), 218–225. https://doi.org/10.1016/j.dss.2012.01.015.

Deci, E. L., & Ryan, R. M. (2008). "Facilitating optimal motivation and psychological well-being across life's domains": Correction to Deci and Ryan (2008). *Canadian Psychology / Psychologie canadienne, 49*, 262–262. doi:10.1037/0708-5591.49.3.262.

Hair, J. F., Howard, M. C., & Nitzl, C. (2020). Assessing measurement model quality in PLS-SEM using confirmatory composite analysis. *Journal of Business Research, 109*, 101–110. https://doi.org/10.1016/j.jbusres.2019.11.069.

Hajibaba, H., Karlsson, L., & Dolnicar, S. (2016). Residents open their homes to tourists when disaster strikes. *Journal of Travel Research, 56*(8), 1065–1078. doi:10.1177/0047287516677167.

Hamari, J., Sjöklint, M., & Ukkonen, A. (2016). The sharing economy: Why people participate in collaborative consumption. *Journal of the Association for Information Science and Technology, 67*(9), 2047–2059. https://doi.org/10.1002/asi.23552.

Howe. (2008). *Crowdsourcing: Why the Power of the Crowd Is Driving the Future of Business*. New York, NY, United States: Crown Publishing Group.

Hsieh, Y.-C., Chiu, H.-C., & Chiang, M.-Y. (2005). Maintaining a committed online customer: A study across search-experience-credence products. *Journal of Retailing, 81*(1), 75–82. https://doi.org/10.1016/j.jretai.2005.01.006.

Ibáñez, Guerrero, Yáñez-Valdés, & Barros-Celume. (2022). Digital social entrepreneurship: The N-Helix response to stakeholders' COVID-19 needs. *The*

Journal of Technology Transfer, *47*(2), 556–579. Available at: https://doi.org/10.1007/s10961-021-09855-4.

Kotler, P. (1986). Global standardization—Courting danger. *Journal of Consumer Marketing, 3*(2), 13–15. doi:10.1108/eb008158.

Kotler, P. (2010). The Prosumer Movement. In B. Blättel-Mink & K.-U. Hellmann (Eds.), Prosumer Revisited: Zur Aktualität einer Debatte (pp. 51–60). Wiesbaden: VS Verlag für Sozialwissenschaften.

Leadbeater, C., & Miller, P. (2004). *The Pro-Am revolution: How enthusiasts are changing our society and economy*: Demos London.

Lindenberg, S. (2001). Intrinsic motivation in a new light. *Kyklos, 54*(2-3), 317–342.

Lucyna, W., & Hanna, H. (2016). Prosumption Use in Creation of Cause Related Marketing Programs through Crowdsourcing. *Procedia Economics and Finance, 39*, 212–218. doi:10.1016/s2212-5671(16)30315-x.

Lusch, Vargo, & O'Brien. (2007). Competing through service: Insights from service-dominant logic. *Journal of Retailing*, *83*(1), 5–18. Available at: https://doi.org/10.1016/j.jretai.2006.10.002.

Möhlmann, M. (2015). Collaborative consumption: determinants of satisfaction and the likelihood of using a sharing economy option again. *Journal of Consumer Behaviour, 14*(3), 193–207. https://doi.org/10.1002/cb.1512.

Nagel, D. M., Cronin Jr, J. J., & Utecht, R. L. (2018). Consumption or prosumption? A question of resources. *Journal of Services Marketing, 32*(6), 739–754. doi:10.1108/JSM-11-2016-0390.

Piller, F. T., & Müller, M. (2004). A new marketing approach to mass customisation. *International Journal of Computer Integrated Manufacturing, 17*(7), 583–593. doi:10.1080/0951192042000273140.

Prahalad, & Ramaswamy. (2004). Co-creation experiences: The next practice in value creation. *Journal of Interactive Marketing*, *18*(3), 5–14. Available at: https://doi.org/10.1002/dir.20015.

Prügl, R., & Schreier, M. (2006). Learning from leading edge customers at The Sims: Opening up the innovation process using toolkits. *R&D Management, 36*(3), 237–250.

Ritzer, G., & Jurgenson, N. (2010). Production, consumption, prosumption: The nature of capitalism in the age of the digital 'prosumer'. *Journal of Consumer Culture, 10*(1), 13–36.

Ritzer, & Miles. (2019). The changing nature of consumption and the intensification of McDonaldization in the digital age. *Journal of Consumer Culture*, *19*(1), 3–20. Available at: https://doi.org/10.1177/1469540518818628.

Sabermajidi, N., Valaei, N., Balaji, M. S., & Goh, S. K. (2020). Measuring brand-related content in social media: a socialization theory perspective. *Information Technology & People, 33*(4), 1281–1302. doi:10.1108/ITP-10-2018-0497.

Shen, L., Chen, Y., & Luo, C. (2019). A Grounded Theory Approach to Reconstruct Brand Value Based on Prosumption Logic in the Era of Sharing Economy Platform. *Theoretical Economics Letters, 9*(8), 2975–2996.

Statista. (2021). Ride-hailing market in Vietnam — Statistics & facts. Available at: https://www.statista.com/topics/8081/ride-hailing-market-in-vietnam/.

Statista. (2022). *Percentage of Brands Creating More Ways for Customers to Interact with Them in 2022, by Global Region*. Available at: https://www.statista.com/statistics/1305881/share-of-brands-planned-customer-brand-interaction-methods/.

Strähle, J., & Grünewald, A.-K. (2017). The prosumer concept in fashion retail: Potentials and limitations. In J. Strähle (ed.), *Green Fashion Retail* (pp. 95–117). Singapore: Springer Singapore.

Tapscott, D. (1997). Strategy in the new economy. *Strategy & Leadership, 25*(6), 8–14. doi:10.1108/eb054601.

Teng, & Tsai. (2020). Can tour leader likability enhance tourist value co-creation behaviors? The role of attachment. *Journal of Hospitality and Tourism Management, 45*, 285–294. Available at: https://doi.org/10.1016/j.jhtm.2020.08.018.

Toffler, A. (1980). The Third Wave. New York: William Morrow and Company. *Inc. Toffler The Third Wave*.

Tussyadiah, I. P. (2016). Factors of satisfaction and intention to use peer-to-peer accommodation. *International Journal of Hospitality Management, 55*, 70–80. https://doi.org/10.1016/j.ijhm.2016.03.005.

Wang. (2021). New frontiers and future directions in interactive marketing: Inaugural editorial. *Journal of Research in Interactive Marketing*, *15*(1), 1–9. Available at: https://doi.org/10.1108/JRIM-03-2021-270.

Watson, M., & Shove, E. (2008). Product, competence, project and practice: DIY and the dynamics of craft consumption. *Journal of Consumer Culture, 8*(1), 69–89. doi:10.1177/1469540507085726

Wei, X., Lo, C. K. Y., Jung, S., & Choi, T.-M. (2021). From co-consumption to co-production: A systematic review and research synthesis of collaborative consumption practices. *Journal of Business Research, 129*, 282–294. https://doi.org/10.1016/j.jbusres.2021.02.027.

Wolf, & McQuitty. (2013). Circumventing traditional markets: An empirical study of the marketplace motivations and outcomes of consumers' do-it-yourself behaviors. *Journal of Marketing Theory and Practice*, *21*(2), 195–210. Available at: https://doi.org/10.2307/23461947.

Xie, Bagozzi, & Troye. (2008). Trying to prosume: Toward a theory of consumers as co-creators of value. *Journal of the Academy of Marketing Science*, *36*(1), 109–122. Available at: https://doi.org/10.1007/s11747-007-0060-2.

https://doi.org/10.1142/9789811286100_0006

Chapter 6

Tourism Destination Management Model in the Transitional Economy

Vo Thi Ngọc Thuy[*,‡], Ho Thi My Linh[*,§], Truong Thi Hong Minh[*,¶] and Thanh-Binh Phung[†,||]

[*]*Hoa Sen University, Vietnam*

[†]*University of Economics and Law, Vietnam National University Ho Chi Minh City, Vietnam*

[‡]*thuy.vothingoc@hoasen.edu.vn*

[§]*linh.hothimy@hoasen.edu.vn*

[¶]*minh.truongthihong@hoasen.edu.vn*

[||]*binhpt@uel.edu.vn*

Abstract

Tourism plays a vital role in the global economy, and its significance becomes increasingly pronounced in the transitional economy, where ensuring sustainable tourism development necessitates effective destination management. This chapter thoroughly examines the involvement of destination management in transition economies and delves into the specific factors within the transitional economy that significantly influence the destination management model. By carefully considering these factors, a comprehensive model for tourism destination management is proposed, offering valuable insights and guidance for

Received on February 10, 2023; accepted on April 7, 2023

managing destinations in transition economies. Moreover, the chapter provides illustrative examples that highlight the factors that affect the development of tourism during periods of economic transition.

Keywords: Tourism destination management, Transitional economy, Tourism development.

1. Introduction

The tourism industry today is one of the most important industries in the economies of all countries. It is one of the world's largest sources of foreign currency, employment, and exports. Creating jobs, promoting foreign exchange, and generating economic growth are some of the benefits of the tourism industry (Shahzad *et al.*, 2017). The World Travel & Tourism Council (WTTC) (2019) reported that international tourist spending in 2019 reached US$1.8 trillion (6.8% of total exports). A 2019 report from WTTC (2019) estimates that before the pandemic, travel and tourism (direct, indirect, and induced impacts) provided one in four new jobs, 10.3% of the global economy, and 10.3% of employment globally. Moreover, an integrated approach to destination management is needed to view destination management as a tourist activity that involves local interests and significant business cooperation (Magaš, 2008). The development of the tourism industry in each country depends on planning, executing, reviewing, and evaluating operations continuously.

Tourism, moreover, encompasses a wide range of industries and fields, each of which is heavily influenced by and significantly influences a country's economic structure and development. It is present in countries in economic transition as well as developed and developing countries. The reality is that many countries such as Vietnam, Thailand, Cambodia, and Slovakia, with tourism resources, contribute significantly to gross domestic product (GDP) growth. The decision to implement the appropriate governance model and tourism development strategy at the appropriate times is an important factor in a country's tourism growth and sustainable development.

This chapter will discuss the role of destination management in the transition economy as well as the transitional economy factors that influence the destination management model. Therefore, the proposed model can serve as a model for governing and managing destinations in transition economies and provide examples of how destination governance has contributed to tourism development during a period of economic transition.

2. Tourism Destination Management Roles in a Transitional Economy

As defined by the Oxford English Dictionary (2006), "transition" refers to the process of changing from one state to another. In the context of a nation's economy, it refers to the change in economic structure as the country experiences reform. It completely disregards each country's current economic, social, cultural, and psychological conditions. A particular example of this can be found in tourism research where transition economies are generally countries that have transitioned to or are transitioning from a state-planned economy to a market economy (Saarinen, 2008).

According to Bergh (1996), economic growth is the result of an increase in a region's or country's GDP, which is regarded as the measurable output per capita (average GDP per individual). It is true that tourism's global economic contribution has grown in tandem with its dramatic expansion in scale and scope. In 2003, international tourism alone generated over $523 billion. By the end of the twentieth century, tourism was the world's highest-value export category. As a result of the extensive range of tourist attractions across many different places around the world, particularly in the Association of Southeast Asian Nations (ASEAN), known as developing countries, 81 million tourists visited ASEAN in 2011, marking an increase of 30% from the 62 million tourists in 2007 (*Tourism — ASEAN Investment*, 2012). The World Travel and Tourism Council also reported that tourism contributed 4.4% to ASEAN's GDP and accounted for 3.2% of employment in 2011. GlobalData estimated that international visitors to the ASEAN region will increase from 129.2 million in 2018 to 155.4 million in 2022, representing a compound annual growth rate of 4.72%.

Furthermore, the World Travel and Tourism Council (2020) reported that domestic tourism accounts for roughly 10% of global GDP and employment, and tourism generates more than 4 trillion USD per year if domestic tourism is included. There is no doubt that tourism is increasing dramatically as seen in the rise in the number of international tourism arrivals from 1.08 billion, amounting to 522.22 billion USD, in 1996, to 2.4 billion arrivals, amounting to 1.8 trillion USD, in 2020 (World

Table 1. Tourist arrivals and receipts for foreign visitors (WTO, 2020).

Countries	International tourism arrival	International tourism, receipts (current USD)
Myanmar	903,000	2,501,000.00
Philippines	1,483,000	2,769,000.00
Vietnam	3,837,000	3,232,000.00
Indonesia	4,053,000	3,533,000.00
Malaysia	4,333,000	3,386,000.00
Thailand	6,700,000	15,360,000.00

Bank Data, 2020). Studying International Tourist Arrivals and Receipts can demonstrate how tourism contributes to economic growth in some developing countries. Table 1 shows the growing contribution of tourism to economic growth in Asian countries (WTO, 2020).

There are an increasing number of destinations in developing countries that are becoming more accessible to international tourism, a key engine of economic development in these countries. Over the past two decades, the number of arrivals in this area has more than doubled and receipts have grown by 121% — both of those figures being twice the global average. Traditionally, the East Asia Pacific (EAP) has been dominated by China, Hong Kong, Thailand, Malaysia, and Singapore, but newer destinations in the region, such as Vietnam, Cambodia, Myanmar, Laos, and Polynesia, have thrived. The number of tourists arriving in developing countries was expected to exceed that of developed countries by 2020, and the number of tourists is expected to exceed 1 billion by 2030 (World Tourism Organization (UNWTO), 2017).

The main focus has been on the economy's direct and indirect benefits from tourism. A significant advantage of tourism is that it promotes the socioeconomic development of a country. It has been shown that tourism promotes job creation through an increase in local investment, an improvement in infrastructure, and an increase in import income (Pedrana, 2013). Tourism is also clearly positioned favorably in the public, private, and non-profit sectors as an economic and developmental driver (Visser and Rogerson, 2004). Developing countries, however, have yet to fully realize their tourism potential (Sanches-Pereira *et al.*, 2017).

3. Factors that Impact Tourism Management in Transitional Economics

Despite the fact that tourism is still relatively young in developing nations, it has risen rapidly in a short period of time, putting unforeseen strain on local infrastructure and human resources. This would necessitate a large financial investment in addition to foreign profits or loans, which seem to be unlikely to exist in developing countries; as a result, their governments have turned to tourism as a quick means of creating the revenue required for industrialization. Supporters of tourism growth in developing countries claim that tourism will reduce urban joblessness and act as an alternative for traditional exports with less certain possibilities.

There are numerous key factors that influence tourism development. These factors have either positive or negative effects, depending on the policy and factors related to the resources and the capacity of the regional tourism department and tourism business management, as shown in the following:

- **Governance and policy factors**
  a. Integrated tourism policy through mechanisms and role of government;
  b. Rebuilding tourism management policies and structures;
  c. Increasing productivity and innovation;
  d. Establishing policies for tourism funding, budgets, and investments;
  e. Boosting business growth through entrepreneurship.

- **Tourism resources and infrastructure factors**
  a. Product development;
  b. Infrastructural connections in the tourism sector;
  c. The marketing capacity, the communication capability, and the ability to attract tourists promoting skill development and employment opportunities;
  d. Improving transport connectivity.

- **Sustainability and nature-related factors**
  a. Sustainable tourism management;
  b. Strategy of digitalization of tourism;

c. Pandemic and tourism recovery;
d. Sustainable tourism management.

These factors affect tourism planning, strategy, and orientation, and this section evaluates key elements that are critical to the development of the tourism and management model in a transitional economy.

3.1. *Governance and policy factors*

3.1.1. *Policy mechanisms that facilitate tourism management*

Many countries rely heavily on tourism for economic, social, and cultural reasons. As a result, governments play an important role in shaping the development of a nation's tourism. A range of shared policy priorities are seen as central to the role of successful tourism administration in any country, particularly in developing countries and countries in transitional economic periods. The following are some examples:

- Increasing the level of sustainability and inclusiveness by promoting and delivering on policy mechanisms.
- Developing innovative tourism structures, policies, and action plans.
- Regulating the sector and monitoring delivery of policies.
- Creating forward-thinking tourism structures, policies, and action plans to achieve strategic goals.
- Developing a competitive and high-quality tourism industry.
- Encouraging entrepreneurship and stimulating business growth.
- Encouraging investment and improvements in the quality of the tourism offerings, as well as the skills of those working in the industry.

Other policy areas are important depending on the stage of development of the sector as well as the nature of the broader economy, including improving connectivity and investing in travel-related infrastructure and services, promoting regional development and encouraging local communities to participate, ensuring safety, and offering a range of tourism products. It is proven that once the government focuses on developing good tourism policies, there are positive effects on tourism development.

As a result, every government has adopted a variety of strategies to promote, develop, or reduce the tourism sector, depending on the system in place, the importance of tourism to the economy, and the degree of demand for tourism. The tourism management structure is influenced by how the government defines tourism's role in the national economy.

Several countries, including Greece and Israel, prioritize tourism and have it handled by a separate ministry, which may reflect the sector's relative importance to the national economy. In many other countries, tourism is overseen by an economic ministry and is closely related to economic growth. This is especially true in the Nordic and Baltic countries, but it is also true in Chile, Thailand, Indonesia, Cambodia, Portugal, Vietnam, etc.

Tourism has been seen as an important economic sector in Vietnam since 2001. Previously, tourism was considered a cultural sector, so this change had a significant impact on the policy and management of tourism. Despite the fact that tourism is an economic sector, it is still managed by the Ministry of Culture, Tourism, and Sport, which facilitates the coordination of various sectors with strong links to tourism. The regional tourism departments are part of the Municipal government of the city/region, but they also integrate policies and programs from the Ministry of Culture, Tourism, and Sport. Furthermore, the Vietnam National Administration of Tourism promotes tourism in Vietnam and assists the regional departments of tourism in implementing some important tourism policies and programs. These policies and programs are intended to promote regional tourism by connecting different regions for launching new routes and promotion programs. In the same way, Colombia established the Superior Tourism Council. Thirteen ministries and other tourism-related agencies are represented on the Council, ensuring a whole-government approach to tourism development. Both Chile and France place a significant emphasis on their tourism economies. Joint organizations have been established between the Chilean Ministry of Economy, Development, and Tourism and the French Ministry of Economy, with the purpose of supporting tourism development as a key component of their respective economies.

In general, in developing countries or countries in the transitional economy period, tourism is defined as an economic sector that makes significant contributions to national economic development. This appears to be relevant. As a result, the tourism development policy and management structure differ from those in other countries where tourism is part of another sector. However, tourism is a unique sector that connects to other sectors when fostering development.

Case study: Tourism in the transitional economy in Slovakia
From 1989 to 1996, Slovakia had seven governments, and a substantial part of the staff of the Ministry of Economy, including the tourism department, changed with almost every succession. As a result of the state socialist legacy, a psychological barrier had to be overcome: most economic ministers in the country had been directors of major industrial enterprises and had little knowledge of the service sector. In the years following 1989, various governments became preoccupied with general transitional issues. In 1989, international tourism was one of the most successful sectors of the Slovak economy but any improvement in the country's social and economic situation was largely attributed to non-specific tourism industry framework factors. Tourism changes were therefore a side effect of the larger transition. A number of significant developments occurred — economic and social stability were maintained, passport and visa barriers were eliminated, and major privatization programs were carried out. The second major set of influences was specific to the tourism industry. The main priorities in 1990–1992 were macroeconomic stabilization, privatization, price liberalization, export reorientation, employment policies, and the establishment of market institutions. These changes had positive effects on the tourism sector in Slovakia in the country's period of transitional economy and politics.

3.1.2. *Rebuilding tourism management policies and structures*

The tourism management structure plays an important role in the effectiveness of government tourism management and the links between government agencies and entrepreneurs. During a country's period of economic transformation, the efficiency of the administrative structure creates such greater favorable outcomes in the country's tourism industry that this is a key factor in the economic growth of tourism. However, while each country is structured differently, there is always an authority that is above the central government that manages the local government. This system creates regulations, rules, and laws regarding which the local government agencies report directly to the local government. Thailand, Vietnam, and Cambodia, are some countries following this structure. The government administrative authority is responsible for the implementation of the law, tourism policy and national tourism, local tourism programs, and local tourism development programs. Participating countries following this model often have more than one general tourism department supporting national tourism promotion activities. The following is another case: that of Denmark, a country improving its tourism management system.

Case study: The case of the public tourism management system in Denmark

Denmark's tourism administration system was mapped by the Ministry of Industry, Business, and Financial Affairs in 2017. Tourism development efforts in this system had to be coordinated across many policy levels which resulted in extensive overlap in marketing activity and affected the effectiveness of other support activities. The main policy initiative in 2018–2019 has been to reform the public tourism administrative system as part of a larger reform of Denmark's business support system. In order to strengthen Danish tourism, the Danish have developed a simpler and more effective management structure and governance regime. Business support laws in Denmark were amended in 2019, reducing administrative burdens. During the revision of the Danish law on business support in 2019, three administrative levels were reduced to two — the national and decentralized levels — and their responsibilities were modified.

At the national level, the Danish Tourism Advisory Board supported the establishment of the National Tourism Forum to lead and coordinate public sector policies in conjunction with the private sector. The number of regional destination management organizations was reduced from 80 to about 20 as part of an agreement with local governments. The role of the decentralized DMO is to organize, coordinate, and operate local business support operations. Furthermore, the Board for Local Business Promotion is in charge of awarding grants to local tourism development programs.

3.1.3. *Increasing productivity and innovation*

Productivity enhancements are being prioritized in a number of countries in order to support tourism firms and strengthen competitiveness. This is a continuous difficulty in the sector related to the intangible, consumable, and heterogeneous nature of tourism services, which is emphasized by the fact that these systems are frequently generated at the same time as they are used (OECD, 2017). Building a more productive and adaptive tourism economy requires innovation that plays a critical role in enhancing tourism's sustainability and leveraging its potential environmental, social, and cultural impacts, as well as incorporating tourism technologies. Low levels of innovative capacity among tourism SMEs, in contrast, are a recognized obstacle that impedes investment.

Furthermore, countries such as Iceland and Portugal use incubating programs to motivate fresh starter and digitalization models, and a similar approach is taken to support the digital transformation of existing tourism businesses in a number of other developing countries such as Vietnam, Austria, Portugal, and Finland. The Estonian government has set up a network of local development institutes that provide services such as consulting and coaching for starting and running businesses. The Tourist Innovation Centre is the foundation of Portugal's Tourism 4.0 initiative, which aims to foster technological change in the Portuguese tourism industry while simultaneously driving creativity and innovation.

3.1.4. *Establishing policies for tourism funding, budgets, and investments*

The tourist industry generates national income which authorities allocate towards spending on infrastructure, training, and education. It is not easy to estimate the amount of government funding because it is channeled through various funding sources and projects. Slightly more than half of OECD nations report an increase in central budget allocations for tourism in comparison to other countries — either maintaining existing levels of expenditure or transferring money across agencies.

Capital is a critical resource for the development of the regional tourism business in Vietnam. It is necessary to have policies that support loans and explore innovative approaches to lending mechanisms to increase the accessibility of loans for organizations and individuals engaged in the tourism business, creating an equal environment in credit access. Moreover, regardless of ownership, it is great to consider using a number of technical measures to increase capital and replicate the model and performance of credit guarantee funds for small and medium enterprises to operate in the tourism industry. Last but not least, encouraging banks and credit funds to lend money to tourism businesses is equivalent to guaranteeing unsecured lending activities.

Some governments raise taxes, costs, or other charges, mostly on visiting overseas guests, to progressively fund promotion or improvement activities and projects and to provide the resources needed to counteract the effects of tourism at the destination level. Slovenia imposes a tourist tax, with earnings going toward tourism marketing. Slovenia has a visitor tax, with a portion of the proceeds going toward tourism promotion. In Portugal, gaming taxes fund over half of the national tourism organization's budget. Visitors are also charged admission fees in Costa Rica, Croatia, and Peru, which are frequently used to fund tourism agencies.

3.1.5. *Boosting business growth through entrepreneurship*

In a country with a transitional economy, the normal structure of the tourism sector is completely biased toward a high number of micro-companies functioning alongside a small number of extremely large businesses. Supporting entrepreneurship and stimulating business growth is thus a primary focus for many tourism administrations. And it is as equally vital for mature tourism economies as it is for growing tourism economies experiencing rapid expansion.

Governments use a variety of policy measures to boost the competitiveness and growth potential of tourist firms. This includes direct support for business owners, such as grants and investment programs, as well as a variety of training and educational programs. Authorities are also passing initiatives to enhance the business environment and deregulate or simplify the regulatory structure in order to decrease the administrative burden on small enterprises which are sometimes impacted by legislation created primarily to regulate larger companies or other industries.

To attain these goals, a variety of tourism policy instruments were developed, including tourism planning, price regulation linked to the goals of social policy, regulations and administrative measures, infrastructure development, promotion and information activities, and vocational training.

In Israel, financial assistance is available, and initiatives are being taken to actively incorporate new entrepreneurs into the sector and stimulate the expansion of tourism SMEs. The governments of various nations have also established tax breaks for company efficiency in order to boost business and tourism growth. The government of Austria decreased VAT/GST on tourism to 10% in 2018. Some governments cut the VAT rate on tourism services as a sector development measure or to encourage employment and activity in reaction to an economic slump. The government of Croatia reduced the VAT rate on food preparation and service activities to 13% in 2020. Similarly, in Vietnam, the government has a policy and a fund for regional department tourism in order to digitize tourism. The government has launched various packages to assist tourism businesses in modernizing their operations. Especially after the COVID-19 pandemic, the government enacted new policies to aid recovery.

3.2. *Tourism resources and infrastructure factors*

3.2.1. *Product development*

Tourists, like customers of any other product, are not all the same; they have varied visions of their ideal vacation, different needs for accommodations, and different budgets. Full comprehension of these aspects is essential to ensure that Ho Chi Minh City can effectively meet the diverse needs and expectations of all types of tourists.

The four primary tourist categories will be introduced and defined in this section, along with the percentage of the total tourist population, total contribution to the City's tourism receipts, and the amount of time spent on each type of product. Then, an analysis of important tourist product segments will be offered, delving deeply into the sub-segments and ranking them in terms of relevance to Ho Chi Minh's position as a tourist destination. Four key tourist segments are identified.

Both domestic and international tourists are primarily leisure travelers. Tourists are divided into groups based on their primary reason for visiting Ho Chi Minh City. Leisure travelers currently account for the majority of domestic and international tourists, more than 71% and 87% of total tourists, respectively. The tourist industry in Vietnam creates seven different types of tourism products. Each region concentrates on developing its dominant type of product. The Vietnam tourist agency has developed numerous clusters to investigate the diversity of tourism resources in the country and increase market share, including the Northwest cluster, Ho Chi Minh City, 13 provinces in the Mekong Delta, and the Central Cluster.

Along with efforts to highlight unexplored regions and new tourist products for tourism development, it is the desire to spread tourist programs and activities throughout the year that brings a lot of benefits, including the probability of a decrease in substantial numbers of tourists during peak seasons, increased business growth, better resource use, and more consistent job possibilities. Many nations, such as Vietnam, Greece, Thailand, and Indonesia, that have effectively built coastal summer urban tourism sites are attempting to expand and produce goods that highlight different territories. As a result of a diversified offering that appeals to both leisure and corporate markets, major cities frequently have flatter seasonal variations. To offset acute seasonal swings, Latvia, for example, is diversifying its offer to include business and medical tourism items. Some aspects of these policies, such as off-peak access to destinations, can be limited by airlines' plans and travel agency timetables. The same is true in Vietnam where medical tourism products or educational tourism products, or meetings, incentives, conferences, and exhibitions tourism (MICE), are strongly built to balance the tourists in the high and low seasons.

Several other countries adopt new policies related to tax reduction or promotion in the off-season period. In Vietnam and countries such as Cambodia, Malaysia, and Slovakia, shopping seasons are launched in the off-season period to attract tourists.

3.2.2. *Marketing capacity, communication capability, and attractiveness of tourists*

The evolving nature of tourist marketing and promotion at home and abroad plays a leading role in destination marketing and promotion operations as the fragmented character of the industry and the small size of tourism enterprises make it difficult for individual businesses to be visible to and attract visitors from remote tourism markets. Recently, nations have started investigating various tourism marketing models that rely on new funding sources, cooperation opportunities, and governance arrangements as well as creating digital techniques to attract tourists (OECD, 2017). The rapid growth of Asian tourism has affected many nations' promotional strategies, which now allow extensive use of digital means of reaching and attracting visitors. Several tour and travel organizations are gradually prioritizing technological platforms above most different traditional types of communication; however, part of this shift is also due to shrinking finances.

Beginning in 2020, a dedicated online platform and better digital marketing strategies in Vietnam were designed to plan to improve the visiting experience for independent travelers. They are provided with suggested trip itineraries and can buy local consumer goods. Indonesia is aggressively investing in branding and marketing, implementing novel tactics such as demand pricing to regulate tourism flows and combining machine learning and big data approaches to identify important target audiences.

Several patterns have emerged in the past two years. In light of the quick shift to digital sales and distribution, several countries are seeking innovative methods for their small and micro-tourism company segments to be used by big online travel agents and facilitators; these countries include South Africa, Vietnam, Croatia, Greece, Turkey, Ireland, and Indonesia.

- Some nations attempting to diversify and develop into new markets or segments have a more seasonal offer and an over-reliance on a small number of high-volume uncomplicated markets. This can include extending the season as well as fostering demand for less popular regions. Croatia, Greece, and Turkey have all made firm commitments to the use of this strategy.

- The effective utilization of artificial intelligence and big data in travel advertisement and branding is still in an early phase despite the fact that substantial investment has already been made in tourism-related applications. As an example, in Indonesia, a competing destination marketing approach is being utilized to target promotional messages to important consumers by using machine learning and big data tools.
- As part of the upstream marketing mix, it is evident that a larger focus is placed on the creation of booked online products and services to promote outside tourists, which has resulted in significant investment and particular initiatives, such as those in Ireland.
- Despite the rise of digital advertising, traditional advertising activities still play a vital role, especially for certain markets targeted by tourists, such as major trade fairs, international tourism development, media relations, and marketing. Other components of the tourist system, such as dependable transportation infrastructure, a liberalized visa policy, and visitor services, are required for successful overseas marketing. To encourage employees to spend their vacation time on things they enjoy, Slovakia has launched a tourist reward campaign.

3.2.3. *Promoting skill development and employment opportunities*

Tourism is a significant job creator, and the industry relies heavily on qualified workers to develop and deliver a competitive tourism offering. However, finding and maintaining qualified employees remains a challenge in the business, exacerbated in some countries by demographic changes and other factors diminishing the available talent pool.

Young employees regularly work in the seasonal tourism industry in Iceland. Due to Iceland's low population and high unemployment rate, a rising proportion of these jobs are filled by foreign workers. This poses challenges since, in the absence of highly trained employees, output, competitiveness, and the strength of the brand of the tourism sites may suffer. Enhancing the abilities, performance, and efficiency of the tourism staff is thus a primary priority. As a result, in 2017, the state created and funded the Tourism Skills Centre Iceland which has the following responsibilities: to influence and collaborate with the traditional classroom framework to modify current and future academic studies programs to meet the requirements of corporate companies, to increase training within Icelandic tourism enterprises, and to mobilize digital solutions for more effective tourism administration.

In recent years, due to economic transitions, there has been a shift of employees in many countries from the tourism sector to the real estate, technology, and industrial sectors. The tourism industry lacks highly qualified employees, so the government recommends internal training for staff in tourism organizations. Furthermore, the provincial department of tourism management has a policy and a modest fund for public training in the tourism sector.

3.2.4. *Improving transport connectivity*

By facilitating tourist movement in and out of each country's areas, tourism synergies can raise tourists' enjoyment and sustain the economic viability of public transport and other amenities by serving both residents and tourists. However, the facilitation of tourist movement remains a key issue in the growth of the tourism and transitional economy. In order to maximize and spread tourism's socio-economic advantages, the government should consider the tourism industry's medium- to long-term needs when planning transportation access and infrastructure.

Global aviation connectivity plays an essential role in a flourishing tourism industry, particularly in coastal areas. Since 2006, the government of Malta has been following a policy to increase the number of direct pathways, with the variety of pathways almost tripling from 45 to 110 in the 12 years to 2018. Over this time, the number of international tourist arrivals has doubled, with 2.6 million visitors in 2018 compared to 1.3 million in 2010. Meanwhile, Ireland's Regional Co-operative Market Connectivity plan fosters direct air and sea connections by matching funding from tourism stakeholders. The same approach, as undertaken since 2013, and several policies, such as significant advancements in the aviation sector, have helped develop pathways between Vietnam and relatively nearby places in Vietnam in recent years. Vietjet Air, for example, launched new direct flights between Ho Chi Minh City and Phuket, Ho Chi Minh City and Chiang Mai, and Da Lat and Bangkok, bringing more Thai visitors to Vietnam. More flights from several source nations, including China, Taiwan, and South Korea, have also been added. More importantly, both the Vietnamese government and other promotion initiatives by organizations have had a significant impact on recent track records of global aviation. Because of increased flight coverage throughout the region, the number of overseas visitors has grown, resulting in increased international tourist expenditure in Vietnam. International tourist expenditure has increased by +7% per year, from roughly 6 billion USD in 2013 to around 8 billion USD in 2017. The World Tourism Organization's (UNWTO) yearly publications indicate that hotels accounted for around 2.6 billion USD, or more than 30% of the total foreign visitor expenditure in 2017, which is the highest level in the world, followed by retail and eating (UNWTO, 2019). Domestic travelers have also contributed significantly to the positive increase in tourism. Domestic tourism expenses have increased by +21% each year, from roughly 2.9 billion USD in 2013 to 7.5 billion USD in 2018. Leisure and recreational activity demand has risen over time, aided by more economical airline options and improved road infrastructure.

Furthermore, in recent years, a large project to build motorways has been initiated and is being implemented connecting the North to Central Vietnam and the Central to South of Vietnam, and connecting 13 Delta Mekong provinces. Traffic problems between the three regions have been a major impediment to Vietnam's tourism development for many years.

Public transportation accessibility in a city influences tourists' movements between tourism destinations based on their length of stay. That is why it is critical to build internal routes and various modes of mobilization within the metropolis in tourist cities. In Slovenia, for example, once tourists arrive at their location, the prospects for cycling and walking are made visible. The local governments are recognizing the opportunity for tourists to cycle and stroll once they arrive at their traveling destinations, and therefore cycling and walking routes are being prioritized, financed by the local housing tax. It has been established in Belgium that there are usable greenways in Wallonia, as well as the Welcome Bike program, which provides cyclists with offerings, while Ireland is constructing biking trails along old train lines as a way to promote industrial development, a strategy which can also be applied to Vietnamese cities like Hue, Danang, Nha Trang, and Ho Chi Minh.

Internal transportation has been prioritized in Ho Chi Minh City (Vietnam's largest tourism city) in recent years. Subway line projects have been planned; however, due to financial concerns, the start date has been pushed to the early 2020s. The program now has two lines in the pipeline; due to funding issues with Line 1, the project completion date had been pushed back to 2020. Construction on Line 2 was previously slated to begin in 2013, with operations beginning in 2018. However, local governments asked the Prime Minister to postpone the construction of the second line until 2020. According to CBRE, these two subway lines will have around 180,000 riders each day. The building of subway lines aims to serve a wide range of stakeholders and visitors as well. Traffic congestion will decrease, allowing residents to move around the city in at least half the time (according to CBRE). Furthermore, these newly created train lines may provide more options for vendors to open shops at train stations, resulting in increased purchase traffic for shops and stores nearby. In addition to the metro line developments, the government has planned eight new highway projects to connect Ho Chi Minh City with neighboring provinces. This planning intends to alleviate traffic congestion in the city and reduce travel time to crucial southern provinces.

3.3. *Sustainability and nature-related factors*

3.3.1. *Sustainability in tourism*

While the tourist industry is an important force for economic development, it has many negative impacts, such as causing climate change, increasing local population growth, damaging the biodiversity in sensitive areas, and damaging the country's cultural heritage. It has repeatedly been argued that tourism is incompatible with the principles of sustainable development (Agrawal, 2014; Lélé, 1991). Therefore, tourism activities and the transition economy must be planned and managed very conscientiously.

According to the UNWTO (2004), sustainable tourism is known as "tourism that takes full account of its current and future economic, social and environmental impacts, taking into account the needs of visitors, industry, the environment and host communities". This means that tourism policymakers need to consider these impacts to make all tourism more sustainable. Since these impacts are frequently measured, they can improve each destination's shortcomings and build on its strengths while also addressing the threats and capitalizing on the opportunities that the industry brings (Lozano-Oyola *et al.*, 2019).

There are five pillars or essential areas that future initiatives and interventions might target (UNWTO, 2004b):

1. Sustainable tourism is recognized as an important part of tourist strategy and legislation.
2. The profitability, investment, and efficiency of the tourism sector are taken into account as well as the business and investment environment and trade liberalization.
3. Planning the human resources necessary to meet the sector's needs is at the core of labor, professionalism, and productive capacity.
4. There is a significant focus on how tourism contributes to poverty eradication and social equality.
5. The maintenance of the heritage and cultural industries is a key issue of sustainable tourism, so there must be strategies and measures in place to preserve the asset base.

Each agency or delegation sets its country's tourism priority level and programs, which are agreed upon through discussions with the government. Changes in the program cycle schedule can impact priorities, potentially limiting the program's flexibility as it endeavors to secure support in new areas. These could be related to broader development and sustainability issues, including resource use, health, well-being, employment, and livelihoods, as well as supporting factors and processes such as effective governance, education, and development skills. For example, in Cambodia's Poverty Reduction Strategy Paper (UNWTO, 2013), Cambodia prioritized the first pillar, sustainable tourism, and began reporting on tourism. The chapter made a significant contribution to identifying the importance of the field, which promotes sustainable growth in the country and reduces poverty. It also states that tourism is "vital to the prosperity of the nation". Furthermore, the fundamental potential for future tourism growth is based on reasonable exploitation of the country's invaluable cultural and natural resources, which was outlined in the chapter. Pursuing a pro-poor tourism policy and reducing the negative impact of tourism have been highlighted in a number of statements on the future shape of tourism.

Among these was the formation of an inter-ministerial working group to ensure an integrated approach, the creation of development zones where tourism can best contribute to poverty alleviation, the use of public–private partnerships to help businesses, and a new focus on specific national and international target markets. Vietnam prioritized the fourth pillar in the development of a plan for sustainable tourism (APEC, 2005). Vietnam is an example of the success of the "proponents of growing poverty" in the developing world. The Vietnam National Administration of Tourist (VNAT) planned to incorporate and/or replicate a poverty eradication program into a tourism effort and promote it as a sustainable tourist product operated by the community. The World Heritage-listed Kim Bong village in Hoi An put it into practice in 2004. Kim Bong Village is home to a variety of natural and cultural resources. Visitors to the city often visit the famous traditional carpentry workshops and the picturesque river landscape. However, due to inadequate advertising, appearance, labeling, and customer satisfaction, its tourist industry has been unable to grow, and its sales have remained low. As a result, it did not benefit from the "spillover effect" of Hoi An's flourishing traveling industry. The Visitor Center is now a point of contact for incoming tours. Thanks to on-the-job training for the local community, more than 30 villagers have been able to join the local tourism cooperative and participate in the project. The tourism products have also been updated with new attractions such as village walks and bicycle trails, which were promoted during the Quang Nam Festival. In the first year, Kim Bong Tourism earned an additional $16,000 from ticket sales for the numerous walks and cycling trails. A part of this revenue is donated through a community fund to the 400 residents of Kim Bong. In addition, sales of local products have increased and new jobs for local tour guides and hospitality service providers have been created as a result of the new sustainable tourism flows. Although developing or transitional countries are working hard to achieve sustainable tourism, they still face many challenges in that area. One of the biggest challenges is that tourism exploitation is not tightly controlled, as tourist destinations focus on quick profits rather than slow and sustainable tourism. In addition, there is a lack of, or insufficient, awareness among the tourism industry of the United Nation's Sustainable Development Goals. Therefore, the government, authorities, and regulators have to pay more attention to the tourism sector to ensure that tourism is done sustainably during this period.

3.3.2. *Strategy of digitalization of tourism*

Technology is the primary driver of growth in market economies. Technology has established itself as a significant factor in the global tourism business, allowing travelers to select new experiences throughout their journey. Online channels have widespread acceptance across all age groups. Currently, online channels are becoming an important platform for travelers to make decisions on hotels, destinations, and restaurants while on vacation. Figures 1 and 2 are some instances of the use of online channels at each phase of a tourist's journey (Roland Berger, TripAdvisor, TripBarometer, 2019):

- *Pre-trip*: During the pre-trip phase, tourists use online channels to study, plan, and book hotels, among other things. The internet is the best place to organize both leisure and business travel. Search engines

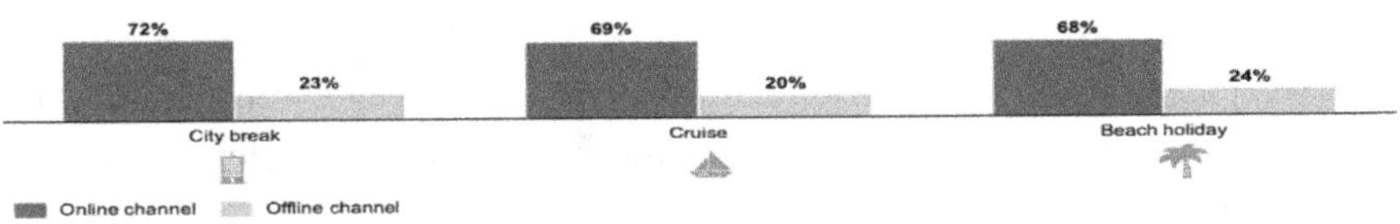

Figure 1. Channels for booking accommodation across holiday types.

Source: Roland Berger, TripAdvisor (2019).

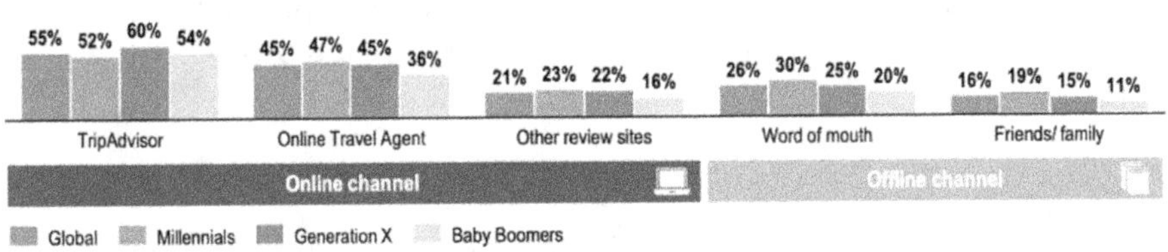

Figure 2. Channels used to book accommodation.

Source: Roland Berger, TripAdvisor, TripBarometer (2019).

are the most commonly used online planning tool, particularly among leisure travelers.

- *During the trip*: Once at their location, tourists rely on a variety of web sources to plan their activities. They utilize internet channels to obtain preliminary information about the destination and reviews or photos uploaded by recent visitors.
- *Post-trip*: After returning from a vacation, travelers may provide comments about their journey using the social networks (e.g., Facebook, Twitter, and Instagram) and digital services that they used to organize their trip in the first place.

Travelers of all ages are increasingly booking their accommodations and planning their journeys online. In spite of the fact that baby boomers use online channels less frequently than other segments of the population, they have generally become more comfortable with using them.

With the help of a digital dashboard, the Indonesian Ministry of Tourism tracks Indonesia's tourism reputation on social media 24/7, both nationally and internationally. Additionally, mobile positioning technologies are used to track tourism quantity and distribution. The data collected by this system enable decision-makers to better analyze visitor patterns and attitudes, respond to problems as they arise, and make more educated marketing decisions based on this information. Digitalization activities involve a digital academy for tourism start-ups, as well as small and medium-sized businesses, along with the development of new products and prototypes.

Meanwhile, tourism digitization has been implemented by the Vietnam Ministry of Tourism since late 2020. There have been several cities and provinces that have led the way. Since the COVID-19 epidemic began two years ago, the program has evolved significantly due to changes in tourist behavior when approaching a site or making decisions using online resources.

3.3.3. *Pandemic and tourism recovery*

Natural disasters or health crises, such as SARS in 2003 and H1N1 in 2009, have always had a great influence on the travel business (Vărzaru *et al.*, 2021), but the effects were always local and manageable. However, due to the global nature of the COVID-19 crisis, the tourist industry has been the one economic area that has been most impacted by the change (Ma *et al.*, 2022); hotels, restaurants, airlines, and travel agencies were forced to suspend operations for an extended period of time. International tourism was expected to drop by 80% (OECD, 2020). A 78% drop in tourist arrivals in 2020 resulted in a 1.2 trillion USD drop in visitor spending, threatening over 100 million direct tourism jobs. The COVID-19 pandemic was the catalyst for these changes. Although the tourism industry is considered to be one of the biggest employers in the world, the COVID-19 pandemic caused a significant drop in visitor numbers and massive unemployment in the tourism labor market (Chang *et al.*, 2020).

Furthermore, there is such a tight relationship between tourism and other economic areas (Faber and Gaubert, 2019) that the negative effects of COVID-19 on the tourism industry have spillover effects on related industries (Henseler *et al.*, 2022). Countries with high tourism sector contributions to GDP in particular are facing a significant economic impact, as are transitioning and developing countries (Chou, 2013; Khan *et al.*, 2020).

There will be a difference in the recommendations to be made to these countries as a response to the challenges posed by COVID-19, and global events will undoubtedly affect the rate and scope of restoration. However, one significant prospect that can be explored to reduce the consequences of the pandemic is for governments to create a "new normal" for destination marketing. The following are some creative tourist industry operations that have been implemented in the wake of the pandemic:

- Government economic policies that promote tourism (e.g., taxation and trade reform): Some governments have provided financial aid to the industry, either directly or through soft loans and guarantees.
- New measures to revitalize the tourist industry may be able to help many tourist industry countries that are constrained by appropriate value capacity.
- A continued change toward sustainable tourism conservation and local job creation can provide a boost to the fast and growing travel industry.

- Digital platforms can also play a vital role as they are increasingly being utilized as the primary vehicle for consumer engagement and transitional as well as for the development of new business models and concepts, particularly in the tourist industry (Omarova *et al.*, 2021).
- Diversify some tourism-dependent countries' economies (Goretti *et al.*, 2021): Some tourism-dependent countries may have to embark on a long and difficult journey to achieve their goals. Investing in non-tourism sectors is a long-term goal that could be aided by improving the links between tourism and locally produced agriculture, manufacturing, and entertainment.

Case study: Thailand's tourism after the COVID-19 pandemic

Tourism is regarded as one of Thailand's most significant businesses, accounting for around 20% of the country's GDP (Thaicharoen *et al.*, 2022). With 40 million tourists, Thailand placed seventh in the world in terms of foreign tourist arrivals in 2019. Domestic and international tourism brought in $90 billion for the country. Unfortunately, as a result of the pandemic and its associated restrictions, foreign travel has declined significantly. In September 2021, the number of foreign travelers flying to Thailand fell by 95%, and the nation's hotels only filled 9% of their rooms (Saxon *et al.*, 2021). However, the country is working to support its tourism industry while also preparing for international travel to recover further.

The Rao Tiew Duay Gun (We Travel Together) program, which received an estimated $640 million in Thai government funding, was launched in August 2020 (Newsroom, 2020). The government paid for six million hotel stays at a 40% discount. The maximum incentive was 3,000 baht ($100) per night for up to five nights. Meals would only be subsidized up to 600 baht ($20) per room, per night. Domestic flight passengers would also be entitled to a 40% government refund on their ticket price. A total of 2 million tickets were offered, with each seat costing 1,000 baht ($32).

In addition, Thailand launched the "Phuket Sandbox" in 2021 in an effort to recapture demand from international travelers. During the first three months of the program, more than 125 million USD were produced as the main profit for Phuket, and nearly 300 million USD were created as socializing funds for Thailand's economy (Thaicharoen *et al.*, 2022).

Because of the spread of the coronavirus pandemic, digital technologies are more important than ever. The travel industry and various digital firms are increasingly experimenting with ways to use virtual reality travel to provide customers with the experience of going on a trip physically. For example, the Tourism Council of Thailand is working with Singapore-based Is Where to build a digital-marketing platform to help tourist company operators better run their company and participate with a relatively great amount of local and international travelers. The platform already reached 600 million digital customers globally through cooperation with a big IT business. As a consequence, Thailand's Tourism Authority announced intentions to form a private digital business to focus on establishing a digital infrastructure for tourism, including the use of big data and the introduction of blockchain-based e-vouchers.

4. Model of Tourism Destination Management in Transitional Economy

The tourism destination management model during the transitional economy period varies across countries, sharing both common and distinct elements. This is attributed to the integrated nature of the tourism industry, influenced not only by the economic development model but also by diverse factors such as tourism resources encompassing nature, culture, infrastructure, human and social aspects and the global trends in tourism. The analysis, the results, and reality in different countries strongly show again that, in the transitional economy, there are some key and decisive factors that affect the model and efficiency of tourism management. These are related to policy and the role of the government, national and regional tourism departments, and considerations such as tourism geography and tourism mechanisms, as well as the components and the capacity of entrepreneurship in tourism (Table 2).

Figure 3 suggests the relationship between these elements and reflects the model of tourism management in the transitional economy.

Table 2. Research in different countries about destination management factors.

Factors	Author	Year	Destination	Key points
1. Governance and policy factors				
1.1. Integrated tourism policy through mechanisms and role of government	Zhang	1999	China	Without question, the government has played a significant part in the current prosperity of the sector through its diverse roles at pivotal moments. The growth of China's tourist policy has placed a strong emphasis on adaptability, and it is important to recognize this as the various governmental functions evolve.
1.2. Rebuilding tourism management policies and structures	Dai *et al.*	2017	China	Understanding China's outbound tourism growth, in addition to being an academic issue, is also important for China's future tourism policy. To further facilitate China's outbound tourism market's growth, orderly guidance and discretionary market policies are recommended.
1.3. Establishing policies for tourism funding, budgets, and investments	Şengel *et al.*	2022	All countries	Providing an examination of countries' financial policies implemented during the pandemic period is the objective of the study.
1.4. Increasing productivity and innovation	Romão *et al.*	2019	European region	The principles for smart specialization plans in European areas and the potential for cross-border regional tourism collaboration are taken into consideration when discussing policy consequences.

Table 2. (*Continued*)

Factors	Author	Year	Destination	Key points
1.5. Boosting business growth through entrepreneurship	Dahles	1998	Indonesia	This examines how small-scale entrepreneurs in tourism manage their social worlds in everyday life, and it asks questions about how they deal with the restrictions imposed by the Indonesian government's tourism policy in general along with the opportunities that small-scale tourism developments in particular provide.
2. Tourism resources and infrastructure factors				
2.1. Product development	Thaicharoen *et al.*	2022	Thailand	This article analyzes how Thailand's tourism industry coped with the COVID-19 pandemic, with a lesson from the pilot Phuket Tourism Sandbox project.
2.2. Tourism human resources	Singh	1997	India	There are several specific ingrained social and economic factors that may be the main contributors to the nation's current tourism situation. An attempt has been made to put up workable suggestions for gauging the performance of India's efforts to produce quality human resources.
2.3. Infrastructural connections in the tourism sector	Sharma *et al.*	2022	China	Long-term findings show a favorable and strong relationship between infrastructural development, word-of-mouth, and ICT and international visitor arrivals in India. ICT does, however, also have an immediate, beneficial, and large impact on visitor arrivals. The findings point to a long-term, one-way, causal relationship between infrastructure, ICT, governance, currency rate, and tourist arrivals.

(*Continued*)

Table 2. (*Continued*)

Factors	Author	Year	Destination	Key points
2.4. The marketing capacity, the communication capability, and the ability to attract tourists	Kokkranikal *et al.*	2011	South Africa	According to the "chain of influence" theory in destination marketing and image-making, those who develop such materials, such as tour operators and destination marketing companies, influence the content of marketing materials based on how tourists perceive South Africa's destinations.
2.5. Promoting skill development and employment opportunities	Kaplan	2004	South Africa	Skill development is essential to change and improve the tourism industry in developing nations effectively and sustainably, as well as, in the case of South Africa, to ensure that the country's poorest citizens start to profit from this business.
2.6. Improving transport connectivity	Khadaroo and Seetanah	2007	Mauritius	The transportation system on the island of Mauritius is notably responsive to visitors from Europe/North America and Asia. European and American citizens, in particular, demonstrate sensitivity to aspects beyond transportation infrastructure. In the tourism demand equation, both types of infrastructure, as well as visitor income, travel time, and relative costs, play significant roles.
3. Sustainability and nature-related factors				
3.1. Sustainable tourism management	Khan *et al.*	2021	Malaysia	This studies the complex relationship between sustainability policy, management, and tourist behavior.
3.2. Pandemic and tourism recovery	Omarova *et al.*	2021	Kazakhstan	This study analyzes innovative activities in the field of tourism as they were impacted by the COVID-19 pandemic.

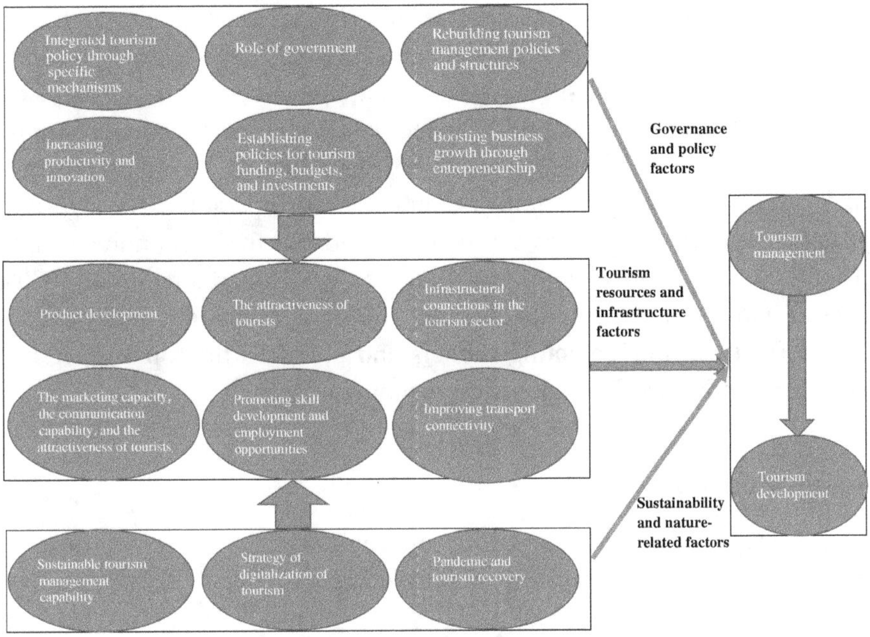

Figure 3. Model of tourism destination management.

We propose that the implementation of this model in any specific country should be tailored to the unique conditions of that country. However, the rules governing its management are expected to share the same or similar elements across different implementations.

5. Conclusion

To conclude, tourism destination management in a transitional economy is essential to ensure the sustainable development of the tourism industry in a transitional economy. A sustainable tourism destination management strategy maximizes the economic benefits of tourism while minimizing the negative impacts on the environment and local communities. Managing tourism in a transitional economy requires negotiating a combination of governance and policy factors, tourism resources, and infrastructure factors, along with encouraging marketing and promotion, revenue management, and stakeholder collaboration, as well as considering sustainability and environmental factors. As a powerful driver of economic growth and development, tourism can also promote environmental and responsible tourism practices when such strategies and practices are implemented. Moreover, tourism destination management in a transitional economy requires collaboration among a variety of stakeholders, including government agencies, local governments, and tourism operators. As a result, sustainable tourism practices can be promoted and the economic benefits of tourism shared between all stakeholders through partnerships and alliances. Finally, in a transitional economy, tourism destination management should focus on implementing models and practices that optimize tourism's economic benefits and ensure sustainable growth.

Acknowledgement

We are deeply grateful to the editor and reviewers for taking the time to review our manuscript carefully and providing valuable feedback that has significantly improved its quality.

References

Agrawal, A. (2014). Indigenous and scientific knowledge: Some critical comments. *Antropologi Indonesia, 3*(3). Available at: https://doi.org/10.7454/ai.v0i55.3331.

Bergh, J. C. J. M. van den. (1996). *Ecological Economics and Sustainable Development: Theory, Methods and Applications*. Aldershot, U.K.: Edward Elgar.

Chang, C.-L., McAleer, M., & Ramos, V. (2020). A charter for sustainable tourism after COVID-19. *Sustainability, 12*, 3671. Available at: https://doi.org/10.3390/su12093671.

Chou, M. C. (2013). Does tourism development promote economic growth in transition countries? A panel data analysis. *Economic Modelling, 33*, 226–232. Available at: https://doi.org/10.1016/j.econmod.2013.04.024.

Dahles, H. (1998). Tourism, government policy, and petty entrepreneurs in Indonesia. *South East Asia Research, 6*(1), 73–98. Available at: https://doi.org/10.1177/0967828X9800600105.

Dai, B., Jiang, Y., Yang, L., & Ma, Y. (2017). China's outbound tourism — Stages, policies and choices. *Tourism Management, 58*, 253–258. Available at: https://doi.org/10.1016/j.tourman.2016.03.009.

Faber, B. & Gaubert, C. (2019). Tourism and economic development: Evidence from Mexico's coastline. *American Economic Review*, *109*(6), 2245–2293. Available at: https://doi.org/10.1257/aer.20161434.

Goretti, M., Leigh, L. Y., Babii, A., Cevik, S., Kaendera, S., Muir, D. V., Nadeem, S. & Salinas, G. (2021). Tourism in the post-pandemic world: Economic challenges and opportunities for Asia-Pacific and the Western hemisphere. *Departmental Papers*, *2021*(002). Available at: https://doi.org/10.5089/9781513561905.087.A001.

Henseler, M., Maisonnave, H., & Maskaeva, A. (2022). Economic impacts of COVID-19 on the tourism sector in Tanzania. *Annals of Tourism Research Empirical Insights*, *3*(1), 100042. Available at: https://doi.org/10.1016/j.annale.2022.100042.

Jena Tesse Fox. (2019). Report: Southeast Asia tourist arrivals to reach 155M by 2022. *Hotel Management*. Available at: https://www.hotelmanagement.net/own/report-southeast-asia-tourist-arrivals-to-reach-155-4m-by-2022.

Kaplan, D. (2004). South Africa's national research and development strategy: A review. *Science, Technology and Society*, *9*(2), 273–294. Available at: https://doi.org/10.1177/097172180400900204.

Khadaroo, J. & Seetanah, B. (2007). Transport infrastructure and tourism development. *Annals of Tourism Research*, *34*(4), 1021–1032. Available at: https://doi.org/10.1016/j.annals.2007.05.010.

Khan, A., Bibi, S., Lorenzo, A., Lyu, J., & Babar, Z. U. (2020). Tourism and Development in developing economies: A policy implication perspective. *Sustainability*, *12*(4), 1618. Available at: https://doi.org/10.3390/su12041618.

Khan, M. R., Khan, H. U. R., Lim, C. K., Tan, K. L., & Ahmed, M. F. (2021). Sustainable tourism policy, destination management and sustainable tourism development: A moderated-mediation model. *Sustainability*, *13*(21), Article 21. Available at: https://doi.org/10.3390/su132112156.

Kokkranikal, J., Cronje, P., & Butler, R. (2011). Tourism policy and destination marketing in developing countries: The chain of influence. *Tourism Planning & Development*, *8*(4), 359–380. Available at: https://doi.org/10.1080/21568316.2011.603885.

Lélé, S. M. (1991). Sustainable development: A critical review. *World Development*, *19*(6), 607–621. Available at: https://doi.org/10.1016/0305-750X(91)90197-P.

Lozano-Oyola, M., Blancas, F. J., González, M., & Caballero, R. (2019). Sustainable tourism tags to reward destination management. *Journal of Environmental Management*, *250*, 109458. Available at: https://doi.org/10.1016/j.jenvman.2019.109458.

Ma, Y., Khurshid, A., Rauf, A., Zhang, J., Wang, X., & Boghicevici, C. (2022). COVID-19, tourism and the economy-evidence from pandemic epicenters of Europe. *Romanian Journal of Economic Forecasting*, *xxv*, 65–82.

Magaš, D. (2008). *Destination Management: Models and Techniques*. Opatija: University of Rijeka, Faculty of Tourism and Hotel Management. Available at: https://urn.nsk.hr/urn:nbn:hr:191:752500.

Newsroom, T. A. T. (2020, June 17). Thailand approves domestic tourism package worth 22.4 billion Baht. *TAT Newsroom*. Available at: https://www.tatnews.org/2020/06/thailand-approves-domestic-tourism-package-worth-22-4-billion-baht/.

OECD. (2017). A review of the policy framework for tourism marketing and promotion. OECD. Available at: https://doi.org/10.1787/096d0ace-en.

Omarova, A., Nurumov, A., Karipova, A., Kabdullina, G., Aimurzina, B., & Kamenova, M. (2021). Analysis of the development of innovative activities of the tourism industry in the influence of pandemic. *Journal of Environmental Management and Tourism*, *12*(6), Article 6. Available at: https://doi.org/10.14505//jemt.v12.6(54).02.

Pedrana, M. (2013). Local economic development policies and tourism: An approach to sustainability and culture. *Regional Science Inquiry Journal*, *5*(1), 91–99.

Romão, J., Okada, M., Machino, K., & Nijkamp, P. (2021). Destination management and sustainable development through the common lens of the Commons. *REGION*, *8*(1), 75–95. Available at: https://doi.org/10.18335/region.v8i1.286.

Saarinen, J. (2008). Special issue: Tourism in transition economies. *Tourism Geographies*, *10*(4), 409–409. Available at: https://doi.org/10.1080/14616680802434023.

Sanches-Pereira, A., Onguglo, B., Pacini, H., Gómez, M. F., Coelho, S. T., & Muwanga, M. K. (2017). Fostering local sustainable development in Tanzania by enhancing linkages between tourism and small-scale agriculture. *Journal of Cleaner Production*, *162*, 1567–1581. Available at: https://doi.org/10.1016/j.jclepro.2017.06.164.

Şengel, Ü., Işkın, M., Çevrimkaya, M., & Genç, G. (2022). Fiscal and monetary policies supporting the tourism industry during COVID-19. *Journal of Hospitality and Tourism Insights*, *ahead-of-print*(ahead-of-print). Available at: https://doi.org/10.1108/JHTI-08-2021–0209.

Shahzad, S. J. H., Shahbaz, M., Ferrer, R., & Kumar, R. R. (2017). Tourism-led growth hypothesis in thc top ten tourist destinations: New evidence using the quantile-on-quantile approach. *Tourism Management*, *60*, 223–232. Available at: https://doi.org/10.1016/j.tourman.2016.12.006.

Sharma, M., Mohapatra, G., & Giri, A. K. (2022). Assessing the role of ICT, governance, and infrastructure on inbound tourism demand in India. *Journal of Economic and Administrative Sciences*, *ahead-of-print*(ahead-of-print). Available at: https://doi.org/10.1108/JEAS-03-2022-0064.

Singh, S. (1997). Developing human resources for the tourism industry with reference to India. *Tourism Management*, *18*(5), 299–306. Available at: https://doi.org/10.1016/S0261-5177(97)00018-6.

Steve Saxon, Jan Sodprasert, & Voramon Sucharitakul. (2021). *Reimagining Travel: Thailand Tourism after the COVID-19 Pandemic* (p. 10). McKinsey. Available at: https://www.mckinsey.com/industries/travel-logistics-and-infrastructure/our-insights/reimagining-travel-thailand-tourism-after-the-covid-19-pandemic.

Thaicharoen, S., Meunrat, S., Leng-ee, W., Koyadun, S., Ronnasiri, N., Iamsirithaworn, S., Chaifoo, W., Tulalamba, W., & Viprakasit, V. (2022). How Thailand's tourism industry coped with COVID-19 pandemics: A lesson from the pilot Phuket Tourism Sandbox project. *Journal of Travel Medicine*, taac151. Available at: https://doi.org/10.1093/jtm/taac151.

Tourism | ASEAN Investment. (2012). Available at: https://investasean.asean.org/tourism.

UNWTO. (2004). *UNWTO Tourism Highlights, 2004 Edition*. World Tourism Organization. Available at: https://www.e-unwto.org/doi/epdf/10.18111/9789284407910.

UNWTO. (2013). *UNWTO Tourism Highlights, 2013 Edition*. World Tourism Organization. Available at: https://www.e-unwto.org/doi/epdf/10.18111/9789284415427.

UNWTO (ed.) (2019). *International Tourism Highlights, 2019 Edition*. World Tourism Organization (UNWTO). Available at: https://doi.org/10.18111/9789284421152.

Vărzaru, A. A., Bocean, C. G., & Cazacu, M. (2021). Rethinking tourism industry in pandemic COVID-19 period. *Sustainability*, *13*(12), 6956. Available at: https://doi.org/10.3390/su13126956.

Visser, G. & Rogerson, C. M. (2004). Researching the South African tourism and development nexus. *GeoJournal*, *60*(3), 201–215.

World Bank Data. (2020). International tourism, receipts (% of total exports). *Data*. Available at: https://data.worldbank.org/indicator/ST.INT.RCPT.XP.ZS?end=2020&most_recent_year_desc=false&start=1995&view=char.

UN World Tourism Organization (UNWTO). (2017). *UNWTO Tourism Highlights: 2017 Edition*. World Tourism Organization (UNWTO). Available at: https://doi.org/10.18111/9789284419029.

World Tourism Organization (WTO) (2020). *WTO | Publications — WTO Annual Report 2020*. Available at: https://www.wto.org/english/res_e/publications_e/anrep20_e.htm.

WTTC. (2019). *Travel & Tourism Economic Impact | World Travel & Tourism Council (WTTC)*. Available at: https://wttc.org/research/economic-impact.

Zhang, H. Q., Chong, K., & Ap, J. (1999). An analysis of tourism policy development in modern China. *Tourism Management*, *20*(4), 471–485. Available at: https://doi.org/10.1016/S0261-5177(99)00020-5.

https://doi.org/10.1142/9789811286100_0007

Chapter 7

Immersive Technologies: A Critical Success Factor for Modern Retailers

Dong Phong Nguyen*, Huong Ho Xuan†, Truong Thi Hoang Oanh‡, Vo Kim Nhan§ and Angelina Nhat Hanh Le¶

**University of Economics Ho Chi Minh City, Vietnam*

†School of International Business - Marketing, University of Economics Ho Chi Minh City, Vietnam

§Campus in Vinh Long, University of Economics Ho Chi Minh City, Vietnam

¶School of Management, University of Economics Ho Chi Minh City, Vietnam

**phongnd@ueh.edu.vn*

†huonghx@ueh.edu.vn

‡oanhtth@ueh.edu.vn

§nhanvk@ueh.edu.vn

¶hanhln@ueh.edu.vn

Abstract

The retail industry has undergone a massive transformation in recent years due to rapid technological advancements. Immersive technologies such as augmented reality (AR), virtual reality (VR), and mixed reality (MR) have become essential elements for modern retailers to enhance their customer experience and

Received on March 14, 2023; accepted on April 19, 2023

stay ahead of their rivals. Based on 107 scholarly papers, this chapter provides a comprehensive review and synthesis of technological features in addition to the variety of benefits that existing and emerging immersive technologies can bring to retailers and consumers. In particular, the two main categories of immersive technology features are identified: sensory stimuli and perceptual stimuli. The benefits that these technologies offer to the success of contemporary retailers in terms of gaining new consumers, keeping existing ones, and cultivating new ones are revealed and analyzed. In addition, a set of values for customers that are made possible by immersive technologies throughout the consumer shopping journey, which consists of pre-, during-, and post-purchase phases, are presented and synthesized. Not only will academics benefit greatly from our findings but so will those in charge of running retail businesses.

Keywords: Immersive Technologies, Modern Retailers.

1. Introduction

Retailing is the act or practice of selling products/services directly to end users or ultimate customers (Peterson and Balasubramanian, 2002). It includes all activities, beginning with acquiring items from manufacturers, suppliers, wholesalers, or agents and ending with delivering them to final customers for consumption (Reinartz *et al.*, 2019). Retailers sell a wide variety of items in relatively modest quantities to many customers. Over the last few decades, a number of formats and distribution channels such as in-store/physical, mobile, online, and social media have emerged within the realm of modern retailing (Ho *et al.*, 2022; Souiden *et al.*, 2019). With the popularity of smart devices, the development of mobile applications, and the advancement of immersive technologies, a variety of online and offline retailing channels are being integrated, allowing modern retailers to provide customers with a streamlined, problem-free, seamless, and unified experience (Ishfaq *et al.*, 2022; Vo *et al.*, 2022).

Immersive technologies such as augmented reality (AR), virtual reality (VR), and mixed reality (MR) are different forms of technology that blur the border between the physical and virtual worlds, allowing users to interact with the virtual environment and experience a sense of presence or immersion (Nussipova *et al.*, 2020; Vo *et al.*, 2022). According to Suh and Prophet (2018), immersive technologies have been utilized in a variety of disciplines during the past decade and thus represent a significant technological trend. The goal of improving consumers' immersive experiences is shared by AR and VR technology. Whereas VR completely immerses users in a computer-generated simulated environment which serves as a substitute for perceived reality (Xi and Hamari, 2021), AR integrates digital information and virtual items into the real world, thus augmenting perceived reality (Vo *et al.*, 2022). Riar *et al.* (2022) proposed a difference between the objectives of applying AR and VR: AR aims to modify the current world as we perceive it, whereas VR aims to replace it. MR is viewed as a hybrid of VR and AR in which virtual objects are superimposed on the actual world with increasing degrees of integration. Nowadays, immersive technologies are becoming increasingly important, with retailers using them as a tool for improving the customer experience in a more convenient, personalized, and engaging manner (Sung *et al.*, 2021). Thus, deploying these technologies offers unique approaches that have an enormous potential to attract and serve both existing and future consumers, ultimately leading to success for modern retailers.

Immersive technologies have the potential to change the way customers interact, experience, and engage in their shopping and decision-making processes (Caboni and Hagberg, 2019). A number of modern retailers have applied these immersive technologies to reshape or redesign the pre-purchase, purchase, and post-purchase stages of the customer shopping journey (Qin *et al.*, 2021; Rauschnabel *et al.*, 2022; Rudkowski *et al.*, 2020). During the pre-purchase stage, immersive technologies can be used to create virtual stores, allowing customers to go shopping as if they were in a physical store (Roggeveen and Sethuraman, 2020). Retailers can easily take consumers through several virtual journeys across the history and values of a brand/company, or present step-by-step illustrations of how products are manufactured and which material sourcing and sustainability practices are conducted. Some immersive technologies allow customers to get involved in the development of products, as they become co-designers of what they intend to buy (Li *et al.*, 2022). Those advantages of immersive technologies create a deeper level of customer participation and involvement by providing more comprehensive knowledge about brands and products during this pre-purchase stage.

During the purchase stage, retailers can adopt immersive technologies that allow consumers to browse and purchase products anywhere and anytime at their convenience and from the comfort of their own physical locations (e.g., homes, offices) (Reinartz *et al.*, 2019). Based on customers' interests and preferences, those advanced technologies can provide customized and personalized recommendations about specific products and brands that customers are consciously seeking out, or perhaps even those they subconsciously desire (Hoyer *et al.*, 2020). More realistic and detailed features and benefits of products are visualized, while virtual try-on opportunities can also be provided during this augmented and virtual shopping stage (Song *et al.*, 2020). These allow customers to see and compare how different/alternative products look and perform in real life in different contexts/environments and subsequently decide upon the most suitable products for their needs (Zhang *et al.*, 2019). In short, a convenient, personalized, and well-informed purchase experience enabled by immersive technologies is the foundation for retailers to build and develop a strong and truthful relationship with customers in the long term.

At the post-purchase stage, immersive technologies can create social experiences that allow consumers to connect with family members and friends from all over the world (Hudson *et al.*, 2019), as they can share their unique, transparent, and immersive experience as well as the photographs of their purchased products on social networks such as Facebook and Instagram. Modern retailers can create immersive games and promotion activities that allow consumers to continuously engage with brands at a deeper level (Sung *et al.*, 2021). This can lead to increased brand loyalty and repeat business.

As previously stated, a rich customer experience entails utilizing immersive technology to enhance the customer experience at every stage of the customer journey, including the pre-purchase, purchase, and post-purchase stages (Pangarkar *et al.*, 2022). However, alongside technical studies, empirical studies currently concentrate on adopting guidelines on how to utilize immersive technologies in the context of both online and brick-and-mortar retail (Hilken *et al.*, 2017; 2022). The great advantages and potential of immersive technologies are undeniably shown in studies focusing on the role of immersive technologies in the different industries of games (Feng *et al.*, 2020), education (Tang *et al.*, 2022), entertainment (Lee *et al.*, 2020), advertising (Sadamali Jayawardena *et al.*, 2023), tourism (Fan *et al.*, 2022), e-commerce (Martínez-Navarro *et al.*, 2019), and even retailing (Erdmann *et al.*, 2021; Vo *et al.*, 2022). Other studies have evaluated the antecedents and consequences of immersion in VR/AR/MR

(Lee *et al.*, 2020). The academic literature also notes the ambiguity and misunderstanding of phrases, notions, and immersive technology types (Rauschnabel *et al.*, 2022). This demonstrates the lack of work in comprehensively understanding the different types of existing and emerging technologies as well as the set of possible benefits that such technologies can offer to modern retailers, thus resulting in researchers or practitioners not being competent to adequately grasp both their applications and boundaries (Li *et al.*, 2022). Our work aims to fill this gap by reviewing and synthesizing the potential of different immersive technologies in the modern retailing sector, thus providing retail scholars and managerial executives with comprehensive knowledge of the studied matter.

The structure of this chapter is as follows. First, we introduce the general definition and history of immersive technologies, as well as current applications of immersive technologies in the retail sector. Next, we describe our research methodology to find relevant research papers that help us conduct a thorough review and synthesis of technological features and a set of benefits that existing and emerging immersive technologies can bring to retailers and consumers. The advantages of those new technologies that can fetch success to modern retailers in attracting, retaining, and growing customers will be presented and discussed. Furthermore, the value for customers in the pre-, during, and post-purchase stages of their shopping journey is synthesized. Finally, we draw conclusions about the current circumstances and future of immersive technologies in the modern retail sector.

2. Background

2.1. *Definition of immersive technologies*

Immersive technologies usually refer to cutting-edge technologies that blur the lines between the real and virtual worlds by engaging multiple senses such as sight, hearing, and touch to make users feel as though they are truly present in a digital or simulated environment (Prabhakaran *et al.*, 2022). Generally speaking, "immersion" is used to describe the status of being completely engrossed and involved in an activity such as watching a movie or playing a video game (Kitson *et al.*, 2018). However, in the context of technology, in line with Slater and Wilbur (1997, p. 3), immersion refers to the "extent to which the computer displays are capable of delivering an inclusive, extensive, surrounding and vivid illusion of reality to the senses of a human participant" (Meißner *et al.*, 2020). Slater (2009) is one of the pioneers who define immersive technologies as those that provide users with a high level of sensory fidelity, whether it be visual, audio, haptic, or involving other senses. Sensory fidelity is a key feature of immersive technologies: each sense that is triggered by the technology subsequently triggers an expected stimuli response in the brain (Yung *et al.*, 2021). Thus, a feeling of presence, immersion, and interaction, linking abstract events with real-time contexts, is created, leading to interactive and dynamic experiences for users (Ho *et al.*, 2022; Le *et al.*, 2022; Nussipova *et al.*, 2020; Vo *et al.*, 2022).

AR, VR, and MR are typical examples of immersive technologies representing different levels of the reality–virtuality continuum (Bec *et al.*, 2019; see Figure 1). Physical and virtual environments are the two ends of the continuum/spectrum in which the world is entirely made up of real and virtual things, respectively. On the relatively far left, AR is a technology that superimposes digital content such as images, text, or animations onto the real world through various devices such as smartphones, tablets, and wearable headsets (Suh and Prophet, 2018). Marker-based AR is one of the simplest types of AR. This technology entails using a camera or similar device to detect a QR code, which then generates a virtual object that appears over the location of the code. In contrast to marker-based AR, markerless AR does not require the use of QR codes (Brito and Stoyanova, 2018). Instead, it uses location data and the orientation of the mobile device to provide information such as navigation routes. Superimposition-based AR, on the other hand, requires the technology (i.e., camera and other sensors) to accurately recognize real-world objects and landscapes so that virtual objects can be superimposed onto them

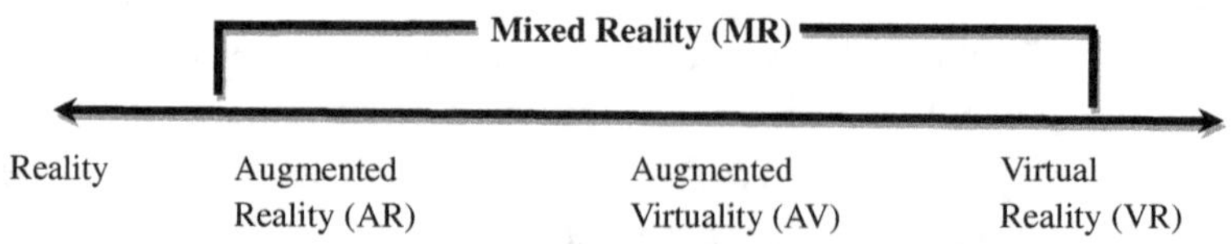

Figure 1. Reality–virtuality continuum (Adapted from Milgram and Kishino, 1994).
Source: Bec *et al.* (2019, p. 118).

(Dargan *et al.*, 2023). This form of AR is frequently used in the retail industry to display products such as furniture and apparel in real-world settings.

Augmented virtuality (AV) is a term used to describe a technology that combines aspects of both AR and VR to create an MR experience. Both AR and AV are categorized as MR technologies, situated between the two extremes where the boundaries between the real and virtual worlds are blurred (Suh and Prophet, 2018). However, unlike AR, AV starts with a virtual environment and integrates real-world components into it. This can be achieved by using a camera and sensors to capture physical objects and incorporate them into the virtual world, or by employing headsets with cameras that allow users to observe their real-world surroundings while being immersed in a virtual environment (Wolf *et al.*, 2022). Recently, virtual objects have been seamlessly incorporated into the real environment using the most recent MR technology such as superior computer vision, tracking, and display technologies, thus allowing users to interact with virtual objects in real time in a more intuitive and natural manner (Tang *et al.*, 2022).

Located at the extreme right end of the reality–virtuality continuum, VR is a technology that employs computer-generated simulations to create a realistic, immersive virtual environment (Bec *et al.*, 2019; Tang *et al.*, 2022). VR often makes use of a head-mounted display (HMD) that detects the user's head movements and displays a 3D scene in front of the eyes, enabling users to fully interact with virtual worlds and characters and providing the sense of existing within a virtual world. VR is divided into three categories: non-immersive VR, semi-immersive VR, and fully immersive VR (Cipresso *et al.*, 2018). The first form, non-immersive VR, involves displaying virtual content on a computer screen and allowing users to interact with it using more conventional online interfaces, including a keyboard and mouse, in a virtual setting (Suh and Prophet, 2018; Xi and Hamari, 2021). Semi-immersive VR, the second type, provides users with a view of the virtual environment wherein they can interact by moving their HMD in which a 3D picture is projected onto a monitor (Tuena *et al.*, 2020). The third type, and the most common, is fully immersive VR, which employs advanced tracking systems like motion-tracking HMDs/headsets, specialized haptic gloves, and multi-directional treadmills to allow users to interact with and immerse themselves in sensory experiences to a greater depth (Suh and Prophet, 2018). The employment of such cutting-edge technology provides consumers with a wholly engrossing experience.

2.2. *History of immersive technologies*

Immersive technology has evolved tremendously over the past few decades and continues to move forward (Prabhakaran *et al.*, 2022). One of the first forms of immersive technology is referred to as immersive images, i.e., stereoscopic images, which were widely used in the 1600s (Li *et al.*, 2022). These pictures create the illusion of real objects, even though they were painted on canvas (Li *et al.*, 2022). This invention also belongs to the early days of photography, wherein immersive static pictures called stereoscopes were widely used (Kumar, 2022). Later, researchers attempted to print photographs taken from slightly different angles and display them to the left and right eyes of viewers on small devices. With present-day digital technologies, photographs can be shown dynamically to induce dynamic illusions and display virtual environments (Kumar, 2022).

Perhaps the most important milestone in immersive technology was innovated by the famous pioneer Morton Heilig, a cinematographer who wanted to enhance the audience's experience by involving all human senses (Kumar, 2022). The first real multisensory VR system — Sensorama — was created and patented in 1962 (Steinicke, 2016). It featured a 3D display that allowed users to experience a motorcycle journey across Manhattan, including scent, vibration, and wind, in addition to sights and sounds (Sherman and Craig, 2018). For users to fully immerse themselves in the movie, immersive technologies were made available in other ways, such as speakers, fans, smell machines, and vibrating chairs (Kumar, 2022).

The creation of Headsight by Charles Comeau and James Bryan in 1961, the first HMD made with a motion-tracking mechanism identifying the orientation of the head, was another significant turning point (Steinicke, 2016). The HMD, however, was not connected to any virtual world because head movements were linked to a camera that moved in accordance to display video from a real remote place. Ivan Sutherland, hailed as "one of the godfathers of computer graphics" (Steinicke, 2016, p. 19), proposed the idea in 1965 of immersing users in a digital world identical to the actual world. This encompassed realism in terms of how the virtual environment appeared, sounded, moved, felt, and even reacted in real time (Steinicke, 2016). Sutherland developed the first HMD that could be used in a virtual environment in 1968, which is now regarded as the first actual HMD system in the VR industry (Mihelj *et al.*, 2014; Steinicke, 2016). The helmet, known as the "Sword of Damocles", gave the wearer the impression that an object was 3D by projecting 2D pictures in front of their eyes. The monitor adapted the image shown to the user as they moved by using a head position sensor (Steinicke, 2016). The device's disadvantage was that because the motion tracking equipment was mounted on the ceiling, the display needed to be very large. Even though advances in immersive technology had been significant, an essential aspect of interaction was still lacking (Steinicke, 2016). This gap was filled in 1969 by computer artist Myran Krueger, who created the first virtual world that responded to user actions and gestures (Steinicke, 2016). In order to decide how to move virtual items, the system used pressure sensors on the floor and video cameras (Mihelj *et al.*, 2014). The word "virtual reality" was first used and widely accepted in 1985 by VR pioneer Jaron Lanier (Mihelj *et al.*, 2014). He also founded Visual Programming Lab (VPL), which produced and sold the first commercial VR HMD, the EyePhone, as well as the first motion recognition gloves, the VPL Dataglove, in the late 1980s (Steinicke, 2016; Mihelj *et al.*, 2014). In fact, AR and VR were first used in the military and by airlines in the 1970s and 1980s, but because of their prohibitive costs, they did not gain popularity until the invention of smartphones (Kumar, 2022).

From the 1990s onwards, immersive technologies made significant advancements, and many businesses adopted them to reduce expenses, increase productivity, and improve team collaboration (Mabrook and Singer, 2019; Stanney *et al.*, 2020). The development of the CAVE (Cave Automatic Virtual Environment), a cube-shaped room made of screens (Cruz-Neira *et al.*, 1993), was another important historical turning point (Prabhakaran *et al.*, 2022).

The well-known Gartner Hype Cycle for emerging technologies is employed to analyze the subsequent years of the development of immersive technology. It demonstrates how response to new technologies often develop, from initial interest and enthusiasm in the innovation to disappointment and finally to ultimate broad adoption (Blosch and Fenn, 2018; Liao and Iliadis, 2021). Immersive technology was included in the first Hype Cycle ever published in 1995, which at the time placed it in the "Trough of Disillusionment" stage (Steinicke, 2016). Thereafter, the initial iPhone and Android smartphone releases coincided with the appearance of some of the earliest AR browsers. By entering the market in late 2008 and early 2009, Layar and Wikitude both asserted themselves to be the first mobile AR browsers (Liao and Iliadis, 2021). After briefly disappearing from the Hype Cycle, VR made a comeback in 2013, albeit while still in the Trough of Disillusionment (Steinicke, 2016). This return was sparked by the release of the Oculus Rift DK1, an HMD for video game developers created by Oculus VR through a Kickstarter effort that earned more than $2 million (Kickstarter, 2016).

By 2016, due to further developments like Facebook's acquisition of Oculus Rift, Google's introduction of Cardboard, and HTC's release of Vive, immersive technologies had become widely accepted and had climbed the Enlightenment Slope. At this point, the full benefit of technology was becoming more apparent, and an increasing number of businesses were exploring its prospective uses (Laurell *et al.*, 2019). Immersive technologies made little progress toward the Productivity Plateau between 2016 and 2017, and it was expected to reach this level within 5 years. The market penetration of the target population was between 5% and 20% in 2018 (Blosch and Fenn, 2018).

Recently, shopping apps utilizing immersive technologies have been released by Chinese e-commerce giant Alibaba, US department store Macy's, Swedish furniture maker IKEA, French hypermarket Carrefour, travel giant Marriott International, and the largest retailer of consumer electronics in Europe (SATURN) (Meißner *et al.*, 2020). The use of VR and AR in retail has the potential to boost sales and give businesses a competitive edge (Inman and Nikolova, 2017). Shopping apps for VR and AR are profitable for retailers. Customers who shopped in Macy's 69 pilot shops that offered VR spaces in its interior division, for instance, placed orders with an average order value that was 60% greater than customers who made their purchases in traditional non-virtual settings (Meißner *et al.*, 2020).

Gartner (2022) recognized some key new technologies that improve technology delivery, broaden immersive experiences, and accelerate AI automation. Decentralized identity (DCI), digital humans, internal talent marketplaces, the metaverse, non-fungible tokens (NFT), super apps, and Web3 are particularly important technologies for immersive experiences (Gartner, 2022). In 2020, the global consumer market for immersive technology generated around \$6.3 billion in revenue (Statista, 2022). By 2023, it was anticipated that the market for VR and AR would reach a value of \$160 billion due to the rising popularity of consumer devices that make these technologies possible (Statista, 2022).

The development of general and fundamental technology is accelerating the development of immersive technologies. Better visuals, quicker processing, and more accurate tracking are all possible because of the increasingly powerful and sophisticated technology utilized in immersive technologies like HMDs, sensors, and controllers (Prabhakaran *et al.*, 2022). Through improvements in hand and body tracking, voice recognition, and haptic feedback, immersive technologies are becoming more intuitive and natural to use, enabling users to interact with virtual environments more realistically (Dwivedi *et al.*, 2022; Liu *et al.*, 2021). Additionally, as more people — including both companies and consumers — have access to less expensive HMDs and other devices, immersive technologies are becoming more widely available (Mabrook and Singer, 2019; Stanney *et al.*, 2020). Furthermore, cutting-edge technologies like artificial intelligence, cloud computing, and the Internet of Things are working in tandem with immersive technologies to create more complex and immersive experiences (Zhang *et al.*, 2022). Overall, the development of immersive technologies continues to open new commercial and consumer options, with the potential to completely change how we engage with the digital world.

2.3. *Applications of immersive technologies in the retail sector*

Immersive technologies are being applied in several industries like education, tourism, entertainment, medicine, retail, and marketing (Kumar, 2021), as well as higher education (Radianti, 2020). This article focuses on the application of immersive technologies such as VR, AR, and MR within the retail sector.

Recent studies have shown the potential of using immersive technologies as a means of intervening in the shopping process and augmenting customer experience (Ho *et al.*, 2022; Xi and Hamari, 2021; Vo *et al.*, 2022). VR has been used as a tool to assist in the investigation of almost every consumer-related research question, including information searches, product evaluation, decision-making, and post-purchase evaluation (Xi and Hamari, 2021). With current VR technology, shopping environments facilitate consumer discovery of products such as food preferences and consumption (Lombart *et al.*, 2019). Managers can easily and accurately track consumer activities such as searches, reviews, selection, and even post-purchase evaluation (Xi and Hamari, 2021). One of the greatest application areas of VR in a business context is shopping and retail (Cowan and Ketron, 2019; Xi and Hamari, 2021). Therefore, VR technology is believed to solve limitations of space and time and to enable the replication and creation of any shopping environment that is accessible to consumers at any time (Serrano *et al.*, 2016). VR applications in retailing include virtual stores, product design and prototyping, brand activation and marketing, virtual try-on, virtual showrooms, event marketing, in-store experiences, data visualization, and virtual training and consultation. Descriptions and specific examples of VR applications in retailing are summarized in Table 1. Evidence shows that VR technologies are effective in retail marketing strategies for customer elevation. One specific example is Adidas applying VR to design and test new shoe prototypes, reducing the need to create physical prototypes and allowing users to explore new designs in an interactive manner. More prominently, the Virtual Try-On app and virtual galleries are increasingly being used as with Ray-Ban's "Virtual Try-On" which allows customers to try on virtual sunglasses using their smartphone camera (Plotkina and Saurel, 2019).

Various AR applications in retailing have also been identified. Table 2 provides the key so-called "trending" AR applications, including virtual trials, location-based services, packaging design, product visualization, product information, video games, interactive advertising, enhanced packaging, enhanced in-store displays, personalized recommendations, brand storytelling, and integrations on social media — specifically, by utilizing

Table 1. VR applications and examples in retailing.

Application	Description	Examples
Virtual Stores	Retailers can create a virtual store environment for customers to explore and shop from anywhere in the world (Breugelmans and Campo, 2011).	Tommy Hilfiger's "VR Runway Show" allows customers to experience a virtual fashion show (Jin *et al.*, 2021). Alibaba's "Buy+" allows customers to shop in virtual stores from anywhere in the world (Yuan *et al.*, 2023).
Product Design and Prototyping	VR technology can be used to design and test products before they are produced, reducing costs and increasing speed to market (Choi and Cheung, 2008; Zhou *et al.*, 2023).	IKEA offers a home furnishing customization service using VR that allows consumers to create, experience, customize, and share their own home ensemble in a virtual living room. The Gravity Sketch 3D design tool applies VR for quick and easy sketching of 3D design prototypes that can be completed by selecting different components, functions, or design elements to customize the available options replacement (Zhou *et al.*, 2023).
Virtual Try-On	Customers can try on products virtually, reducing the need for in-person try-ons and increasing convenience (Kim and Forsythe, 2008; Plotkina and Saurel, 2019).	Ray-Ban's "Virtual Try-On" allows customers to try on virtual sunglasses using their smartphone camera (Plotkina and Saurel, 2019). Topshop's "VR Catwalk" allows customers to experience a virtual fashion show and try on virtual clothing (Van Kerrebroeck *et al.*, 2017).
Virtual Showrooms	Some retailers are creating virtual showrooms that allow customers to experience products within a virtual environment (Ma *et al.*, 2023).	JD and Dewu established online virtual showrooms, displaying products in a stereoscopic manner to improve the accuracy of the consumer's prior perception and subsequently reduce product evaluation uncertainty (Ma *et al.*, 2023).

(*Continued*)

Table 1. (*Continued*)

Application	Description	Examples
Event Marketing	Retailers can use VR to create immersive experiences at events and trade shows (Farah *et al.*, 2019).	Toms Shoes created a VR experience that allowed customers to take a virtual trip to Peru and see how the company's "One for One" program is helping to provide shoes for children in need (Jin *et al.*, 2021). Mercedes-Benz advertised its SL model with a virtual drive on the Pacific Coast Highway in California, allowing users to explore the new design in an interactive manner (Farah *et al.*, 2019). Oreo used VR to promote its new cupcake-flavored cookies through a mystical wonderland filled with the Milky Way and a chocolate canyon (Farah *et al.*, 2019).
In-Store Experiences	VR can be used to create engaging in-store experiences that help to draw customers in and keep them in the store longer (Roggeveen *et al.*, 2020; Bonfanti and Yfantidou, 2021).	Nike created a VR experience that allowed customers to explore a virtual basketball court and practice their skills (Bonfanti and Yfantidou, 2021).
Data Visualization	VR can be used to create interactive data visualizations that help retailers better understand customer behavior and preferences (Zhang *et al.*, 2020).	The *Wall Street Journal's* VR narrative, which uses a time series of the NASDAQ's price/earnings ratio over 21 years as a roller coaster track that the reader then rides from one end to the other, is one of the few engaging examples of an immersive data story (Lee *et al.*, 2020).
Virtual Training and Consultation	VR can be used to provide training and consultation services to customers (Trappey *et al.*, 2022).	Chatbots can be used as virtual assistants (Trappey *et al.*, 2022).

Table 2. AR applications and examples in retailing.

Application	Description	Examples
Virtual Try-On	AR can be used to allow consumers to virtually try on products such as clothing, accessories, and makeup, thus reducing the need for in-person try-ons and reducing the likelihood of returns (Lee *et al.*, 2022; Wanick *et al.*, 2023).	Sephora's Virtual Artist app allows customers to try on makeup virtually using their smartphone cameras. Uniqlo's "Magic Mirror" allows customers to try on virtual clothing and see how it looks on them before making a purchase (Wanick *et al.*, 2023).
Location-Based Services	AR technology can be used to provide in-store navigation and product information (Jung *et al.*, 2021).	Target's "See It In Your Space" feature allows customers to view furniture and decor in their own space using their smartphone cameras (Anastasiya Tolocka, 2023).
Packaging Design and Augmented Packaging	AR technology can be used to enhance the design of product packaging and create interactive product labels (Cascini *et al.*, 2020; Vanderroost *et al.*, 2017; Zhao and Balagué, 2015).	Nestlé's "KitKat AR" app allows customers to scan KitKat packaging and play interactive games using AR technology (Zhao and Balagué, 2015).
Product Visualization	AR can be used to provide customers with an interactive and immersive way to view and learn about products (Hilken *et al.*, 2022).	3D holograms of food and drinks from a café's menu are given (Hilken *et al.*, 2022).
Product Information	AR can be used to provide customers with additional product information, such as product specifications, reviews, and ratings (Tan *et al.*, 2022).	Lego's "AR Studio" app allows customers to see 3D versions of Lego sets and provides additional information about the sets. LEGO's Hidden Side AR app offers new ways of enjoying products after customers make purchases (Tan *et al.*, 2022).

(*Continued*)

Table 2. (*Continued*)

Application	Description	Examples
Gamification	AR can be used to create interactive and engaging experiences for customers, such as games and contests (Ponis *et al.*, 2020).	Vuzix Smart Glasses for Warehousing use an ongoing enhanced AR application (Gamification in order picking) for stocking, selecting, and controlling inventory (Ponis *et al.*, 2020).
Interactive Advertising	AR can be used to create interactive and engaging advertisements that allow customers to interact with products in new and innovative ways (Feng and Mueller, 2019).	Pepsi's "Pepsi Max Unbelievable" campaign used AR technology to create a bus shelter that appeared to be transparent, allowing customers to see through it and interact with virtual objects (Feng and Mueller, 2019). IKEA's products in real-time feature realistically rendered true-to-scale 3D products based on room dimensions (Wang, 2021).
Enhanced In-Store Displays	AR can be used to create enhanced in-store displays that provide customers with an immersive and interactive way to learn about products (Caboni and Hagberg, 2019).	Adidas' "Virtual Footwear Wall" uses AR technology to allow customers to see and learn about different shoe styles in an interactive and engaging manner. Amazon offers an AR-view feature based on 3D models (Caboni and Hagberg, 2019).
Personalized Recommendations	AR can be used to provide customers with personalized product recommendations based on their preferences and past purchase history (Alimamy and Gnoth, 2022; Riegger *et al.*, 2021).	The NomadX store in Singapore includes facial recognition features, so that when registered customers approach a touchscreen terminal in the store, they receive recommendations that reflect their online purchase history (Riegger *et al.*, 2021).

Table 2. (*Continued*)

Application	Description	Examples
Brand Storytelling	AR can be used to tell the story of a brand and its products in an immersive and engaging manner (Xue *et al.*, 2023).	Lacoste's "LCST" app uses AR technology to tell the story of the brand's history and products in an interactive and engaging manner (Xue *et al.*, 2023). Adidas and the German AR company Eye Candy Lab created the AR in-store storytelling experience "For The Oceans" (Rauschnabel *et al.*, 2022).
Social Media Integration	AR can be integrated into social media platforms to allow customers to share their AR experiences with friends and followers (Appel *et al.*, 2020).	Snapchat's "Shoppable AR" feature allows customers to try on and purchase products within the Snapchat app using AR technology (Appel *et al.*, 2020).

"virtual trial and education of the product" and gamification to enhance the customer experience. By presenting additional product information as virtual content, AR apps can assist consumers in their product decisions. AR enhances the customer experience, decision-making, and feedback. Furthermore, AR allows for the enhancement of the design of product packaging and create interactive product labels. For example, Nestlé's "KitKat AR" app allows customers to scan KitKat packaging and play interactive games using AR technology. AR can be used to provide customers with personalized product recommendations based on their preferences and past purchase history. For example, the NomadX store in Singapore includes facial recognition features, so that when registered customers approach a touchscreen terminal in the store, they receive recommendations that reflect their online purchase history (Riegger *et al.*, 2021). Another potential extension of AR is the creation of an AR-based social network, as the technology offers the opportunity for immersive reality. In general, consumers find applications on AR to be relatively easy-to-use, novel experiences.

MR embraces both real-world components (real objects and their conditions in real-world space) and virtual ones (virtual models and virtual conditions) in immersive applications. In practical terms, MR is helping to transform the retail consumer market, but applying MR technology in the retail context is difficult (Sung *et al.*, 2021). MR technology can, however, be used to educate consumers about products and brands. In addition, the MR smartphone app also enhances the consumer's in-store shopping experience, ultimately influencing purchase decisions with techniques such as enhanced customer service, interactive product demos, windows MR devices, and an enhanced in-store shopping experience (see Table 3). For example, the evolution of the capabilities of MR devices — as was the case with the HTC Vive and Microsoft HoloLens — has allowed them to be used as part of the MR interface to effectively

Table 3. MR applications and examples in retailing.

Application	Description	Examples
Enhanced Customer Service	MR can be used to enhance the customer service experience by providing real-time information and assistance to customers (Jain *et al.*, 2023).	Amazon's global shopping platform offers all kinds of products for supporting MR shopping assistants (e.g., at the physical point of sale) on the go or at home (Jain *et al.*, 2023).
Interactive Product Demos	Prototyping and design are areas in which firms are already realizing the benefits of MR (Rauschnabel *et al.*, 2022).	Ford is using mixed-reality applications to add new features to existing vehicles before the physical production of a prototype (Rauschnabel *et al.*, 2022).
Windows MR devices	MR can be used at low cost and ease of use and allows retailers to create a gamified and unique in-store shopping experience for customers (Dehghani *et al.*, 2020).	ASUS, Acer, and Dell applied smart phone-based window MR applications and launched their headsets for commercial devices (Dehghani *et al.*, 2020).
Enhanced in-store shopping experience	The MR smartphone app also enhances consumers' in-store shopping experience and influences purchasing decisions (Sung *et al.*, 2021).	A musical and MR hologram talk show and an MR media art show (e.g., Proto) were released (Sung *et al.*, 2021).

provide remote expertise between geographically dispersed users (Dehghani *et al.*, 2020).

3. Methodology

This study follows the guidelines of the systematic literature review process proposed by Kitchenham (2004) and Brereton *et al.* (2007) consisting of several stages, starting with the formulation of the research objectives, followed by a literature search, screening of the identified literature, evaluation of the eligibility of the remaining studies, data extraction, critical assessment, and finally a synthesis of the literature.

The preliminary search was carried out in the Web of Science database and produced 963 publications. The Web of Science database was queried using the following search string: TITLE-ABS-KEY ("augmented reality" OR AR OR "virtual try-on" OR "virtual reality" OR VR OR "mix* reality" OR "extended reality") AND TITLE-ABS-KEY (shop* OR retail* OR mall OR supermarket OR store OR commerce OR business). The keywords "augmented reality" OR AR OR "virtual try-on" OR "virtual reality" OR VR OR "mix* reality" OR "extended reality" were used to include all forms of the term "immersive technologies" and its abbreviations. The keywords "shop* OR retail* OR mall OR supermarket OR store OR commerce OR business" were used to comprise varying terminology in the literature related to shopping or the retail experience. The search was limited to peer-reviewed articles and journals in the SSCI databases to ensure source credibility (Podsakoff *et al.*, 2005). Multiple processes were included in the screening and eligibility process of this study. Firstly, we investigated the titles and abstracts of the records to find instances of duplication. Next, we superficially screened documents that had some connection to immersive technologies (e.g., VR, AR, or MR) or retail to see whether they were relevant. We then used our reference searches to find more relevant records. As illustrated in Figure 2, a manual search process was conducted to ensure articles in leading journals were captured.

After checking the abstract and main text for relevance to the keywords, the next stage was to apply inclusion and exclusion criteria. All included studies focused on immersive technologies (e.g., VR, AR,

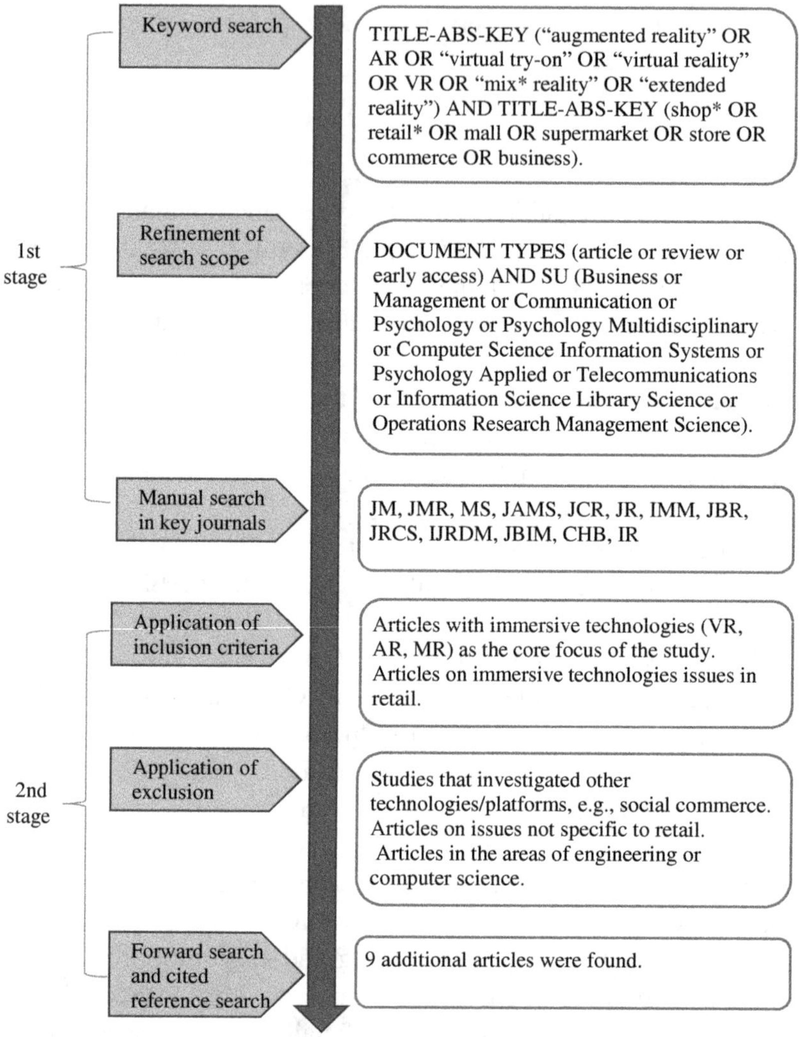

Figure 2. Literature search and inclusion.

or MR) and dealt with problems that arise while using these technologies in both online and physical stores. Studies that looked at other types of technologies/platforms, did not focus on retail at all, or were primarily concerned with engineering or computer science were excluded. Ninety-eight studies met the criteria and were thus selected for further analysis.

Seven additional publications were discovered through a forward search of the identified articles. To make sure that all relevant studies were found, we double-checked our search phrases in a third search engine, EBSCO. The search strategy was validated by using cited references as a secondary source, although it only produced two new papers.

The final sample of 107 papers is reviewed and narratively summarized to identify the features of immersive technologies comparing AR, VR, and MR. Moreover, the merits associated with attracting, maintaining, and developing customers that AR, VR, and MR can bring to the success of modern retailers are disclosed and discussed. Furthermore, a set of values for customers enabled by AR, VR, and MR in the pre-, during, and post- purchase stages of customer shopping journey are presented and synthesized.

4. Analysis Results

4.1. *Technological features of immersive technologies that are applied in the retailing industry*

At the heart of immersive technologies are the affordances that involve/engage/absorb users in immersive environments, thereby delivering an immersive experience. Based on certain characteristics of immersive systems, we have identified two main clusters of system characteristics: sensory stimuli and perceptual stimuli.

The first stream of research investigated the effects of visual displays (Mishra *et al.*, 2021), auditory modalities (Petit *et al.*, 2019; Ringler *et al.*, 2021), haptic interfaces (Alzayat and Lee, 2021; Branca *et al.*, 2023), and movement tracking (Luangrath *et al.*, 2022; Pfeiffer *et al.*, 2019) (see Table 4). Visual display refers to the presentation of digital information or graphics overlaid onto a user's view of the real world and determines the effective horizontal and vertical angles through which the virtual environment is seen (Ho *et al.*, 2022; Le *et al.*, 2022; Wedel *et al.*, 2020). Stationary display, head-based display, and hand-based display of the visual display are three of the key feature systems of immersive technologies. To create the virtual environment in accordance with the users's point of view, head-based displays often include sensors that measure head

Table 4. Sensory stimuli of immersive technologies in the context of modern retail.

Sensory stimuli	System feature	Immersive technologies		
		VR system	**AR system**	**MR system**
Visual display (Suh and Prophet, 2018; Sung *et al.*, 2021; Wedel *et al.*, 2020)	• Stationary display	— Non-headset VR experiences on monitors or projection systems	— AR applications on TV screens — Projection-based AR systems	— MR projection-based systems
	• Head-based display	— Oculus Rift — HTC Vive — PlayStation VR	— Google Glass — Microsoft HoloLens — Magic Leap One	— Microsoft HoloLens 2
	• Hand-based display	— VR experiences on smartphones with Google Cardboard or Samsung Gear VR	— Smartphone/ tablet-based AR apps (e.g., Gap, IKEA, Amazon, or other virtual try-on apps)	— Microsoft HoloLens 2
Auditory modality (Heller *et al.*, 2019; Petit *et al.*, 2019; Ringler *et al.*, 2021; Suh and Prophet, 2018; Wedel *et al.*, 2020)	• Stationary auditory modality (surround or stereo speakers)	— Computer-generated audio from virtual objects and environments in 3D sound	— Audio from digital overlays or holograms, combined with audio from real-world sources in 3D sound	— Audio seamlessly blended from both digital and physical objects and environments in 3D sound, creating a coherent and interactive audio experience

	• Head-position-based auditory modality (headphones)	— VR headsets with integrated headphones or separate headphones connected to the system	— AR glasses or devices with integrated headphones, or separate headphones connected to the AR device	— MR headsets with integrated headphones or separate headphones connected to the MR system
Haptic interface (Alzayat and Lee, 2021; Branca *et al.*, 2023; Cowan *et al.*, 2021; Gatter *et al.*, 2022; Ivanov *et al.*, 2023; Luangrath *et al.*, 2022)		— Haptic gloves, controllers, vests, and other wearables that provide tactile feedback	— Haptic devices, such as wearables or handheld controllers providing tactile feedback in conjunction with digital overlays	— Haptic wearables and devices that provide tactile feedback when interacting with both digital and physical objects
Movement tracking (Hoffmann *et al.*, 2022; Meissner *et al.*, 2020; Pfeiffer *et al.*, 2019; Schnack *et al.*, 2021; Xi and Hamari, 2021)	• Sensor-based tracking • Vision-based tracking • Marker-based tracking • Hybrid tracking	— Cameras and sensors integrated into the VR headset — VR headset or controllers with embedded markers (e.g., infrared)	— Cameras and sensors integrated into AR glasses or devices — Mobile devices with AR capabilities utilizing built-in cameras and sensors	— Cameras and sensors integrated into MR headsets or devices, combining the tracking capabilities of both VR and AR technologies

position, orientation, and movement, all of which simulate visual perception when the users moves their body or head. With the use of a handheld display, users may combine virtual and real-world scenes and objects by tracking their location and orientation in space. In stationary auditory modalities (surround or stereo speakers) and head-position-dependent auditory modalities (headphones), sounds can be reproduced with extremely high fidelity. However, approximating the physical processes involved in simulating sound propagation in real time in virtual environments is an exceedingly difficult task (Wedel *et al.*, 2020). Previous research (e.g., Heller *et al.*, 2019; Petit *et al.*, 2019) found that higher levels of engagement and presence resulted in multisensory AR having a greater behavioral modulating effect.

Haptics refers to the sensation of touch and its integration into virtual environments, rooted in our somatosensory system throughout "the body that senses contact with, and temperature of, the skin, and force, balance, pose (proprioception) and movement (kinesthesis) of body parts, including the arms, hands, and fingers" (Wedel *et al.*, 2020). In the context of modern retailing, touch as a sensory control is essential for obtaining haptic information and kinesthetic properties (Heller *et al.*, 2019; Luangrath *et al.*, 2022). The active inference of sensorimotor actions resembling touch plays a crucial role in reducing the mental intangibility of a product for consumers. By simulating the tactile sensations of a product in a virtual space, users are better equipped to evaluate the item and make informed purchasing decisions, leading to a more satisfactory shopping experience. Moreover, for consumers to conduct purchasing in VR in a natural and efficient manner, there is a high demand for accurate and multimodal tracking technologies that enable consumers to interact with various virtual objects (Xi and Hamari, 2021; Suh and Prophet, 2018). Such monitoring technologies can range from a typical pointing device, such as a cursor, to a direct neural link. In the existing literature on VR purchasing, movement-based input modalities are classified into sensor-based tracking, vision-based tracking, marker-based tracking, and hybrid tracking, all of which employ consumer psychology and behavior within the context of virtual shopping.

According to the vividness theory, communication success increases when information is provided in a vivid and rich format (Steuer, 1992).

Immersive technologies (i.e., VR, AR, and MR) are very rich sensory mediums for information transfer because they allow users to feel like they are a part of the scene and experience sensory stimulation just as they would in the actual world (Grewal *et al.*, 2020).

According to Heller *et al.* (2019) and Mishra *et al.* (2020), sensory stimuli cause stronger emotional arousal (such as emotions of shame and empathy), which then motivates people to give more money and take part in more charitable activities. An outstanding representation of real-world experiences is given by the technological features of immersive technologies (Yim *et al.*, 2017; Suh and Prophet, 2018). Modern retailers have adaptively applied media richness according to features and services, and deployed "avatar sales agents" to successfully simulate human touch, increasing customer well-being and purchase intentions as a result (Chen *et al.*, 2022; Kumar, 2022). Moreover, immersive technologies offer a sensory-rich, aesthetically pleasing, and visually attractive interactive environment (Nussipova *et al.*, 2019; Suh and Prophet, 2018). This should increase consumers' perceptions of visual and emotional attractions (Mishra *et al.*, 2020; Simmonds *et al.*, 2020) while enhancing decision-making evaluation, customer engagement, and brand perceptions in online retailing (Chen *et al.*, 2022; Kumar, 2022).

The other stream of research on system features examines the effects of perceptual stimuli on the user experience and focuses on user perception of features of immersive technologies. A comprehensive literature review indicates that descriptions of immersive technologies have focused on three key characteristics: interactivity, vividness, and novelty. Interactivity is defined as a system feature that detects a user's input (i.e., a gesture) and responds immediately to the new activity (Steuer, 1992). Vividness — which is defined as a medium's level of representational richness — is an essential component for creating immersive experiences (Steuer, 1992), which render an online simulation experience more authentic by applying various sensory stimulations and multiple cues (Ho *et al.*, 2022; Le *et al.*, 2022). According to Yim *et al.* (2017), novelty — the perceived uniqueness or newness of stimuli — is the third most important characteristic of immersive technology such as AR, VR, and MR. The important distinguishing characteristics have been explored in relation to consumer cognition in the context of immersive technologies, with particular emphasis on the sense of self-location and possible action (i.e., embodiment) (Huang and Liao, 2017; Huang *et al.*, 2019; Ho *et al.*, 2022; Scholz and Smith, 2016; Vo *et al.*, 2022). A positive affective reaction is created by interactivity as it entertains and immerses users (Yim and Park, 2019). Simulated physical control is defined as "the visual integration of virtual content into a person's real-world environment", whereas environmental embedding refers to "the ability of AR to simulate physical control over an offering as embodiment" (Hilken *et al.*, 2017, p. 886). Two types of characteristics also play a significant role in facilitating mental imagery (imagery generation and imagery transformation) which promotes the senses of presence and immersion and reduces the mental burden, thus enhancing experiential value creation (Fan *et al.*, 2020; Hilken *et al.*, 2017, 2018; Huang, 2019; Song *et al.*, 2020). The reviewed literature further considered perceived ease of use and perceived usefulness as perceptual stimuli of immersive technologies (Chiang *et al.*, 2022; McLean and Wilson, 2019). Modern retailers have been applying these characteristics to enhance the customer experience in a more convenient, personalized, and engaging manner. Table 5 also provides a summary of the perceptual stimuli that have been investigated in previous studies.

Table 5. Perceptual stimuli of immersive technologies in the context of modern retail.

Perceptual stimuli	**System feature**	**Studies**
Interactivity	Motion tracking, gesture detection, voice recognition, haptic feedback, object manipulation, and other system features enable users to interact with and manipulate virtual objects in a way that feels natural and intuitive.	Chen *et al.*, 2023; Kim *et al.*, 2023; Kim *et al.*, 2021; McLean and Wilson, 2019; Parise *et al.* 2016; Park and Yoo, 2020; Poushneh, 2018; Yim *et al.* 2017; Riar *et al.*, 2023; Yim and Park, 2019
Vividness/Media richness	Realistic graphics, spatial audio, 360-degree video, and social interaction are some essential elements of vividness and media richness in immersive technology systems.	Chen *et al.*, 2023; de Amorim *et al.*, 2022; Kim *et al.*, 2023; Kim *et al.*, 2021; McLean and Wilson, 2019; Riar *et al.*, 2023; Yim *et al.*, 2017

Table 5. (*Continued*)

Perceptual stimuli	System feature	Studies
Novelty/ Innovativeness	The concept that customers can have new and different experiences thanks to novelty and innovativeness, including virtual try-on, interactive product showcases, AR product information, virtual store tours, and personalized product suggestions.	Arghashi, 2022; McLean and Wilson, 2019; Yim *et al.*, 2017
Sense of self-location	The feeling that an online consumer is located in the virtual retail world.	Huang and Liao, 2017; Huang *et al.*, 2019; Scholz and Smith, 2016
Possible action	Consumers feel themselves to be authentically taking possible actions within the virtual environment.	Huang and Liao, 2017; Huang *et al.*, 2019; Scholz and Smith, 2016
Simulated physical control	The ability of immersive technology to simulate physical control over an offering as an embodiment.	Fan *et al.*, 2020; Hilken *et al.*, 2017, 2018; Huang, 2019; Song *et al.*, 2020
Environmental embedding	The visual integration of virtual content into a person's real-world environment.	Fan *et al.*, 2020; Hilken *et al.*, 2017, 2018; Huang, 2019; Song *et al.*, 2020
Perceived ease of use	An easy-to-use technological system enabling people to finish activities, enhance production, while also improving their performance and efficiency.	Castillo and Bigne, 2021; Chiang *et al.*, 2022; McLean and Wilson, 2019; Pillai *et al.*, 2020; Zhang *et al.*, 2019
Perceived usefulness	The perception of consumers that using certain immersive technologies would improve their performance.	Castillo and Bigne, 2021; Chiang *et al.*, 2022; McLean and Wilson, 2019; Pillai *et al.*, 2020; Qin *et al.*, 2021

Table 6. The value of immersive technologies for modern retailers.

Stage	Value for modern retailers
Attracting	• Information (information provided, information quality/product presentations) • Product contextuality/complexity • Modern retail environment (reshape or redesign/retail space) • Communication (creative and interactive advertising, sales promotion)
Maintaining	• Response time/responsiveness • System quality/service excellence • Recommendations/point-of-view sharing
Developing	• Brand image, brand awareness, customer loyalty • Brand engagement • Brand love • Increased sales volume

Source: Caboni and Hagberg (2019).

4.2. *Benefits that immersive technologies provide for modern retailers*

According to the examined literature, immersive technologies can contribute to enriching the retail setting, both online and in physical stores (Caboni and Hagberg, 2019). In particular, the reviewed literature revealed that immersive technologies have emerged as an effective method of attracting potential customers, maintaining existing ones, and developing strong relationships with customers.

The analyzed studies showed that AR/VR/MR technology enables modern retailers to develop immersive customer-engaging experiences that captivate the attention of consumers. Examining how immersive technologies might assist consumers' informativeness is one important benefit of immersive technologies for modern retailers that seems to be more relevant now than ever, not least because of the growing trend toward online purchasing (Nussipova *et al.*, 2019; Riar *et al.*, 2023). The reviewed literature looked at how immersive technologies can improve informativeness through their rich and interactive product presentations, and also revealed that higher levels of informativeness and high-quality information in immersive technologies can decrease product uncertainty, boost perceived usefulness, and positively affect choice confidence (Kowalczuk *et al.*, 2021). By encouraging a distinct style of consumer perceptions and sense-making and by utilizing several features connected to the five senses (Grewal *et al.*, 2020; Heller *et al.*, 2019; Mishra *et al.*, 2020), immersive technologies allow modern retailers to reshape/redesign their retail service spaces. Retailers can utilize immersive technologies to provide customers with the chance to virtually try on items to assist them in identifying which products are most suited to their needs (Ivanov *et al.*, 2023; Kumar and Srivastava, 2022; Vo *et al.*, 2022). Immersive technologies have become an excellent opportunity for modern retailer advertising and increasing customer attendance.

According to the examined literature, beneficial aspects related to maintaining existing consumers, such as real-time/quick responses and service excellence (Grewal *et al.*, 2020; Khoi and Le, 2023; Riar *et al.*, 2023), have also been investigated. Moreover, modern retailers can promote point-of-view sharing between consumers and encourage consumer recommendations in the immersive systems to engage/maintain extant customers (Heller *et al.*, 2019; Hilken *et al.*, 2017, 2018). Retailers also benefit from these technologies which facilitate a quicker understanding of their customers' habits, psychology, and behaviors and, as a result, can provide better assistance at the point of sale, which in turn may enhance customers' overall shopping experiences (Dacko, 2017; Flavián *et al.*, 2019). Also, immersive technologies enable modern retailers to achieve multiple objectives within their advertising and marketing strategy, including attracting customers to their store (online and/or offline), increasing brand awareness, customer loyalty, brand engagement, and brand love. By allowing customers to do their own pre-purchase evaluations using mobile, web, and in-store applications, immersive technologies provide modern retailers with a chance to boost sales (Dacko, 2017). Immersive technologies are thus becoming increasingly valuable to shops as a way to create a memorable customer experience and increase consumer engagement (Nussipova *et al.*, 2019; Riar *et al.*, 2023).

4.3. *Value for retail consumers afforded by immersive technologies*

4.3.1. *Value for consumers in the pre-purchase stage*

As noted earlier, immersive technologies (VR, AR, or MR) have been used to enhance the consumer experience across the pre-purchase,

purchase, and post-purchase stages of the customer shopping journey (Qin *et al.*, 2021; Rauschnabel *et al.*, 2022; Rudkowski *et al.*, 2020). In the pre-purchase stage of a modern retail consumer's journey, these immersive technologies play a crucial role in fostering mental imagery (Heller *et al.*, 2019, Hilken *et al.*, 2021), mental stimulation/simulation (Heller *et al.*, 2019; Petit *et al.*, 2019; Wedel *et al.*, 2020), illustration of products, and enhancement of learning experiences (Wedel *et al.*, 2020). The market size for immersive technologies in communication/advertising has grown considerably with research showing that these immersive technologies elicit positive brand attitudes, stimulate purchase intentions, and result in higher engagement than standard online ads. These immersive technologies contribute to mental stimulation by enabling interactive exploration of products, while also providing essential information about production, content, and design. By blurring the lines between advertising and retailing, they allow consumers to make purchases in the same medium, simplifying the process.

Another form of immersive technology allows consumers to interact with print and outdoor media through applications, typically by scanning a QR code which leads to an AR or VR interface. This interactivity enriches mental imagery, product information, and contextualization while making interactions trackable. Haptic ads, which utilize the vibration motor of mobile devices, introduce a tactile dimension to the consumer's experience. By stimulating a multisensory experience, haptic ads help enhance brand awareness and engagement. Outdoor digital AR advertising creates awareness, engagement, and free publicity through social media sharing. These creative applications overlay virtual objects, products, animals, or people in the real world, further enhancing mental imagery. Some applications even enable content personalization based on facial or emotion recognition, allowing consumers to interact with virtual objects in a more meaningful way. Product placement is facilitated through AR, contextualizing products by showing them in use within a desirable virtual environment. This provides mental imagery and allows consumers to better visualize themselves using the product. Finally, 360°, 3D, and immersive video ads can be placed in games, virtual stores, and VR sports broadcasts to target specific consumer interactions within the virtual environment. This enhances mental stimulation, ensuring a more captivating and informative experience during the pre-purchase stage.

Moreover, immersive technology experiences in the pre-purchase stage can be categorized as embedded, embodied, shared, or adaptive, and there is a wide range of research on the potential of embedded and embodied experiences to influence consumer behavior (Chen *et al.*, 2021; Hilken *et al.*, 2017, 2018). Immersive technologies enable greater customer satisfaction, resulting in more meaningful customer engagement (Jessen *et al.*, 2020), aiding the decision-making process and enhancing consumer comprehension through the digitization of services (Huang and Liao, 2015; Parise *et al.*, 2016; Heller *et al.*, 2020).

4.3.2. *Value for consumers in the purchase stage*

During the purchase stage, immersive technologies can be used to create virtual stores such as ShelfZone® (Pizzi *et al.*, 2019) and ViCoS (Schnack *et al.*, 2019). Customers may visually test products out in their homes, on themselves, or on avatars — for instance, using mobile AR applications (Chen *et al.*, 2023; de Amorim *et al.*, 2022; Kim *et al.*, 2023; Kim *et al.*, 2021; McLean and Wilson, 2019; Riar *et al.*, 2023; Yim *et al.*, 2017). By making things fun while simultaneously providing rational reasons for buying products, immersive technologies offer hedonic shopping value as well as utilitarian shopping value (Vieira *et al.*, 2022). Firms such as Ikea, Nestle, and Baker Furniture have been using immersive technologies to improve their products' technical aspects as well.

Customers feel more comfortable and confident making decisions as a consequence, which in turn increases customer satisfaction and lowers risk perception (Heller *et al.*, 2019; Hilken *et al.*, 2017, 2018, 2022). By easing the fitting process in physical establishments, in-store technologies like smart mirrors and holograms largely target fashion and luxury goods, fostering decision confidence and purchase happiness. Additionally, in-store navigation, in addition to online product discovery, and mobile VR and AR applications, provides practical value by streamlining the shopping experience. Along with enhancing the overall shopping experience, interactive digital displays or virtual signage that provide product information, suggestions, and promotions also serve the customer's hedonistic and practical demands. By offering hedonic value via immersive settings and utilitarian value through specialized assortments and items, virtual pop-up shops and simulated retail locations provide distinctive and individualized shopping experiences (Lin *et al.*, 2022). Customers may choose shops, goods, locations, and other characteristics in a single visit thanks to this customized approach to retail, which also reduces the sense of risk and further improves decision comfort, confidence, and purchase pleasure (Lin *et al.*, 2022) (see Figure 3).

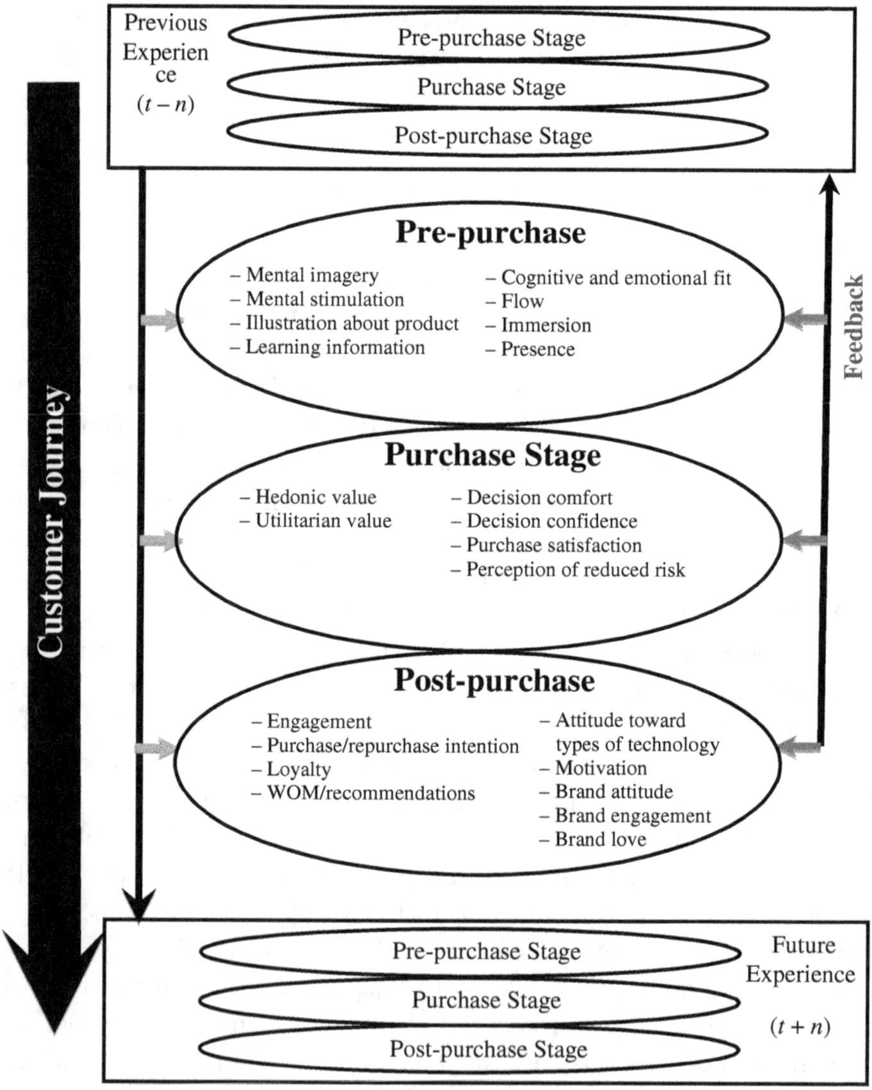

Figure 3. Value for consumers during the shopping journey.

4.3.3. *Value for consumers in the post-purchase stage*

The post-purchase stage is a vital part of the retail customer experience, and the incorporation of VR, AR, and MR technologies at this stage presents a special chance to improve engagement, loyalty, and general brand image (Heller *et al.*, 2019; Petit *et al.*, 2019; Wedel *et al.*, 2020). Through the creation of interactive, customized, and immersive environments, these technologies may improve post-purchase experiences and eventually help consumers feel more strongly connected to their favorite brands. The interaction of customers with VR, AR, and MR apps can significantly influence on their post-purchase intentions for both new and repeat purchases. These technologies enable consumers to connect with goods by providing a platform for product modification or co-creation, which then boosts customer incentive to keep using the technology and improves their perception of it. A better attitude fosters brand love and encourages consumer loyalty, which in turn improves brand attitude and engagement.

Customers feel encouraged and more appreciated while using these technologies, which strengthens their brand loyalty and motivates them to spread the word about the company. These technologies also give rise to instruction, gamification, and contextualized usage experiences. Finally, by supplying more contextual information or enabling users to relive the process of consumption, VR and AR apps may improve post-consumption experiences and assessments. Increased consumer happiness, brand loyalty, and more favorable word-of-mouth recommendations are all benefits of this improved post-purchase experience.

5. Conclusions and Recommendations for Modern Retailers

This book chapter has demonstrated that immersive technologies have the potential to offer significant advantages to modern retailers. By leveraging AR, VR, and MR, retailers can create highly personalized and engaging experiences that attract and retain customers, as well as fostering brand loyalty. Immersive technologies also provide retailers with valuable insights into consumer behavior, enabling them to make more informed decisions about inventory, marketing, and customer engagement strategies. Furthermore, our analysis has revealed that immersive technologies offer value to customers during all stages of the shopping journey, including pre-purchase, purchase, and post-purchase. For example, retailers can use immersive technologies to provide customers with more detailed product information before making a purchase decision, as well as enhancing the in-store shopping experience. Additionally, immersive technologies can facilitate post-purchase engagement by offering personalized follow-up experiences such as virtual try-ons or product tutorials.

As consumer expectations continue to rise, retailers must embrace immersive technologies to stay relevant and competitive in the market. We predict that immersive technologies will continue to evolve and play a significant role in shaping the future of retailing. The following are some projections of enhancements in immersive technologies that will influence retailers in various manners. First, the future of immersive technologies will be heavily influenced by advancements in hardware. The development of lightweight and comfortable AR and VR headsets will make immersive experiences more accessible and user-friendly. Next, the integration of sensors and haptic feedback technologies can enhance the sensory experience of immersive technologies. Additionally, the advent of 5G networks and edge computing can support more seamless and responsive immersive experiences. With faster data transfer speeds and lower latency, retailers can provide real-time and immersive experiences that feel more natural and intuitive. Moreover, computer vision and machine learning technologies can enhance the functionality and accuracy of immersive technologies. For example, by using machine learning algorithms, retailers can create more accurate and personalized recommendations for customers based on their preferences and past purchases.

Furthermore, spatial computing, which refers to the use of AR, VR, and MR technologies to create 3D spatial experiences, has the potential to revolutionize the retail industry. By allowing customers to interact with virtual products in the physical space, spatial computing can provide more intuitive and engaging experiences. The use of blockchain technology in the retail industry can help ensure the security and authenticity of products, particularly with regard to luxury goods and fashions. By using blockchain-based tracking and authentication systems, retailers can provide customers with a more transparent and trustworthy shopping experience. Natural Language Processing (NLP) technology can enable more natural and intuitive interactions between customers and immersive technologies. For example, by using NLP-based chatbots, retailers can provide personalized recommendations and support their customers in real time. Finally, the use of biometric sensors in immersive technologies can enhance the accuracy and personalization of experiences. For example, using biometric sensors to track a customer's heart rate, temperature, and other physiological signals can provide insights into their emotional state, allowing retailers to provide more closely tailored experiences.

In short, the future of immersive technologies in the retail industry looks promising; retailers who quickly adopt and effectively utilize these technologies will be better positioned to attract and retain customers, and ultimately succeed in a highly competitive marketplace.

Acknowledgement

This research is funded by University of Economics Ho Chi Minh City, Vietnam.

References

Alimamy, S. & Gnoth, J. (2022). I want it my way! The effect of perceptions of personalization through augmented reality and online shopping on customer intentions to co-create value. *Computers in Human Behavior*, *128*, 107105.

Alzayat, A. & Lee, S. H. (Mark). (2021). Virtual products as an extension of my body: Exploring hedonic and utilitarian shopping value in a virtual reality retail environment. *Journal of Business Research*, *130*, 348–363. Available at: https://doi.org/10.1016/J.JBUSRES.2021.03.017.

Anastasiya Tolocka. (2023). *Augmented Reality for Furniture Industry: Make Your Customers Go Wow*. Zolak Tech. Available at: https://zolak.tech/blog/augmented-reality-for-furniture-industry.

Appel, G., Grewal, L., Hadi, R., & Stephen, A. T. (2020). The future of social media in marketing. *Journal of the Academy of Marketing Science*, *48*(1), 79–95.

Arghashi, V. (2022). Shopping with augmented reality: How wow-effect changes the equations! *Electronic Commerce Research and Applications*, *54*, 101166. Available at: https://doi.org/10.1016/J.ELERAP.2022.101166.

Bec, A., Moyle, B., Timms, K., Schaffer, V., Skavronskaya, L., & Little, C. (2019). Management of immersive heritage tourism experiences: A conceptual model. *Tourism Management*, *72*(November 2018), 117–120. Available at: https://doi.org/10.1016/j.tourman.2018.10.033.

Blosch, M. & Fenn, J. (2018). *Understanding Gartner's Hype Cycles*. Gartner Inc. Available at: https://www.gartner.com/en/documents/3887767.

Bonfanti, A. and Yfantidou, G. (2021). Designing a memorable in-store customer shopping experience: Practical evidence from sports equipment retailers. *International Journal of Retail & Distribution Management*, *49*(9), 1295–1311. Available at: https://doi.org/10.1108/IJRDM-09-2020-0361.

Branca, G., Resciniti, R., & Loureiro, S. M. C. (2023). Virtual is so real! Consumers' evaluation of product packaging in virtual reality. *Psychology and Marketing*, *40*(3), 596–609. Available at: https://doi.org/10.1002/mar.21743.

Brereton, P., Kitchenham, B. A., Budgen, D., Turner, M., & Khalil, M. (2007). Lessons from applying the systematic literature review process within the software engineering domain. *Journal of Systems and Software*, *80*(4), 571–583.

Breugelmans, E. & Campo, K. (2011). Effectiveness of in-store displays in a virtual store environment. *Journal of Retailing*, *87*(1), 75–89.

Brito, P. Q. & Stoyanova, J. (2018). Marker versus markerless augmented reality. Which has more impact on users? *International Journal of Human–Computer Interaction*, *34*(9), 819–833.

Caboni, F. & Hagberg, J. (2019). Augmented reality in retailing: A review of features, applications and value. *International Journal of Retail and Distribution Management*, *47*(11), 1125–1140. Available at: https://doi.org/10.1108/IJRDM-12-2018-0263.

Cascini, G., O'Hare, J., Dekoninck, E., Becattini, N., Boujut, J.-F., Guefrache, F. Ben, Carli, I., Caruso, G., Giunta, L., & Morosi, F. (2020). Exploring the use of AR technology for co-creative product and packaging design. *Computers in Industry*, *123*, 103308.

Castillo S, M. J. & Bigne, E. (2021). A model of adoption of AR-based self-service technologies: A two country comparison. *International Journal of Retail & Distribution Management*, *49*(7), 875–898. Available at: https://doi.org/10.1108/IJRDM-09-2020-0380.

Chen, R., Perry, P., Boardman, R., & McCormick, H. (2022). Augmented reality in retail: A systematic review of research foci and future research agenda.

International Journal of Retail & Distribution Management, *50*(4), 498–518. Available at: https://doi.org/10.1108/IJRDM-11-2020-0472.

Chiang, L.-L. (Luke), Huang, T.-L., & Chung, H. F. L. (2022). Augmented reality interactive technology and interfaces: A construal-level theory perspective. *Journal of Research in Interactive Marketing*, *16*(4), 683–698. Available at: https://doi.org/10.1108/JRIM-06-2021-0156.

Choi, S. H. & Cheung, H. H. (2008). A versatile virtual prototyping system for rapid product development. *Computers in Industry*, *59*(5), 477–488.

Cipresso, P., Giglioli, I. A. C., Raya, M. A., & Riva, G. (2018). The past, present, and future of virtual and augmented reality research: A network and cluster analysis of the literature. *Frontiers in Psychology*, *9*(NOV), 1–20. Available at: https://doi.org/10.3389/fpsyg.2018.02086.

Cowan, K., Spielmann, N., Horn, E., & Griffart, C. (2021). Perception is reality… How digital retail environments influence brand perceptions through presence. *Journal of Business Research*, *123*, 86–96. Available at: https://doi.org/10.1016/J.JBUSRES.2020.09.058.

Cruz-Neira, C., Sandin, D. J., & DeFanti, T. A. (1993). Surround-screen projection-based virtual reality: The design and implementation of the CAVE. *Proceedings of the 20th Annual Conference on Computer Graphics and Interactive Techniques*, 135–142.

Dacko, S. G. (2017). Enabling smart retail settings via mobile augmented reality shopping apps. *Technological forecasting and social change*, *124*, 243–256. Available at: https://doi.org/10.1016/j.techfore.2016.09.032.

Dargan, S., Bansal, S., Kumar, M., Mittal, A., & Kumar, K. (2023). Augmented reality: A comprehensive review. *Archives of Computational Methods in Engineering*, *30*(2), 1057–1080.

de Amorim, I. P., Guerreiro, J., Eloy, S., & Loureiro, S. M. C. (2022). How augmented reality media richness influences consumer behaviour. *International Journal of Consumer Studies*, *46*(6), 2351–2366. Available at: https://doi.org/10.1111/ijcs.127904.

Dehghani, M., Lee, S. H. M., & Mashatan, A. (2020). Touching holograms with windows mixed reality: Renovating the consumer retailing services. *Technology in Society*, *63*, 101394.

Dwivedi, Y. K., Hughes, L., Baabdullah, A. M., Ribeiro-Navarrete, S., Giannakis, M., Al-Debei, M. M., Dennehy, D., Metri, B., Buhalis, D., & Cheung, C. M. K. (2022). Metaverse beyond the hype: Multidisciplinary perspectives on emerging challenges, opportunities, and agenda for research, practice and policy. *International Journal of Information Management*, *66*, 102542.

Erdmann, A., Mas, J. M., & Arilla, R. (2021). Value-based adoption of augmented reality: A study on the influence on online purchase intention in retail. *Journal of Consumer Behaviour*, *22*(4), 912–932. Available at: https://doi.org/10.1002/cb.1993.

Fan, X., Jiang, X., & Deng, N. (2022). Immersive technology: A meta-analysis of augmented/virtual reality applications and their impact on tourism experience. *Tourism Management*, *91*, 104534. Available at: https://doi.org/10.1016/j.tourman.2022.104534.

Fan, X., Chai, Z., Deng, N., & Dong, X. (2020). Adoption of augmented reality in online retailing and consumers' product attitude: A cognitive perspective. *Journal of Retailing and Consumer Services*, *53*, 101986. Available at: https://doi.org/10.1016/J.JRETCONSER.2019.101986.

Farah, M. F., Ramadan, Z. B., & Harb, D. H. (2019). The examination of virtual reality at the intersection of consumer experience, shopping journey and physical retailing. *Journal of Retailing and Consumer Services*, *48*, 136–143.

Feng, Y. & Mueller, B. (2019). The state of augmented reality advertising around the globe: A multi-cultural content analysis. *Journal of Promotion Management*, *25*(4), 453–475.

Feng, Z., González, V. A., Mutch, C., Amor, R., Rahouti, A., Baghouz, A., Li, N., & Cabrera-Guerrero, G. (2020). Towards a customizable immersive virtual reality serious game for earthquake emergency training. *Advanced Engineering Informatics*, *46*, 101134. Available at: https://doi.org/10.1016/J.AEI.2020.101134.

Flavián, C., Ibáñez-Sánchez, S., & Orús, C. (2019). The impact of virtual, augmented and mixed reality technologies on the customer experience. *Journal of Business Research*, *100*, 547–560. Available at: https://doi.org/10.1016/j.jbusres.2018.10.050.

Gartner. (2022). *What's new in the 2022 Gartner Hype Cycle for Emerging Technologies*. Gartner Inc. Available at: https://www.gartner.com/en/articles/what-s-new-in-the-2022-gartner-hype-cycle-for-emerging-technologies.

Gatter, S., Hüttl-Maack, V., & Rauschnabel, P. A. (2022). Can augmented reality satisfy consumers' need for touch? *Psychology and Marketing*, *39*(3), 508–523. Available at: https://doi.org/10.1002/mar.21618.

Grewal, D., Noble, S. M., Roggeveen, A. L., & Nordfalt, J. (2020). The future of in-store technology. *Journal of the Academy of Marketing Science*, *48*, 96–113. Available at: https://doi.org/10.1007/s11747-019-00697-z.

Heller, J., Chylinski, M., de Ruyter, K., Mahr, D., & Keeling, D. I. (2019). Touching the untouchable: Exploring multi-sensory augmented reality in the context of online retailing. *Journal of Retailing*, *95*(4), 219–234. Available at: https://doi.org/10.1016/J.JRETAI.2019.10.008.

Hilken, T., de Ruyter, K., Chylinski, M., Mahr, D., & Keeling, D. I. (2017). Augmenting the eye of the beholder: Exploring the strategic potential of augmented reality to enhance online service experiences. *Journal of the Academy of Marketing Science*, *45*(6), 884–905. Available at: https://doi.org/10.1007/s11747-017-0541-x.

Hilken, T., Chylinski, M., Keeling, D. I., Heller, J., de Ruyter, K., & Mahr, D. (2022). How to strategically choose or combine augmented and virtual reality for improved online experiential retailing. *Psychology & Marketing*, *39*(3), 495–507.

Hilken, T., Heller, J., Chylinski, M., Keeling, D. I., Mahr, D., & de Ruyter, K. (2018). Making omnichannel an augmented reality: The current and future state of the art. *Journal of Research in Interactive Marketing*, *12*(4), 509–523. Available at: https://doi.org/10.1108/JRIM-01-2018-0023.

Ho, X. H., Nguyen, D. P., Cheng, J. M. S., & Le, A. N. H. (2022). Customer engagement in the context of retail mobile apps: A contingency model integrating spatial presence experience and its drivers. *Journal of Retailing and Consumer Services*, *66*, 102950.

Hoffmann, S., Joerß, T., Mai, R., & Akbar, P. (2022). Augmented reality-delivered product information at the point of sale: When information controllability backfires. *Journal of the Academy of Marketing Science*, *50*(2022), 743–776. Available at: https://doi.org/10.1007/s11747-022-00855-w.

Hoyer, W. D., Kroschke, M., Schmitt, B., Kraume, K., & Shankar, V. (2020). Transforming the customer experience through new technologies. *Journal of Interactive Marketing*, *51*(1), 57–71. Available at: https://doi.org/10.1016/j.intmar.2020.04.0.

Huang, T. L. & Liao, S. L. (2017). Creating e-shopping multisensory flow experience through augmented-reality interactive technology. *Internet Research*, *27*(2), 449–475. Available at: https://doi.org/10.1108/IntR-11-2015-0321.

Huang, T.-L., Mathews, S., & Chou, C. Y. (2019). Enhancing online rapport experience via augmented reality. *Journal of Services Marketing*, *33*(7), 851–865. Available at: https://doi.org/10.1108/JSM-12-2018-0366.

Hudson, S., Matson-Barkat, S., Pallamin, N., & Jegou, G. (2019). With or without you? Interaction and immersion in a virtual reality experience. *Journal of Business Research*, *100*, 459–468. Available at: https://doi.org/10.1016/j.jbusres.2018.10.062.

Inman, J. J. & Nikolova, H. (2017). Shopper-facing retail technology: A retailer adoption decision framework incorporating shopper attitudes and privacy concerns. *Journal of Retailing*, *93*(1), 7–28.

Ishfaq, R., Davis-Sramek, B., & Gibson, B. (2022). Digital supply chains in omnichannel retail: A conceptual framework. *Journal of Business Logistics*, *43*(2), 169–188. Available at: https://doi.org/10.1111/jbl.12277.

Ivanov, A., Head, M., & Biela, C. (2022). Mobile shopping decision comfort using augmented reality: The effects of perceived augmentation and haptic imagery. *Asia Pacific Journal of Marketing and Logistics*, *ahead-of-p*(ahead-of-print). Available at: https://doi.org/10.1108/APJML-06-2022-0518.

Jain, S., Obermeier, G., Auinger, A., Werth, D., & Kiss, G. (2023). Design principles of a mixed-reality shopping assistant system in omnichannel retail. *Applied Sciences*, *13*(3), 1384.

Jessen, A., Hilken, T., Chylinski, M., Mahr, D., Heller, J., Keeling, D. I., & de Ruyter, K. (2020). The playground effect: How augmented reality drives creative customer engagement. *Journal of Business Research*, *116*, 85–98. Available at: https://doi.org/10.1016/j.jbusres.2020.05.002.

Jin, B., Kim, G., Moore, M., & Rothenberg, L. (2021). Consumer store experience through virtual reality: Its effect on emotional states and perceived store attractiveness. *Fashion and Textiles*, *8*, 1–21.

Jung, T. H., Bae, S., Moorhouse, N., & Kwon, O. (2021). The impact of user perceptions of AR on purchase intention of location-based AR navigation systems. *Journal of Retailing and Consumer Services*, *61*, 102575.

Khoi, N. H. & Le, A. N. H. (2023). Real-time interactivity and impulsive buying in livestreaming commerce: The focal intermediary role of inspiration. International *Journal of Human–Computer Interaction*, 1–16. Available at: https://doi.org/10.1080/10447318.2023.2176987.

Kickstarter (2016). *Oculus Rift: Step Into The Game*. Available at: https://www.kickstarter.com/projects/1523379957/oculus-rift-step-into-the-game

Kim, J. & Forsythe, S. (2008). Adoption of virtual try-on technology for online apparel shopping. *Journal of Interactive Marketing*, *22*(2), 45–59.

Kim, J. H., Kim, M., Park, M., & Yoo, J. (2023). Immersive interactive technologies and virtual shopping experiences: Differences in consumer perceptions between augmented reality (AR) and virtual reality (VR). *Telematics and Informatics*, *77*, 101936. Available at: https://doi.org/10.1016/J.TELE.2022.101936.

Kim, J.-H., Kim, M., Park, M., & Yoo, J. (2021). How interactivity and vividness influence consumer virtual reality shopping experience: The mediating role of telepresence. *Journal of Research in Interactive Marketing*, *15*(3), 502–525. Available at: https://doi.org/10.1108/JRIM-07-2020-0148.

Kitchenham, B. (2004). Procedures for performing systematic reviews. *Keele, UK, Keele University*, *33*(2004), 1–26.

Kitson, A., Prpa, M., & Riecke, B. E. (2018). Immersive interactive technologies for positive change: A scoping review and design considerations. *Frontiers in Psychology*, *9*(AUG). Available at: https://doi.org/10.3389/fpsyg.2018.01354.

Kowalczuk, P., Siepmann, C., & Adler, J. (2021). Cognitive, affective, and behavioral consumer responses to augmented reality in e-commerce: A comparative study. *Journal of Business Research*, *124*, 357–373. Available at: https://doi.org/10.1016/j.jbusres.2020.10.050.

Kumar, H. (2022). Augmented reality in online retailing: A systematic review and research agenda. *International Journal of Retail & Distribution Management*, *50*(4), 537–559.

Laurell, C., Sandström, C., Berthold, A., & Larsson, D. (2019). Exploring barriers to adoption of virtual reality through social media analytics and machine learning — An assessment of technology, network, price and trialability. *Journal of Business Research*, *100*, 469–474.

Le, A. N. H., Ho, H. X., Nguyen, D. P., & Cheng, J. M. S. (2022). Dataset for cognition processes, motivations, spatial presence experience, and customer engagement in retail mobile apps. *Data in Brief*, *42*, 108198.

Lee, B., Brown, D., Lee, B., Hurter, C., Drucker, S., & Dwyer, T. (2020). Data visceralization: Enabling deeper understanding of data using virtual reality. *IEEE Transactions on Visualization and Computer Graphics*, *27*(2), 1095–1105.

Lee, H., Xu, Y., & Porterfield, A. (2022). Antecedents and moderators of consumer adoption toward AR-enhanced virtual try-on technology: A stimulus-organism-response approach. *International Journal of Consumer Studies*, *46*(4), 1319–1338.

Lee, H., Jung, T. H., tom Dieck, M. C., & Chung, N. (2020). Experiencing immersive virtual reality in museums. *Information & Management*, *57*(5), 103229. Available at: https://doi.org/10.1016/J.IM.2019.103229

Li, F., Trappey, A. J. C., Lee, C.-H., & Li, L. (2022). Immersive technology-enabled digital transformation in transportation fields: A literature overview. *Expert Systems with Applications*, 117459.

Liao, T. & Iliadis, A. (2021). A future so close: Mapping 10 years of promises and futures across the augmented reality development cycle. *New Media and Society*, *23*(2), 258–283. Available at: https://doi.org/10.1177/1461444820924623.

Lin, M. Y. C., Nguyen, T. T., Cheng, E. Y. L., Le, A. N. H., & Cheng, J. M. S. (2022). Proximity marketing and Bluetooth beacon technology: A dynamic mechanism leading to relationship program receptiveness. *Journal of Business Research*, *141*, 151–162.

Liu, R., Peng, C., Zhang, Y., Husarek, H., & Yu, Q. (2021). A survey of immersive technologies and applications for industrial product development. *Computers & Graphics*, *100*, 137–151.

Luangrath, A. W., Peck, J., Hedgcock, W., & Xu, Y. (2022). Observing product touch: The vicarious haptic effect in digital marketing and virtual reality. *Journal of Marketing Research*, *59*(2), 306–326. Available at: https://doi.org/10.1177/00222437211059540.

Ma, Y., Zhang, C., & Li, Y. (2023). Strategies for the retail platform to counteract match uncertainty: Virtual showroom and return or exchange policy. *Computers & Industrial Engineering*, *176*, 108832.

Mabrook, R. & Singer, J. B. (2019). Virtual reality, 360 video, and journalism studies: Conceptual approaches to immersive technologies. *Journalism Studies*, *20*(14), 2096–2112.

Martínez-Navarro, J., Bigné, E., Guixeres, J., Alcañiz, M., & Torrecilla, C. (2019). The influence of virtual reality in e-commerce. *Journal of Business Research*, *100*, 475–482. Available at: https://doi.org/10.1016/J.JBUSRES.2018.10.054.

McLean, G. & Wilson, A. (2019). Shopping in the digital world: Examining customer engagement through augmented reality mobile applications. *Computers in Human Behavior*, *101*, 210–224. Available at: https://doi.org/10.1016/J.CHB.2019.07.002.

Meissner, M., Pfeiffer, J., Peukert, C., Dietrich, H., & Pfeiffer, T. (2020). How virtual reality affects consumer choice. *Journal of Business Research*, *117*, 219–231. Available at: https://doi.org/10.1016/J.JBUSRES.2020.06.004.

Mihelj, M., Novak, D., & Beguš, S. (2014). *Virtual Reality Technology and Applications*. Springer Dordrecht.

Mishra, R., Singh, R. K., & Koles, B. (2021). Consumer decision-making in omnichannel retailing: Literature review and future research agenda. *International Journal of Consumer Studies*, *45*(2), 147–174. Available at: https://doi.org/10.1111/ijcs.12617.

Nussipova, G., Nordin, F., & Sörhammar, D. (2020). Value formation with immersive technologies: An activity perspective. *Journal of Business & Industrial Marketing*, *35*(3), 483–494. Available at: https://doi.org/10.1108/JBIM-12-2018-0407.

Pangarkar, A., Arora, V., & Shukla, Y. (2022). Exploring phygital omnichannel luxury retailing for immersive customer experience: The role of rapport and social engagement. *Journal of Retailing and Consumer Services*, *68*

(December 2021), 103001. Available at: https://doi.org/10.1016/j.jretconser.2022.103001.

Parise, S., Guinan, P. J., & Kafka, R. (2016). Solving the crisis of immediacy: How digital technology can transform the customer experience. *Business Horizons*, *59*(4), 411–420. Available at: https://doi.org/10.1016/j.bushor.2016.03.004.

Peterson, R. A. & Balasubramanian, S. (2002). Retailing in the 21st century: Reflections and prologue to research. *Journal of Retailing*, *78*(1), 9–16. Available at: https://doi.org/10.1016/S0022-4359(01)00062-8.

Petit, O., Velasco, C., & Spence, C. (2019). Digital sensory marketing: Integrating new technologies into multisensory online experience. *Journal of Interactive Marketing*, *45*(1), 42–61. Available at: https://doi.org/10.1016/j.intmar.2018.07.0.

Pfeiffer, J., Pfeiffer, T., Meißner, M., & Weiß, E. (2020). Eye-tracking-based classification of information search behavior using machine learning: Evidence from experiments in physical shops and virtual reality shopping environments. *Information Systems Research*, *31*(3), 675–691. Available at: https://doi.org/10.1287/ISRE.2019.0907.

Pillai, R., Sivathanu, B., & Dwivedi, Y. K. (2020). Shopping intention at AI-powered automated retail stores (AIPARS). *Journal of Retailing and Consumer Services*, *57*, 102207. Available at: https://doi.org/10.1016/J.JRETCONSER.2020.102207.

Plotkina, D. & Saurel, H. (2019). Me or just like me? The role of virtual try-on and physical appearance in apparel M-retailing. *Journal of Retailing and Consumer Services*, *51*, 362–377.

Podsakoff, P. M., MacKenzie, S. B., Bachrach, D. G., & Podsakoff, N. P. (2005). The influence of management journals in the 1980s and 1990s. *Strategic management journal*, *26*(5), 473–488.

Ponis, S. T., Plakas, G., Agalianos, K., Aretoulaki, E., Gayialis, S. P., & Andrianopoulos, A. (2020). Augmented reality and gamification to increase productivity and job satisfaction in the warehouse of the future. *Procedia Manufacturing*, *51*, 1621–1628.

Prabhakaran, A., Mahamadu, A. M., & Mahdjoubi, L. (2022). Understanding the challenges of immersive technology use in the architecture and construction industry: A systematic review. *Automation in Construction*, *137*(2020), 104228. Available at: https://doi.org/10.1016/j.autcon.2022.104228.

Qin, H., Osatuyi, B., & Xu, L. (2021). How mobile augmented reality applications affect continuous use and purchase intentions: A cognition-affect-conation perspective. *Journal of Retailing and Consumer Services*, *63*, 102680. Available at: https://doi.org/10.1016/J.JRETCONSER.2021.102680.

Radianti, J., Majchrzak, T. A., Fromm, J., & Wohlgenannt, I. (2020). A systematic review of immersive virtual reality applications for higher education: Design elements, lessons learned, and research agenda. *Computers & Education*, *147*, 103778. Available at: https://doi.org/10.1016/J.COMPEDU.2019.103778.

Rauschnabel, P. A., Felix, R., Hinsch, C., Shahab, H., & Alt, F. (2022). What is XR? Towards a Framework for Augmented and Virtual Reality. *Computers in Human Behavior*, *133*(May 2021), 107289. Available at: https://doi.org/10.1016/j.chb.2022.107289.

Rauschnabel, P. A., Babin, B. J., tom Dieck, M. C., Krey, N., & Jung, T. (2022). What is augmented reality marketing? Its definition, complexity, and future. *Journal of Business Research*, *142*, 1140–1150. Available at: https://doi.org/10.1016/j.jbusres.2021.12.084.

Reinartz, W., Wiegand, N., & Imschloss, M. (2019). The impact of digital transformation on the retailing value chain. *International Journal of Research in Marketing*, *36*(3), 350–366. Available at: https://doi.org/10.1016/j.ijresmar.2018.12.002.

Riar, M., Xi, N., Korbel, J. J., Zarnekow, R., & Hamari, J. (2023). Using augmented reality for shopping: A framework for AR induced consumer behavior, literature review and future agenda. *Internet Research*, *33*(1), 242–279. Available at: https://doi.org/10.1108/INTR-08-2021–0611.

Riegger, A.-S., Klein, J. F., Merfeld, K., & Henkel, S. (2021). Technology-enabled personalization in retail stores: Understanding drivers and barriers. *Journal of Business Research*, *123*, 140–155.

Ringler, C., Sirianni, N. J., & Christenson, B. (2021). The power of consequential product sounds. *Journal of Retailing*, *97*(2), 288–300. Available at: https://doi.org/10.1016/J.JRETAI.2020.09.002.

Roggeveen, A. L. & Sethuraman, R. (2020). Customer-interfacing retail technologies in 2020 & beyond: An integrative framework and research directions. *Journal of Retailing*, *96*(3), 299–309. Available at: https://doi.org/10.1016/j.jretai.2020.08.001.

Roggeveen, A. L., Grewal, D., & Schweiger, E. B. (2020). The DAST framework for retail atmospherics: The impact of in-and out-of-store retail journey touchpoints on the customer experience. *Journal of Retailing*, *96*(1), 128–137.

Rudkowski, J., Heney, C., Yu, H., Sedlezky, S., & Gunn, F. (2020). Here today, gone tomorrow? Mapping and modeling the pop-up retail customer journey.

Journal of Retailing and Consumer Services, *54*, 101698. Available at: https://doi.org/10.1016/j.jretconser.2018.11.003.

Sadamali Jayawardena, N., Thaichon, P., Quach, S., Razzaq, A., & Behl, A. (2023). The persuasion effects of virtual reality (VR) and augmented reality (AR) video advertisements: A conceptual review. *Journal of Business Research*, *160*, 113739. Available at: https://doi.org/10.1016/J.JBUSRES.2023.113739.

Schnack, A., Wright, M. J., & Holdershaw, J. L. (2021). Does the locomotion technique matter in an immersive virtual store environment? — Comparing motion-tracked walking and instant teleportation. *Journal of Retailing and Consumer Services*, *58*, 102266. Available at: https://doi.org/10.1016/J.JRETCONSER.2020.102266.

Scholz, J. & Smith, A. N. (2016). Augmented reality: Designing immersive experiences that maximize consumer engagement. *Business Horizons*, *59*(2), 149–161. Available at: https://doi.org/10.1016/J.BUSHOR.2015.10.003.

Sherman, W. R. & Craig, A. B. (2018). *Understanding Virtual Reality: Interface, Application, and Design*. Morgan Kaufmann.

Simmonds, L., Bellman, S., Kennedy, R., Nenycz-Thiel, M., & Bogomolova, S. (2020). Moderating effects of prior brand usage on visual attention to video advertising and recall: An eye-tracking investigation. *Journal of Business Research*, *111*, 241–248. Available at: https://doi.org/10.1016/j.jbusres.2019.02.062.

Slater, M. (2009). Place illusion and plausibility can lead to realistic behaviour in immersive virtual environments. *Philosophical Transactions of the Royal Society B: Biological Sciences*, *364*(1535), 3549–3557.

Slater, M. & Wilbur, S. (1997). A framework for immersive virtual environments (FIVE): Speculations on the role of presence in virtual environments. *Presence: Teleoperators & Virtual Environments*, *6*(6), 603–616.

Song, H. K., Baek, E. & Choo, H. J. (2020). Try-on experience with augmented reality comforts your decision: Focusing on the roles of immersion and psychological ownership. *Information Technology & People*, *33*(4), 1214–1234. Available at: https://doi.org/10.1108/ITP-02-2019-0092.

Souiden, N., Ladhari, R., & Chiadmi, N. E. (2019). New trends in retailing and services. *Journal of Retailing and Consumer Services*, *50*(2018), 286–288. Available at: https://doi.org/10.1016/j.jretconser.2018.07.023.

Stanney, K., Lawson, B. D., Rokers, B., Dennison, M., Fidopiastis, C., Stoffregen, T., Weech, S., & Fulvio, J. M. (2020). Identifying causes of and solutions for cybersickness in immersive technology: Reformulation of a research and development agenda. *International Journal of Human–Computer Interaction*, *36*(19), 1783–1803.

Statista. (2022). Immersive technology consumer market revenue worldwide from 2018 to 2023, by segment. Statista.Com. Available at: https://www.statista.com/statistics/936078/worldwide-consumer-immersive-technology-market-revenue/.

Steinicke, F. (2016). *Being Really Virtual*. Springer. Available at: https://doi.org/10.1007/978-3-319-43078-2.

Steuer, J., Biocca, F., & Levy, M. R. (1995). Defining virtual reality: Dimensions determining telepresence. *Communication in the Age of Virtual Reality*, *33*, 37–39.

Suh, A. & Prophet, J. (2018). The state of immersive technology research: A literature analysis. *Computers in Human Behavior*, *86*, 77–90. Available at: https://doi.org/10.1016/J.CHB.2018.04.019.

Sung, E. C., Bae, S., Han, D. I. D., & Kwon, O. (2021). Consumer engagement via interactive artificial intelligence and mixed reality. *International Journal of Information Management*, *60*, 102382. Available at: https://doi.org/10.1016/j.ijinfomgt.2021.102382.

Sung, E. C., Bae, S., Han, D.-I. D., & Kwon, O. (2021). Consumer engagement via interactive artificial intelligence and mixed reality. *International Journal of Information Management*, *60*, 102382.

Tan, Y.-C., Chandukala, S. R., & Reddy, S. K. (2022). Augmented reality in retail and its impact on sales. *Journal of Marketing*, *86*(1), 48–66.

Tang, Y. M., Chau, K. Y., Kwok, A. P. K., Zhu, T., & Ma, X. (2022). A systematic review of immersive technology applications for medical practice and education-trends, application areas, recipients, teaching contents, evaluation methods, and performance. *Educational Research Review*, *35*, 100429. Available at: https://doi.org/10.1016/j.edurev.2021.100429.

Trappey, A. J. C., Trappey, C. V, Chao, M.-H., & Wu, C.-T. (2022). VR-enabled engineering consultation chatbot for integrated and intelligent manufacturing services. *Journal of Industrial Information Integration*, *26*, 100331.

Tuena, C., Pedroli, E., Trimarchi, P. D., Gallucci, A., Chiappini, M., Goulene, K., Gaggioli, A., Riva, G., Lattanzio, F., & Giunco, F. (2020). Usability issues of clinical and research applications of virtual reality in older people: A systematic review. *Frontiers in Human Neuroscience*, *14*, 93.

Van Kerrebroeck, H., Brengman, M., & Willems, K. (2017). When brands come to life: Experimental research on the vividness effect of Virtual Reality in transformational marketing communications. *Virtual Reality*, *21*, 177–191.

Vanderroost, M., Ragaert, P., Verwaeren, J., De Meulenaer, B., De Baets, B., & Devlieghere, F. (2017). The digitization of a food package's life cycle:

Existing and emerging computer systems in the logistics and post-logistics phase. *Computers in Industry*, *87*, 15–30.

Vo, K. N., Le, A. N. H., Thanh Tam, L., & Ho Xuan, H. (2022). Immersive experience and customer responses towards mobile augmented reality applications: The moderating role of technology anxiety. *Cogent Business & Management*, *9*(1), 2063778. Available at: https://doi.org/10.1080/23311975.2022.2063778.

Wang, C. L. (2021). New frontiers and future directions in interactive marketing: Inaugural Editorial. *Journal of Research in Interactive Marketing*, *15*(1), 1–9.

Wanick, V., Stallwood, J., & Bazaki, E. (2023). The Use of augmented reality to enhance consumer experience: The case of Kohl's snapchat virtual closet and Sephora virtual artist. In *Reinventing Fashion Retailing: Digitalising, Gamifying, Entrepreneuring* (pp. 55–71). Springer.

Wedel, M., Bigné, E., & Zhang, J. (2020). Virtual and augmented reality: Advancing research in consumer marketing. *International Journal of Research in Marketing*, *37*(3), 443–465. Available at: https://doi.org/10.1016/j.ijresmar.2020.04.004.

Wolf, M., Teizer, J., Wolf, B., Bükrü, S., & Solberg, A. (2022). Investigating hazard recognition in augmented virtuality for personalized feedback in construction safety education and training. *Advanced Engineering Informatics*, *51*, 101469.

Xi, N. & Hamari, J. (2021). Shopping in virtual reality: A literature review and future agenda. *Journal of Business Research*, *134*, 37–58. Available at: https://doi.org/10.1016/J.JBUSRES.2021.04.075.

Xue, L., Parker, C. J., & Hart, C. A. (2023). How augmented reality can enhance fashion retail: A UX design perspective. *International Journal of Retail & Distribution Management*, *51*(1), 59–80.

Yim, M. Y.-C., Chu, S.-C., & Sauer, P. L. (2017). Is augmented reality technology an effective tool for e-commerce? An interactivity and vividness perspective. *Journal of Interactive Marketing*, *39*(1), 89–103. Available at: https://doi.org/10.1016/j.intmar.2017.04.001.

Yuan, C., Wang, S., Liu, Y., & Ma, J. W. (2023). Factors influencing parasocial relationship in the virtual reality shopping environment: The moderating role of celebrity endorser dynamism. *Asia Pacific Journal of Marketing and Logistics*, *35*(2), 398–413.

Yung, R., Khoo-Lattimore, C., & Potter, L. E. (2021). Virtual reality and tourism marketing: Conceptualizing a framework on presence, emotion, and intention.

Current Issues in Tourism, *24*(11), 1505–1525. Available at: https://doi.org/10.1080/13683500.2020.1820454.

Zhang, T., Wang, W. Y. C., Cao, L., & Wang, Y. (2019). The role of virtual try-on technology in online purchase decision from consumers' aspect. *Internet Research*, *29*(3), 529–551. Available at: https://doi.org/10.1108/IntR-12-2017-0540.

Zhang, Y., Liu, H., Kang, S.-C., & Al-Hussein, M. (2020). Virtual reality applications for the built environment: Research trends and opportunities. *Automation in Construction*, *118*, 103311.

Zhang, Z., Wen, F., Sun, Z., Guo, X., He, T., & Lee, C. (2022). Artificial intelligence-enabled sensing technologies in the 5G/internet of things era: From virtual reality/augmented reality to the digital twin. *Advanced Intelligent Systems*, *4*(7), 2100228.

Zhao, Z. & Balagué, C. (2015). Designing branded mobile apps: Fundamentals and recommendations. *Business Horizons*, *58*(3), 305–315.

Zhou, F., Zhang, N., Wang, N., & Mou, J. (2023). Design affordance in VR and customization intention: Is customer inspiration a missing link? *Technological Forecasting and Social Change*, *192*, 122594. Available at: https://doi.org/10.1016/J.TECHFORE.2023.122594.

https://doi.org/10.1142/9789811286100_0008

Chapter 8

The Impact of Leaders' Curiosity on the Intention to Introduce IoT-Based Products: The Case of Vietnam

Manh Phan Dinh[*,†,§] and Le Tran Thi Huynh[‡,II]

[†]*Department of Business Administration, Graduate School of International Social Sciences, Yokohama National University, Japan*

[‡]*Faculty of Economics and Tourism, Kien Giang University, Vietnam*

[§]*phan-manh-dj@ynu.jp*
[II]*tthle@vnkgu.edu.vn*

Abstract

This study explores the relationships between leaders' curiosity and the intention to introduce Internet of Things (IoT)-based products (or product innovation); and the moderating role of different moderators on the above relationships. The chapter uses the survey-based methodology and scanning electron microscope (SEM) analysis technique with the sample collected in Vietnam. The findings show that there is a positive impact of the curiosity of leaders on the intention to introduce IoT-based products at firms and the effects of different variables negatively moderating the above relationships. Accordingly, people with more curiosity may lead them to accelerate the innovation to introduce IoT-based products

[*]Corresponding author.
Received on December 5, 2022; accepted on March 23, 2023

at firms. Our study is one of the first to demonstrate the impact of leaders' characteristics in driving IoT adoption and, more broadly, innovation at companies. The second theoretical contribution is our research findings have introduced two new moderating variables for business research on the impact of personal traits of leaders on innovation (in the case of IoT-based products). The implications of this research are also presented.

Keywords: IoT-based Products, Leadership Traits, Curiosity, IoT Adoption.

1. Introduction and Motivation

The Internet of Things (IoT) is a contemporary wireless communication paradigm. According to the basic assumption, many aspects of our environment interact with one another to accomplish shared objectives (Giusto *et al.*, 2010). The IoT's main strength is its substantial effect on prospective users' behavior and everyday lives. From the user's perspective, the IoT is most apparent at work and at home. The new paradigm could soon play significant roles in home automation, life support, electronic health, and reinforcement learning applications.

Business users perceive the most apparent benefits in automation and industrial production, logistics, business/process management, intelligent people, and goods transportation. Therefore, it's no surprise that the US National Information Council named IoT one of six possible disruptive civil engineering technologies (National Intelligence Council, 2008). By 2025, Internet nodes can be found in food, furniture, and printed papers. It is expected that "public demand coupled with technological advancements would likely result in broad deployment of IoT".

Concerning leaders and their reasonings and styles to decide on innovative activities at firms, the paper by Aarum (2000) offers some ideas. Accordingly, this subject is addressed via a study of 200 managers from eight companies. Based on Jung's typology, Aarum questions whether managers' intuition is a valuable contribution to their organizations and examines the problem-solving and decision-making styles of 33 managers regarding organizational effectiveness. Twenty-three percent of managers exhibited a "creative-innovative" decision-making approach. This article claims that intuition as a decision-making style appears to be associated with organizational efficiency. Multiple administrators are intuitive.

It remains to be established whether intuitive managers are more effective than others. Thus, intuitive thinking plays a specific role in explaining some aspects of the science of decision-making.

Regarding the leadership-relevant drivers determining the decision to adopt technology like IoT, the present literature addresses two leadership approaches, technical (or hard facets) and artistic/intuitive (or soft facets). The task (or technical) group is becoming more critical in established businesses focusing on productivity and cost reduction. However, in the context of IoT and other 4.0 technologies, artistic viewpoint (or soft aspects, like curiosity) appears to play a more significant role. This is because the latter group can assist companies in organizing resources, fostering creativity and innovation, and addressing problems arising from IoT technology's unique features.

At the same time, recent research indicates that curiosity (as an indicator of intuition) should be promoted in the workplace as a good predictor of job success (Mussel, 2013; Mussel *et al.*, 2012). Additionally, Dewett (2007) and Walsh and Nagaoka (2009) report that creative performance is more motivated by internal task motivation than by extrinsic (monetary) incentives. Curiosity or the "want to know" is probably at the heart of this intrinsic drive (Schiefele *et al.*, 1992), since it leads efforts toward investigation and enables the connection of new signals to chances to learn, develop, and create (Kashdan *et al.*, 2004). As a result, more curious individuals might seek fresh ideas and solutions even before the situation deteriorates to a crisis level, just because they are naturally interested in comprehending and gaining new information and abilities. Curiosity is therefore considered an important trait that accelerates the process of making decisions on adopting IoT for product development at Vietnamese firms.

The current business and academic gaps in the above arguments inspire us to conduct this study to explore the mechanism of intuitive styles concerning curiosity in the process of making decisions to introduce IoT-based products in the case of Vietnam. The relevant moderators are also introduced to test the conditions in which the impact of intuitive components of leaders' curiosity will be activated, leading to decisions to introduce IoT-based products at firms.

2. Literature Review

2.1. *The role of intuitive mindsets in strategic decision-making to adopt IoT*

2.1.1. *Rational versus intuitive strategic decision-making styles*

Academic research on planning and strategic decision-making has typically contrasted technocratic (rational) with intuitive decision-making styles (Elbanna, 2010), arguing that the former produces superior choices. A technocratic style is characterized by a highly rational and well-organized (systematic) procedure that prompts managers to divide a problem into smaller pieces necessary for resolution, to search for and evaluate relevant objective information, and prefers the use of quantitative tools when evaluating and selecting among alternatives (Grünig *et al.*, 2005). On the other hand, an intuitive approach entails the application of "a multitude of facts, patterns, ideas, methods, abstractions, and generally what we refer to as formal knowledge or beliefs that are imprinted on our brains" (Simon, 1987).

2.1.2. *Research on rational and intuitive reasoning processes with cross-cultural differences*

In terms of cultural perspective, cultural psychologists have shown that the Chinese think more holistically and intuitively than Westerners (Masuda and Nisbett, 2001). Westerners were shown to value formal reasoning above intuition more than Chinese and Korean people. In comparison to European Americans, Chinese and Korean individuals were seen to depend more on intuitive methods of making decisions (Norenzayan *et al.*, 2002). Not only are there cultural variations in terms of proclivity for intuitive vs analytical thinking, but Buchtel and Norenzayan (2008) also discovered cultural disparities in terms of the perceived importance of analytical (rational) versus intuitive reasoning. East Asians regarded intuitive thinking as more essential and reasonable than Western participants. This finding could be because East Asians have a more holistic, field-dependent form of attention, while Westerners demonstrate a more concentrated, analytical, field-independent mode of attention (Masuda and Nisbett, 2001).

Additionally, Westerners prefer to categorize ideas using deterministic principles, while East Asians depend more on similarities and connections between objects (Norenzayan *et al.*, 2002). When confronted with contradictions, Westerners are prone to encounter conceptual conflicts and polarize their choices, that is, to choose between opposing views on a principled basis. In contrast, East Asians want to avoid such confrontations and are eager to find a middle ground between diametrically opposed views (Peng and Nisbett, 1999).

However, there is a growing reservoir of data that refutes the conventional dichotomy between an intuitive East and an analytic West. For instance, a study of Chinese and American adult students enrolled in higher education (Huang and Sisco, 1994) showed that their analytical and synthesis thinking processes were identical. Allinson and Hayes (2000) found that British corporate managers were more intuitive than Singaporean managers in their study of cross-cultural differences in cognitive style. Similarly, Abramson and colleagues discovered that Canadian MBA students outperformed their Japanese counterparts on the "intuiting" element of the cognitive thinking style (Abramson *et al.*, 1993). In contrast to what one would anticipate from the intuitive East, a subsequent expansion of this research revealed that Japanese participants made slower and more deliberate decisions than Canadians or a similar group of Americans (Abramson *et al.*, 1996).

2.1.3. *The limitations of rational reasoning process and the important role of intuitive reasoning processes in accelerating innovation at firms*

Previous research has shown that certain decision features, such as choice uncertainty (Elbanna and Child, 2007), decision frequency of occurrence (Papadakis *et al.*, 1998), or decision motivation, can affect decision outcomes and decision processes (Papadakis *et al.*, 1998). Based on these findings, evaluating strategic decision-making within its specific environment is essential.

Ilori and Irefin (1997) highlighted the need to use rational-analytic and intuitive-emotional approaches while making technical decisions. They assert that these processes interact and are influenced by contextual factors such as varying degrees of ambiguity, certainty, risk, and pressure.

These interactions take place at various levels within the organization, including lower-level technical personnel who, according to the authors, initiate the decision-making process; middle-level management who become emotionally invested in a particular issue; and upper-level management who have the final say. According to Kester *et al.* (2011), extensive decision processes (rationality) are harmful to new product performance when faced with considerable technical and demand uncertainty due to the challenges of data gathering.

Other academics have discovered evidence that, depending on the complexity of the task, intuitive thought can be just as effective and accurate as analytical (Dijksterhuis, 2004). When jobs cannot be completed through analysis, such as when they demand pattern identification or are complex and time-sensitive, intuition could be the superior mode of thought (Wilson, 2002).

2.2. *Some discussions for the intuitive reasoning process for making decisions to apply IoT to new products in Vietnam*

Relationship (or soft or intuitive) facets are essential to promote firm performance as well as innovation. Therefore, researching soft facets is the key to exploring the factors that impact innovation adoption. Further exploration is even more critical in the case of IoT, as this technology is so complex that many issues are out of leaders' reach. Thus, soft skills with intuitive capability will emerge to solve these untraditional issues.

The above literature has shown that a rationally based decision-making style is popular for a stable environment and long-term orientation with abundant data and information so that the leaders can analyze and set strategic plans. In contrast, intuitive decision-making is popular for dynamic and complex environments and short-term orientation with limited data and information. Therefore, leaders must rely on their observation of similar cases and sensing capacity to make strategic decisions. From another perspective of culture, the rational decision-making style is prevalent in Western cultures like the US or European countries. In contrast, the intuitively-based decision-making style is most dominant in

Eastern cultures like Japan, South Korea, and China (although the opposite is sometimes true).

In the case of Vietnam, it can be inferred that Vietnamese leaders are more oriented toward the intuitive style to promote IoT-based product development. Vietnamese culture is closer to the Eastern group, similar to Japan, China, or South Korea. Moreover, IoT-based products have complex characteristics from both the technology and market demand perspectives that require intuitive styles to undergo a quick decision-making process. This process is especially suitable during the emergence of COVID-19, which exacerbates the uncertainty of the business environment, requiring leaders to be sensitive to the challenges and opportunities to make decisions on adopting IoT technology with new products.

2.3. *The role of curiosity as a component of intuition-related traits*

Curiosity is the urge to investigate new, uncertain, complicated, and ambiguous situations. There is a sense of curiosity in a setting in which learning is possible. There is a drive to seek out new experiences, to see what occurs or how others respond. Curiosity is a psychological concept that includes openness to experience, novelty seeking, desire for cognition, intrinsic motivation, tolerance of ambiguity, uncertainty, frustration tolerance, and sensation seeking (Kashdan *et al.*, 2018). Additionally, early accounts of exploratory behavior depicted curiosity as a rather unpleasant emotion, whereas modern theories define it as a highly joyful one (Litman and Jimerson, 2004). However, these contradictory views on the nature of curiosity are not mutually exclusive. Keller *et al.* (1994) found that most motivating systems involve negative and positive emotional experiences. Similarly, it has been observed that curiosity involves two distinct types of reactions to novelty, both of which help to stimulate exploration: (a) pleasant emotions of interest and (b) somewhat unpleasant feelings of uncertainty (Litman and Jimerson, 2004).

Comparably, the concept and nature of intuitive decision-making in particular have received considerable attention in the organizational psychology literature and have been articulated as a managerial means of moving beyond the reliance on rational, numerical, and complex flows of data to make quicker or post-doc rationalized judgments based on what research participants have described as "gut feelings" recognizable within the business environment (Lank and Lank, 1995). Thus, when comparing the characteristics of curiosity and attributes of intuition, the shared components of these two traits of the people who own them depend on the feelings and sensational capacity in terms of psychological activities. We can therefore conclude that curiosity could be a component of a person's intuition. In other words, a person with more curiosity will use more intuition in his or her life.

2.4. *Technical interoperability barriers to IoT adoption and the need for curiosity*

2.4.1. *The IoT-based products across the industries*

IoT-based products are present and utilized in many industries. The use of IoT devices varies greatly in the healthcare industry. Wearable gadgets, such as fitness trackers and smartwatches, medical devices, such as pacemakers and insulin pumps, and hospital equipment, such as IV pumps and ventilators, are some of the most popular IoT device types being used in healthcare. All of these gadgets gather information that can be utilized to enhance patient care and boost the effectiveness of healthcare institutions.

In the manufacturing industries, to increase the effectiveness of production lines and decrease waste, IoT devices are utilized. IoT gadgets can be used to track product manufacturing, keep an eye on equipment health, and manage the material flow. IoT devices can also be utilized to provide information about product quality and to increase worker safety. The industrial sensor is one of the most popular IoT device types used in production. Industrial sensors are used to keep tabs on material flow, equipment health, and product output. Additionally, data about product quality and worker safety can be provided via industrial sensors, which are making it possible for manufacturers to increase the effectiveness of manufacturing lines and decrease waste.

IoT gadgets are utilized in retail to enhance customer satisfaction and boost revenue. Inventory tracking, customer loyalty programs, and data collection on consumer behavior are all possible with IoT devices. IoT devices can also be utilized to offer real-time customer support, targeted marketing, and personalized suggestions. The retail industry is transforming in a number of ways thanks to IoT devices. By giving retailers access to real-time information about the behavior of their customers, IoT devices are transforming retail in one of the most significant ways possible. Retailers can offer a more specialized shopping experience thanks to this data. IoT devices are also being utilized to boost the effectiveness of retail operations, including consumer loyalty programs and inventory management.

In transportation areas, to increase driver safety and ease traffic congestion, IoT devices are being employed in the transportation sector. Vehicle tracking, speed regulation, and condition monitoring are all possible with IoT devices. Additionally, IoT gadgets can be utilized to offer information on traffic conditions and boost the effectiveness of transportation systems. The GPS tracker is one of the most popular IoT device types utilized in the transportation industry. Vehicles' locations are tracked using GPS trackers, which can also be used to monitor their speed and motion. To increase the effectiveness of transportation systems, GPS trackers can also be employed to offer information regarding traffic conditions.

In agricultural industries, IoT devices have grown more and more important. They are being used to increase agricultural productivity and use less water and fertilizers in agriculture. IoT devices can be used to track the whereabouts of farm animals, keep an eye on the health of crops, and regulate irrigation water flow. By using less water and fertilizers, these advances are assisting farmers in increasing the production of their crops. Farmers can make better decisions about planting, irrigation, and crop upkeep because of the data acquired by IoT devices.

With regards to smart home industries, IoT devices are the core of systems used in smart homes, which are gaining popularity. Homes are utilizing IoT devices to increase home security, cut down on energy use, and enhance the quality of life. They can be used to keep an eye on the state of the house, locate family members, and manage the performance of home appliances. Additionally, data from IoT devices about air quality can be used to boost the effectiveness of home security systems. IoT devices will eventually be utilized to operate a wide range of home systems and appliances and will be a crucial component of the future smart home.

In the aviation industry, the use of IoT devices is also extensive. IoT devices are being utilized to increase the safety of passengers and crew members in the aviation industry, which is one of the most strictly regulated sectors in the world. By supplying information that may be utilized to increase the safety of pilots and passengers, IoT is revolutionizing the aviation sector. IoT gadgets can be used to track an aircraft's location, manage its speed, and keep an eye on its health. To increase the effectiveness of aircraft operations and offer data on the weather, IoT devices can also be deployed, which could ultimately result in cheaper airline costs.

2.4.2. *Technical interoperability barriers to IoT adoption and the need for curiosity*

According to Hans and Anthony (2008), technical interoperability is "the ability to operate software and exchange information in a heterogeneous network, i.e., one large network made of several different local area networks [or computer systems]". IoT interoperability is the capacity for multiple components within an IoT deployment to effectively communicate, share data, and perform together to achieve a shared outcome. Organizations must be able to transmit and understand data throughout all connections from devices to the cloud (Pratt, 2021).

The lack of automatic, widespread interoperability not only slows the consumer or home IoT markets but also hinders progress in civic and commercial IoT deployments. Smart city projects can require hundreds or thousands of devices in numerous categories to work in concert to achieve the technology's full advantages. Industrial IoT investments with different device requirements and physical barriers could also necessitate the use of multiple communication protocols (Pratt, 2021).

2.4.3. *The need for curiosity to solve technical interoperability barriers to develop IoT-based products*

To achieve technical interoperability, the company can license or make its intellectual property available to others in a variety of mutually beneficial ways. Several companies can also collaborate to facilitate interoperability between their respective products. Finally, the industry can adopt technical standards that, where implemented, facilitate technical interoperability.

Many within the IoT community, including manufacturers and engineers who design connected ecosystems for use, work together to develop standards that address interoperability challenges. Multiple standards organizations have rallied around the cause, but there's no dominant common standard that's applicable in every IoT use case. Many competing government organizations, standards bodies, industry coalitions, corporations, academic institutions, and even individual contributors make contributions in this space, with significant variance by industry and even location sometimes in the same industry (Pratt, 2021).

To overcome the technical interoperability barriers mentioned above, leaders need to be curious and seek to understand the technical problems and solutions so that they can select the right technology for their IoT-based projects.

2.5. *The role of curiosity to develop IoT-based products in the context of Vietnamese culture*

Vietnamese culture is a low uncertainty avoidance culture that is relevant to high curiosity: According to a research project by Hofstede (2001), Vietnam scores 30 on this dimension of uncertainty avoidance, which means that practice is more important than ideals in low uncertainty avoidance cultures, and deviation from the norm is more readily accepted. People in low uncertainty avoidance cultures think regulations should be simple and clear, and confusing or ineffective rules should be abandoned or modified. Work is done when it is needed, but not for its purpose; accuracy and punctuality are not natural; and innovation is not seen as a threat.

Furthermore, uncertainty avoidance, a critical cultural dimension, is closely associated with information seeking and risk tolerance and can reflect cultural differences. Cultures with high uncertainty avoidance display more rigidity and a lack of openness to innovation, as compared to low uncertainty avoidance cultures, in which people are more tolerant of ambiguity and display a willingness to take risks (Hofstede, 2001). This suggests a lack of inhibition to approaching problems.

At the same time, curiosity is associated with pleasure derived from discoveries, stimulating positive effects, and facilitating positive outcomes from the information learned (Lauriola *et al.*, 2015). Curiosity is associated with openness to experience, extraversion, fun-seeking, and developing new ideas in the workplace (Litman and Mussel, 2013), which suggests a moderate to high tolerance for uncertainty. This perspective was further reiterated by Litman (2010), who finds ambiguity tolerance to be positively associated with curiosity. Moreover, curiosity underlies carefree intellectual bent of mind and knowledge exploration (Lauriola *et al.*, 2015). For instance, curiosity is associated with pleasure derived from discoveries, stimulating positive affects, and facilitating positive outcomes from information (Kashdan *et al.*, 2004). As a result, curiosity to some extent has a positive association with low uncertainty avoidance. In this case, curiosity is an important and compulsory trait of leaders to introduce IoT-based products in Vietnamese companies.

2.6. *Research gaps, research objectives, and research questions*

2.6.1. *Research gaps and the necessity of our paper*

For the case of IoT-based products, due to the radical changes in technology and relevant products, leading to an insufficient workforce with relevant skills and pre-knowledge as well as the absence of business cases for this new technology, there is a need for entrepreneurship, adventure-based spirits, and quick and intuitive decision-making styles that can be traced back to the curiosity trait of managers. When leaders are more curious, they are more likely to accumulate the necessary knowledge and the nature of a variety of phenomena and events related to IoT technology to solve the problems of technical interoperability. Furthermore, owing to the effect of situations that moderate the relationship between the personal trait of curiosity (of leaders) and the intention to introduce IoT-based products, this chapter presents two moderators: job variety and educational backgrounds in social sciences, arts, and humanities.

2.6.2. *Research objectives*

RO1: To test the impact of the curiosity of leaders on the intention to introduce IoT-based products at firms.

RO2: To test the moderating effect of job variety of leaders on the above relationship.

RO3: To test the moderating effect of leaders' educational backgrounds in social sciences, arts, and humanities on the above relationship.

2.6.3. *Research questions*

RQ1: How does the curiosity of leaders impact the intention to introduce IoT-based products at firms?

RQ1: How does the job variety of leaders moderate the relationship between the curiosity of leaders and the intention to introduce IoT-based products at firms?

RQ1: How do educational backgrounds (of leaders) in social sciences, arts, and humanities moderate the relationship between the curiosity of leaders and the intention to introduce IoT-based products at firms?

3. Research Framework and Hypothesis Development

3.1. *Research framework (Figure 1)*

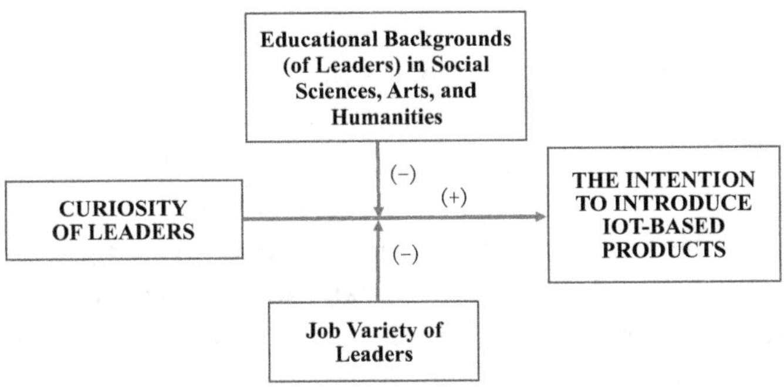

Figure 1. Research framework.

3.2. *Rationales for hypotheses*

3.2.1. *Curiosity and the intention to introduce IoT-based products*

Curiosity encourages enthusiastic and curious leaders to learn about a wide range of occurrences and events, which helps them address technological interoperability issues. It is possible that two different types of epistemic curiosity, diversive and particular, are components of one underlying epistemic curiosity dimension, namely a desire to know, triggered by knowledge gaps. Curiosity seems to be distinct from experience-seeking and worry. Curiosity is linked to cognitive needs, intellectual engagement, and receptivity to new ideas. Curious individuals love the process of learning and thinking (Mussel, 2010) and work hard to manage their attention and self-regulation (Schmeichel *et al.*, 2003). Due to dramatic changes in technology and products, there is a need for entrepreneurship and an adventure-based attitude that can be linked to the curiosity of leaders (C-level). Curiosity encourages leaders to learn about a wide range of phenomena and events to solve the issues related to the nature of IoT technology. Thus, executives' curiosity can anticipate their firms' desire to introduce IoT-based products:

H1: The curiosity of leaders has a positive relationship with the intention to introduce IoT-based products to firms.

3.2.2. *Job variety as a moderator*

Job variety is described by Hackman and Lawler (1971) as "the degree to which workers must execute a broad range of activities and/or utilize a diversity of equipment and procedures in their work" (p. 265). In other words, job variety involves utilizing diverse abilities and talents and engaging in various activities (Hackman and Oldham, 1976). Job variety (a significant number of jobs that the leaders have to do at work) also indicates that the jobs are *complex and mentally challenging* (Hackman and Lawler, 1971), and individuals are expected to discover new strategies for performing them. The perception of challenge can help individuals "invest more efforts to successfully fulfill the demands entailed by the job" (Cohen-Meitar *et al.*, 2009, p. 364) and will result in greater creativity. A meta-analysis conducted by Marinova *et al.* (2015) reveals that high-complexity jobs stimulate change-oriented behaviors. High-complexity jobs are multifaceted, are less specified (Humphrey *et al.*, 2007), and offer tremendous potential for creativity. In high-complexity jobs, leaders have more chances to discover new ideas, look for novel solutions and methodologies, and solve nontraditional problems in their work (Shalley and Gilson, 2004). At the same time, complex jobs are more mentally challenging and require the use of diverse advanced skills (Tierney and Farmer, 2002) and the development of new skills to address the challenging job demands (Audenaert *et al.*, 2016).

Pan *et al.* (2012) found that empowered employees working in organic structures, in which the jobs are complex and challenging, displayed higher levels of creativity than employees working in mechanistic structures. In the case of IoT-based products, the job of the leaders (who have the significant onus to make decisions to plan to introduce IoT-based products) is highly varied, signaling that it is very mentally challenging and complex. The complexity and challenging nature of the jobs of the leaders will naturally lead the leaders to innovate. In this case, the greater the variety of the assignments, the less likely the leaders will be to activate their traits to innovate (because the job requires a high level of multi-task problem-solving capacity). However, when the job is less varied, the work environment is less open to multi-task solutions (the basics for innovation ideas at firms), and the leaders have to activate their traits of curiosity to innovate to compensate for the failure of the work environment. The above argument has led us to hypothesize the following:

H2: Job variety negatively moderates the relationship between the curiosity of leaders and The intention to introduce IoT-based products at firms.

3.2.3. *Educational backgrounds (of leaders) in social sciences, arts, and humanities (EDU) as a moderator*

EDUs in social sciences, arts, and humanities cover a wide range of research disciplines, and there is an internal diversity as rich as in these sciences. The fields included in the arts and humanities research base include archaeology, classics, and community arts. At a broad level, social sciences, arts, and humanities research contributes to a constantly growing body of knowledge on human experience, agency, identity, and expression, as constructed through language, literature, artifacts, and performance.

Be Creative and Exercise Critical Thinking: Leaders must be analytical and innovative in their approach, encouraging empathy and awe at the complexity of our planet. Literature, philosophy, religion, reading, writing, and listening skills improve the linkages between the humanities and STEM fields of leaders. Individuals with higher education in social sciences, arts, and humanities are expected to offer novel solutions to global problems. Programs in social sciences, arts, and humanities place a premium on critical thinking and innovation. While creativity generates new ideas and discoveries, critical thinking facilitates their implementation. They have the potential to create substantial synergies for global development (Hughes, American poet and columnist) (Langford, in British Academy Report, 2004). Therefore, people with a wide variety of knowledge in social sciences, arts, and humanities usually follow rationality or politically based decisions. Such behavior indicates that they care less about the short-term or tactic plans but follow the long-term and critically determined goals. So, the more comprehensive the knowledge in social sciences, arts, and humanities the leaders have, the less likely the leaders will be to use intuitive styles in their decision-making. Thus, they will be less likely to activate their curiosity to promote the IoT adopted in their product development. The aforementioned arguments can lead us to the following hypothesis:

H3: Educational backgrounds (of leaders) in social sciences, arts, and humanities will negatively moderate the relationship between the curiosity of leaders and the intention to introduce IoT-based products at firms.

4. Measurement of Constructs

4.1. *Measurement of curiosity (CURI)*

Curiosity is measured by the scales developed by Kashdan *et al.* (2018) using items on a seven-point Likert Scale ranging from strongly disagree

(1) to strongly agree (7). Stress tolerance (S.TOLE), deprivation sensations (D.SEN), joyous exploratory (J.EXP), social curiosity (SO.CU), and thrill-seeking (THR.SK) are indications of curiosity. The scale items are as follows:

Items for Curiosity (Independent Variables)
Joyous Exploration

J.EXP1	I view challenging situations as an opportunity to grow and learn.
J.EXP2	I am always looking for experiences that challenge how I think about myself and the world.
J.EXP3	I seek out situations where it is likely that I will have to think in depth about something.
J.EXP4	I enjoy learning about subjects that are unfamiliar to me.
J.EXP5	I find it fascinating to learn new information.

Deprivation Sensitivity

D.SEN1	Thinking about solutions to difficult conceptual problems can keep me awake at night.
D.SEN2	I can spend hours on a single problem because I just can't rest without knowing the answer.
D.SEN3	I feel frustrated if I can't figure out the solution to a problem, so I work even harder to solve it.
D.SEN4	I work relentlessly at problems that I feel must be solved.
D.SEN5	It frustrates me not to have all the information I need.

Stress Tolerance (Reverse Questions)

S.TOLE1	The smallest doubt can stop me from seeking out new experiences.
S.TOLE2	I cannot handle the stress that comes from entering uncertain situations.
S.TOLE3	I find it hard to explore new places when I lack confidence in my abilities.
S.TOLE4	I cannot function well if I am unsure whether a new experience is safe.
S.TOLE5	It is difficult to concentrate when there is a possibility that I may be taken by surprise.

Social Curiosity

SO.CU1	I like to learn about the habits of others.
SO.CU2	I like finding out why people behave the way they do.
SO.CU3	When other people are having a conversation, I like to find out what it's about.
SO.CU4	When around other people, I like listening to their conversations.
SO.CU5	When people quarrel, I like to know what's going on.

Thrill-Seeking

THR.SK1	The anxiety of doing something new makes me feel excited and alive.
THR.SK2	Risk-taking is exciting to me.
THR.SK3	When I have free time, I want to do things that are a little scary.
THR.SK4	Creating an adventure as I go is much more appealing than a planned adventure.
THR.SK5	I prefer excitingly unpredictable friends.

4.2. *Measurement of job variety (VARI)*

Job variety is measured using an instrument developed by Sims *et al.* (1976). Previous research (Dodd and Ganster, 1996) has demonstrated the validity of the measures. Five items were used to assess the coaches' job variety. Respondents give feedback to each item using a 7-point Likert-type scale from 1 (*strongly disagree*) to 7 (*strongly agree*). These scale items are as follows:

Items for Job Variety

VARI1	I have a lot of variety in my job.
VARI2	My duties at work are repetitious.
VARI3	My workday usually consists of performing the same task over and over.
VARI4	I have the opportunity to do a number of different things in my job.
VARI5	My job has a lot of variety.

4.3. *Measurement of educational backgrounds (EDU) in social sciences, arts, and humanities*

This study applies self-developed question items that have been critically evaluated by academicians and tested by a pilot study. Respondents give feedback to each item using a 7-point Likert-type scale from 1 (*strongly disagree*) to 7 (*strongly agree*). These scale items are as follows:

Items for Education Background

EDU1 My main academic courses and projects at the university level (including bachelor, master, and/or Ph.D. if applicable) are in social sciences, arts, or/and humanities areas.

EDU2 My main lifetime self-study materials (except for academic courses) are in social sciences, arts, or/and humanities areas.

4.4. *Measurement of the intention to introduce IoT-based products*

These are the question items adapted from Yoon and George (2013). Respondents give feedback to each item using a 7-point Likert-type scale from 1 (*strongly disagree*) to 7 (*strongly agree*). These scale items are as follows:

Items for IoT-based Products

IOT1 My organization intends to introduce IoT-based products.

IOT2 It is likely that my organization will take steps to introduce IoT-based products.

IOT3 How soon do you think your organization will introduce IoT-based products? (This question item is used just for the provision of information, not for the purpose of combining with other items to formulate the construct).

5. Data Collection and Analytical Methodology

5.1. *Primary data*

A questionnaire was sent to CEOs, chairmen, or other leaders in companies in Vietnam to collect the data. We chose Vietnam because it is suitable for our framework and because it is seriously considering digital transformation.

5.2. *Population and sampling*

Experts from a variety of industries participated in the research and had a say in whether or not their companies should employ cutting-edge solutions. CEOs, managers, chairmen, and other executives with considerable decision-making authority over the adoption of new products and technologies by Vietnamese businesses are the participants who are being targeted. We collected 193 cases between February and July 2021, of which 186 were used for analysis after being assessed (other observations are removed because they omitted many items).

5.3. *Analytical methodology*

The research model is tested using partial least squares (PLS), a component-based structural equation modeling technique that enables path analytic modeling using latent variables (Chin *et al.*, 2003). PLS is regarded as an appropriate statistical tool for theory exploration (Jöreskog and Wold, 1982), which is the case in our study. Path significance is assessed using bootstrap statistics with a total of 500 resamples (Lohmöller, 1982). Moderating relationships are estimated using the product indicator method first developed by Kenny and Judd (1984) and later implemented in PLS by Chin *et al.* (2003), in which interaction terms are created by multiplying the indicators of the predictor and moderator constructs. Each indicator of moderator and predictor is centered before multiplication is performed.

5.4. *Demographic backgrounds*

Figures 2–4 show the respondents' backgrounds. They show that the targets of the leader respondents at firms have been achieved with C-level leaders from a variety of age groups and various industries. The respondents are the people who make key decisions at firms, including the IoT adoption of new products.

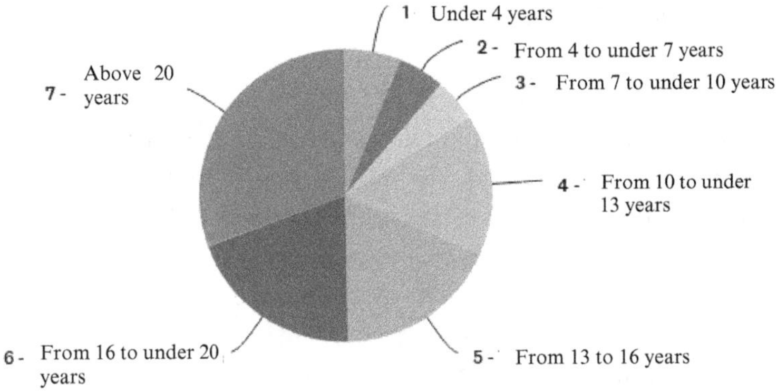

Figure 2. Number of years of working in the company.

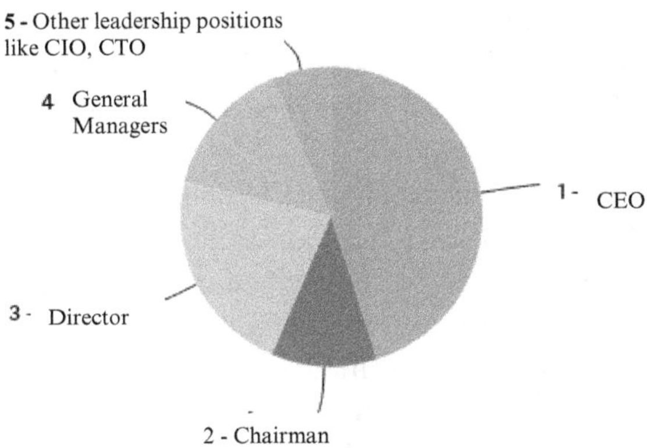

Figure 3. Positional backgrounds of respondents.

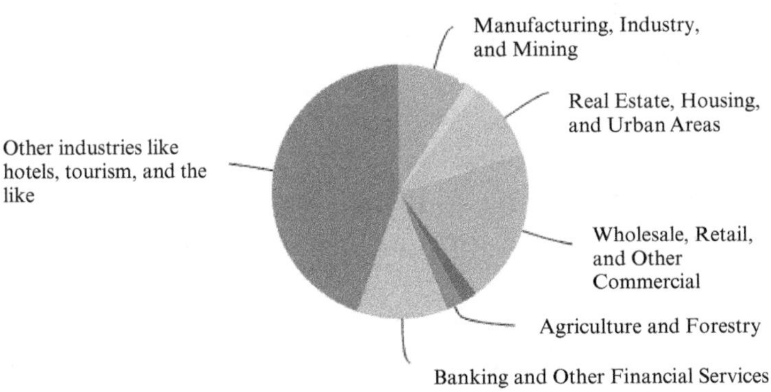

Figure 4. Industry backgrounds of respondents.

6. Measurement Model

6.1. *First-order analysis*

Each latent variable's discriminant and convergent validity must be evaluated during scale development. An item is considered to have adequate convergent validity when it assesses a latent concept. The factor loadings of the items in this research are used to evaluate convergent validity. Items with high loading (>0.5) on the parent concept (Hair *et al.*, 2010; Schumacker and Lomax, 2012) have excellent convergent validity.

S.TOLE1 through S.TOLE5 (–0.571, –0.509, –0.254, –0.812, –0.629) have negative signs, so they are removed from the list of subconstructs that can be used to formulate the main construct of curiosity. The *p*-values are utilized as validation parameters in confirmatory factor analysis, according to Schumacker and Lomax (2012). All subconstructs have *p*-values below 0.000 in Table 1 (after removing the subconstruct of stress tolerance (S.TOLE)).

Average variance extracted (AVE) is employed to evaluate a construct's discriminant validity. If a construct's square root of AVE is more significant than its correlations with others, it has strong discriminant validity, according to Fornell and Larcker (1981). As indicated in Table 4, this criterion is fulfilled in the present research. Table 2 shows that most subconstructs are judged to function well (their AVEs are above the critical value of 0.6 and the relationship with other subconstructs).

6.2. *Second-order analysis*

Hair *et al.* (2006) propose that a higher-order construct be evaluated similarly to a lower-order construct. As a result, in addition to the theoretical evaluation, statistical validations for validity and reliability employed at the first-order level are also relevant for evaluating the second-order construct.

Similarly, deprivation, joyous exploration, social curiosity, and thrill-seeking become four indicators of curiosity. These indicators were created using factor scores of deprivation sensations, joyous exploratory, social

Table 1. First order — Loadings and alpha analysis.

Items	Loadings	*t* Statistics	*p* Values	Alpha
D.SEN1	0.548	6.236	0.000	0.676
D.SEN2	0.654	8.31	0.000	
D.SEN3	0.775	19.342	0.000	
D.SEN4	0.767	19.445	0.000	
D.SEN5	0.541	6.831	0.000	
EDU1	0.571	3.444	0.000	0.643
EDU2	0.857	11.809	0.000	
EDU3	0.820	8.268	0.000	
IOT1	0.842	20.959	0.000	0.767
IOT2	0.946	74.567	0.000	
J.EXP2	0.686	10.464	0.000	0.634
J.EXP3	0.713	13.841	0.000	
J.EXP4	0.647	8.21	0.000	
J.EXP5	0.714	13.854	0.000	
SO.CU1	0.745	17.347	0.000	0.752
SO.CU2	0.655	9.368	0.000	
SO.CU3	0.710	9.024	0.000	
SO.CU4	0.770	10.452	0.000	
SO.CU5	0.640	6.683	0.000	
THR.SK1	0.711	17.441	0.000	0.677
THR.SK2	0.764	18.876	0.000	
THR.SK3	0.590	8.33	0.000	
THR.SK4	0.636	9.243	0.000	
THR.SK5	0.591	10.467	0.000	
VARI1	0.584	5.932	0.000	0.775
VARI2	0.703	7.658	0.000	
VARI3	0.790	11.993	0.000	
VARI4	0.762	11.429	0.000	
VARI5	0.776	12.983	0.000	

Table 2. First order — Discriminant validity test.

Items	D.SEN	EDU	IOT	J.EXP	SO.CU	THR.SK	VARI
D.SEN	**0.665**						
EDU	0.153	**0.760**					
IOT	0.338	0.246	**0.896**				
J.EXP	0.386	0.100	0.237	**0.691**			
SO.CU	0.206	0.226	0.232	0.241	**0.706**		
THR.SK	0.405	0.253	0.356	0.419	0.403	**0.662**	
VARI	0.339	0.040	0.312	0.314	0.062	0.335	**0.727**

Table 3. Second order — Loadings and alpha analysis.

Items	Loadings	Significant	Alpha
D.SEN	0.740	0.000	0.677
J.EXP	0.681	0.000	
SO.CU	0.598	0.000	
THR.SK	0.816	0.000	
EDU1	0.572	0.000	0.643
EDU2	0.857	0.000	
EDU3	0.819	0.000	
IOT1	0.839	0.000	0.767
IOT2	0.948	0.000	
VARI1	0.583	0.000	0.775
VARI2	0.704	0.000	
VARI3	0.791	0.000	
VARI4	0.762	0.000	
VARI5	0.776	0.000	

curiosity, and thrill-seeking generated by Smart-PLS. The output (Table 3) shows that deprivation, joyous exploratory, social, and thrill-seeking aspects had significant loadings on curiosity (above 0.5, $p < 0.001$). The reliability of curiosity was confirmed with Cronbach's alpha of 0.677. Table 4 further supports the discriminant validity of curiosity with the square root of AVE that was higher than the maximum shared variance

Table 4. Second order — Discriminant validity test.

Items	CURI	EDU	IOT	VARI
CURI	**0.713**			
EDU	0.259	**0.760**		
IOT	0.418	0.246	**0.895**	
VARI	0.384	0.040	0.313	**0.727**

among the constructs. Accordingly, the square root of AVE of curiosity is 0.713, higher than the highest shared variance with other constructs.

7. Structural Model

Tables 5 and 6 summarize the *R* square and hypothesis testing outcome. Accordingly, the *R* square of the model is 25%. This means that the model explains 25% of the variation in the intention to introduce IoT-based products at firms. All three hypotheses are supported.

The summary of hypothesis testing results, extracted from Table 6, is as follows:

H1: The curiosity of leaders has a positive relationship with the intention to introduce IoT-based products to firms. Based on Table 6, we hypothesize that the curiosity of leaders has a positive relationship with the intention to introduce IoT-based products at firms; this hypothesis is supported, with $\beta = 0.266$, $p < 0.01$ from the one-tailed test.

H2: Job variety negatively moderates the relationship between the curiosity of leaders and the intention to introduce IoT-based products at firms. According to Table 6, our hypothesis that job variety negatively moderates the relationship between the curiosity of leaders and the intention to introduce IoT-based products at firms is supported, with $\beta = (-0.107)$, $p < 0.05$ from the one-tailed test.

H3: Social sciences, arts, and humanities backgrounds of leaders negatively moderate the relationship between the curiosity of leaders and the intention to introduce IoT-based products at firms. According to Table 6, we hypothesize that the social sciences, arts, and humanities backgrounds

Table 5. *R* square.

Dependent variable	*R* square	*R* square adjusted
IOT	0.250	0.211

Table 6. Structural model.

Proposed hypotheses	Signs of hypotheses	Data coefficients	Decisions
H1	+	0.266***	Supported
H2	–	(–0.107)**	Supported
H3	–	(–0.091)*	Supported

Note: ***Significant at 0.01; **significant at 0.05; *significant at 0.1.

of leaders will negatively moderate the relationship between the curiosity of leaders and the intention to introduce IoT-based products at firms; this hypothesis is supported, with $\beta = (-0.091)$, $p < 0.1$ from the one-tailed test.

8. Results and Discussions

8.1. *Curiosity and the intention to introduce IoT-based products*

Due to the dramatic changes in technology and products, there is a need for entrepreneurship and an adventure-based attitude that can be linked back to the curiosity of leaders. Curiosity encourages leaders to learn about various occurrences and events, which helps them address technological interoperability. Recent research shows that epistemic curiosity is a good predictor of job success (Mussel, 2013; Mussel *et al.*, 2012). Intrinsic task motivation drives creative performance more than an extrinsic (monetary) incentive, according to Dewett (2007) and Walsh and Nagaoka (2009). That is, epistemic curiosity drives attention toward exploration and enables the connection of new signals with chances to learn, develop, and create (Schiefele *et al.*, 1992). As a result, more curious individuals tend to seek fresh ideas and solutions before the issue deteriorates to a crisis level (Kashdan *et al.*, 2004). To examine the connection between individual worker-related curiosity and worker creativity, Storme *et al.* (2016) claim that personal work-related curiosity predicts worker creativity. Curiosity at work promotes exploratory abilities, which enhance innovative skills. Similarly, the curiosity of leaders thus accelerates their decision-making with the intention to introduce IoT-based products at firms.

8.2. *Job variety as a moderator*

The data show that job variety negatively moderates the relationship between the curiosity of leaders and the intention to introduce IoT-based products at firms (Figure 5).

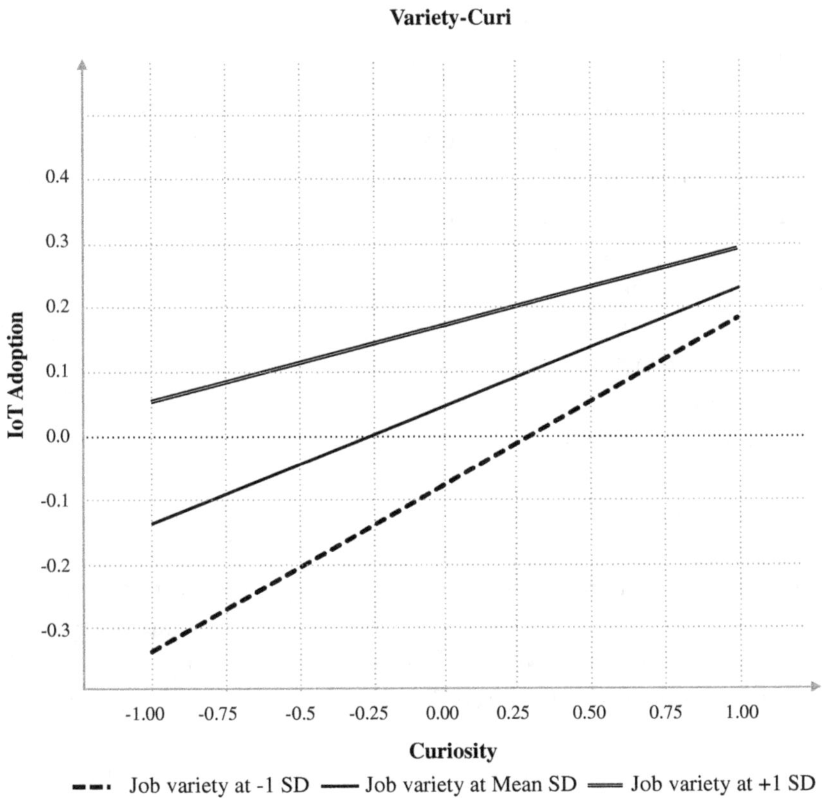

Figure 5. Moderating effects of job variety.

Note: Variety-curi means the interaction of job variety and curiosity with the intention to introduce IoT-based products. Variety at −1 SD means job variety is low, while job variety at +1 SD means job variety is high. It can be seen that the slope of the line of the relationship between curiosity and the intention to introduce IoT-based products is steeper when job variety is higher.

According to some studies, CEO/leaders' job variety is described as the degree to which CEOs prefer to perform several tasks concurrently rather than one at a time (Alipour *et al.*, 2017; Slocombe and Bluedorn, 1999). The research on job variety in strategy is scarce and has primarily focused on positive implications (e.g., Souitaris and Maestro, 2010). On the positive side, job variety promotes creativity and cognitive diversity by exposing people to a broad range of ideas and allowing them to solve new problems by combining information domains (Kaplan, 2008; Persing, 1999). However, working on several tasks simultaneously leads to attention fragmentation and a superficial rather than thorough assessment of problems (Mohammed and Harrison, 2013; Mohammed and Nadkarni, 2014).

IoT is a dynamic technology with changing circumstances requiring various innovative approaches. Because future technology developments, market needs, and competitor actions cannot be foreseen (Bergh and Lawless, 1998), flexibility and openness to various initiatives are critical to business innovation (Garg *et al.*, 2003; Simerly and Li, 2000). The cognitive diversity of job variety and idea cross-fertilization benefit business innovation in dynamic settings. CEOs with job variety acquire diverse ideas and cross-fertilize them by simultaneously evaluating several positions (Bluedorn, 2002; Madjar and Oldham, 2006).

As aforementioned, IoT is a dynamic technology that requires job variety to foster creativity and cognitive variety by exposing individuals to a wide range of ideas and by presenting opportunities for novel problem-solving through cross-fertilization of diverse information domains (Kaplan, 2008; Persing, 1999). When the job is varied, leaders spend too much time on a variety of projects, and the nature of these jobs (with passive effects to follow the various procedures and processes of multiple jobs) will lead to innovation like IoT adoption. In this case, the need for active curiosity (traits) of leaders is less critical (active curiosity has little value at this stage). In other words, people with high job variety don't need to activate innovation ideas because well-defined roles and resources automatically drive leaders to innovate. Therefore, leaders do not need to activate their curiosity capacity to seek ideas for IoT-based projects.

8.3. *Social sciences, arts, and humanities backgrounds of leaders as moderators*

The data show that leaders' educational backgrounds in social sciences, arts, and humanities negatively moderate the relationship between the curiosity of leaders and the intention to introduce IoT-based products at firms.

Accordingly, curiosity has two obstacles, according to Francesca (2018). Despite the advantages of curiosity, many companies discourage it, but not because leaders don't appreciate it. Instead, both executives and workers recognize that curiosity benefits their organizations. According to a recent study of over 3,000 employees, curiosity is a driver of work happiness, motivation, creativity, and high performance. However, CEOs' behaviors frequently contradict this. Specific companies like 3M and Facebook indeed allow workers to pursue hobbies, but they are uncommon. Achieving a quarterly sales target or releasing a new product on the schedule are common short-term performance objectives that take away from workers' time to explore new methods for their job or come up with creative ideas (Figure 6).

8.3.1. *People with high curiosity are exploring in the wrong way*

Companies may fear that letting workers pursue their curiosity will result in expensive disasters. According to Francesca Gino's recent study (2018) of 520 chief learning officers and chief talent development officers, leaders frequently avoid fostering curiosity because they think it would make the business more difficult to manage. They also believe that disputes and delays in decision-making will increase company costs. According to research, people who identify creativity as a goal often reject innovative ideas when confronted with them. This is because exploration via curiosity requires challenging the status *quo* and doesn't necessarily provide valuable data.

Clearly, some companies encourage efficiency and stability in political approaches rather than entertain curiosity and exploration. In this scenario, the military and political (or rational) models of business choices are appropriate to manage the internal environments in the firm. These styles could be acquired via knowledge of social sciences, arts, and humanities.

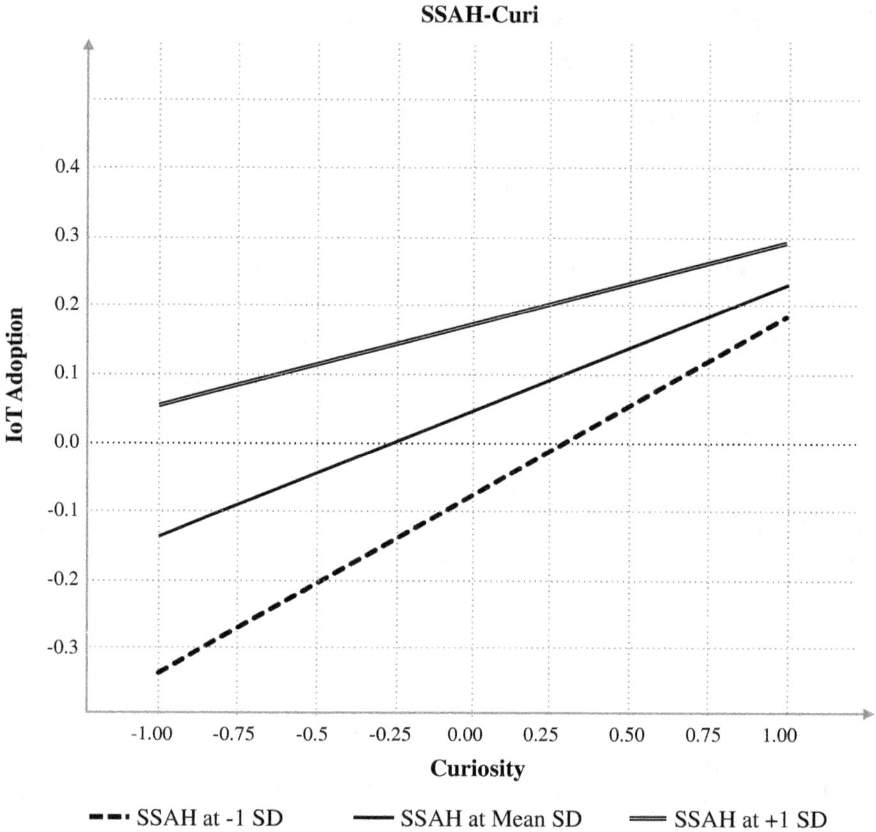

Figure 6. The moderating effects of education background.

Note: SSAH-Curi means the interaction of leaders' educational background in SSAH and leaders' curiosity on the intention to introduce IoT-based products. Edu at −1 SD means leaders' educational backgrounds in SSAH is low, while Edu at +1 SD means leaders' educational backgrounds in SSAH is high education in social sciences, arts, and humanities. It can be seen that the slope of the line of the relationship between curiosity and the intention to introduce IoT-based products is steeper when job variety is higher.

8.3.2. *Educational backgrounds (of leaders) in social sciences, arts, and humanities (EDU): Supplementary to curiosity traits*

People in the social sciences, arts, and humanities have a broader vision than just a desire for information. People with knowledge in social sciences, arts, and humanities are more long-term focused, strategic, and politically and rationally motivated than those with STEM knowledge backgrounds. These traits are further described, as follows.

8.3.3. *People in the social sciences, arts, and humanities know the world and its people*

In an ever-changing global economy, individuals from all socioeconomic backgrounds acquire a global perspective by studying cultures worldwide. As technology extends our boundaries, learners greatly respect different cultures and viewpoints. Obtaining knowledge in social sciences, arts, and humanities can teach learners how the human body works or that every action has a reversal. Our global community's residents and their responses aren't always predictable. The social sciences, arts, and humanities, such as literature, poetry, philosophy, and history, equip learners with the skills to traverse the human experience.

8.3.4. *Boost intellectual base*

Knowledge in social sciences, arts, and humanities broadens our intellectual base. These fields teach us that "most human situations defy single correct answers, that life itself is rarely as precise as a math problem and as clear as an elegant equation" (Fitzgerald, 2014). Learners studying the social sciences, arts, and humanities will discover "how people, organizations, and countries act on their concerns". They acquire historical and cultural knowledge, critical thinking abilities, and the ability to listen, explain, and inspire (Fitzgerald, 2014).

An educational background in social sciences, arts, and humanities helps people accumulate knowledge from the big picture at political, national, and cultural levels that are related to strategic management. At the same time, curiosity is more oriented to the narrow tactic picture and individual habit and concern, and the sphere of impact is limited to some specific people or projects and moments. In this case, educational backgrounds in social sciences, arts, and humanities help people develop broad strategic and political skills. Their decisions are not related to curiosity but to the perspective on the political or global standard with rational styles. Thus, leaders with educational backgrounds in social sciences, arts, and humanities do not need to activate curiosity to find solutions for introducing IoT-based products. In this case, curiosity is less critical for the leaders to explore new solutions to promote IoT-based products at firms.

9. Theoretical Contributions and Practical Implications

9.1. *Theoretical contributions*

9.1.1. *Psychology perspective: Curiosity and innovation*

Our findings confirm that the individual curiosity of leaders is a good predictor of business innovation in the specific case of IoT-based products in Vietnam. This finding follows other researchers' predictions (Mussel, 2013; Mussel *et al.*, 2012) and the current research on motivational antecedents of workplace creativity (Madrid and Patterson, 2015). Curiosity is linked to exploration, and exploration is related to creative potential and innovation (Runco and Acar, 2012). The findings show that the greater the people's degree of curiosity, the more varied and numerous their innovations and the faster their adaptation. Our study is among the first to demonstrate the impact of leaders' characteristics in driving IoT adoption and, more broadly, innovation at companies in Vietnam. With a broader perspective, we then contribute to the theory of intuition in the business decision-making process to reach innovative solutions. The intuitive decision-making styles with the representation of curiosity impact decision-making for innovation like IoT in the case of Vietnam.

9.1.2. *Contributions to the situational and contextual leadership approach (as moderators)*

The second theoretical contribution is that our research findings introduce two new moderating variables for business research on the impact of personal traits (of leaders) on innovation in the case of IoT-based products.

9.1.2.1. Situation 1: Job variety of leaders as moderators

The effect of previous experience on strategic decision-making and performance is a recurring topic in strategic leadership studies (Carpenter *et al.*, 2004; Finkelstein *et al.*, 2009). Crossland *et al.* (2014) more recently created the concept of CEOs' job variety, referring to the leader of the executive group's professional experience from different fields of competence and institutional contexts. According to this research, CEOs' job variety experience negatively moderates the relationship between curiosity and innovation. Our case contributes to this theory with the focus on the intention to introduce IoT-based products. We then contribute to the current research with new insights into the academic field in trait-situation interaction.

9.1.2.2. Situation 2: Educational backgrounds (of leaders) in social sciences, arts, and humanities as moderators

Our chapter is the first project to mention knowledge (Educational Backgrounds) in social sciences, arts, and humanities as a moderator (or situation) moderating a relationship in business and management. We then contribute to the current research with new insights into the academic field in trait–situation interaction. Education in the social sciences, arts, and humanities is essential to a good, well-rounded education. Studies in these fields not only assist in producing excellent citizens and leaders but also reinforce cultural and ethical duties and values in those citizens and leaders (Fitzgerald, 2014). Leaders with an education background in social sciences, arts, and humanities have strategic, political, and long-term orientation in their essential decision-making process. For the first time, our study looks at how a person's education influences the relationship between his or her personality characteristics and the ability to promote innovation (as in the case of IoT adoption). The moderating role of educational backgrounds in social sciences, arts, and humanities will differentiate the impacts of personal traits of leaders on the intention to introduce IoT-based products in particular or innovation activity in general. Accordingly, leaders with educational backgrounds in social sciences, arts, and humanities will be more likely to use rational decision-making styles to decide on innovation activities instead of using intuitive capacities like curiosity.

9.2. *Practical implications*

Regarding the managerial implications for selecting and developing leaders for IoT projects, our findings provide several contributions.

9.2.1. *For practical implications related to curiosity*

One of our findings clearly shows the relationship between curiosity and the intention to introduce IoT-based products. Practically, when companies plan to introduce IoT-based products in the market, they must hire or promote people with high curiosity to the position in charge of organizing and managing the IoT-based products in case the company needs to combine a variety of technologies as well as employ knowledge from a bundle of disciplines and fields. In this case, people with higher curiosity will have more capability to solve this requirement more appropriately. In particular, IoT is an integrated technology that needs the combination of many separate technologies and ideas. Thus, curiosity can help leaders, in this case, to accelerate the IoT-based product development project more smoothly.

To improve curiosity, a person could be supported by a group of intelligent, inquisitive coworkers who can share fresh perspectives from around the globe. He or she might aggressively encourage people to engage in and pursue extracurricular activities to foster that curiosity. To strengthen their culture, firms might routinely invite many lecturers, thinkers, and activists to the office. The goal is to assemble a mix of concepts, narratives, assumptions, and insights that will compel individuals to naturally wonder why and how these concepts affect their work. The corporation pushes a range of things into the ether of its culture, creating a welcoming environment for ideas, in the belief that the confluence of those ideas will produce uniqueness.

9.2.2. *For practical implications related to moderators*

Companies could administer tests to get insights into whether potential candidates have backgrounds and knowledge in social sciences, arts, and humanities and whether their job is very varied or not. The people who score high in indicators related to social sciences, arts, and humanities, have strategic, political, and rational styles. Thus, companies should develop robust and rigorous strategic plans and actions so that leaders will automatically manage to develop IoT-based products as they do not need to use their curiosity for business management activities.

In the case of people with high scores in job variety, they also have opportunities to work many jobs and take on several responsibilities with diverse functions and tasks. The nature of the jobs with a great variety of skills accumulated will automatically promote IoT adoption at firms. Leaders with high job variety thus do not need to activate curiosity to find solutions for introducing IoT-based products at firms. In this case, the company must focus on facilitating environments with a great variety of jobs for the leaders so that leaders will successfully promote innovation. This is very true in the case of high technology areas like IoT, which has a vast number of separate technologies like RFID, AI, big data, and robots.

10. Conclusions, Limitations, and Future Research

10.1. *Conclusions*

Our findings show the positive impact of the curiosity of leaders on the intention to introduce IoT-based products at firms and the roles of different moderators that negatively affect the above relationships. The findings show that people with greater degree of curiosity can innovate more effectively, as seen in the case of the intention to introduce IoT-based products. Our study is among the first to demonstrate the impact of leaders' characteristics on driving IoT adoption to introduce new products and, more broadly, innovation at companies. The second theoretical contribution is that our findings introduce two new moderating variables for business research on the impact of personal traits of leaders on innovation-related decisions (as in the case of IoT-based products).

10.2. *Limitations*

There are limitations to our paper. First, although this research concerns the intention to introduce IoT-based products, a mode of innovation, the applications to other technologies and innovation are limited due to the unique characteristics of IoT, which is a very radical technology, including a combination of many technologies and expansion through social and technical areas (with high complexity). In addition, IoT is among the most general of technologies with a diversity of knowledge and expertise required to run it, and it has increased the potential for scalability in diverse industries. In contrast, other technologies usually focus on a single area or specialist field relevant to just some industries. These differences show the need for a unique model for IoT cases with new moderator variables, which would be different to some extent from the model of other industries like automobiles, or even the closest industries in information technology areas like RFID or ERP.

Second, the model applies to the Vietnamese case with a culture different from those of other countries like Europe or North America or even countries with close cultural norms like East Asian countries. This is because this model is related to psychology, which is affected by local culture. This presents a limitation as well as an opportunity to widen our research topic to other countries with different cultures like Japan and other ASEAN nations, Europe, and North America.

10.3. *Future research*

This study presents some suggestions for future research. We can provide a separate research paper on the actual adoption of IoT in introducing new products at firms because our chapter focuses on the intention to adopt greater innovation in firms in Vietnam, while the actual adoption action could offer a different story. Future research could also thus focus on other countries like Japan, other ASEAN nations, and European and North American countries, to test whether our model can run in different geographic regions with different cultures and management systems.

Acknowledgement

We would like to give our greatest thanks to the respondents including managers who got involved in our data collection processs. They ares such kind managers that although they managed multiple tasks in the workplaces, they were very generous when they spent around 20 minutes engaging in discussions with me and the doing the survey.

We also give respects to academicians and scholars who gave us comments and reviews for the theoretical frameworks and hypotheses. Without their helps, we cannot proceed the papers. Finally, we give greatest thanks to the Coordinators of ACBES conference for giving us a chance to publish this paper.

References

Aarum, A. J. (2000). Intuition in managers: Are intuitive managers more effective? *Journal of Managerial Psychology*, *15*(1), 46–63.

Abramson, N., Lane, H., Nagai, H., & Takagi, H. (1993). A Comparison of Canadian and Japanese cognitive styles: Implications for management interaction. *Journal of International Business Studies*, *24*, 575–587.

Abramson, N. R., Keating, R. J., & Lane, H. W. (1996). Cross-national cognitive process differences: A comparison of Canadian and Japanese managers. *Management International Review*, *36*, 123–148.

Alipour, K. K., Mohammed, S., & Martinez, P. N. (2017). Incorporating temporality into implicit leadership and followership theories: Exploring inconsistencies between time-based expectations and actual behaviors. *The Leadership Quarterly*, *28*(2), 300–316.

Audenaert, M., Decramer, A., George, B., Verschuere, B., & Van Waeyenberg, T. (2019). When employee performance management affects individual innovation in public organizations: The role of consistency and LMX. *The International Journal of Human Resource Management*, *30*, 815–834.

Bergh, D. D. & Lawless, M. W. (1998). Portfolio restructuring and limits to hierarchical governance: The effects of environmental uncertainty and diversification strategy. *Organization Science*, *9*(1), 87–102.

Berlyne, D. E. (1978). Curiosity and learning. *Motivation and Emotion*, *2*(2), 97–175.

Bluedorn, A. C. (2002), *The Human Organization of Time: Temporal Realities and Experience.* Stanford, CA: Stanford University Press.

Buchtel, E. E. & Norenzayan, A. (2008). Which should you use, intuition or logic? Cultural differences in injunctive norms about reasoning. *Asian Journal of Social Psychology*, *11*(4), 264–273.

Carpenter, M. A., Geletkanycz, M. A., & Sanders, W. G. (2004). Upper echelons research revisited: Antecedents, elements, and consequences of top management team composition. *Journal of Management*, 30, 749–778.

Chin, W. W., Marcolin, B. L., & Newsted, P. R. (2003). A partial least squares latent variable modeling approach for measuring interaction effects: Results from a Monte Carlo simulation study and an electronic-mail emotion/adoption study. *Information Systems Research*, *14*(2), 189–217.

Cohen-Meitar, R., Abraham, C., & David, A. W. (2009). Linking meaningfulness in the workplace to employee creativity: The intervening role of organizational identification and positive psychological experiences. *Creativity Research Journal*, *21*(4), 361–375.

Crossland, C., Zyung, J., Hiller, N. J., & Hambrick, D. C. (2014). CEO career variety: Effects on firm-level strategic and social novelty. *Academy of Management Journal*, *57*(3), 652–674.

Dewett, T. (2007). Linking intrinsic motivation, risk-taking, and employee creativity in an R&D environment. *R&D Management*, *37*(3), 197–208.

Dijksterhuis, A. (2004). Think different: The merits of unconscious thought in preference development and decision making. *Journal of Personality and Social Psychology*, *87*, 586–598.

Dodd, N. G. & Ganster, D. C. (1996). The interactive effects of variety, autonomy, and feedback on attitudes and performance. *Journal of Organizational Behavior*, *17*(4), 329–347.

Elbanna, S. (2010). *Making Strategic Decisions: A State of the Art Review and Empirical Evidence from a Cultural Perspective*. Dudweiler Landstr: Lambert Academic Publishing.

Elbanna, S. & Child, J. (2007). Influences on strategic decision effectiveness: Development and test of an integrative model. *Strategic Management Journal*, *28*(4), 431–453.

Finkelstein, S., Hambrick, D. C., & Cannella, A. A. (2009). *Strategic Leadership: Theory and Research on Executives, Top Management Teams, and Boards.* New York: Oxford University Press.

Fornell, C. & Larcker, D. F. (1981). Evaluating structural equation models with unobservable variables and measurement error. *Journal of Marketing Research*, *18*(1), 39–50.

Garg, V. K., Walters, B. A., & Priem, R. L. (2003). Chief executive scanning emphases, environmental dynamism, and manufacturing firm performance. *Strategic Management Journal*, *24*(8), 725–744.

Grünig, R., Kühn, R., Clark A., & O`Dea, C. (2005). *Successful Decision Making: A Systematic Approach to Complex Problems*. Heidelberg: Springer-Verlag Berlin.

Hackman, J. R. & Lawler, E. E. (1971). Employee reactions to job characteristics. *Journal of Applied Psychology*, *55*(3), 259–286.

Hair, J. F., Black, W. C., Babin, B. J., & Anderson, R. E. (2010). *Multivariate Data Analysis* (7th edn.). Upper Saddle River. NJ, USA: Prentice-Hall, Inc.

Hair, J. F., Black, W. C., Babin, B. J., Anderson, R. E., & Tatham, R. L. (2006). *Multivariate Data Analysis* (6th edn.). New Jersey: Pearson Prentice Hall.

Hans, V. & Anthony, W. (2008). Achieving technical interoperability — The ETSI approach. *ETSI White Paper*, *3*, 1–29.

Hofstede, G. (2001). *Culture's Consequences: Comparing Values, Behaviors, Institutions, and Organizations Across Nations.* Thousand Oaks, CA: Sage Publications.

Huang, J. & Sisco, B. R. (1994). Thinking styles of Chinese and American adult students in higher education: A comparative study. *Psychological Reports*, *74*(2), 475–480.

Humphrey, S. E., Nahrgang, J. D., & Morgeson, F. P. (2007). Integrating motivational, social and contextual work design features: A meta-analytic summary and theoretical extension of the work. *Journal of Applied Psychology*, *92*, 1332–1336.

Ilori, M. O. & Irefin, I. A. (1997). Technology decision-making in organizations. *Technovation*, *17*(3), 153–160.

Ji, L. J., Peng, K., & Nisbett, R. E. (2000). Culture, control, and perception of relationships in the environment. *Journal of Personality and Social Psychology*, *78*(5), 943–955.

Joreskog, K. G. & Wold, H. (1982). The ML and PLS techniques for modeling with latent variables: Historical and comparative aspects. In Joreskog, K. G., & Wold, H. (eds.), *Systems under Indirect Observation: Causality, Structure, Prediction, Part I* (pp. 263–270). Amsterdam: Elsevier.

Kaplan, S. (2008). Polychronicity in work team: A theoretical examination of antecedents and consequences. In Roe, R. A., Waller, M. J., & Clegg, S. R. (eds.), *Time in Organizational Research.* Routledge, Abingdon, VA (pp. 103–126).

Kashdan, T. B., Rose, P., & Fincham, F. D. (2004). Curiosity and exploration: facilitating positive subjective experiences and personal growth opportunities. *Journal of Personality Assessment*, *82*(3), 291–305.

Kashdan, T. B., Stiksma, M. C., Disabato, D. J., McKnight, P. E., Bekier, J., Kaji, J., & Lazarus, R. (2018). The five-dimensional curiosity scale: Capturing the bandwidth of curiosity and identifying four unique subgroups of curious people. *Journal of Research in Personality*, *73*, 130–149.

Kashdan, T. B., Rose, P., & Fincham, F. D. (2004). Curiosity and exploration: Facilitating positive subjective experiences and personal growth opportunities. *Journal of Personality Assessment*, *82*(3), 291–305.

Keller, H., Schneider, K., & Henderson, B. (1994). Preface: The study of exploration. In Keller, H., Schneider, K., & Henderson, B. (eds.), *Curiosity and Exploration* (pp. 199–212). Berlin: Springer-Verlag.

Kenny, D. A. & Judd, C. M. (1984). Estimating the nonlinear and interactive effects of latent variables. *Psychological Bulletin*, *96*, 201–210.

Kester, L., Griffin, A., Hultink, E. J., & Lauche, K. (2011). Exploring portfolio decision-making processes. *Journal of Product Innovation Management*, *28*(5), 641–661.

Lauriola, M., Litman, J., Mussel, P., Santis, R. D., Crowson, H. M., & Hoffman, R. R. (2015). Epistemic curiosity and self-regulation. *Personality and Individual Differences*, *83*, 202–207.

Litman, J. A. & Jimerson, T. L. (2004). The measurement of curiosity is a feeling of deprivation. *Journal of Personality Assessment*, *82*(2), 147–157.

Litman, J. A. & Spielberger, C. D. (2003). Measuring epistemic curiosity and its diversive and specific components. *Journal of Personality Assessment*, *80*(1), 75–86.

Loewenstein, G. (1994). The psychology of curiosity: A review and reinterpretation. *Psychological Bulletin*, *116*(1), 75–98.

Lohmoller, J. B. (1989), *Latent Variable Path Modeling with Partial Least Squares*. Heidelberg: Physica-Verlag.

Madjar, N. & Oldham, G. R. (2006). Task rotation and polychronicity: Effects on individuals' creativity. *Human Performance*, *19*(2), 117–131.

Madrid, H. P. & Patterson, M. G. (2016). Creativity at work as a joint function between openness to experience, the need for cognition, and organizational fairness. *Learning and Individual Differences*, *51*, 409–416.

Marinova, J., Janneke, P., & Chantal, R. (2016). Gender diversity and firm performance: Evidence from Dutch and Danish boardrooms. *The International Journal of Human Resource Management*, *27*(15), 1777–1790.

Masuda, T. & Nisbett, R. E. (2001). Attending holistically versus analytically: Comparing the context sensitivity of Japanese and Americans. *Journal of Personality and Social Psychology*, *81*(5), 922–934.

Mohammed, S. & Harrison, D. A. (2013). The clocks that time us are not the same: A theory of temporal diversity, task characteristics, and performance in teams. *Organization Behavior and Human Decision Processes*, *122*(2), 244–256.

Mohammed, S. & Nadkarni, S. (2014). Are we all on the same temporal page? The moderating effects of temporal team cognition on the polychronicity diversity — Team performance relationship. *Journal of Applied Psychology*, *99*(3), 404–422.

Mussel, P. (2010). Epistemic curiosity and related constructs: Lacking evidence of discriminant validity. *Personality and Individual Differences*, *49*(5), 506–510.

Mussel, P. (2013). Introducing the construct curiosity for predicting job performance. *Journal of Organizational Behavior*, *34*(4), 453–472.

Mussel, P., Spengler, M., Litman, J. A., & Schuler, H. (2012). Development and validation of the German work-related curiosity scale. *European Journal of Psychological Assessment*, *28*(2), 109–117.

Norenzayan, A., Smith, E. E., Kim, B. J., & Nisbett, R. E. (2002). Cultural Preferences for Formal versus Intuitive Reasoning. *Cognitive Science*, *26*(5), 653–684.

Pan, W., Sun, L. Y., & Chow, I. H. S. (2012). Leader-member exchange and employee creativity: Test of a multilevel moderated mediation model. *Human Performance*, *25*, 432–451.

Papadakis, V. M., Lioukas, S., & Chambers, D. (1998). Strategic decision-making processes: The role of management and context. *Strategic Management Journal*, *19*(2), 115–147.

Peng, K. & Nisbett, R. E. (1999). Culture, dialectics, and reasoning about contradiction. *American Psychologist*, *54*(9), 741–754.

Persing, D. L. (1999). Managing in polychronic times: Exploring individual creativity and performance in intellectually intensive venues. *Journal of Managerial Psychology*, *14*(5), 358–373.

Pratt, M. K. (2021). IoT interoperability standards complicate IoT adoption. Available at: https://www.techtarget.com/iotagenda/tip/IoT-interoperability-standards-complicate-IoT-adoption (Accessed 25 January 2023).

Runco, M. & Acar, S. (2012). Divergent thinking as an indicator of creative potential. *Creativity Research Journal*, *24*(1), 66–75.

Schiefele, U., Krapp, A., & Winteler, A. (1992). Interest as a predictor of academic achievement: A meta-analysis of research. In Renninger, K. A., Hidi, S., & Krapp, A. (eds.), *The Role of Interest in Learning and Development* (pp. 183–212). Mahwah, NJ: Lawrence Erlbaum Associates.

Schmeichel, B. J., Vohs, K. D., & Baumeister, R. F. (2003). Intellectual performance and ego depletion: Role of the self in logical reasoning and other information processing. *Journal of Personality and Social Psychology*, *85*(1), 33–46.

Schumacker, R. E. & Lomax, R. G. (2012). *A Beginner's Guide to Structural Equation Modeling* (3rd edn.). Hoboken: Taylor and Francis.

Shalley, C. E. & Gilson, L. L. (2004). What leaders need to know: A review of social and contextual factors that can foster or hinder creativity. *The Leadership Quarterly*, *15*(1), 33–53.

Simerly, R. L. & Li, M. (2000). Environmental dynamism, capital structure, and performance: A theoretical integration and an empirical test. *Strategic Management Journal*, *21*, 31–50.

Simon, H. A. (1987). Making management decisions: The role of intuition and emotion. *Academy of Management Executive*, *1*(1), 57–64.

Sims, H., Szilagyi, A., & Keller, R. (1976). The measurement of job characteristics. *Academy of Management Journal*, *19*, 195–212.

Slocombe, T. E. & Bluedorn, A. C. (1999). Organizational behavior implications of the congruence between preferred polychronicity and experienced work-unit polychronicity. *Journal of Organizational Behavior*, *20*(1), 75–99.

Souitaris, V. & Maestro, B. M. M. (2010). Polychronicity in top management teams: The impact on strategic decision processes and performance of new technology ventures. *Strategic Management Journal*, *31*(6), 652–678.

Storme, M., Tavani, J. L., & Myszkowski, N. (2016). Psychometric properties of the French ten-item personality inventory (TIPI). *Journal of Individual Differences*, *37*(2), 81–87.

Tierney, P. & Farmer, S. M. (2002). Creative self-efficacy: Its potential antecedents and relationship to creative performance. *Academy of Management Journal*, *45*(6), 1137–1148.

Walsh, J. P. & Nagaoka, S. (2009). Who invents? Evidence from the Japan-US inventor survey. Technical report. The Research Institute of Economy, Trade and Industry, Tokyo. RIETI Discussion Paper Series 09-E-034, pp. 1–68.

Wilson, T. D. (2002). *Strangers to Ourselves: Discovering the Adaptive Unconscious.* Cambridge, MA: Harvard University Press.

Yoon, T. & George, J. (2013). Why aren't organizations adopting virtual worlds? *Computers in Human Behavior*, *29*, 772–790.

Zuckerman, M. (1994). *Behavioral Expressions and Biosocial Bases of Sensation Seeking*. Cambridge: Cambridge University Press.

https://doi.org/10.1142/9789811286100_0009

Chapter 9

Market Orientation of Public Organizations in a Transitional Economy

Thi Thuy Hang Le[*,‡] and Toan Luu Duc Huynh[†,§]

[*]*University of Finance — Marketing (UFM), Ho Chi Minh City, Vietnam*

[†]*College of Technology and Design, University of Economics Ho Chi Minh City, Vietnam*

[‡]*ltt.hang@ufm.edu.vn*

[§]*toanhld@ueh.edu.vn*

Abstract

This chapter covers the transformation of a market-oriented economy and the advancements in exchange efficiency and effectiveness crucial to a successful transition. A key characteristic of transition economies is that the market is only partially exploited as a mechanism for economic exchange. Thus, rather than being influenced primarily by market forces, corporate behavior may be significantly more affected by factors like government regulation and ownership structure. Excessive regulations that restrict competition and insufficient regulations of the operating mechanism of economic sectors according to market supply and demand characterize countries transitioning from a planned economy to a market economy. The old plan-driven economy left behind anticompetitive regulation that makes achieving economic growth targets difficult. Therefore, the government should play a role in encouraging healthy competition among businesses and supplement regulations to develop a market economy.

Keywords: Market orientation, Public organizations, Transitional economy.

Received on December 20, 2022; accepted on April 16, 2023

1. Introduction

The fact that the drivers and pathways to success in transition economies are largely defined by the socially and institutionally managed environment is a characteristic of business performance in these countries. Economic sector activities have been hampered by formal institutional restraints such as state control mechanisms, government agencies, the market architecture of regulatory organizations, and planning skills. Non-state-owned enterprises (non-SOEs), such as private businesses, seek market-oriented growth prospects, whereas SOEs are equitized (Peng, 2001).

In the post-reform age, markets are becoming more competitive and complex, raising an intriguing question: How do local state collectivism, regulatory networks, and market-oriented attitudes relate to corporate performance in the economy? Recent events seem to indicate that the impact of local community governments on the operations of firms in transition economies has greatly decreased, especially when dealing with increasing privatization. Business managers in transition economies appear to be shifting their focus from managing networks of interpersonal ties to adopting competitive market behaviors (Peng and Shekshnia, 2001).

Despite growing empirical data demonstrating the positive effects of market orientation, market orientation development-related issues have received less attention in empirical investigations (Jaworski and Kohli, 1996; Savitt, 1999). The main problem is the difficulty of market-oriented development in a transition economy such as the Czech Republic. According to Savitt (1999), expanded market orientation is hampered by restructuring without tightly controlled programs and processes working in a market economy, as well as continuous intervention by senior management from the previous system.

Many countries with transition economies claim to be market economies, but many aspects of economic activity expressed through exchange and interest rates are still tightly regulated. Within the context of an economy in transition, government regulations can have positive and negative effects on market orientation. The results imply that policymakers should pay close attention to how applicable regulations are set up as they affect business, to the extent that encouraging market orientation is considered desirable to increase the competitiveness of enterprises in transition economies. The value of regulations that limit competition and defend existing businesses will negatively affect expanded market orientation. Furthermore, by offering solutions to a lack of management expertise, governments in transition economies can assist enterprises in becoming more market-oriented. Government policy has a great deal of opportunity to increase the supply of qualified and market-oriented managers for domestic businesses as a significant provider and funder of education and training (Liu *et al.*, 2000; Ambler *et al.*, 1999).

The market-oriented transition economy reached new heights following the institutionalization of additional opening-up policies and collective ownership reform throughout the 1990s. The major results of transformational economic change include enhanced institutions that support market economies and steady growth in market competitiveness (Child and Tse, 2001). Based on the above practice, this study provides an overview of market orientation of governments in transition economies worldwide and empirical evidence that market orientation affects Vietnam's economic growth. The transition to a market economy occurred in different countries with various trends and starting points. The Soviet Union and Eastern Europe primarily focused on the degree of financial liberalization. Some countries open up completely, accepting that the economy will experience shock but taking advantage of opening up. Some countries determine when and how much to open their economies to suit the circumstances and avoid economic damage. China had a completely different economic transition. China focused on the structure of its economic sectors, paying attention to the protection of SOEs, gradually loosening the control of other economic sectors, and being cautious in the use of international cooperation to increase domestic market competitiveness. Given these factors, this chapter addresses the following:

1. What are the shortcomings of planned economies transitioning to a market economy?
2. How does a planned economy transition to a typical market economy worldwide?
3. How do state market-oriented economic management activities affect economic growth in Vietnam?

Study materials on the market-based transition economy are presented in Section 2. The market orientation processes of some representative transition economies around the world are presented in Section 3. Given the empirical approach of the research model, the estimated results are presented and discussed in Section 4. Finally, Section 5 provides conclusions.

2. The Reform Process and the Existence of Market-Oriented Transition Economies

Partial reforms in a market-oriented transition economy are characterized by the establishment of an institutional setting where mixed forms outperform other planned economic structures based on transaction costs. These parameter changes also result in decreased transaction costs for private enterprises and relatively increased costs for mixed-governance arrangements as the institutional underpinnings of market economies gradually develop (Williamson, 1991). The relatively wider range of market institutions managing the economy, changes in ownership structure, and the steady shift from redistributive to regulatory mechanisms are key explanations for the rapid growth of mixed forms and private enterprises. The economic efficiency of SOEs declines while privately owned and marketized businesses quickly expand due to changes in the institutional framework (Nee, 1989).

Reform during the 1980s focused on decentralizing power to businesses and local government, which is most evident in profit-sharing and retention arrangements. By strengthening its decision-making power, the state sought to provide industrial enterprises with flexibility and an incentive to improve economic performance (Zhang and Zhang, 1987). Therefore, businesses are permitted to keep 70% of the non-budget fund to invest in the physical assets of the plant or to distribute it to staff members through an annual bonus program. Meanwhile, the state gives local governments more control over finances and budgets (CASS, 1989). After paying the central government a portion of the agreed-upon local taxes, local governments, like businesses, are permitted to keep excess funds. The administrative rigidity associated with central planning must be eliminated to foster local government enthusiasm that supports the pursuit of market-oriented economic development. The accompanying revenue-sharing agreements forge partnerships between local government and industry.

The economics of transaction costs explain the emergence of affiliates to save on transaction costs in inter-organizational relationships when the parties to the transaction maintain autonomy (Williamson, 1991). Local authorities support collective enterprises, which receive very little support from the state, to ensure reliable access to the resources businesses need, especially those in short supply. Local governments also monitor the local labor market and appoint managers for collective enterprises, act as intermediaries in important negotiations with banks for access to credit, fix local prices for certain commodities, and approve and coordinate investments by non-budget funds under their authority and projects proposed by the collective enterprise. Local corporatism can improve corporate competitiveness in domestic and international markets through subsidies, facilitate horizontal and vertical economic integration, provide access to credit, and invest in infrastructure such as schools, roads, public transportation, and other services. These micro-interventions by local governments can ease corporate budget constraints. In conclusion, local governments can offer help and assets to enterprises to compete successfully in an economy defined by partial reform in which institutions are dispersed. As with submarket institutions, the dominant distribution system engages in market forces (Wong, 1986, 1987, 1990).

Local governments and collective firms have a close working relationship supported by bilateral reliance and the ownership structure. In a shortage economy, collective enterprises — those at the bottom of the industrial enterprise food chain — must rely on connections supplied by local governments to acquire needed financing and resources. Similarly, municipal governments depend more heavily on money from joint ventures. When the institutional framework supporting the market is weak, local corporatism reduces transaction costs. To strengthen their negotiating positions, collective business managers engage in cooperative talks with local governments. For SOEs and foreign corporations, obtaining business contracts with local government backing can reduce transaction costs by offering a formal guarantee that the conditions of the contract will be fulfilled on time.

Despite local governments' propensity for protectionism, larger collective firms behave in ways that promote international trade. Because of these collective firms, the market becomes increasingly important to their success. Collective businesses rely on local governments to access resources allocated through the plan, but such resources are limited. For this reason, they must turn to specialized markets to purchase multiple-factor resources. This activity often involves importing foreign investments and technologies to sustain economic growth. Likewise, products produced by collective enterprises not intended for domestic consumption but for sale abroad are more readily sold in regional markets than redistributed by the consuming state. An additional market dynamic stems from government agencies setting below-market prices for most commodities. Businesses that can purchase factor resources at subsidized state prices and sell some of their products at a higher market price have developed a keen interest in arbitrage. Collective enterprises quickly orient their production to the market and contribute to rapid market expansion (Bonnell, 1980).

Private firms are small and lack capital because access to factor resources is restricted, and capitalists and merchants are continuously rejected in a communist society. Additionally, Private entrepreneurs' states of abandonment drives them to make short-term investment choices to obtain rapid returns from corporate expansion. Numerous private businesses work to establish tight relationships with local government, frequently paying fees to access those resources. The absence of clearly defined and consistently upheld private property rights, however, poses the biggest threat to the competitiveness of private enterprises.

The transition economy has produced a new diversity of ownership structures and organizational forms. The spectrum extends continually from formal, hierarchical SOEs to modest, family-run firms operated by rural businesspeople. The progressive change of collective companies into a mixed form of organization — the marketized redistributive corporation — was one of the effects of the 1980s' strong market-oriented economic growth (equitized company). Marketed enterprises are an intermediary asset class that has been shaped by increasing demands for efficiency and adaptability in contexts that are rapidly changing and where market forces have gradually supplanted the state redistribution mechanism

(Powell, 1988). The organizational ownership structure is dynamic. Local governments transition communal companies into mixed ownership when they lease them to private operators; in this case, the local government and private operators jointly own the company. Synergies in transitional capitalist economies are organizational formations that pool resources from several organizations or use their governance systems, just like in mature capitalist economies. The participation of local governments in the rural industry is viewed as a local reform distortion that undercuts the successful goals of market-based economic reform. The shift of economic protectionism from central ministries to local governments exacerbated it due to the protectionist attitude of local politicians and the legacy of closed local economies (Borys and Jemison, 1989).

A marketized corporation has stronger access to factor markets than a private company does under partial reform. Since the asset ownership structure in collective ownership ties the local government in partnership with the market company, local governments may give marketized enterprises access to capital, raw materials, and labor with a higher priority than SOEs within their jurisdictions. A marketed company's expansion and profitability have a greater and more immediate impact on local government revenue maximization than unmarketed or privately held companies. Marketized businesses can promote their goods through state supply and marketing channels in addition to having access to the free market system. However, since collective enterprises rely on SOEs in the state marketing system, local governments frequently actively urge marketized firms toward market competitiveness and growth in order to escape restrictions and responsibilities imposed by central ministries (Walder, 1989).

Demarketed businesses receive first dibs on raw materials and centrally allotted funds for investments because they are SOEs. They can only make things for the market once they reach the production goal outlined in the plan. Therefore, the planning system restricts and limits their access to the market. There may not be a level playing field between the economic sectors and the private sector due to cronyism and patronage between political leadership and the private sector (Eglinger, 2021). Although there is a theoretically ample labor pool, workers are allocated to the demarketed company during the planning process. Demarketed businesses mostly rely on permanent employees chosen by the state human resources agency, whereas marketized businesses can hire labor based on market demand. Due to this, marketized businesses have more freedom to change their number or the number of workers than SOEs. As a result, the staff of the organization experiences alternating periods of shortages and layoffs. Since the company's supply of raw materials is also frequently clogged because of strict scheduling, shortages are common (Kornai, 1980).

The salaries and bonuses of marketized businesses have grown substantially faster than those of public sector businesses in employee compensation. Compared with employees in the demarketed state sector, wages and benefits for workers in marketized firms have increased more. Low morale has become a significant issue in government organizations because of the wage gap between workers with secondary education in for-profit businesses and university graduates in the public sector. The public sector experienced waves of labor migration as a result, with workers seeking to transition to the market sector (Vogel, 1989).

Since local governments have official control over them, market-based businesses lack formal autonomy. The goal of corporate reform is to give managers more control over decisions, yet because of the interaction with local governments, local industries are exposed to overt bureaucracy. To the extent that they recognize that successful enterprises generate more income streams, reasonable authorities would be motivated to support effective expansion. Local governments, however, also have a stake in shielding ineffective communal firms from rivalry by limiting the importation of commodities. It is frequently challenging for local governments to abstain from micro-intervening in the operation of collective companies due to the desire to foster economic growth. The issue of inefficiency is made worse by these latter traits (Kornai, 1989; Bekkevold *et al.*, 2020).

3. Market Orientation of Public Organizations in the World's Transition Economy

In 1991, the Soviet Union was split into 16 sovereign entities. The newly independent states had limited independence and sovereignty. However, in 1992, most newly independent countries transitioned their economies to liberalized and democratic market-oriented governing systems (Nepal and Jamasb, 2012). On the other hand, countries in transition following the demise of the communist government in the early 1990s saw a significant economic downturn as output in the state sector declined while the private sector had not developed sufficiently to swiftly bridge the output gap. The early transition was marked by the onset of serious economic and social issues similar to those witnessed with the 1980s' central planning model. Economic growth can influence institutional reform and vice versa (Perenyi *et al.*, 2019).

Some Eastern European countries, such as Lithuania and the Slovak Republic, have used *shock treatment* to open up and liberalize their economies as rapidly as feasible. Reforms in other countries, such as the Commonwealth of Independent States, have been slower. Market fundamentalists say the solution for crisis-hit countries is swift and extensive transformation. On the other hand, some believe that the timing and sequence of reforms are crucial to operational improvement (Staehr, 2005). These actions result in large-scale and complex experiences with economic reforms, leading to a range of outcomes for transition countries.

Since the 1980s, China, historically a planned economy, has been undergoing a fundamental transformation to a market economy. The right of private enterprises to operate freely is frequently granted in the West. In China, however, basic and widespread recognition of the freedom of private companies to operate does not occur immediately (Peng and Luo, 2000). The institutional environment in China is still far from ideal for private firms, since the state retains a dominating role in the economy, and the laws and policies governing the private sector are underdeveloped. Due to state restrictions, management priorities, or relationships, established SOEs, such as state-owned banks and collective enterprises, tend to do business using their own specialized procedures. In other words, the institutional environment for private firms is highly adverse in the early stages of transformation. The economic revolution is a significant milestone in the fight for the legitimacy of private firms (Xin and Pearce, 1996; Hu, 2019).

China's transition from central planning has taken a substantially different path from that of Eastern Europe and the Soviet Union. While Eastern Europe and the Soviet Union abandoned the communist path in favor of Western-style democracies and began rapid state-led transitions to market economies, China steadfastly refused to reform its political institutions and determined that its path would be to rebuild the economic institutions of state socialism through reform rather than revolution. As a result, China, which was considered inventive and daring in the 1980s, is now portrayed as a bulwark of communist resistance to the changes sweeping Eastern Europe and the Soviet republics. Political pressure to maintain the rule of the Communist Party of China has led to a socialist orientation in the transition of the market economy in China (Lee, 2018).

Even before market reform, central planning in China was substantially less than in the Soviet Union and Eastern Europe. The planning process encompasses numerous layers of decision-making, from central ministries to provinces, cities, counties, and towns, with each level of the state structure dispersing significant resources within its authority (Lyons, 1990). Only 6% of China's industrial enterprises are classified as large or medium sized. These SOEs form the core of companies directly supervised by central ministries and centrally planned provincial agencies. Meanwhile, 78% of Chinese enterprises are small-scale, labor-intensive organizations registered under collective ownership (Kueh, 1985). Local governments are in charge of smaller SOEs. It can be argued that the predominance of small businesses in China's industrial economy before reform could explain why China's industrial economy responded more favorably to economic reform than economies of the Soviet Union and Eastern Europe, where the proportions of large and small industrial plants were equal to those in China (Zhang, 2020a, 2020b).

Economic reform from 1978 to 1989 resulted in changes in the power structure of the state and society and a new alignment of interests that favored the marketization of the Chinese economy. First, in the 1980s, organizational and budgetary changes resulted in a considerable transfer of power from the central state apparatus to provincial and local administrations (Tong, 1989). Despite Beijing's efforts to centralize financial regulations, provincial officials currently oversee more than half of China's state budget. Second, as market transactions have become more important, reliance on vertical interactions with state redistributive agencies has diminished for both private manufacturers and industrial firms (Lardy, 1991). Farming households and enterprises, in particular, have gained more liberty as they move production away from a near-monopoly dependency on basic crops and toward more diverse market items. In contrast to the Maoist emphasis on local self-sufficiency, specialization fostered by commercialization has brought to market a diverse range of goods, both agricultural and light industrial (Nee and Su, 1990). The socialist market economy is not a model easily transferred and copied across countries. The achievements of the country's Doi Moi process prove that developing a socialist-oriented market economy is the right choice for countries when transforming into a market-oriented economy. The guideline of being people-centered is the key to the socialist market economy. The socialist market economy is an economic model operating according to the market mechanism in which the state economic sector plays a leading role, especially in building socialism. The socialist market economic structure is not static or immutable but rather a continuous flow between the market, the state, and society, shaped by domestic and international events and trends (Bekkevold *et al.*, 2021).

The influence of reforms on economic growth in transition economies has been thoroughly researched, and a substantial body of literature exists. Fischer *et al.* (1996) pioneered a study with data for the period 1992 to 1994 using transformation indices as the cumulative index, discovering a favorable association between cumulative reform and growth. Following Fischer *et al.*'s study of economic growth in transition economies, Havrylyshyn (2001) performed a comprehensive poll that suggested a high level of agreement on the causes of economic growth. According to Black *et al.* (2000), falling national output is due to inadequacies in transition countries' privatization attempts. Staehr (2005) investigated the relationship between growth and reform and concluded that the sequence of reforms is critical and that favorable outcomes might be reached when changes are hastened.

Aghion and Schankerman (1999) proposed a model demonstrating that investment in physical and institutional infrastructure allows for reduced transaction costs and a high degree of competition while reducing direct costs through indirect or transitional effects. De Macedo and Martins (2008) discovered a connection between governance reform and infrastructure to promote investment efficiency, whereas the interaction between liberalization and financial reform improved investment returns.

Studies show that large-scale privatization leads to worsening health conditions. King *et al.* (2009) attributed the increase in mortality in former communist countries to mass privatization leading to increased deaths, suicides, and heart problems related to alcohol. These factors negatively affect life expectancy. Rapid socioeconomic developments have caused conflict with the aforementioned effects. These views are confirmed by findings by Stiglitz (1999) which suggested that low-income persons, and those who have not generally kept up with the transition, cannot afford higher-end and more expensive private healthcare services. However, the issues in Russia's healthcare system, the greatest of all transition economies experiencing mass privatization, are not related to the status of the economic system (Tompson, 2007). It would be absurd to expect that all aspects, such as educational and health consequences, could not be objectively and explicitly quantified and modeled.

4. Empirical Study of the Government's Market Orientation on Economic Growth in Vietnam

Vietnam has achieved impressive socioeconomic development over the past 35 years. From one of the poorest countries in mid-1986, Vietnam became a low-middle-income country in 2010 (Baum, 2020). Other social indicators such as education, healthcare, and access to basic services have all improved significantly. The national poverty rate decreased from 70% in 1986 to less than 2% in 2021 (World Bank, 2022). From a closed economy and embargo in 1986, Vietnam has become one of the most open economies in the world. Vietnam has established partnerships with 189/193 countries worldwide and signed 185 bilateral agreements and 77 multilateral agreements, including 15 free trade agreements with 57 economies. Vietnam achieved the UN's Millennium Development Goals in 2005 and is making impressive strides toward the Sustainable Development Goals (WTO, 2022).

Despite the remarkable achievements, important challenges remain. The study of the socialist market economy in Vietnam is therefore important not only for Vietnam but also for other countries. The concept of *socialism* refers to a civilized and just society in which the state represents the long-term interests of the nation. The authors discuss how socialist ideology has influenced the country's impressive growth record and its future course (Knutsen and Khanh, 2020). Instead of going through a capitalist transition to achieve the goal of socialism, Vietnam is going through a quite diverse and complex transition to socialism (Gillespie, 2018; Hualing *et al.*, 2018).

4.1. *VECM model*

The transition of planned economies to a market economy is mainly assessed through the control and management policies of the money market adopted by the state. Therefore, the VECM model was chosen because it has the function of variance decomposition and impulse response to measure the impact of a variable on the volatility of other variables. In turn, it is suitable for carrying out transmission-level tests during the conversion process. The Vector Error Correction Model (VECM) tracks the transition of time series data from one equilibrium state to another, facilitating the measurement of how these series adjust and return to equilibrium after a disturbance. The degree of the impact of the variables is felt both in the short and the long runs. In addition, the stationary time series with the same order of difference and the cointegration test indicate the selection and use of the VECM model (Johansen, 1988, 1990).

Forming the VECM Model:

$$y_t - y_{t-1} = (A_1 + A_2 + \cdots + A_p - I)\, y_{t-1} - (A_2 + \cdots + A_p)\,(y_{t-1} - y_{t-2}) - (A_3 + \cdots + A_p)\,(y_{t-2} - y_{t-3}) - \cdots - A_p\,(y_{t-p+1} - y_{t-p}) + u_t$$

$$\Delta y_t = \underset{y_{t-1}}{\prod} + C_1\,\Delta y_{t-1} + C_2\,\Delta y_{t-2} + \cdots + C_{p-1}\,\Delta y_{t-p+1} + u_t$$

in which $\Pi = -(\mathrm{I} - A_1 - A_2 - \cdots - A_p)$; $C_i = -\sum^{p}_{j=i+1} A_j$, $i = 1, 2, \ldots, \mathrm{p} - 1$

The model contains Πy_{t-1} as the correct part of errors in ECM. If y_t and k are cointegration, Π has the form

$$\underset{(k\times r)}{\prod} = \underset{(r\times k)}{\alpha \times \beta}$$

Then, $\Delta y_t = \alpha\beta y_{t-1} + C_1\,\Delta y_{t-1} + C_2\,\Delta y_{t-2} + \cdots + C_{p-1}\,\Delta y_{t-p+1} + u_t$

Set $\mathrm{EC}_{t-1} = \beta y_{t-1}$: nonstop series combos in y_t to become a stationary series; EC_{t-1} is the redundancy of those combinations and EC_{t-1} indicates an imbalance in period $t-1$. Then, α indicates the correction coefficient of Δy_t when an imbalance occurs.

4.2. *Data and model specifications*

The study has six variables: economic growth, USD/VND exchange rate (USDVND00), lending interest rate, credit provided by banks, financial development index, and regional private capital demand. According to Peng's study (2001), the degree of market orientation of transition economies is reflected in two aspects of the state control mechanism. The degree of privatization of the economy will affect economic growth. In fact, the government often uses two tools to intervene in the economy: the exchange rate and the interest rates. Vietnam implements a market-oriented economy, but this has not been widely recognized by international organizations. The main reason is that the factors of the money market, including exchange and interest rates, also have relative intervention from the state bank. Therefore, assessing the market economy is primarily based on state regulation of interest rates, exchange rates, and credit. On the other hand, Vietnam's economic transition has many similarities with that of China. That is, by focusing on the role of the state economic sector compared with other economic sectors and capital needs, domestic competitiveness determines the degree of economic openness. The characteristics of emerging countries like Vietnam are very dependent on the capital provided by the banking system in carrying out transformational economic activities. The study uses the financial development index and the capital demand of the private sector to represent the degree of privatization of the economy and measure the pass-through effect of the economy's degree of transformation on economic growth.

The scope of the study is the relationship between the market-oriented economy and the economic growth of Vietnam; the data are taken quarterly for the period from Q1 2000 to Q1 2022. The GDP of Vietnam is taken as a percentage. The economy's market mechanism is characterized by two main components: the state control mechanism, represented by the USD/VND exchange rate (USDVND00), and the lending interest rate, expressed as a percentage (IRO); credit provided by banks (DCB) and the degree of privatization of the capital demand of the private sector (CLP), respectively. credit provided by banks (DCB) and the degree of privatization of the economy are represented by the financial development index (INF) and the capital demand of the private sector (CLP), respectively. The data series are taken from IMF financial statistics (IFS). USDVND00, DCB, INF, and CLP are trend variables without normal distribution; the deviation level must be very high. The study converts this variable into a logarithmic base of natural form so that the variable has a distribution close to the normal distribution, meeting the input data conditions of the model. At the same time, the real exchange rate is calculated according to the ratio between the annual exchange rate to be calculated and the base year rate (the exchange rate of the first quarter 2000).

4.3. *Tests of the model*

4.3.1. *Unit root test of data*

The results of the unit root test, conducted at a significance level of α = 0.05%, indicate a rejection of the null hypothesis (H0) concerning unit roots for the series GDP, DCB, USDVND00, IRO, INF, and CLP, implying that all these series achieve stationarity at the second level of differencing. Thus, the stopped data series with the same order of difference are shown in Table 1.

4.3.2. *Cointergration test*

The Engle–Granger test (1987) shows that GDP, DCB, USDVND00, IRO, INF, and CLP all stop at the difference level of 2: I(2). Then, we use the

Table 1. Unit root test of data at the second difference ($d = 2$).

Augmented Dickey–Fuller test statistic	*t*-statistic	Prob.*
Null Hypothesis: GDP has a unit root	−5.579	0.000
Null Hypothesis: USDVND00 has a unit root	−11.384	0.000
Null Hypothesis: IRO has a unit root	−11.306	0.000
Null Hypothesis: DCB has a unit root	−7.898	0.000
Null Hypothesis: INF has a unit root	−14.111	0.000
Null Hypothesis: CLP has a unit root	−4.867	0.000

Table 2. Cointegration test.

Hypothesized no. of CE(s)	Eigenvalue	Trace statistic	0.05 critical value	Prob.**
None	0.735	439.907	95.753	0.0001
At most 1	0.685	328.125	69.818	0.0001
At most 2	0.632	230.983	47.856	0.0001
At most 3	0.573	146.805	29.797	0.0001
At most 4	0.425	75.253	15.494	0.0000
At most 5	0.289	28.767	3.841	0.0000

Note: Trace test indicates 5 cointegrating eqn(s) at the 0.05 level.

Johansen test to determine whether GDP, DC, IRO, INF, and CLP have cointegration.

The results obtained from Table 2 show that GDP, DCB, USDVND00, IRO, INF, and CLP have cointegration at a significance level of $\alpha = 0.05$; when $k = 0$ (None), the p-value $= 0.000 < \alpha$ should reject the hypothesis Ho: $r = 0$ (non-cointegration between variables).

4.3.3. *Optimal latency test*

The criteria in LR, FPE, and AIC will be used to determine the optimal delay for the model, although many information standards can be used to determine model latency. Johansen (1990) showed that the lag of VECM is lower than the latency of VAR at the 1 level. In the analysis, the authors define their proposed lag as $p = 3$ (Table 3).

4.3.4. *Stability check*

The AR root test is applied to test the stability of the VECM model by considering whether the test or the individual values are less than 1 or are in the unit circle; the VECM model achieves stability (Figure 1).

The estimation shows solutions in the unit circle, so the VECM model is stable. Thus, the tests show that stationary chains are at the same level of difference, and the cointegration test shows cointegration, ensuring that the VECM model selection is reasonable. With 3 as the appropriate

Table 3. Optimal latency test for model.

VAR lag order selection criteria						
Lag	**LogL**	**LR**	**FPE**	**AIC**	**SC**	**HQ**
0	−19.745	NA	7.55e−08	0.627	0.804	0.698
1	53.050	133.164	3.08e−08	−0.269	0.963	0.225
2	142.085	149.838	8.58e−09	−1.563	0.726*	−0.643
3	208.282	101.717	4.25e−09	−2.299	1.046	−0.956*
4	255.041	65.007*	3.50e−09*	−2.561*	1.840	−0.794
5	284.282	36.372	4.64e−09	−2.397	3.062	−0.205

Notes: *Indicates the lag order selected by the criterion. LR: sequential-modified LR test statistic (each test at 5% level); FPE: Final prediction error; AIC: Akaike information criterion; SC: Schwarz information criterion; HQ: Hannan–Quinn information criterion.

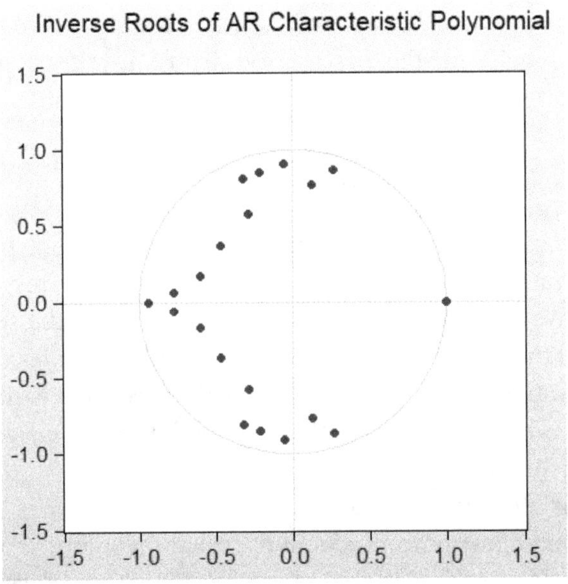

Figure 1. Stability test of the model.

selected latency, the VECM model is guaranteed to be stable and suitable for regression. From there, the authors analyzed variance decomposition and impulse response functions as the basis for the conclusions.

4.4. *Results and discussion*

After testing the VECM model, the results of the VECM regression model are obtained as follows.

The cointegration equation shows long-term relationships between variables in the form:

$$u = -\text{GDP} + 130.205\text{CLP} - 140.659\text{DCB} - 0.1002\text{INF} - 2.024\text{IRO} + 221.219\text{USDVND00} + 0.019$$

$$\text{GDP} = 0.019 + 130.205\text{CLP} - 140.659\text{DCB} - 0.1002\text{INF} - 2.024\text{IRO} + 221.219\text{USDVND00} - u$$

In the long run, GDP has a positive relationship with CLP and USDVND00 and an inverse relationship with the variables DCB, IRO, and INF.

$\text{EC}(t-1) = 0.064$ shows that with an imbalance in the previous period by 1 unit, the dependent variable will adjust in the same direction with the equilibrium of 6.4% in the first period. Thus, it takes two periods to restore equilibrium at the significance level $\alpha = 0.05$ (Table 4).

4.5. *Impulse response function*

Private sector capital demand volatility shocks represent the degree to which privatization of the economy leads to an initial response to real GDP. They have a particularly large impact on GDP in the second phase. It is explained that Vietnam, like other transition economies, is increasing economic privatization in line with the market economy's tendency. The private sector is becoming more efficient, and it has made significant contributions to economic growth (Figure 2).

Vietnam is a developing country; when the economy is boosted with capital, it encourages more production, hence favorably promoting economic growth. However, in the long run, the GDP reaction varies inversely with bank credit sources and financial depth. Poor capital management and utilization are prevalent problems in emerging economies. Although capital is critical to economic growth, effective capital use is always challenging for developing countries.

Table 4. VECM regression results.

Vector error correction estimates	
Cointegrating Eq:	**Coint Eq1**
GDP1(−1)	1.000
CLP1(−1)	130.205
	(24.749)
	[5.260]
DCB1(−1)	−140.659
	(24.311)
	[−5.7857]
INF1(−1)	−0.100
	(0.014)
	[−6.973]
IRO1(−1)	−2.024
	(0.290)
	[−6.960]
USDVND1(−1)	221.219
	(27.296)
	[8.104]
C	0.019

Note: Coint Eq1 = 0.064.

When there are fluctuations in financial depth, interest rates, and exchange rates, the responses of GDP are not especially large. Since Vietnam and other transition countries always regard market orientation as merely a component, the state continues to control and defend the economy using monetary policy tools. As a result, fluctuations in interest and currency rates do not accurately represent market realities and have little impact on economic growth. However, the state's ability to intervene in the money market through interest rates, exchange rates, and financial instruments will increasingly be limited. Vietnam joined the WTO; thus, it must follow through on its commitment to allow the economy to self-regulate through market mechanisms while gradually reducing state intervention.

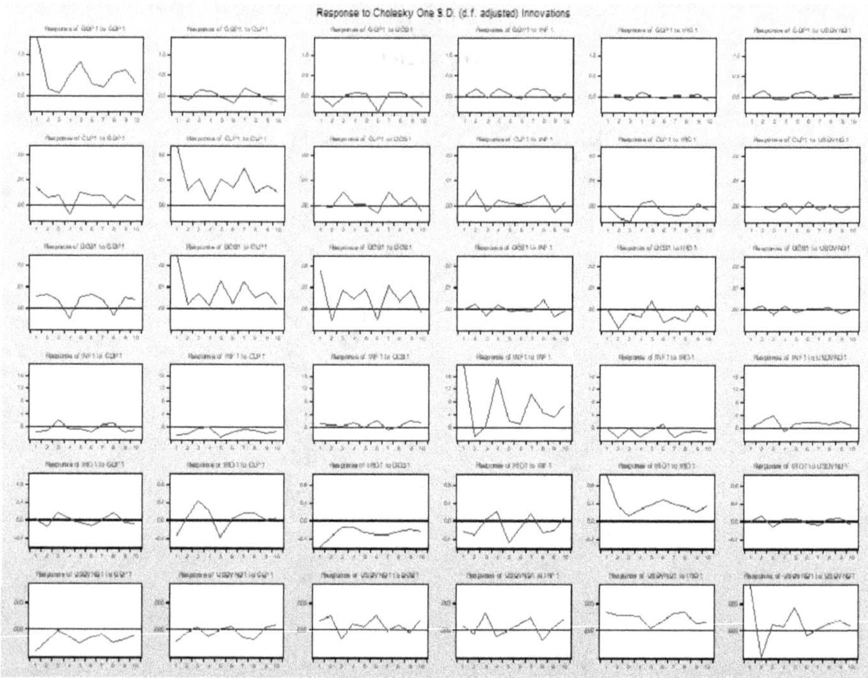

Figure 2. Impulse response function.

4.6. *Variance decomposition*

When forecasting variables in the VECM model, variance decomposition is used to distinguish the contribution of other time series as well as the time series itself in the variance of the forecast error. The variance decomposition results match well with the results of the impulse response function (Table 5). Although the prediction error in GDP attributable to variations in private sector capital demand is approximately 2%, it has been sustained and extended in subsequent periods, with no indications of decreasing. The variation in bank credit was over 5% compared to the variation in GDP from the sixth period. Exchange and interest rate variables have little impact on economic growth. This is completely consistent with the operating policy of the exchange rate; interest rates in Vietnam are still regulated by the state much more than the regulation of the market.

Table 5. Variance decomposition.

The variance decomposition of GDP1							
Period	**Std. error**	**GDP**	**CLP**	**DCB**	**INF**	**IRO**	**USDVND00**
1	1.397	100.000	0.000	0.000	0.000	0.000	0.000
2	1.454	93.318	0.784	3.278	1.623	0.034	0.959
3	1.465	92.002	1.512	3.232	1.709	0.456	1.086
4	1.559	90.631	1.610	3.001	2.792	0.785	1.178
5	1.755	92.309	1.350	2.454	2.210	0.631	1.043
6	1.827	87.279	2.257	6.319	2.170	0.661	1.311
7	1.856	85.609	3.122	6.240	2.989	0.657	1.380
8	1.939	86.079	2.933	5.848	3.266	0.601	1.269
9	2.037	86.910	2.727	5.346	3.224	0.584	1.205
10	2.086	84.828	2.996	7.057	3.206	0.732	1.178

4.7. *Further analysis*

Vietnam has different features in the process of transforming the economy from a centralized subsidy mechanism to a market mechanism. The study continues to use the NARDL model to examine whether there is a disproportionate impact of the mechanism of transition on economic growth. The subsample of data was taken from the first quarter of 2008 to the first quarter of 2022. The year 2008 marked Vietnam's accession to the WTO, which meant that Vietnam cannot control the economy closely and financial liberalization is required. The economy follows the market mechanism more clearly than in previous periods. NARDL model regression results are shown in Table 6.

This research tested the statistical significance of NARDL and performed a stability test of the estimated parameters using Cusum and Cusumsq as shown in Figure 3. The results confirmed that Cusum and Cusumsq are within the critical lines with a significance factor of 5%, so the model is stable and does not suffer from sudden shocks or structural breaks.

The results of the cumulative dynamic multiplier graphs (Figure 4) show that there is no disproportionate impact of factors when converting

Table 6. NARDL model for the sub-sample analysis.

Method: NARDL				
Variable	**Coefficient**	**Std. error**	***t*-statistic**	**Prob.***
DGDP(−1)	−0.216	0.158	−1.363	0.191
DGDP(−2)	−0.637	0.142	−4.465	0.000
DGDP(−3)	−0.251	0.145	−1.734	0.102
DCLP_POS	−29.897	19.878	−1.503	0.152
DCLP_POS(−1)	−128.940	23.847	−5.406	0.000
DCLP_NEG	−96.126	22.795	−4.216	0.000
DCLP_NEG(−1)	−6.797	18.801	−0.361	0.722
DCLP_NEG(−2)	−61.734	14.769	−4.179	0.000
DDCB_POS	10.730	15.286	0.701	0.492
DDCB_POS(−1)	37.418	16.835	2.222	0.041
DDCB_POS(−2)	−28.134	15.145	−1.857	0.081
DDCB_POS(−3)	−39.437	14.912	−2.644	0.017
DDCB_NEG	124.863	21.895	5.702	0.000
DDCB_NEG(−1)	−42.349	13.943	−3.037	0.007
DINF_POS	0.079	0.031	2.523	0.022
DINF_POS(−1)	−0.000	0.041	−0.011	0.991
DINF_POS(−2)	0.090	0.037	2.411	0.028
DINF_POS(−3)	0.061	0.030	2.016	0.060
DINF_NEG	−0.118	0.036	−3.257	0.004
DINF_NEG(−1)	0.051	0.031	1.658	0.116
DINF_NEG(−2)	0.045	0.027	1.652	0.118
DINF_NEG(−3)	0.096	0.025	3.809	0.001
DIRO_POS	1.986	0.415	4.777	0.000
DIRO_POS(−1)	−0.340	0.484	−0.702	0.492
DIRO_POS(−2)	−0.659	0.365	−1.805	0.089
DIRO_POS(−3)	−0.300	0.311	−0.964	0.349
DIRO_NEG	−0.260	0.400	−0.651	0.524
DIRO_NEG(−1)	0.517	0.497	1.038	0.314
DIRO_NEG(−2)	0.263	0.348	0.756	0.460

Table 6. (*Continued*)

Method: NARDL				
Variable	**Coefficient**	**Std. error**	***t*-statistic**	**Prob.***
DUSDVND_POS	–54.127	20.627	–2.624	0.018
DUSDVND_POS(–1)	99.048	36.166	2.738	0.014
DUSDVND_NEG	42.706	33.355	1.280	0.218
DUSDVND_NEG(–1)	–70.541	25.246	–2.794	0.013
DUSDVND_NEG(–2)	–17.453	25.835	–0.675	0.509
DUSDVND_NEG(–3)	–59.983	19.702	–3.044	0.007
C	–8.686	5.713	–1.520	0.147
R-squared	0.928	Mean dependent var		0.036
Adjusted *R*-squared	0.771	S.D. dependent var		1.118
S.E. of regression	0.534	Akaike info criterion		1.789
Sum squared resid	4.564	Schwarz criterion		3.140
Log likelihood	–10.528	Hannan–Quinn criterion		2.307
F-statistic	5.932	Durbin–Watson stat.		2.561
Prob(*F*-statistic)	0.000			

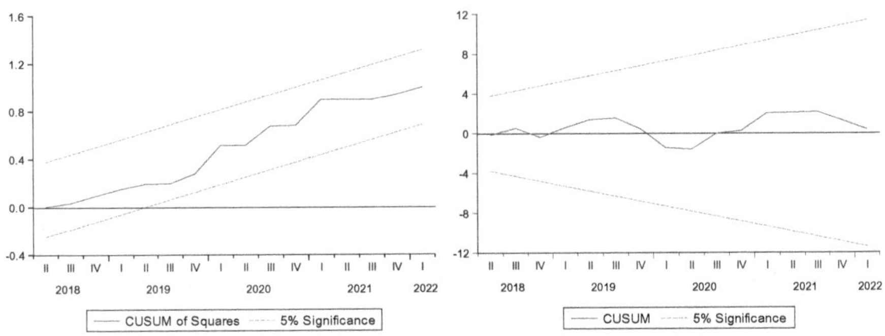

Figure 3. Plots of CUSUM and CUSUMSQ tests.

from a centralized subsidy mechanism to a market mechanism on Vietnam's economic growth. This shows that the government's operating policy during the transition is relatively consistent. Vietnam has learned from the experiences of other countries, especially China, in the process

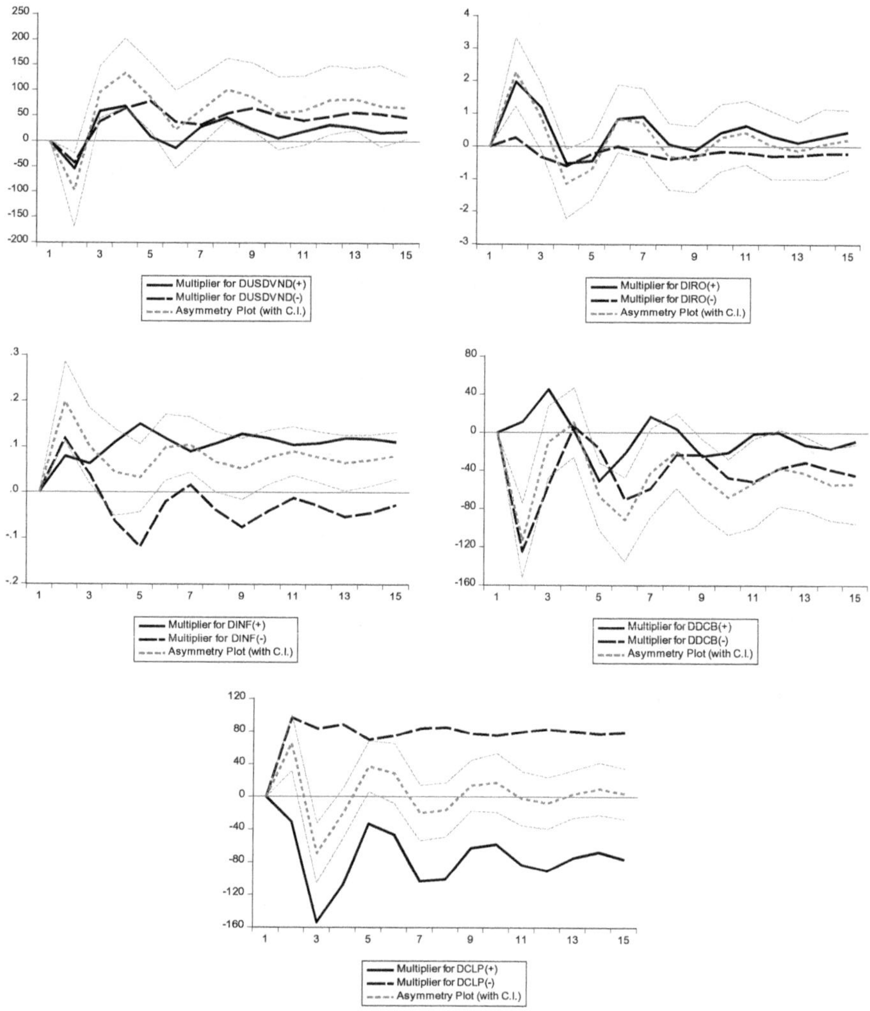

Figure 4. NARDL dynamic multiplier effect graphs of economic growth.

Note: The ultra-thin line is the boundary.

of economic transformation. The economy's potential is still weak, so it is not possible to carry out the transformation to a market-oriented economy immediately, but it must be done step by step. The transformation process requires the intervention of the State to support domestic actors to survive and develop, gradually improve competitiveness, and promote domestic potential.

Our findings indicate that the reform process in transition economies is complicated and has diverse effects on several aspects of economic growth as countries experience rapid and significant changes. The most important result is that while the reform has had a beneficial influence, policy issues and fiscal policy packages remain critical. The importance of privatization is reaffirmed. The harmful consequence of bank credit is a critical future lesson.

According to Lawrence and Lorsch (1967), no uniform organizational form is ideally suited to all institutional situations. Classical state socialism's formal and hierarchical features are best adapted to a homogeneous and stable environment. Organizations that are more flexible, informal, and open to entrepreneurship, on the other hand, will display higher flexibility in times of fast change and institutional uncertainty (Piore and Sabel, 1984). Hansen *et al.* (2020) argue that the socialist market economic model in China, Vietnam, and Laos works better than the economic systems of countries with similar per capita incomes in many areas.

4.8. *Development index*

The emergence of enterprises from non-state sectors in transition economies is a phenomenon that evolved during the 1980s' economic reform. The rapid growth of these private sectors has challenged the status quo of central planning and provided an impetus for transition economies to continue with economic reforms. Non-SOEs are the most active force in the transition economy today and embody the fundamental character of a market economy. The transition economy's non-SOEs have various ownership arrangements, including collectively owned enterprises, private enterprises, joint-stock cooperatives, and even international joint ventures. The number of SOEs has shrunk dramatically in recent years. In contrast to SOEs, transition economies have seen tremendous growth in private enterprises (Bruton *et al.*, 2000).

5. Conclusion

Local state collectivism contributes to corporate entrepreneurship for several reasons. The first reason is that in some transition economies, local community governments are part of a powerful authority structure with various authoritative entities. Their assistance can give nearby companies and other stakeholders a sense of security, help them avoid administrative hassles, and increase economic efficiency. Second, capable local organizations can be crucial in accessing outside resources, particularly bank loans. Third, they can provide suggestions and guarantee market efficiency within the region. We can conclude that local state collectivism encourages social entrepreneurship by reducing costs and generating market-oriented commercial activity.

The development of private enterprise within transition economies was neither planned nor anticipated by central governments (Byrd and Lin, 1989). Instead, they evolved initially from the increasing government acceptance of non-SOEs in the 1970s and received formal recognition and encouragement in the 1980s when it was found that non-SOEs are an important means of economic promotion. More importantly, they can absorb large amounts of surplus labor without much financial support from the state (Jin and Qian, 1998).

Private businesses grow outside the planned economy in transition economies because they do not operate under the planned regime, instead following market orientation over the model of government-run businesses. In general, three factors — governance institutions, management networks, and market orientation — can direct the commercial activities of non-SOEs (Deng and Dart, 1999).

Companies cannot execute market transactions effectively in transition economies because of the lack of transparent laws and regulations, as well as policy uncertainty. As a result, creating a solid and stable network of connections between business managers and public authorities is promoted (Peng and Luo, 2000).

Acknowledgements

Thi Thuy Hang Le acknowledges all lecturers and managers of the University of Finance – Marketing, Ho Chi Minh City, Vietnam. Besides, this research is supported by the University of Finance – Marketing.

References

Aghion, P. & Schankerman, M. (1999). Competition, entry and the social returns to infrastructure in transition economies. *Economics of Transition*, *7*(1), 79–101.

Ambler, T., Chris, S., & Wang, X. (1999). The effect of channel relationships and Guanxi on the performance of inter-province export ventures in the Peoples' Republic of China. *International Journal of Research in Marketing*, *16*(1), 75–87.

Baum, M. A. (2020). Vietnam's development success story and the unfinished SDG agenda. International Monetary Fund, Washington DC, United States. doi:10.5089/9781513527024.001.

Bekkevold, J. I., Hansen, A., & Nordhaug, K. (2020). Introducing the socialist market economy. *The Socialist Market Economy in Asia*, 3–25. doi:10.1007/978-981-15-6248-8_1.

Bekkevold, J. I., Hansen, A., & Nordhaug, K. (2021). The socialist market economy in China, Vietnam and Laos: A development model to embrace? Developing economics. Available at: https://developingeconomics.org/2021/01/11/the-socialist-market-economy-in-china-vietnam. [Accessed on February 2022].

Black, B., Kraakman, R., & Tarassova, A. (2000). Russian privatization and corporate governance: What went wrong? *Stanford Law Review*, *52*, 1731–1808.

Bonnell, V. (1980). The use of theory, concepts and comparison in historical sociology. *Comparative Studies in History and Society*, *22*, 156–173.

Borys, B. & Jemison, D. B. (1989). Hybrid arrangements as strategic alliances: Theoretical issues in organizational combinations. *Academy of Management Review*, *14*, 234–249.

Bruton, G. D., Lan, H., & Lu, Y. (2000). China's township and village enterprises: Kelon's competitive edge. *Academy of Management Executive*, *14*(1), 19–29.

Byrd, W. A. & Lin, Q. (1989), *China's Rural Industry: Structure, Development, and Reform*. New York, NY: Oxford University Press.

CASS, Study Group for Guidelines for Midterm Reform of the Economic Structure, (1989). Ideas for the midterm (1988–1995) reform of China's economic structure. *Social Sciences of China*, *10*, 39–73.

Center for WTO and International Trade. (2022). Vietnam's FTAs as of January 2022. Available at: https://wtocenter.vn/thong-ke/13814-vietnams-ftas-summary-as-of-april-2019,%202020 [Accessed on February 2022].

Child, J. & Tse, D. K. (2001), China's transition and its implications for international business. *Journal of International Business Studies*, *32*(1), 5–22.

De Macedo, J. B. & Martins, J.O. (2008), Growth, reform indicators and policy complementarities, *Economics of Transition*, *16*(2), 141–164.

Deng, S. & Dart, J. (1999), The market orientation of Chinese enterprises during a time of transition. *European Journal of Marketing*, *33*(5/6), 631–54.

Eglinger, J.-P. (2021). The role of the private economy in the socialist-oriented market economy in Vietnam. *The Russian Journal of Vietnamese Studies*, *5*(5S), 44–51. doi:10.54631/vs.2021.s-44-51.

Fischer, S., Sahay, R., & Vegh, C. A. (1996), Economies in transition: The beginnings of growth. *American Economic Review*, *86*(2), 229–233.

Gillespie, J. (2018). Is Vietnam transitioning out of socialism or transforming socialism? Searching for answers in commercial regulation. In *Socialist Law in Socialist East Asia* (pp. 319–350). Cambridge, United Kingdom: Cambridge University Press. doi:10.1017/9781108347822.012.

Granger, C. W. J. & Newbold, P. (1987). Spurious regressions in econometrics. *Journal of Econometrics*, *2*, 111–120.

Hansen, A., Bekkevold, J. I., & Nordhaug, K., (2020). *The Socialist Market Economy in Asia: Development in China, Vietnam and Laos*. Singapore: Palgrave Macmillan. doi:10.1007/978-981-15-6248-8.

Havrylyshyn, O. (2001). Recovery and growth in transition: A decade of evidence. *IMF Staff Papers*, *48*(Special Issue), 53–87.

Hu, J. (2019). Analysis of the innovation and development of the socialist market economy theory. *China Political Economy*, *2*(1), 85–97. doi:10.1108/cpe-04-2019-0006.

Hualing, F., Gillespie, J., Nicholson, P., & Partlett, W. (2018). *Socialist Law in Socialist East Asia* (pp. 3–22). Cambridge: Cambridge University Press. doi:10.1017/9781108347822.001.

Jaworski, B. J. & K. Kohli, K. A (1996). Market orientation: Review, refinement and roadmap. *Journal of Market-focused Management*, *1*(1), 119–135.

Jin, H. & Qian, Y. (1998). Public versus private ownership of firms: Evidence from rural China. *The Quarterly Journal of Economics, August*, *113*(3), 773–808.

Johansen, S. (1988). The statistical analysis of cointegration vectors. *Journal of Economic Dynamics and Control*, *12*(2–3), 231–254.

Johansen, S. (1990). Testing for cointegration using the Johansen methodology when variables are near-integrated. *Journal of IMF Working paper W07/1041*.

King, L., Hamm, P., & Stuckler, D. (2009). Rapid large-scale privatization and death rates in ex-communist countries: An analysis of stress-related and health system mechanisms. *International Journal of Health Services*, *39*, 3, 461–489.

Knutsen, H. M. & Khanh, D. T. (2020). Reforming state-owned enterprises in a global economy: The case of Vietnam. In *The Socialist Market Economy in Asia* (pp. 141–166). Singapore: Palgrave Macmillan. doi:10.1007/978-981-15-6248-8_5.

Kornai, J. (1980). *Economics of Shortage* (2 vols). Amsterdam: North-Holland.

Kornai, J. (1989). The Hungarian reform process: Visions, hopes, and reality. In Victor, N., & Stark, D. (eds.), *Remaking the Economic Institutions of Socialism: China and Eastern Europe* (pp. 32–94). Stanford, CA: Stanford University Press.

Kueh, Y. Y. (1985). Economic planning and local mobilization in post-Mao China. *Research Notes and Studies, Contemporary China Institute School of Oriental and African Studies*, *7*, 1–56.

Lardy, N. (1991). Is China different? The fate of its economic reforms. In Chirot, D. (ed.), *The Crisis of Leninism and the Decline of the Left: The Revolutions of 1989* (pp. 147–162). Seattle: University of Washington Press.

Lawrence, P. R. & Lorsch, J. W. (1967). *Organization and Environment: Managing Differentiation and Integration*. Boston: Graduate School of Business Administration, Harvard University.

Lee, J. Y. (2018). A theoretical revisit to the China's marketization: Reflection on neo-liberal approach to the socialist market economy with Chinese characteristics. *Journal of China Studies*, *21*(2), 37–56. doi:10.20288/jcs.2018.21.2.37.

Liu, S. S., Luo, X., & Shi, Y. (2003). Market-oriented organizations in an emerging economy: a study of missing links. *Journal of Business Research*, *56*, 481–491.

Lyons, T. P. (1990). Planning and interprovincial co-ordination in Maoist China. *China Quarterly*, *121*, 36–60.

Nee, V. & Sijin, S. (1990). Institutional change and economic growth in China: The view from the villages. *Journal of Asian Studies*, *49*, 3–25.

Nee, V. (1989). Peasant entrepreneurship and the politics of regulation in China. In Victor Nee and David Stark (eds.). *Remaking the Economic Institutions of Socialism: China and Eastern Europe* (pp. 169–207). Stanford, CA: Stanford University Press.

Nepal, R. & Jamasb, T. (2012). Reforming the power sector in transition: Do institutions matter. *Energy Economics*, *34*(5), 1675–1682.

Peng, M. W. & Luo, Y. (2000). Managerial ties and firm performance in a transition economy: the nature of a micro-macro link. *Academy of Management Journal*, *43*(3), 486–501.

Peng, M. W. & Shekshnia, S. V. (2001). How entrepreneurs create wealth in transition economies. *Academy of Management Review*, *15*(1), 95–110.

Peng, Y. (2001). Chinese villages and townships as industrial corporations: Ownership, governance, and market discipline. *American Journal of Sociology*, *106*(5), 1338–1370.

Perenyi, A., Esposto, A., & Bamforth, J. (2019). Institutional transformation and development from an economic transition perspective: The case of Argentina. *Journal of Institutional Economics*, *16*(1), 83–104. doi:10.1017/S1744137419000134.

Piore, M. J. & Sabel, C. F. (1984). *The Second Industrial Divide: Possibilities for Prosperity*. New York: Basic Books.

Powell, W. W. (1988). Institutional effects on organizational structure and performance. In Zucker, L. G. (ed.), *Institutional Patterns and Organizations: Culture and Environment* (pp. 115–136). Cambridge, MA: Ballinger.

Savitt, R. (1999). The prospects of becoming market oriented: Evidence from the Czech Republic. In Bastra, R. (ed.), *Marketing Issues in Transitional Economies*. Boston: Kluwer Academic Publishers.

Staehr, K. (2005). Reforms and economic growth in transition economies: Complementarity, sequencing and speed. *The European Journal of Comparative Economics*, *2*(2), 177–202.

Stiglitz, J. (1999). Whither reform? Ten years of transition. In Paper Presented at the *Annual Bank Conference on Development Economics* (pp. 127–171). Washington, DC, April.

Tompson, W. (2007). Healthcare reform in Russia: Problems and prospects. *OECD Economics Department Working Papers* No. 538. Paris: OECD Publishing.

Tong, J. (1989). Fiscal reform, elite turnover and central-provincial relations in post-Mao China. *Australian Journal of Chinese Affairs*, *22*, 1–28.

ul Haq, M. (1996). *Reflections on Human Development.* New York, Oxford: Oxford University Press.

Vogel, E. F. (1989). *One Step Ahead in China: Guangdong under Reform.* Cambridge, MA: Harvard University Press.

Walder, A. G. (1989). Factory and manager in an era of reform. *China Quarterly*, *118*, 242–254.

Williamson, O. E. (1991). Comparative economic organization: The analysis of discrete structural alternatives. *Administrative Science Quarterly*, *36*, 269–296.

Wong, C. P. W. (1986). The economics of shortage and problems of reform in Chinese industry. *Journal of Comparative Economics*, *10*, 363–387.

Wong, C. P. W. (1987). Between plan and market: The role of the local sector in post-Mao China. *Journal of Comparative Economics*, *11*, 385–398.

Wong, C. P. W. (1990). Central-local relations in an era of fiscal decline: The paradox of fiscal decentralization in post-Mao China. *Working Paper* #210. Department of Economics, University of California, Santa Cruz.

World Bank. (2022). The World Bank in Vietnam. Available at: https://www.worldbank.org/en/country/vietnam/overview#1. [Accessed on February 2022].

Xin, K. R. & Pearce, J. L. (1996). Guanxi: Connections as substitutes for formal institutional support. *Academy of Management Journal*, *39*, 1641–1658.

Zhang, S. & Zhang, A. (1987). The present management environment in China's industrial enterprises. In Reynolds, B. (ed.), *Reform in China: Challenges and Choices* (pp. 47–59). Armonk, New York: M. E. Sharpe.

Zhang, Y. (2020a). The contribution of the School of New Marxist Economics to China's Socialist Market Economy. *World Review of Political Economy*, *11*(1), 4–27. doi:10.13169/worlrevipoliecon.11.1.0004.

Zhang, Z. (2020b). The establishment of the theory of socialist market economy in 1992 and its rise as the theoretical pillar for China to deepen reform and opening up. In *Historical Perspectives on Chinese Economics* (pp. 1949–2011). Singapore: Springer. doi:10.1007/978-981-15-8163-2_15.

https://doi.org/10.1142/9789811286100_0010

Chapter 10

The Role of Social Investment in Information, Communication, Science, and Technology on the Productivity Growth of Enterprises in Vietnam

Quang Hai Nguyen

Faculty Business Administration,
Ho Chi Minh City University of Industry and Trade, Vietnam

quangnhai@huit.edu.vn

Abstract

The development of science and technology (ST) and information and communication (IC) has positively affected countries socioeconomically. The aim of this study is to explore the impact of social investment in IC and ST on the output growth of enterprises in different industries. The study focuses on enterprises in 77 Tier-2 industries in Vietnam and is divided into three samples: industry and construction, services, and overall data for the period 2008–2019. The chosen estimator is the panel generalized method of moments (GMM). The results were checked for robustness via comparison with the panel least squares (LS) method. The results confirm that business capital and labor are still the two basic inputs that determine the output value of enterprises. However, social investment in IC and ST also plays a significant role. Different roles of explanatory factors for output value were also found between enterprises in two economic sectors: the industry and construction sector, and the service sector.

Received on December 1, 2022; accepted on March 24, 2023

Enterprises in industry and construction benefit more from society's investment in IC and ST than enterprises in the service sector.

Keywords: Social Investment, Information and Communication, Science and Technology, Productivity Growth, Enterprise.

1. Introduction

In recent decades, the scientific and technological revolution has promoted the growth and development of countries around the world, especially in terms of economy and society. Investments in information technology and communications (ITC) and research and development (R&D) are important drivers of growth worldwide (Edquist & Henrekson, 2017). Thus, insights into how investments in ICT and R&D or science and technology (ST) have affected productivity growth are of interest to many economists and policymakers. Economists have used models derived from production theory to estimate the impact of these factors on economic activities, focusing on topics such as the impact of ICT on productivity growth in the US (Jorgenson *et al.*, 2008) and in developing and developed countries (Dimelis *et al.*, 2010); labor productivity in the EU (Relich, 2017); economic growth in Australia (Shahiduzzaman and Alam, 2014), Asian countries (Pradhan *et al.*, 2015), developed countries (Bahrini and Qaffas, 2019), and OECD countries (Kurniawati, 2020); the impact of ST on the outputs of enterprises in Spain (Parrilli and Elola, 2012); the impact of R&D on economic growth in the EU (McMorrow and Röger, 2009); and the impact of both ICT and R&D on total factor productivity (TFP) growth and value-added across different industries in Sweden (Edquist and Henrekson, 2017) and ten countries in the EU, the US, and Japan (Haider *et al.*, 2021). These studies have shown the positive impact of ICT and IC or R&D in different contexts. However, most of the studies focus on countries and regions with developed, high-income, or upper-middle-income economies (Jorgenson *et al.*, 2008; McMorrow and Röger, 2009; Parrilli and Elola, 2012; Shahiduzzaman and Alam, 2014; Edquist and Henrekson, 2017; Bahrini and Qaffas, 2019; Kurniawati, 2020; Haider và cộng sự, 2021). Research comparing sectors in low-income or lower-middle-income developing countries has received little attention, especially in Asia. The author found only Pradhan *et al.* (2015)

and Dimelis *et al.* (2010) focusing on comparative analysis between developing and developed countries in Asia. Therefore, the role of social investment in IC and ST on the growth of enterprises in general and across sectors in particular is an issue worthy of research attention, especially in Vietnam, a developing economy.

According to the Prime Minister (2018), Vietnam's economic sector system is divided into 21 Tier-1 sectors and 88 Tier-2 sectors. Tier-1 and Tier-2 sectors are grouped into three main economic sectors: (1) agriculture, forestry, and fishing; (2) industry and construction; and (3) service. As of December 31, 2019, Vietnam had over 668,000 operating enterprises with production and business results (the service sector accounted for 67.1%; the industry and construction sector accounted for 31.6%; and agriculture, forestry, and fishing accounted for 1.3%). These enterprises employ 12.5 million employees and use 41 billion VND of capital, contributing about 890 trillion VND in profit and about 60% to the GDP of the country (GSO, 2021). Therefore, enterprises play a key role in the economic development of Vietnam.

Over the years, Vietnamese enterprises have made rapid developments, thanks to increased scale, technological innovation, and social advances including social investment in IC and ST development. According to GSO data, in 2019, Vietnamese enterprises had increased in business capital, labor, revenue, and profit before tax plus income of employees, by 6.70, 1.84, 4.89, and 5.20 times, respectively, since 2008. Investment in IC and ST development helps enterprises expand their knowledge and access new technologies; it also makes transportation and communication more convenient. However, these effects are not the same across sectors. The question is as follows: in which economic sector do enterprises benefit the most from social investment in IC and ST?

The main objective of this chapter is to determine the contribution of basic inputs (capital and labor) and social investment in IC and ST to the productivity growth of enterprises and examine the different roles these factors play across enterprises in different sectors in Vietnam. The study results will be the basis for proposing investment and development policies for IC and ST to promote enterprise development in different sectors.

The remainder of the chapter is organized into four sections. Section 2 presents a literature review. The specification model, definitions of variables and data, and estimation methods are presented in Section 3. Section 4 reports the results of the estimation of the coefficients, checks the certainty, and discusses the research results. Finally, the conclusion in Section 5 presents the main findings, implications, and limitations of the study.

2. Literature Review

2.1. *The role of ICT in economic and productivity growth*

ICT refers to products "intended to fulfill or enable the function of information processing and communications by electronic means, including transmission and display" (OECD, 2009, p. 90). It includes the technologies and services related to computing, data management, telecommunications, and internet provision for information processing and transmission. Therefore, from an investment perspective, the capital invested in IC can be considered an investment in ICT. Today, ICT pervades and develops strongly into all aspects of life and provides new knowledge faster. It helps enterprises and economies improve efficiency with software for information, automated data storage, and management processes. ICT thereby helps enterprises obtain new products and services at lower costs and receive better customer support.

The link between ICT and economic growth is of great interest and has been examined in many different contexts. At the macro level, studies have reinforced the positive impacts of ICT capital or ICT infrastructure on economic growth in different areas, focusing on countries around the world (Vu, 2011) and on specific places such as Australia (Shahiduzzaman and Alam, 2014), Asian countries (Pradhan *et al.*, 2015), developed countries (Bahrini and Qaffas, 2019), and OECD countries (Kurniawati, 2020). From an industry and enterprise perspective, ICT can have both direct and indirect impacts on value-added and productivity growth. Edquist and Henrekson (2017) argue that ICT's direct impact can be measured using growth calculations, assessing the contribution of different inputs to added value, while its indirect effect is its contribution to TFP at the sector level in each specific industry. Thus, data at aggregate, industry, and company levels can be used to estimate direct and indirect impacts.

The neoclassical theory holds that ICT has a direct impact on investment, input substitution, and capital deepening (Stiroh, 2002) and thus has a direct impact on value-added and labor productivity. This implies that industries that invest more in ICT will experience higher TFP growth, due to improved information management, easier data exchange, and faster dissemination (Venturini *et al.*, 2013). Evidence of ICT's direct impact has been found in many studies; value-added has been demonstrated in 10 countries in the EU, the US, and Japan (Haider *et al.* (2021), as well as in Sweden (Edquist and Henrekson, 2017); productivity growth has been demonstrated in the US (Jorgenson *et al.*, 2008); and labor productivity has been demonstrated in the EU (Relich (2017). Additionally, ICT's indirect effect was shown in Van der Wiel and van Leeuwen (2003) for firms in the Netherlands and in Brynjolfsson and Hitt (2003) and Venturini *et al.* (2013) for firms in the US.

2.2. *The role of ST in economic and productivity growth*

ST has long been considered an important determinant of economic growth and has received more attention in recent years, because of the greater emphasis on the role of intellectual property and transferred knowledge (Feldman *et al.*, 2012). The G7 industrialized countries (2017) argue that science, technology, and innovation have long been important drivers of economic growth and human development. Therefore, the United Nations Educational, Scientific and Cultural Organization, UNESCO (2020), has affirmed that investment in these areas is necessary for economic development and social progress. Çalışkan (2015, p. 653) emphasizes that "scientific and technological changes form the motivating power of scientific and economic policies adopted to ensure economic growth and development". Furthermore, Şener and Sarıdoğan (2011) argue that science, technology, and innovation are important variables for long-term economic growth and that technological development brings economic growth because classical growth models show that technological change is exogenously determined. An empirical study by Parrilli and Elola (2012) in Spain shows that the outputs of small and medium enterprises (SMEs) are very sensitive to ST drivers, while Do (2019) shows that science, technology, and innovation play a key role in maintaining high economic growth rates. Many developing countries have positive attitudes toward ST.

Based on this theoretical overview and the related empirical results, this study finds that investment in IC and ST development has a positive impact on the output of enterprises across different sectors.

3. Methods and Data

3.1. *Specification model*

Based on the theoretical overview and the production function theory, this study uses the input factors affecting the outputs of enterprises including business capital, labor volume of enterprises, and social investment into IC and ST (ICST). Due to the lack of access to data on capital for IC and ST in the business capital of each enterprise, it is not possible to separate the K of the enterprise that does not include the enterprise's business capital for ICST. Therefore, it is possible that an amount of investment capital for ICST in Tier-2 industries is included in society's total investment capital in ICST in each observation. However, this is a small amount, so the capital calculated twice is not significant.

The combined value of social investment capital for IC and ST in a single variable is derived from the relationship between them. To be more specific, the products of ST activities may bring about innovations in all sectors of the economy, including IC. In contrast, IC products also help all sectors increase labor productivity and support the development of ST. Combining IC and ST helps assess the overall impact of both. In addition, merged variables often have more values than the variables they are composed of (Bonet and Van Den Briel, 2014). When the independent variables have multicollinearity, researchers often combine them into a single index (O'Brien, 2007).

Regarding the output factor, although Stiroh (2005) points out that there are both advantages and disadvantages to using added value instead of total output, it is the best choice for this study, because it provides nominal value-added sums to GDP. Moreover, it also helps bring about common value when considering enterprises across different industries and sectors. Using value-added instead of total output has been widely applied in studies of economic growth (Zwick, 2003; Edquist and Henrekson, 2017, Haider *et al.*, 2021; Nguyen, 2021). The general model in this study is shown in Equation (1):

$$\mathrm{VA}_{i,t} = K_{i,t}^{\alpha} L_{i,t}^{\beta} \mathrm{ICST}_{t}^{\gamma} \quad (1)$$

where VA denotes the added value; K denotes the amount of capital; L denotes the amount of labor; α, β, and γ are the contribution coefficients of capital, labor, and ICST, respectively, which are expected to be positive; i denotes Tier-2 sectors; and t denotes the time in years.

Equation (2) is the result of taking natural logarithms on both sides of Equation (1):

$$\ln \mathrm{VA}_{i,t} = \alpha \ln K_{i,t} + \beta \ln K_{i,t} + \gamma \ln \mathrm{ICST}_{t} + \varepsilon_{i,t} \quad (2)$$

where $\varepsilon_{i,t}$ denotes the error term.

3.2. *Variables' definitions and data*

Under the income method, value added is determined by the sum of gross profit, interest, taxes, labor costs, and depreciation. In other words, it includes labor cost, depreciation, profit before tax, and interest. Since there are no data on depreciation and interest expense, this study uses profit before tax and employee incomes as a proxy for added value, as in Thanh *et al.* (2019) and Nguyen (2021). The variables of interest are defined in Table 1.

Annual data on average capital and labor, profit before tax, and employee incomes of enterprises from 2008 to 2019 were collected from the Statistical Yearbook of Vietnam. The data include 77 enterprises in

Table 1. Variables' definitions.

Variable	Definition
VA	Employee incomes and profit before tax of enterprises
K	Annual average capital of the enterprise
L	Average total number of employees in the year of the enterprise
ICST	Investment capital of society at current prices in IC and ST activities

Tier-2 industries, with a time series of 12 years. To ensure data stability, cases where the total profit before tax and employee incomes were not positive or were too small were not used. Equation (2) was developed for three samples, namely enterprises in the industry and construction sector (Sample 1), enterprises in the service sector (Sample 2), and overall enterprise data (Sample 3). The samples used in the study are summarized in Table 2.

The descriptive statistics in Table 2 show a significant difference in the size of the panel objects in the samples, namely in terms of capital, labor, and output value; on the other hand, social investment capital in IC and ST was quite stable from 2008 to 2019. This demonstrates strong heterogeneity in panel data. Table 2 also shows that the dependent variable and the explanatory variable are closely correlated with each other in all three samples and provide a solid basis for the estimation models. The correlation between the explanatory variables is generally quite weak, except between the amount of capital and labor in all three samples; this will be tested separately in the econometric specification model.

3.3. *Estimation method*

Different econometric procedures can be applied to fit data and achieve the research objectives. Based on the collected data, this study applies the GMM panel approach for several reasons. First, the total time (T) of 12 years is much lower than the number of cross-sections (*N* values for Samples 1, 2 and 3 are 37, 40, and 77, respectively). Second, it is considered an effective method due to the dynamic nature of panel data (Roodman, 2009). Third, the GMM approach also addresses the expected correlation between the error term and object-fixed effects and solves the endogeneity and heterogeneity issues (Bakhsh *et al.*, 2021). Furthermore, Nickell (1981) argues that, in general, when T is small, the first difference method is not suitable. In the GMM approach, a two-step system produces more efficient estimators than a one-step system (Bakhsh *et al.*, 2021); thus, such a system is applied in this study. By default, the lag of the dependent variable is chosen to be 1. This is consistent with the data with small T in this study, like the lag of the dependent variable applied in

Table 2. Descriptive statistics and correlation.

		Descriptive statistics					Correlation				
	Variable	Unit	Mean	Maximum	Minimum	Std. Dev.	K	L	ICST	VA	Note
Sample 1	K	billion VND	197,434	1,784,642	125	274,076	1.000				Industries (*N*): 37 Observations: 420
	L	People	216,146	1,598,372	264	293,376	0.392***	1.000			
	ICST	billion VND	36,588	41,815	29,671	3,249	0.128**	0.041	1.000		
	VA	billion VND	24,586	237,103	16	31,706	0.611***	0.711***	0.127***	1.000	
Sample 2	K	billion VND	336,007	11,147,158	263	1,167,022	1.000				Industries (*N*): 40 Observations: 468
	L	People	99,075	1,422,696	1,306	190,419	0.425***	1.000			
	ICST	billion VND	36,566	41,815	29,671	3,236	0.072	0.058	1.000		
	VA	billion VND	14,676	219,770	17	30,253	0.848***	0.755***	0.108***	1.000	
Sample 3	K	billion VND	270,466	11,147,158	125	870,247	1.000				Industries (*N*): 77 Observations: 888
	L	People	154,446	1,598,372	264	251,332	0.277***	1.000			
	ICST	billion VND	36,576	41,815	29,671	3,241	0.070**	0.047	1.000		
	VA	billion VND	19,363	237,103	16	31,325	0.658***	0.724***	0.116***	1.000	

Note: *** and ** for statistical significance at 0.01 and 0.05 levels, respectively.

Bakhsh *et al.* (2021). From Equation (2), the econometric specification model for the GMM approach is expressed in Equation (3):

$$\ln \mathrm{VA}_{i,t} = \delta \ln \mathrm{VA}_{i,t-1} + \alpha \ln K_{i,t} + \beta \ln K_{i,t} + \gamma \ln \mathrm{ICST}_{t} + \varepsilon_{i,t} \quad (3)$$

where δ denotes the elasticity coefficient lnVA with a lag of 1 year.

$\ln \mathrm{VA}_{i,t-1}$ indicates the lagged value of the output quantity, a proxy variable for value added of enterprises in industry *i* at time *t*, which represents the dynamic nature of the model. The lag of the dependent variable is associated with the error term. The first difference of the variables, selected to prevent an industry-specific effect, is called the GMM difference (Arellano and Bond, 1991). This study proposes using the lag of the dependent variable and the explanatory variable as an instrument.

The appropriateness of the GMM approach was confirmed by the reasonable number of instrumental variables, the endogeneity was tested using the Hansen test (*J*-statistic test), and the phenomenon of series correlation was taken from Arellano and Bond (1991). In addition, robustness tests were performed by estimating the coefficients of the explanatory variable using an alternative estimator which fit the data. Data were processed and analyzed by the software Eviews 10.

4. Results and Discussion

4.1. *Estimated coefficients*

Estimation results by Panel GMM on the impact of inputs on the three samples' outputs are summarized in Table 3. For each sample, the necessary statistics are presented to test for a reasonable number of instrumental variables, endogeneity, and series correlation.

The estimated results are presented in Table 3. The explanatory variables — lnK, lnL, and lnICT — in the three samples are all significant at the 0.01 or 0.05 level, so they are accepted. The significant effect coefficients of LnK, LnL, and LnICST are positive in all three samples as expected, but their values are significantly different. *P* values of *J*-statistics are all greater than 0.05, showing that the model achieves endogeneity for all three samples. The numbers of instrumental variables generated for the

Table 3. Estimation results by panel GMM.

	Sample 1		Sample 2		Sample 3	
Variable	**Coefficient**	***t*-Statistic**	**Coefficient**	***t*-Statistic**	**Coefficient**	***t*-Statistic**
Estimates						
LnVA(−1)	0.2994	56.79***	0.2485	44.15***	0.3472	28.62***
LnK	0.4112	78.49***	0.0776	8.35***	0.2412	8.85***
LnL	0.5046	67.71***	1.3014	51.40***	0.8217	14.14***
LnICST	0.1170	3.02***	0.0472	3.09***	0.1308	2.53**
Statistics						
Cross-sections included	37		40		77	
Instrument rank	37		40		55	
J-statistic	31.8611		37.8350		61.0493	
Prob(*J*-statistic)	0.5237		0.3855		0.1583	
Serial correlation test						
AR(1) (*p*-value)	0.0123		0.5901		0.0006	
AR(2) (*p*-value)	0.8687		0.7719		0.3072	

Note: LnVA is dependent variable; *** and ** for statistical significance at 0.01 and 0.05 levels, respectively; constant added to instrument list.

three samples are 37, 40, and 55, respectively; these are less than or equal to the numbers of cross-sections in the panel data (37, 40, and 77). The number of instrumental variables created in the research samples is reasonable, and the results estimated by the GMM approach to overcome endogenously are appropriate. The *p*-values of the variables lnVA(−1) are all significant at the 0.01 level, indicating that there is an endogenous variable in all three samples. Finally, the *p*-value at AR(2) of the three samples is greater than 0.05, showing that the model in the samples does not display the Arellano Bond series correlation phenomenon. These test results indicate that the estimated results are reliable.

4.2. *Robustness tests*

To select an alternative estimator that is appropriate for the data, stationary tests for all variables were performed using the panel unit root test.

Table 4. Panel unit root tests.

	Deterministic	lnK	lnL	lnICST	lnVA
Sample 1	Intercept	225.79***	137.30***	173.96***	250.19***
	Intercept and trend	192.43***	141.92***	109.61***	136.72***
Sample 2	Intercept	153.83***	275.65***	186.65***	167.82***
	Intercept and trend	236.60***	156.27***	107.81***	237.79***
Sample 3	Intercept	379.62***	412.94***	360.61***	418.02***
	Intercept and trend	429.03***	298.18***	217.42***	374.50***

Note: Automatic lag length selection based on SIC; Newey–West automatic bandwidth selection and Bartlett kernel; *** for statistical significance at the 0.01 level.

Since panel data are not balanced and heterogeneous, the PP-Fisher Chi-square test with the assumed "individual unit root process" was chosen to report unit root test results. It was implemented for both "intercept" and "intercept and trend" patterns. Table 4 reports the panel unit root test results for the three samples studied.

The results of the stationary test in Table 4 show that the variables are stationary at the 1% significance level for all three samples. Therefore, the panel least squares (LS) method can be applied and chosen as an alternative to check the robustness of the GMM approach. This study used both fixed effects (FE) and random effects (RE) estimators, then used the Hausman test to choose a more appropriate estimator and compare it with the GMM approach's estimated results. Table 5 reports the estimation results using the panel LS method to check the robustness of the estimated results from the GMM approach.

As shown in Table 5, the adjusted R-squared in the samples give values from 69.80% to 94.44%, and the F-statistics in the samples give values from 164.70 to 747.39 (all p-values = 0.000), so the estimated models are suitable. The Hausman test gives p-values greater than 0.05 in all three samples, so FE estimate is more appropriate than RE and it is chosen. The estimated coefficients for the selected method (FE) are all significant at the 1% or 5% level, except for the lnICST variable in Sample 1, which

Table 5. Results of panel LS.

		Sample 1		Sample 2		Sample 3	
Variable		**FE**	**RE**	**FE**	**RE**	**FE**	**RE**
Estimates							
C	Coefficient	–8.5487	–6.8414	–7.5775	–7.7777	–8.3450	–7.8631
	t-Statistic	–3.56***	–2.97***	–3.57***	–4.01***	–5.07***	–5.36***
LnK	Coefficient	0.6357	0.6892	0.4279	0.4480	0.5152	0.5512
	t-Statistic	13.95***	17.97***	5.07***	7.31***	8.56***	12.96***
LnL	Coefficient	0.5530	0.3449	0.7324	0.6368	0.6348	0.4948
	t-Statistic	5.79***	6.39***	3.76***	4.80***	4.32***	5.75***
LnICST	Coefficient	0.4163	0.4195	0.3506	0.4445	0.4366	0.4978
	t-Statistic	1.85*	1.89*	1.61	2.29**	2.47**	3.28***
Statistics							
R-squared		0.9407	0.7001	0.9482	0.7336	0.9494	0.7172
Adj *R*-squared		0.9347	0.6980	0.9431	0.7318	0.9444	0.7163
F-statistic		154.70	323.78	185.34	425.85	191.78	747.39
Prob(*F*-statistic)		0.0000	0.0000	0.0000	0.0000	0.0000	0.0000
Hausman test		7.2138*		0.9690		1.4309	

Note: ***, **, and * for statistical significance at the 0.01, 0.05, and 0.10 levels, respectively.

is only significant at the 10% level. This level of significance is still acceptable for comparison with the results from the GMM approach. Table 6 compares the estimated results of the GMM and FE methods for the three samples.

According to Table 6, both methods show that capital, labor, and investment in information, communication, science, and technology have a positive impact on the added value of enterprises in general as well as the added value of enterprises in both the industry and construction sector and the service sector. However, the values of the estimated coefficients show certain differences. This evidence supports the GMM estimation results and shows that they are robust.

Table 6. Differences in coefficients by GMM and FE.

	Sample 1			Sample 2			Sample 3		
Variable	**GMM**	**FE**	**Bias**	**GMM**	**FE**	**Bias**	**GMM**	**FE**	**Bias**
C		−6.8414			−7.5775			−7.8631	
lnVA(−1)	0.2994			0.2485			0.3472		
lnK	0.4112	0.6892	−0.2780	0.0776	0.4279	−0.3503	0.2412	0.5512	−0.3100
lnL	0.5046	0.3449	0.1597	1.3014	0.7324	0.5690	0.8217	0.4948	0.3269
lnICST	0.1170	0.4195	−0.3025	0.0472	0.3506	−0.3034	0.1308	0.4978	−0.3670

4.3. *Discussion*

The results of the data analysis confirm that, in addition to capital and labor (the two basic inputs that determine the output of enterprises), society's investment in IC and ST also contribute significantly to the output value of enterprises in Vietnam. Labor contributes the most, followed by capital. To be more specific, 1% increase in the amount of labor, business capital, and social investment in IC and ST will help Vietnamese enterprises increase value-added by 0.82%, 0.24%, and 0.13%, respectively. In general, this study's results are consistent with many others on the role of ST and ICT. Others have found that the outputs of SMEs are sensitive to ST drivers in Spain (Parrilli and Elola, 2012); ST plays a key role in maintaining a high economic growth rate (Do, 2019); and capital investment in ICT increases labor productivity in the US (Jorgenson *et al.*, 2008), positively contributes to economic output in Australia (Shahiduzzaman and Alam, 2014), and increases value added in EU countries, the US, and Japan (Haider *et al.*, 2021). Our study found that the role of labor was more significant than that of capital in explaining value added, indicating that most Vietnamese enterprises operate in labor-intensive sectors. This is also consistent with the reality of Vietnam's relative advantage over most developed countries due to its abundant labor force with cheap labor costs.

There is a big difference in how capital and labor explain value added between enterprises in the two research sectors. In the industry and construction sector, labor plays a bigger role than capital but not much (the sensitivities of labor and capital are 0.52 and 0.41, respectively). However, in the service sector, the difference is much larger; the sensitivity of labor (1.30) is much higher than the sensitivity of capital (only 0.08). This can be explained by the fact that, at the same capital size, enterprises in the service sector are usually more labor-intensive. In other words, the ratio of capital per worker in the industry and construction sectors is often much higher than in the service sector. The contribution of social capital invested in IC and ST to added value is also significantly different between the two enterprise sectors. The sensitivity of enterprises in the industry and construction sector is 0.12, nearly 2.5 times higher than that of enterprises in the service sector. This result confirms that enterprises in the industry and construction sector have benefited more than enterprises in the service sector from social investment in IC and ST.

The 1-year lagged value of a dependent variable represents the dynamic nature of the output productivity growth (value added) based on capital, labor, and social investment in IC and ST. The values for all enterprises, the industry and construction sector, and the service sector are 0.35, 0.3, and 0.25, respectively. In addition to the studied value added explanatory variables, a fairly large number of other factors account for about 22.47% of the value added for enterprises in the industry and construction sector and 14.84% for enterprises in the service sector. TFP is one of these factors. It reflects technological innovation, rationalization of production, improvement of management, and improvement of the labor skills of employees in each enterprise and each industry.

5. Conclusion and Implications

This study examines the effect of social investment in IC and ST on the output value of enterprises and how it differs across enterprises in the industry and construction sector and the service sector. The production function, consisting of two basic inputs (capital and labor) combined with social investment in IC and ST, is used to estimate output value. Employee incomes and enterprises' profits before tax are used as a proxy for added value, which reflects the output value of different enterprises. The two-step panel GMM approach is used with datasets from enterprises in 77 Tier-2 industries between 2008 and 2019 and deployed for three samples.

The estimation method is evaluated for suitability by confirming a reasonable number of instrumental variables, endogeneity, and the series correlation phenomenon. Moreover, the robustness of the selected model is checked by comparison with the panel LS method.

Research results confirm that capital and labor are still the two basic inputs that determine the output of enterprises in Vietnam. Social investment in IC and ST has also contributed significantly to their output value. Among the explanatory variables for value added, labor contributes the most, followed by capital. This shows that most Vietnamese enterprises operate in labor-intensive sectors. In addition, the role of endogenous factors is also quite significant, which reflects that factors not included in the model, such as TFP, may be important. The roles of capital, labor, and social investment in IC and ST also differ between the two studied economic sectors. Labor plays a key role in explaining the output value of enterprises in the service sector and remains the most important factor for enterprises in the industry and construction sector. However, enterprises in the industry and construction sector benefit more than those in the service sector from social investment in IC and ST.

The results of this study suggest that Vietnamese enterprises, especially those in the service sector, need to continue to exploit their relative advantage of low-cost labor to grow. The state and society need to constantly invest in IC and ST development. This not only helps access and expand new knowledge and technologies for general socioeconomic development but also promotes the growth of enterprises. In addition to capital and labor, enterprises need to promote other factors contributing to growth, especially TFP, by constantly innovating technology, rationalizing production, improving management, and improving the skill levels of employees.

This empirical study adds to the theoretical foundation of the productivity growth of enterprises, with the input variables being capital, labor, and social investment in IC and ST, as well as other endogenous factors. It shows the role of input variables in the productivity of enterprises in different economic sectors, serving as a basis for notable measures to increase the productivity of enterprises in these economic sectors. However, due to the lack of access to data on IC and ST costs for each enterprise, the study did not consider the role of enterprises' investment in IC and ST. This issue represents an area with potential for further study.

Acknowledgement

The author would like to thank Ho Chi Minh City University of Industry and Trade for supporting this research.

References

Arellano, M. & Bond, S. (1991). Some tests of specification for panel data: Monte Carlo evidence and an application to employment equations. *The Review of Economic Studies*, *58*(2), 277–297. Available at: https://doi.org/10.2307/2297968.

Bahrini, R. & Qaffas, A. A. (2019). Impact of information and communication technology on economic growth: Evidence from developing countries. *Economies*, *7*(1), 21. Available at: https://doi.org/10.3390/economies7010021.

Bakhsh, S., Yin, H., & Shabir, M. (2021). Foreign investment and CO2 emissions: do technological innovation and institutional quality matter? Evidence from system GMM approach. *Environmental Science and Pollution Research*, *28*(15), 19424–19438. Available at: https://doi.org/10.1007/s11356-020-12237-2.

Bonet, B. & Van Den Briel, M. (2014). Flow-based heuristics for optimal planning: Landmarks and merges. In *Proceedings of the International Conference on Automated Planning and Scheduling*, 24, 47–55. Available at: https://doi.org/10.1609/icaps.v24i1.13643.

Brynjolfsson, E. & Hitt, L. M. (2003). Computing productivity: Firm-level evidence. *Review of Economics and Statistics*, *85*(4), 793–808. Available at: https://doi.org/10.1162/003465303772815736.

Çalışkan, H. K. (2015). Technological change and economic growth. *Procedia-Social and Behavioral Sciences*, *195*, 649–654. Available at: https://doi.org/10.1016/j.sbspro.2015.06.174.

Dat, T. T., Thanh, T. T., Cuong, C. S., Duong, N. A., Ha, N. H., Huyen, N. T. T., Minh, D. T., Nam, P. X., Ngoc, T. A., Phuong, L. T., Quynh, L. T. N., Thanh, T. T., Toan, P. N., Trang, N. Q., Trinh, B., & Van, N. T. C. (2020). Improving labor productivity in the digital economy context. *Annual Vietnam Economic Review 2019*. Hanoi: National Economics University.

Dimelis, S. P. & Papaioannou, S. K. (2010). FDI and ICT effects on productivity growth: A comparative analysis of developing and developed countries. *The European Journal of Development Research*, *22*(1), 79–96. Available at: https://doi.org/10.1057/ejdr.2009.45.

Do, H. T. (2019). Science, Technology and innovation policies in developed and developing countries, *VNU Journal of Science: Policy and Management Studies*, *35*(1), 8–20. Available at: https://doi.org/10.25073/2588-1116/vnupam.4150.

Edquist, H. & Henrekson, M. (2017). Do R&D and ICT affect total factor productivity growth differently? *Telecommunications Policy*, *41*(2), 106–119. Available at: https://doi.org/10.1016/j.telpol.2016.11.010.

Feldman, M. P., Link, A. N., & Siegel, D. S. (2012). The economics of science and technology: An overview of initiatives to foster innovation, entrepreneurship, and economic growth.

G7 (2017). New economic growth: The role of science, technology and infrastructure. *G7 Academies' Joint Statements 2017*. Available at: https://royalsociety.org/~/media/about-us/international/g-science-statements/2017-may-3-new-economic-growth.pdf?la=en-GB.

General Statistics Office (GSO, 2021). *Statistical Yearbook 2020*.

Haider, F., Kunst, R., & Wirl, F. (2021). Total factor productivity, its components and drivers. *Empirica*, *48*(2), 283–327. Available at: https://doi.org/10.1007/s10663-020-09476-4.

Jorgenson, D. W., Ho, M. S., & Stiroh, K. J. (2008). A retrospective look at the US productivity growth resurgence. *Journal of Economic Perspectives*, *22*(1), 3–24. doi:10.1257/jep.22.1.3.

Kurniawati, M. A. (2020). The role of ICT infrastructure, innovation and globalization on economic growth in OECD countries, 1996–2017. *Journal of Science and Technology Policy Management*. Available at: https://doi.org/10.1108/JSTPM-06-2019-0065.

McMorrow, K. & Röger, W. (2009). R&D capital and economic growth: The empirical evidence. *EIB Papers*, *14*(1), 94–118. Available at: https://www.econstor.eu/bitstream/10419/44909/1/618780394.pdf.

Nguyen, H. Q. (2021). Total factor productivity growth of Vietnamese enterprises by sector and region: Evidence from panel data analysis. *Economies*, *9*(3), 109. Available at: https://doi.org/10.3390/economies9030109.

Nickell, S. (1981). Biases in dynamic models with fixed effects. *Econometrica: Journal of the Econometric Society*, 1417–1426. Available at: https://doi.org/10.2307/1911408.

O'brien, R. M. (2007). A caution regarding rules of thumb for variance inflation factors. *Quality & Quantity*, *41*, 673-690. Available at: https://doi.org/10.1007/

s11135-006-9018-6OECD (2009). Guide to Measuring the Information Society. 2nd Edition. Paris: OECD. Available at: http://www.oecd.org/dataoecd/25/52/43281062.pdf.

Parrilli, M. D. & Elola, A. (2012). The strength of science and technology drivers for SME innovation. *Small Business Economics*, *39*(4), 897–907. Available at: https://doi.org/10.1007/s11187-011-9319-6.

Pradhan, R. P., Arvin, M. B., & Norman, N. R. (2015). The dynamics of information and communications technologies infrastructure, economic growth, and financial development: Evidence from Asian countries. *Technology in Society*, *42*, 135–149. Available at: https://doi.org/10.1016/j.techsoc.2015.04.002.

Prime Minister (2018). Decision 27/2018/QD-TTg dated July 6, 2018 on promulgating the system of economic sub-sectors of Vietnam.

Relich, M. (2017). The impact of ICT on labor productivity in the EU. *Information Technology for Development*, *23*(4), 706–722. Available at: https://doi.org/10.1080/02681102.2017.1336071.

Roodman, D. (2009). A note on the theme of too many instruments. *Oxford Bulletin of Economics and Statistics*, *71*(1), 135–158. Available at: https://doi.org/10.1111/j.1468-0084.2008.00542.x.

Şener, S. & Sarıdoğan, E. (2011). The effects of science-technology-innovation on competitiveness and economic growth. *Procedia-Social and Behavioral Sciences*, *24*, 815–828. Available at: https://doi.org/10.1016/j.sbspro.2011.09.127.

Shahiduzzaman, M. & Alam, K. (2014). The long-run impact of information and communication technology on economic output: the case of Australia. *Telecommunications Policy*, *38*(7), 623–633. Available at: https://doi.org/10.1016/j.telpol.2014.02.003.

Stiroh, K. J. (2002). Are ICT spillovers driving the new economy? *Review of Income and Wealth*, *48*(1), 33–57. Available at: https://doi.org/10.1111/1475-4991.00039.

Stiroh, K. J. (2005). Reassessing the impact of IT in the production function: A meta-analysis and sensitivity tests. *Annales d'Economie et de Statistique*, 529–561. Available at: https://doi.org/10.2307/20777587.

UNESCO (2020). *Investing in Science, Technology and Innovation*. Available at: https://en.unesco.org/themes/investing-science-technology-and-innovation.

Van der Wiel, H. & van Leeuwen, G. (2003). Do ICT spillovers matter; evidence from Dutch firm-level data (No. 26). CPB Netherlands Bureau for Economic Policy Analysis. Available at: https://www.cpb.nl/sites/default/files/publicaties/download/do-ict-spillovers-matter-evidence-dutch-firm-level-data.pdf.

Venturini, F., Rincon-Aznar, A., & Vecchi, M. (2013). ICT as a general purpose technology: spillovers, absorptive capacity and productivity performance (No.

416). National Institute of Economic and Social Research. Available at: https://www.niesr.ac.uk/wp-content/uploads/2021/10/dp416_0-5.pdf.

Vu, K. M. (2011). ICT as a source of economic growth in the information age: Empirical evidence from the 1996–2005 period. *Telecommunications Policy*, *35*(4), 357–372. Available at: https://doi.org/10.1016/j.telpol.2011.02.008.

Zwick, T. (2003). The impact of ICT investment on establishment productivity. *National Institute Economic Review*, *184*, 99–110. Available at: https://doi.org/10.1177/0027950103184001009.

https://doi.org/10.1142/9789811286100_0011

Chapter 11

Factors Affecting Retail Investors' Intentions to Use Financial Robo-Advisors in the Middle of COVID-19 in Vietnam

Thuy Chung Phan[*,‡], Dao Quynh Dam Nguyen[*,§], Lam Van Le[*,¶] and Kurniawan Saefullah[†,||]

[*]*School of Banking, College of Business, University of Economics Ho Chi Minh City, Vietnam*

[†]*Faculty of Economics and Business, Universitas Padjadjaran, Indonesia*

[‡]*phanthuy@ueh.edu.vn*

[§]*ngquynh2912@gmail.com*

[¶]*levanlamtcnh@ueh.edu.vn*

[||]*kurniawan.saefullah@unpad.ac.id*

Abstract

This study aims to identify factors influencing retail investors' intentions to use automated financial advisors (or financial robo-advisors) during the COVID-19 pandemic in Vietnam. We used an online survey to collect data through a structured questionnaire. We then adopted the structural equation modeling (SEM) approach to test the conceptual model on 333 respondents without experience with robo-advisors. The results show that trust, the tendency to rely on robo-advisors, financial knowledge, and the COVID-19 pandemic are key driving

Received on December 8, 2022; accepted on April 4, 2023

factors that affect retail investors' intentions to use robo-advisors in their investment processes. Our results suggest managerial implications for financial service providers to develop their business strategies in line with the rise and development of fintech.

Keywords: Intention to Use, Financial Robo-Advisors, COVID-19 Pandemic, Fintech.

1. Introduction

The financial industry and academia have recently shown a growing interest in financial robo-advisors, thanks to the high market demand for cost-effective portfolio management methods (Gan *et al.*, 2021; Hohenberger *et al.*, 2019). Jung *et al.* (2018) propose many potential advantages of robo-advisors, such as reduced biases and errors in human judgment as well as better accuracy and precision in forecasting. With these potential advantages, robo-advisors suit retail investors with different socio-economic backgrounds better than more conventional financial advisors. Brenner and Meyll (2020) predict that AI-based financial services can replace human advisory services due to the former's ease of access and cost-effective advice.

Over the past 2 years, due to the COVID-19 pandemic, the WHO recommended various measures to limit human contact and gatherings of people, leading to many companies adopting digital technology and even transforming their business models (Mckinsey, 2020). This shift toward digitalization is also evident in the financial sector (Duchin and Harford, 2021). Despite the growing literature on robo-advisors, how the pandemic has affected their adoption remains unclear. Ben and Sade (2020) found that people were more willing to adopt financial advisors, regardless of whether they were human or robots, during the pandemic. Similarly, Ben-David *et al.* (2021) reported that individuals were less sensitive to the type of advisor during the pandemic than at regular times. Recently, Gan *et al.* (2021) conducted one of the few studies examining the factors influencing the adoption of robo-advisors during the pandemic, particularly in developing countries such as Malaysia. They found that restricted close contact due to the pandemic might have led individuals to trust robo-advisors more as an alternative to human-based financial advisors. However, they failed to investigate the direct impact of COVID-19 on customers' willingness to adopt robo-advisors.

Although robo-advisors have been appearing since 2015, they have not flourished much in Vietnam. Statistica (2022) shows that fintech firms are expanding in Vietnam, from 144 in 2018 to 249 in 2022. However, their financial services are limited, primarily e-wallets and payment facilitators. Only a few fintech firms provide robo-advisory services for stock and forex trading. Still, most Vietnamese customers know little about robo-advisors (Hai Ngo, 2020). Therefore, the study's main aim is to investigate the adoption of robo-advisors among Vietnamese retail investors while controlling for the effect of COVID-19.

The data were collected through an online survey by Vietnamese retail investors who had never used robo-advisors. A sample of 333 valid respondents was then analyzed using the structural equation model (SEM) in AMOS version 24 to test the proposed research hypotheses. The results show that trust, the tendency of retail investors to rely on robo-advisors, financial knowledge, and the impact of the pandemic are positively related to their intentions to use robo-advisors in Vietnam.

This study contributes to the growing robo-advisory literature in which the pandemic effect has been discussed. We take a further step by investigating the direct impact of the pandemic on retail investors' adoption of robo-advisors. Moreover, we also provide empirical evidence of the intention of retail investors to use robo-advisors during the pandemic while considering all the effects of various factors at once. The advantage of this approach is that it will help us gain a deeper understanding of investors' behaviors and attitudes toward robo-advisory services, which can help financial institutions propose appropriate policies to advance robo-advisors in developing countries like Vietnam. Improving the functional quality of robo-advisors will also provide a solid foundation for bringing Vietnam closer to financial and technological advancement in both the region and the world. With the cost-effective approach, robo-advisors help bridge the gap between the Vietnamese and developed markets and make it easier for inexperienced investors to manage their investments.

The rest of this chapter is structured as follows. Section 2 introduces an overview of financial robo-advisors, related studies on adopting robo-advisors, the theoretical framework, and hypothesis development. Data, research models, measurement of variables, and research methods are described in Section 3. Research results are presented in Section 4. The final section discusses research results, limitations, and future direction for related research.

2. Research Overview

2.1. *Overview of financial robo-advisors*

Robo-advisors are computerized platforms offering automated, online algorithm-based financial investment, portfolio management, and investment services with minimal human intervention. These platforms usually request users to complete an online survey about their financial status, savings, investment horizons, and goals to generate investment advice tailored to each client's financial objectives.

These robo-advisors use AI to automate portfolio management and selection. Upon a customer's registration, the platform gathers information about their socio-economic background, financial goals, and risk tolerance using a questionnaire. Subsequently, the cataloging process starts right away. The robo-advisors' algorithms create a portfolio that a professional investor pre-sets according to Nobel Prize-winning models. In addition, the robo-advisors apply rebalancing as needed to keep the portfolio consistent with the initial distribution. At the same time, they manage the portfolio to improve tax. They also carry out operational support or adjustment tactics depending on the market situation.

Robo-advisors are often built with many complex algorithms based on classical economic theories. One of them is the most popular modern portfolio theory (MPT), developed by Harry Markowitz in 1952. This theory proposes that a portfolio is most effective when it either maximizes the expected return while considering risk tolerance or minimizes risk while ensuring a scheduled return. Following this, the investment portfolio should comprise assets with varying levels of risk and predetermined weights. Moreover, the investment process should also involve automatically buying or selling different financial products based on the current market context to balance the risk weight of the portfolio (Hoya, 2020).

Due to their broad diversification, many robo-advisors include ETFs in investment recommendations that match an investor's risk profile, investment horizon, and financial goals. When an investor buys into an

ETF, robo-advisors make many purchases of stocks and other bond investments. In addition, some robo-advisory providers allow their customers to adjust their asset allocation, and the fees for using robo-advisors are usually fixed annually or pro rata. Besides, some robo-advisors enable customers to use some financial services for free, such as Ally Invest, Goodment, SoFi Invest, Schwab IntelliGant Portfolio, and Wealthfront (Robo Advisors Information Guide, 2019).

In 2019, the global market size of the robo-advisory industry was estimated to be $4.51 billion. This estimation is because the sector has seen a surge in growth due to the rise in adopting robo-advisors for effective asset management. Robo-advisors offer many advantages, such as low-cost, high-quality investment portfolio construction, loss tax collection, powered judgments based on real-time statistics and current economic conditions, and eliminating the possibility of credit risk. The untapped potential of emerging economies, along with the rise in government support and initiatives for robo-advisors, is also anticipated to create a profitable opportunity to expand the robo-advisory market in the foreseeable future. Another factor is the rapid digitization in financial services, which has fueled the growth of the market trend in robo-advisors. Indeed, the robo-advisory business grew exponentially in the first and second quarters of 2020, comprising more than 7.8% of users of investment advice in 2019. According to Corporate Vision Magazine, the number of subscriptions to robo-advisory services in the first quarter of 2020 increased sharply at a growth rate of 3.1%.

When segmenting the global robo-advisory market by region, including North America, Europe, Asia-Pacific, Latin America, and the Middle East and Africa, North America is projected to hold the largest share due to the increasing adoption of advanced technology in wealth management. The Asia-Pacific region is also anticipated to experience rapid growth thanks to the rise in digital investment, the consulting scene supported by an increase in the number of companies and start-ups, and several government initiatives to develop fintech in countries such as China, India, and Japan (Deloitte, 2019).

Being part of the global development cycle of fintech, Vietnam has also witnessed this field's intense and extensive development in recent years. Among the personal finance apps in Vietnam, robo-advisors are the least popular. Similar to developed financial markets such as the US, the

UK, Germany, Canada, Singapore and South Korea are countries that could potentially develop this field in Asia. However, the concept is still relatively new to consumers in Vietnam, which has only seen a few pioneering companies (Hai Ngo, 2020).

In Vietnam, Techcom Securities (TCBS), a subsidiary of Techcombank, introduced the first robo-advisory service, named TCWealth, to the financial market in May 2017. In the same year, a start-up called Finhay launched an app enabling users to start investing with as little as $2. Finhay has received funding from domestic and foreign investors and was recognized as one of the top 100 fintech companies globally in 2019, as reported by KPMG. Although the Tan Viet Securities Joint Stock Company's Individual Retirement Account (IRA) and BIDV Securities' (BSC) iBroker were only introduced to the market in 2019, they appear to be gaining market awareness, as indicated by survey results. Over the past two years, many companies have added robo-advisory services to the offering, aiming to satisfy customers' increasing needs in line with the market context. In 2020, MBS launched two financial tools, Power Rank and CANSLIM, that operate under the robo-advisory application system.

The market for robo-advisor solutions in Vietnam is promising because of the high demand for individual investment advice. According to data provided by Statistica (2022), the assets managed by robo-advisors in Vietnam are predicted to attain a total of $1,658 million, with an annual growth rate of 30.73%, equivalent to $4,842 million in 2025. Furthermore, the expected number of users will reach over 3 million people by 2025.

2.2. *Related studies on customers' adoption of financial robo-advisors*

Jung *et al.* (2018) were among the first to investigate robo-advisors from a consumer-centric perspective. They found that trust was the main factor influencing inexperienced users' attitudes with low budgets and low-risk tolerance toward robo-advisors. Ruhr *et al.* (2019) examined 171 German university students' choices of investment management services when they had 5,000 EUR and four advisory service options, such as automated robo-advisor, human advisors, authorized human advisors, and hybrid advisors. They discovered that performance expectancy and perceived risk were significant factors in forecasting the respondents' behavioral intention. Also, the use of algorithms by robo-advisors caused high performance, increasing the possibility of using this digital advisory service. In a later study with 148 university students in Germany, Ruhr (2020) concluded that the impact of automation on the behavioral intention to use robo-advisors was reversed in favor of robo-advisors in hybrid automation, as the participants valued the automation provided by the hybrid advisor.

Milani (2019) investigated the acceptance and usage of robo-advisors in the Italian market using the Unified Theory of Acceptance and Use of Technology (UTAUT) with a sample of 635 employees from the professional services company PricewaterhouseCoopers (PwC). The result showed that individuals with higher education, investment experience, and a better understanding of robo-advisors were more likely to use them. Milani (2019) also concluded that perceived use, trust, effort expectancy, and social influence were positively associated with individuals' attitudes toward robo-advisors. In a similar study using the extended Technology Acceptance Model (TAM), Belanche *et al.* (2019) found that customers' attitudes toward robo-advisors were strongly influenced by their perceived usefulness and ease of use. Sa *et al.* (2018) found similar results showing that ease of use and perceived usefulness encouraged the adoption of robo-advisors. Lourenco *et al.* (2020), while focusing on the characteristics of robo-advisory providers, found that individuals' perceptions of the expertise and level of trust in the firm mediated the relationship between the type of firm and their acceptance of robot financial advisors.

In the Asian context, Cheng (2020) discovered that to continue using robo-advisors, Taiwanese customers must perceive robo-advisors as applicable, satisfying, and having experience. Gan *et al.* (2021) surveyed 285 Malaysian residents, of whom only 20% were familiar with robo-advisors. According to their findings, Malaysian consumers' intentions of adopting robo-advisors during the COVID-19 pandemic were impacted by performance expectancy, social influence, trust, perceived financial knowledge, and willingness to rely on robo-advisors.

In short, the findings on customers' adoption of robo-advisors across studies were somewhat contextual. It is also important to note that this topic is still new and relatively understudied in developing countries like Vietnam, particularly in the context of the COVID-19 pandemic. Therefore, this provides a strong motivation for our study.

2.3. *Theoretical framework and hypothesis development*

The theoretical framework for this research is grounded in the UTAUT model, which was initially proposed by Venkatesh *et al.* (2003). The model identified four significant constructs while determining the adoption habits of technology users, including performance expectancy, effort expectancy, social influence, and facilitating conditions. However, previous studies that applied the UTAUT framework showed that the four components were limited to predicting customers' behavioral intentions, particularly in the evolution of fintech (i.e., Gan *et al.*, 2021; Le, 2021). Therefore, our study extends the UTAUT model to incorporate five additional variables in the proposed research model: trust, security and privacy, the tendency to rely on robo-advisors, financial knowledge, and especially the impact of COVID-19, which enhances the relevance of the research in the new context.

2.3.1. *Performance expectancy*

Performance expectancy is an individual's perception or belief that using a particular system or technology will enhance their performance or ability to accomplish a task (Venkatesh *et al.*, 2003). In the case of robo-advisors, customers' performance expectancy is their perception that these systems can aid in financial and investment management. With the COVID-19 pandemic causing difficulties in meeting face-to-face with financial advisors, customers are turning to robo-advisors for assistance with managing their finances and investing more efficiently. Ruhr *et al.* (2019) and Gan *et al.* (2021) share some typical results showing that performance expectancy positively impacts the intention to use robo-advisors. Therefore, we suggest the following hypothesis:

H1: Performance expectancy positively affects investors' intentions to use robo-advisors in Vietnam during the pandemic.

2.3.2. *Effort expectancy*

Effort expectancy is characterized by the degree of ease and convenience that a user experiences when employing a system, as defined by Venkatesh *et al.* (2003). In the context of robo-advisory services, customers' effort expectancy can be characterized as their belief that robo-advisors can help them achieve higher efficiency with minimal effort. Customers may also prefer robo-advisors that are easy and comfortable to use. Milani's (2019) study in Italy indicated that effort expectancy positively correlated with adopting robo-advisors. As a result, we propose the following hypothesis:

H2: Effort expectancy positively affects investors' intentions to use robo-advisors in Vietnam during the pandemic.

2.3.3. *Social influence*

Social influence refers to an individual's inclination to consider the opinions of others when making decisions about adopting or using a particular system or technology (Venkatesh *et al.*, 2003). Therefore, the social impact becomes important when customers rely on the views of their friends and family members when using robo-advisors. The pandemic has highlighted the significance of financial planning due to its impact on people's income (Fox and Bartholomae, 2020). Thus, consumers may be more inclined to seek low-cost financial advice when they observe their friends and family members doing the same. Milani (2019) and Gan *et al.* (2021) found that social influence positively affected the intention of users to adopt robo-advisors. Other studies have also suggested that social impact can indirectly affect attitudes toward new technology by increasing relative advantages and reducing perceived risks. Thus, even if the number of robo-advisor users is low, their impact can still be significant in enhancing the attitudes of those who rely on their opinions and trust their judgment. Based on this, we propose the following hypothesis:

H3: Social influence positively affects investors' intentions to use robo-advisors in Vietnam during the pandemic.

2.3.4. *Facilitating conditions*

Facilitating conditions refer to the availability of infrastructure, organization, and technology to support the use of a system. Though the UTAUT model only suggests a correlation between facilitating conditions and the intention to use a system, previous research has demonstrated that promoting conditions can encourage users to make behavioral choices toward the system. For example, Rahman *et al.* (2020) found that there is a direct influence of facilitating behavioral intention on actual behavior when consumers adopt mobile financial services. Similarly, studies have shown that consumers' behavioral choices when using e-wallets and digital payments increase with the degree of facilitation (Soodan and Rana, 2020). During the COVID-19 crisis, precautions that limited personal interaction and close contact constituted barriers to participation in traditional financial advisory services. Therefore, to encourage customers to adopt robo-advisors, facilitating conditions were implemented, as robo-advisors provided services without human connection or intervention. Additionally, the ubiquity of mobile computing devices, such as mobile phones and laptop computers, made it easier for customers to set up and effectively use robo-advisors during the COVID-19 pandemic (Gan *et al.*, 2021). Based on these findings, we propose the following hypothesis:

H4: Facilitating conditions positively affect investors' intentions to use robo-advisors in Vietnam during the pandemic.

2.3.5. *Trust*

Trust is a crucial factor that affects the inclination to use robo-advisors for investment activities. Bui and Bui (2018) incorporated trust into the UTAUT model to examine mobile payment acceptance in Vietnam and found a significant relationship between consumer trust and behavioral intentions to adopt mobile payments. Similar trends were found in various studies focusing on digital wallet adoption (Singh and Sinha, 2020; Widodo *et al.*, 2019) and online referral agents (Nilashi *et al.*, 2016). Trust also influences consumer behavior toward fintech (Alwi *et al.*, 2019; M.T.H. Le, 2021; Stewart and Jürjens, 2018). These findings demonstrate the significance of trust in shaping the intention to use technology products and, consequently, the preference for robo-advisors. Additionally, using robo-advisors can enhance user confidence during market volatility caused by the pandemic, as these systems are less likely to be affected by emotional biases. Therefore, we propose the following hypothesis:

H5: Trust positively affects investors' intentions to use robo-advisors in Vietnam during the COVID-19 pandemic.

2.3.6. *Security and privacy*

According to Chang *et al.* (2016), data security and privacy are significant factors for consumers' acceptance of digital financial services. Users who download and install apps risk encountering design flaws, malware attacks, and data theft, making them anxious about the possibility of their personal information and bank accounts being stolen or leaked, as highlighted by Noor *et al.* (2019). As evidenced by incidents reported by Byrnes (2020) and Yang *et al.* (2018), inadequate protection for financial systems and information leaks has led to significant monetary losses. Despite such concerns, mobile app downloads worldwide continue to rise (Statista, 2019). Therefore, the data security and privacy of fintech are critical to establishing trust and encouraging users to select such services, as Barth *et al.* (2019) noted. Users typically demand transparency when apps collect their online behavior data. When a high level of data security is perceived to meet users' requirements, their desire to use the service increases, thereby enhancing the service's reputation and competitive advantage (Hu *et al.*, 2019; Stewart and Jürjens, 2018). Therefore, fintech products, such as robo-advisors protected with high-security systems, will likely inspire trust and retain customers over the long term. As a result, we propose the following hypothesis:

H6: Security and privacy positively affect investors' intentions to use robo-advisors in Vietnam during the pandemic.

2.3.7. *Tendency to rely on robo-advisors*

The inclination of customers to trust and utilize robo-advisors instead of traditional financial advisors can impact their behavioral intention toward robo-advisors. According to Mumuni *et al.* (2019), consumers in the United States heavily rely on online product reviews, significantly influencing their attitudes. Similarly, Thoumrungroje (2014) found that reliance on electronic word-of-mouth significantly impacts customers' consumption behavior for conspicuous products. During the outbreak of the COVID-19 pandemic in Malaysia, Gan *et al.* (2021) also demonstrated that customers' tendency to rely on robo-advisors influenced their intention to use them as limited contact made traditional financial advice challenging. As a result, robo-advisors are becoming a popular alternative to conventional financial advice to reduce disease transmission. Therefore, we suggest the following hypothesis:

H7: The tendency to rely on robo-advisors positively affects investors' intentions to use robo-advisors in Vietnam during the pandemic.

2.3.8. *Financial knowledge*

In addition to the factors mentioned earlier, financial knowledge is an essential factor that explains the intention to use robo-advisors and is not included in the UTAUT model. This idea is supported by previous studies that link financial literacy to adopting robo-advisors. According to many studies (i.e., Barber and Odean, 2001, Konan and Balasubramanian, 2005), exposure to new information can lead to a "knowledge illusion", where people's beliefs about their knowledge exceed their actual level of knowledge. Other research has indicated that the perception of financial knowledge has a more significant impact on investment behavior than actual financial knowledge (Allgood and Walstad, 2016; Henager and Cude, 2016).

In addition, Brenner and Meyll (2020) discovered that robo-advisory users have low levels of objective financial literacy. Todd and Seay (2020) found that individuals with high levels of investment knowledge were less likely to use robo-advisors than those with low scores. Therefore, financial literacy is viewed as a positive factor in using robo-advisory platforms (Fan and Chatterjee, 2020). In the context of the pandemic, individuals who are considered financially savvy are expected to rely on cost-effective robo-advisors for financial planning. Additionally, during this volatile market environment, financially savvy individuals may prefer to seek advice from non-human-based advisors, such as robo-advisors, as they are less willing to accept the risks of uncertainty. Based on this, we propose the following hypothesis:

H8: Financial knowledge positively affects investors' intentions to use robo-advisors in Vietnam during the pandemic.

2.3.9. *The impact of the COVID-19 pandemic*

The implementation of social distancing due to the complicated developments of COVID-19 caused many people to face economic difficulties and many professions to face challenges. Regarding the financial field, we must mention financial consulting services. The nature of this work means that it is necessary to meet and discuss with customers to satisfy their needs, carry out procedures, and produce documents according to the regulations. Social distancing is a significant hindrance to this form of counseling. In addition, with the declining economic situation due to the pandemic's impact, many individuals were looking for opportunities to improve their finances while ensuring that the disease does not spread. Robo-advisors are more conspicuous when customers can fully use this service at home and have more effective investment opportunities if they lack investment knowledge and experience but do not want to spend too much. Previous studies on the trend of using fintech during the COVID-19 period have shown the positive impact of this factor on the use of financial technology as the fintech sector grows and different models of fintech get promoted during the COVID-19 crisis (Das, 2019). Fu and Mishra (2020) found that financial users are increasingly adopting digital financial services during the COVID-19 pandemic due to lockdown restrictions and are recognizing the convenience and usefulness of fintech in their daily lives. Moreover, during the pandemic, some consumers utilized digital financial services to purchase goods and services (Fu and Mishra, 2020). Hence, we propose the following hypothesis:

H9: The impact of the COVID-19 pandemic positively affects investors' intentions to use robo-advisors in Vietnam.

Figure 1 summarizes the proposed framework.

3. Research Methodology

3.1. *Data collection*

- **Survey participants**: Retail investors who have never used robo-advisors in the Vietnamese stock market.
- **Data collection method**: Data were collected through an online survey that comprised a structured questionnaire that was sent to retail

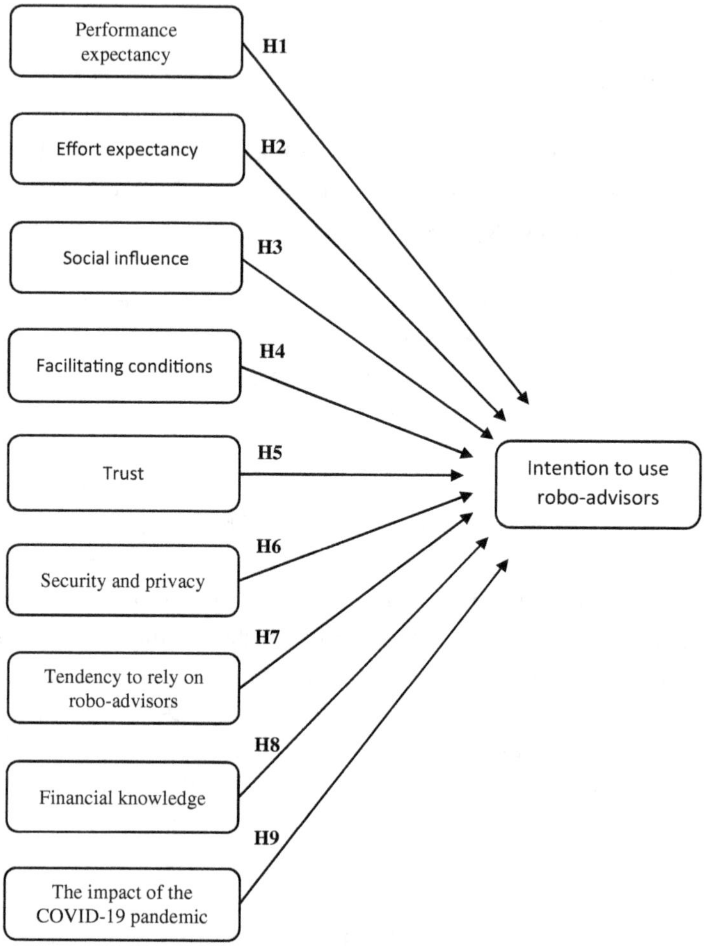

Figure 1. The proposed framework.

investors from various financial institutions (brokerage firms, financial companies, and mutual funds) in Vietnam via a Google Forms link between August and November 2021.

- **Sampling method and cleaning process**: The minimum sample size for a Cronbach's Alpha coefficient test is 100. Conducting an exploratory factor analysis (EFA) requires a minimum sample size of 50 to 100 with a ratio of at least five observations per observed variable (Hair *et al.*, 2006). Thus, with 36 variables, the research sample data must be at least 180. Moreover, the minimum requirement for testing research hypotheses with the SEM is 150. Therefore, the minimum sample size to be collected was 180.

In this research, the total number of questionnaires collected was 416, 61 of which showed that respondents had used robo-advisors before taking the survey. After removing these responses, the sample size for further analysis was 333. Most participants were 20–39 years old (approximately 71%) and had a bachelor's degree (81.8%). More females than males participated in our study (55.86% vs. 44.14%). Over half (57%) reported a monthly income above 10 million VND (equivalent to 435 USD). Finally, approximately 61% of the survey population had at least 1 year of investment experience in the Vietnamese stock market, whereas only 26% worked in the financial industry (see Table 1).

3.2. *Measurement of variables*

The measurement of all constructs used in this study was based on previously validated items from other studies. Following Gan *et al.* (2021), we adopted **seven** items, as follows: performance expectancy, effort expectancy, social influence, facilitating conditions, trust, the tendency to rely on robo-advisors, and financial knowledge. In addition, two factors were adapted from Hu *et al.* (2019), Fu and Mishra (2020), and Le (2021): security and privacy and the impact of the COVID-19 pandemic. Finally, the intention to use robo-advisors was taken from Venkatesh *et al.* (2003, 2012) and adapted for use in this research. This measure was popularly used in many studies (i.e., Jung and Shin, 2019; Le, 2021). The scale items used are shown in Table A.1. All responses were submitted according to a 5-point Likert scale ranging from 1 to 5 (where "1 = strongly disagree" and "5 = strongly agree").

3.3. *Measurement model analysis*

This study analyzed data using SPSS software (version 26) and AMOS (version 24). The data were first examined using Cronbach's alpha with SPSS to measure the scales' internal consistency reliability. In Cronbach's alpha test, the recommended value of Cronbach's alpha coefficients is above 0.7. Afterward, we used both EFA and confirmatory factor analysis (CFA)

Table 1. Descriptive statistics of the sample.

Variables	*N*	%
Gender		
Male	147	44.14
Female	186	55.86
Age		
Below 20	34	10.21
20–29	132	39.64
30–39	102	30.63
40 or above	65	19.52
Education		
High school	10	3.00
College	26	7.81
Bachelor's degree	270	81.08
Postgraduate	27	8.11
Working in finance		
Yes	88	26.43
No	245	73.57
Income (million VND per month)		
Below 10	146	43.85
10–20	85	25.52
20–25	48	14.41
Above 25	54	16.22
Investment experience		
No experience	131	39.34
Below 1 year	68	20.42
1–3 years	54	16.22
3–5 years	40	12.01
Above 5 years	40	12.01
Total sample	*333*	*100.00*

to assess the validity of the measurement model. Outer loadings and average variance extracted (AVE) are measures for evaluating the convergent validity of the observed constructs. Hair *et al.* (2017) state that only items with outer loadings greater than 0.7 can be directly retained. However, those with loadings between 0.3 and 0.7 can be deleted from the model if the removal could increase the outcomes of AVE and composite reliability (CR). In short, the minimum acceptable values of AVE and CR should exceed the cutting point of 0.5 (Fornell and Larcker, 1981). In the next step, the discriminant validity of the measurement model was assessed following the Fornell–Larcker criteria. Fornell–Larcker's rule of thumb is that the square root of the AVE must be greater than its most significant correlations for the rest of the scales in the proposed model. Finally, the study used SEM to test the research hypotheses proposed in the research model.

4. Empirical Results

4.1. *Reliability test and measurement model test*

4.1.1. *Reliability test*

The reliability test results from Cronbach's Alpha scores show that all the scales in the model exceeded 0.7 (Nunnally, 1978), ensuring the scales' reliability (see Table 2).

4.1.2. *Measurement model test*

The results of the outer loadings are also presented in Table 2, which show that all the model's constructs satisfy the recommended value of 0.5 (Hair *et al.*, 2017). Moreover, all the constructs' AVE and CR values were above 0.5 (Fornell and Larcker, 1981). Thus, the measurement model proved the convergent validity.

The discriminant validity of the measurement model was also assessed using the criteria found in Fornell and Larcker (1981). Any construct has guaranteed discriminant validity if the square root of the extracted variance (shown in bold) is higher than all the correlation values of the construct for the rest of the model. The results presented in Table 3 show that all the constructs met this criterion.

Table 2. Test results of reliability and convergent validity.

Constructs	Items	Loadings	AVE	CR	Cronbach's alpha
Performance expectancy (PE)			0.50	0.80	0.80
	PE1	0.77			
	PE2	0.70			
	PE3	0.66			
	PE4	0.70			
Effort expectancy (EE)			0.52	0.81	0.81
	EE1	0.76			
	EE2	0.74			
	EE3	0.70			
	EE4	0.68			
Social influence (SI)			0.50	0.80	0.80
	SI1	0.78			
	SI2	0.71			
	SI3	0.67			
	SI4	0.68			
Facilitating conditions (FC)			0.5	0.80	0.79
	FC1	0.77			
	FC2	0.74			
	FC3	0.70			
	FC4	0.60			
Trust (T)			0.51	0.76	0.75
	T1	0.76			
	T2	0.65			
	T3	0.73			
Security and privacy (SP)			0.52	0.77	0.77
	SP1	0.68			
	SP2	0.79			
	SP3	0.70			

Table 2. (*Continued*)

Constructs	Items	Loadings	AVE	CR	Cronbach's alpha
Tendency to rely on robo-advisors (R)			0.58	0.84	0.84
	R1	0.75			
	R2	0.81			
	R3	0.75			
	R4	0.72			
Financial knowledge (PFK)			0.52	0.81	0.81
	FK1	0.66			
	FK2	0.71			
	FK3	0.67			
	FK4	0.83			
The impact of COVID-19 (CV)			0.69	0.87	0.87
	CV1	0.81			
	CV2	0.86			
	CV3	0.83			
Intention to use robo-advisors (INT)			0.68	0.86	0.86
	INT1	0.74			
	INT2	0.93			
	INT3	0.79			

Table 3. Discriminant validity of measured items according to the criteria found in Fornell–Larcker (1981).

	R	PFK	CV	EE	SI	PE	FC	SP	T	INT
R	**0.76**									
PFK	0.21	**0.72**								
CV	0.02	0.04	**0.83**							
EE	0.06	−0.10	−0.05	**0.72**						
SI	0.07	−0.00	−0.10	−0.03	**0.71**					
PE	0.03	−0.08	−0.06	0.36	0.18	**0.71**				
FC	−0.01	−0.04	−0.02	−0.07	−0.13	−0.09	**0.71**			

(*Continued*)

Table 3. (*Continued*)

	R	PFK	CV	EE	SI	PE	FC	SP	T	INT
SP	0.13	0.03	−0.03	0.12	0.12	0.34	−0.09	**0.72**		
T	0.14	0.27	−0.01	−0.14	0.19	0.07	0.00	0.28	**0.71**	
INT	0.23	0.28	0.28	−0.04	0.10	−0.02	−0.03	0.10	0.28	**0.82**

Note: R: Tendency to reply to a robo-advisor, PFK:-perceived financial knowledge, CV: the impact of COVID-19, EE: effort expectancy, SI: social influence, PE: performance expectancy, FC: facilitating conditions, SP: security and privacy, T: trust, INT: intention to use robo-advisors. Values in bold are the square root of the AVE.

Table 4. SEM results.

Hypothesis	Structural relationship	Unnormalized regression coefficient	Normalized regression coefficient	SE	CR	*p*-value	Decision
H1	INT ← PE	−0.04	−0.04	0.07	−0.54	0.59	Not supported
H2	INT ← EE	0.03	0.03	0.07	0.39	0.69	Not supported
H3	INT ← SI	0.08	0.08	0.06	1.33	0.18	Not supported
H4	INT ← FC	−0.01	−0.01	0.06	−0.08	0.93	Not supported
H5	INT ← T	0.19	0.19	0.07	2.60	0.009***	Supported
H6	INT ← SP	0.03	0.03	0.07	0.40	0.69	Not supported
H7	INT ← R	0.13	0.15	0.05	2.44	0.015**	Supported
H8	INT ← PFK	0.19	0.18	0.07	2.85	0.004***	Supported
H9	INT ← CV	0.25	0.28	0.05	4.89	0.000***	Supported

Note: PE: performance expectancy, EE: effort expectancy, FC: facilitating conditions, SI: social influence, T: trust, SP: security and privacy, R: tendency to reply to robo-advisors, PFK: perceived financial knowledge, CV: the impact of the COVID-19 pandemic, INT: intention to use robo-advisors. *$p < 0.1$, ** $p < 0.05$, ***$p < 0.01$.

4.2. *Research hypotheses testing*

We tested the nine proposed research hypotheses after the model satisfied the SEM requirements. Standardized regression coefficients were used to evaluate the hypotheses. The results are presented in Table 4 and show that trust, the tendency to rely on robo-advisors, financial knowledge, and the impact of the COVID-19 pandemic were significant with p values < 0.05 (Hypotheses H5, H7, H8, and H9, respectively). This observation indicates that these constructs significantly affected the behavioral intentions of retail investors to use robo-advisors. Among constructs that influenced the willingness to adopt robo-advisors, the impact of COVID-19 emerged as the highest predictor ($\beta = 0.28$, $p = 0.000$), followed by perceived trust ($\beta = 0.19$, $p = 0.009$), financial knowledge ($\beta = 0.18$, $p = 0.004$), and the tendency to rely on robo-advisors ($\beta = 0.15$, $p = 0.015$). However, the rest of the constructs, such as PE, EE, SI, FC, and SP, were insignificant with p values > 10% (Hypotheses H1, H2, H3, H4, and H6, respectively) and thus did not directly influence the theoretical model. The study reported the path coefficients and significance levels in Figure 2. Additionally, the results of the PLS-SEM diagram can be found in Figure A.1.

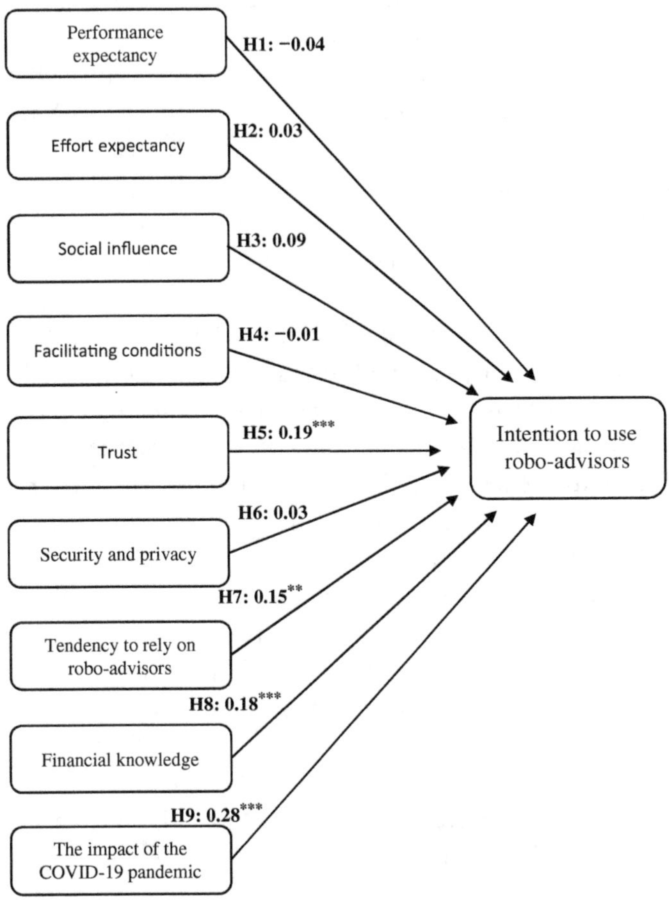

Figure 2. Structural model.

Note: $^{*}p < 0.1$, $^{**}p < 0.05$, $^{***}p < 0.01$.

5. Discussion and Implications

5.1. *Discussion*

Social distancing and evolving fintech amid the pandemic have forced businesses and people to digitalize. In the financial industry, AI-based robo-advisors have become widely used as an alternative to human advisors to assist clients in making decisions during the prohibition of close-contact meetings. In his recent exploration of the status of robo-advisors globally, Canoz (2021) showed that the pandemic had increased the number of robo-advisory users, assets under management, and the penetration rate in 2020. However, robo-advisors have underperformed during the pandemic as the number of investments per person controlled by robo-advisors decreased. This tendency is further confirmed by the average normalized return of robo-advisor portfolios, which was −14.55% during the outbreak of the COVID-19 crisis (Barron, 2020). In emerging markets, the results are still rare (Gan *et al.*, 2021). Therefore, this paper investigated retail investors' perceptions and adoption behaviors toward robo-advisors while controlling for the pandemic effect in emerging markets like Vietnam.

The study's findings indicate that during the pandemic, trust significantly impacted Vietnamese retail investors' intention to adopt robo-advisors. This observation implies that Vietnamese retail investors are more likely to adopt robo-advisors if they have a higher level of trust. We argue that the unprecedented situation related to the pandemic might have caused retail investors to prefer robo-advisors to human-based advisors for their financial and wealth management due to their increased anxiety over their financial situation during the pandemic outbreak. The findings confirmed previous studies showing that trust is crucial in establishing customers' perception of robo-advisors and subsequent acceptance of such online automated systems (Bruckes *et al.*, 2019; Lourenco *et al.*, 2020).

The results of this study also suggest that a higher tendency to rely on robo-advisors had a positive impact in Vietnam during the COVID-19 pandemic (H7), which is consistent with Thoumrungroje (2014), who found a positive relationship between reliance and behavior in consumption of conspicuous products. This finding could be explained by the reduction of close contact during the pandemic outbreak which might have increased the likelihood of Vietnamese retail investors switching from traditional advisory services to virtual platforms that could help them make financial decisions more conveniently. In addition to these external factors, the study provided empirical evidence to confirm the link between perceived financial knowledge and the intention to adopt robo-advisors, supporting H8. This finding is consistent with previous studies emphasizing the role of financial knowledge in stimulating customers' acceptance of robo-advisors (i.e., Fan and Chatterjee, 2020; Todd and Seay, 2020), especially during rare disasters like the COVID-19 crisis (Gan *et al.*, 2021). In this study, we argue that retail investors with higher financial knowledge are more likely to be aware of the market volatility triggered by the pandemic than those with lower financial knowledge. Moreover, they might also be more aware of the benefits of robo-advisors compared to their human counterparts. Altogether, this might affect their willingness to adopt robo-advisors to manage their investments more efficiently.

Interestingly, the impact of COVID-19 was the strongest predictor for the intention to use robo-advisors among Vietnamese retail investors (H9). The research results imply that the more apparent the pandemic effect, the more the retail investors prefer using robo-advisors in Vietnam. Due to the adverse impact of the pandemic on their economic status and quality of life (Tran *et al.*, 2020), we argue that retail investors in Vietnam might be more likely now to seek financial advice to manage their financial issues. This tendency might result in their acceptance of robo-advisory services, given that they provide automated financial planning at a low cost.

Surprisingly, however, this study found that none of the constructs suggested by the UTAUT models significantly affected the adoption of robo-advisors among retail investors in Vietnam during the pandemic (H1, H2, H3, H4, and H6). These results are inconsistent with recent findings in emerging markets such as Malaysia (Gan *et al.*, 2021). One possible explanation for this variation is that robo-advisory services have tailored their offerings to a certain extent (Bhatia *et al.*, 2020; Jung *et al.*, 2018b), so using robo-advisory apps might require much effort and assistance. It can also be argued that because of the unpopularity of robo-advisors in Vietnam (Hai Ngo, 2020), customers' perceptions and attitudes play a relatively minor role in predicting technology adoption behaviors. The result could be related to the recent findings of Yeh *et al.* (2022), who reported an indirect relationship between the core constructs of UTAUT, such as performance expectancy, effort expectancy, and social influence, when using this technology in Taiwan.

5.2. *Implications*

5.2.1. *Managerial implications*

This study will help academics and practitioners better understand the perceptions of retail investors and particularly the underlying factors driving their behavioral intentions to use robo-advisors in Vietnam. The results showed that financial knowledge, trust, and the tendency to rely on robo-advisors directly affect the adoption behavior of potential investors toward the services. Therefore, developers of robo-advisors may consider initiatives such as awareness campaigns and advertisements to highlight the competitive advantages of robo-advisors over human-based financial advisors. During the pandemic, online training programs could have also been considered to increase customers' knowledge and confidence levels when using robo-advisory services. Following our study, the pandemic also helped predict retail investors' intentions to use robo-advisors in Vietnam. Hence, robo-advisory service providers may consider developing robo-advisors' capabilities to provide quality investment performance across different countries' contexts and situations to attract more potential customers.

5.2.2. *Theoretical implications*

This study advances the literature on robo-advisors, which has been considered an evolving topic in the financial advice industry. First, we contribute to the AI adoption literature by identifying key determinants of retail investors' intention to use robo-advisors, focusing on a wide range of investors and the AI-related factors in the pandemic context. The results suggest that improving retail investors' financial knowledge can significantly affect their willingness to use robo-advisors. Furthermore, the tendency to rely on robo-advisors and their perception of the pandemic effect can be good predictors of the intention to use robo-advisors. We also embraced the perspective that stresses the importance of the trust framework.

Second, our study showed that the relationship between the core constructs of the UTAUT model, such as PE, EE, SI, and FC, and the user's perception toward security and privacy is insignificant. The findings not only fill the gaps in discovering customers' behavioral intentions toward new technology but also propose a comprehensive framework that extends the existing UTAUT model by explaining the reasons for adopting robo-advisors in the setting of emerging markets.

5.3. *Limitations and future directions*

The present study has certain limitations that need to be acknowledged. First of all, it extended the UTAUT model by introducing five different constructs. However, future research might want to consider incorporating other variables that could provide a more comprehensive understanding of the adoption of robo-advisors, such as perceived financial risk and expertise. Second, while the study established the impact of trust, financial knowledge, reliance on robo-advisors, and the pandemic effect on adopting robo-advisors among retail investors, the underlying reasons were not examined in detail. Further research is necessary to explore these reasons more thoroughly. Third, the study was conducted with a limited sample of retail investors in Vietnam, and thus the results may not be generalizable to other financial markets. Finally, the data were collected at a particular time during the COVID-19 pandemic. Therefore, future research utilizing longitudinal data collection methods might offer a better way to handle data.

Acknowledgments

This research was funded by the University of Economics Ho Chi Minh City, Vietnam (Grant ID No. 2023-01-05-1318).

References

Allgood, S. & Walstad, W. B. (2016). The effects of perceived and actual financial literacy on financial behaviors. *Economic Inquiry*, *54*(1), 675–697.

Alwi, S., Salleh, M. N., Razak, S. A., & Naim, N. (2019). Consumer acceptance and adoption toward payment-type fintech services from a Malaysian perspective. *International Journal of Advanced Science and Technology*, *28*, 148–163.

Bachmann, K. & Hens, T. (2015). Investment competence and advice-seeking. *Journal of Behavioral and Experimental Finance*, *6*, 27–41.

Barber, B. M. & Odean, T. (2001). The internet and the investor. *Journal of Economic Perspective*, *15*(1), 41–54.

Barron (2020). The robo report first quarter 2020. Available at: https://storage.googleapis.com/gcs.backendb.com/wordpress/media/2021/02/2020-Q1-Robo-Report.pdf [Accessed on March 8, 2021].

Barth, S., Jong, M. D. T., Junger, M., Hartel, P. H., & Roppelt, J. C. (2019). Putting the privacy paradox to the test: Online privacy and security behaviors among users with technical knowledge, privacy awareness, and financial resources. *Telematic Informations*, *41*, 55–69.

Belanche, D., Casal'o, L. V., & Flavi'an, C. (2019). Artificial intelligence in Fintech: Understanding robo-advisors adoption among customers. *Industrial Management & Data Systems*, *119*, 1–21.

Ben-David, D. & Sade, O. (2021). Robo-advisor adoption, willingness to pay, and trust — Before and at the outbreak of the COVID-19 pandemic. Available at SSRN: Available at: https://ssrn.com/abstract=3361710.

Brenner, L. & Meyll, T. (2020). Robo-advisors: A substitute for human financial advice? *Journal of Behavioral and Experimental Finance*, *25*, 100275.

Bruckes, M., Westmattelmann, D., Oldeweme, A., and Schewe, G. (2019). Determinants and barriers of adopting robo-advisory services. *ICIS 2019 Proceedings*, 2. Available at: https://aisel.aisnet.org/icis2019/blockchain_fintech/blockchain_fintech/2.

Bui, T. T. & Bui, H. T. (2016). Gamification impact on the acceptance of mobile payment in Ho Chi Minh city, Vietnam. *International Journal of Social Science and Economic Research*, *3*(9), 4822–4837.

Byrnes, S. (2020). Can consumer data privacy coexist with how businesses want to use data? *Forbes*. Available at: https://www.forbes.com/sites/forbestechcouncil/2020/04/27/can-consumer-data-privacy-coexist-with-how-businesses-want-to-use-data/?sh=705ce33f2818.

Canoz, I. (2021). An Exploration into the Posture of Robo-Advisor Globally. In Musleh Al-Sartawi, A. M., Razzaque, A., & Kamal, M. M. (eds.) *Artificial Intelligence Systems and the Internet of Things in the Digital Era. EAMMIS 2021. Lecture Notes in Networks and Systems* (p. 239). Cham.: Springer.

Chang, Y., Wong, S. F., Lee, H., & Jeong, S. P. (2016, August 17–19). What motivates Chinese consumers to adopt fintech services: A regulatory focus theory [Paper presentation]. In *Proceedings of the 18th Annual International Conference on Electronic Commerce: E-Commerce in Smart Connected World*, Suwon, Republic of Korea.

Cheng, Y. M. (2020). Will robo-advisors continue? Roles of task-technology fit, network externalities, gratifications, and flow experience in facilitating continuance intention. *Kybernetes*, *50*, 1751–1783.

Das, S. R. (2019). The future of fintech. *Financial Management*, *48*(4), 981–1007.

Duchin, R. & Harford, J. (2021). The COVID-19 crisis and the allocation of capital. *Journal of Financial and Quantitative Analysis*, *56*(7), 2309–2319.

Fan, L. & Chatterjee, S. (2020). The utilization of robo-advisors by individual investors: An analysis using diffusion of innovation and information search frameworks. *Journal of Financial Counseling and Planning*, *31*(1), 130–145.

Fornell, C. & Larcker, D. F. (1981). Structural equation models with unobservable variables and measurement error: Algebra and statistics. *Journal of Marketing Research*, *18*(3), 328–388.

Fox, J. & Bartholomae, S. (2020). Household finances, financial planning, and COVID-19. *Financial Planning Review*, *3*(4), e1103.

Fu, J. & Mishra, M. (2020). The global impact of COVID-19 on FinTech adoption. *Swiss Finance Institute Research Paper*, 20–38.

Gan, L. Y., Khan, M. T. I., & Liew, T. W. (2021). Understanding consumer's adoption of financial robo-advisors at the outbreak of the COVID-19 crisis in Malaysia. *Financial Planning Review*, e1127.

Hai, N. (2020). *Emerging Personal Finance Applications In Vietnam. In Industry Reviews*. B&Company Vietnam. Available at: https://b-company.jp/emerging-personal-finance-applications-in-vietnam/.

Hair, J., Black, W., Babin, B., Anderson, R., & Tatham, R. (2006). *Multivariate Data Analysis* (6th ed.). Upper Saddle River, NJ: Pearson Prentice Hall.

Hair, J. F., Hult, G. T. M., Ringle, C. M., Sarstedt, M. (2017). *A Primer on Partial Least Squares Structural Equation Modeling (PLS-SEM)* (2nd ed.). Sage, Thousand Oaks.

Henager, R. & Cude, B. J. (2016). Financial literacy and long-and short-term financial behavior in different age groups. *Journal of Financial Counseling and Planning*, *27*(1), 3–19.

Hohenberger, C., Lee, C., & Coughlin, J. F. (2019). Acceptance of robo-advisors: Effects of financial experience, affective reactions, and self-enhancement motives. *Financial Planning Review*, *2*(2), e1047.

Hoya, T. N. (2020). *Development of Investor-Facing Robo-Advisors in Indonesia.* Tilburg Law School.

Hu, Z., Ding, S., Li, S., Chen, L., & Yang, S. (2019). Adoption intention of fintech services for bank users: An empirical examination with an extended technology acceptance model. *Symmetry*, *11*(3), 340.

Jung, D., Dorner, V., Weinhardt, C., & Pusmaz, H. (2018). Designing a robo-advisor for risk-averse, low-budget consumers. *Electronic Markets*, *28*(3), 367–380.

Jung, J.-H., Shin, J.-I. (2019). The effect of choice attributes of internet specialized banks on integrated loyalty: The moderating effect of gender. *Sustainability*, *11*(24), 7063.

Konana, P. & Balasubramanian, S. (2005). The social-economic psychological model of technology adoption and usage: An application to online investing. *Decision Support Systems*, *39*(3), 505–524.

Kwon, D., Jeong, P., & Chung, D. (2022). An empirical study of factors influencing the intention to use robo-advisors. *Journal of Information & Knowledge Management*, *21*(3), 2250039.

Le, M. T. H. (2021). Examining factors boosting intention and loyalty to use Fintech post-COVID-19 lockdown as normal behavior. *Heliyon*, *7*(8), e078212.

Lourenco, C. J., Dellaert, B. G., & Donkers, B. (2020). Whose algorithm says so: The relationships between type of firm, perceptions of trust and expertise, and the acceptance of financial Robo-advice. *Journal of Interactive Marketing*, *49*, 107–124.

Mckinsey (2020). Available at: https://www.mckinsey.com/business-functions/strategy-and-corporate-finance/our-insights.

Milani, A. (2019). The role of risk and trust in the adoption of robo-advisory in Italy. PricewaterhouseCoopers Byrnes Advisory. Available at: https://www.pwc.com/it/it/publications/assets/docs/Report-robo-advisors.pdf.

Moore, G. C. & Benbasat, I. (1991). Development of an instrument to measure the perceptions of adopting an information technology innovation. *Information Systems Research*, *2*(3), 192–222.

Mumuni, A. G., Lancendorfer, K. M., O'Reilly, K. A., & MacMillan, A. (2019). Antecedents of consumers' reliance on online product reviews. *Journal of Research in Interactive Marketing*, *13(*1), 26–46.

Nilashi, M., Jannach, D., Ibrahim, O. B., Esfahani, M. D., & Ahmadi, H. (2016). Recommendation quality, transparency, and website quality for trust-building in recommendation agents. *Electronic Commerce Research and Applications*, *19*, 70–84.

Noor, U., Anwar, Z., Amjad, T., & Choo, K.-K. R. (2019). A machine learning-based fintech cyber threat attribution framework using high-level indicators of compromise. *Future Generation Computer Systems*, *96*, 227–242.

Nunnally, J. C. (1978). An overview of psychological measurement. *Clinical Diagnosis of Mental Disorders*, 97–146.

Park, J., Konana, P., & Gu, B. (2010). Confirmation bias, overconfidence, and investment performance: Evidence from stock message boards. *McCombs Research Paper Series*, 1–56. Available at: http://misrc.umn.edu/wise/papers/p1-3.pdf.

Rahman, S. A., Alam, M. M., & Taghizadeh, S. K. (2020). Do mobile financial services ensure the subjective well-being of microentrepreneurs? An investigation is applying the UTAUT2 model. *Information Technology for Development*, *26*(2), 1–24.

Robb, C. A., Babiarz, P., & Woodyard, A. (2012). The demand for financial professionals' advice: The role of financial knowledge, satisfaction, and confidence. *Financial Services Review*, *21*, 291–305.

Robo Advisors Information Guide (2019). Available at: https://www.inbestme.com/en/information/robo-advisor. [Accessed on March 8, 2022].

Robots are here: The rise of robo-advisers in the Asia Pacific. (2019, November 20). *Deloitte*. Available at: https://www2.deloitte.com/vn/en/pages/financial-services/articles/robo-advisers-asia-pacific.html.

Ruhr, A. (2020). Robo-advisor configuration: An investigation of user preferences and the performance-control dilemma. *Research Papers*, *94*.

Ruhr, A., Berger, B., & Hess, T. (2019). Can I control my robo-advisor? Trade-offs in automation and user control in (digital) investment management. *Twenty-fifth Americas Conference on Information Systems*, *2*, 1–10.

Sa, J. H., Lee, K. B., Cho, S. I., Lee, S. H., & Gim, G. Y. (2018). A study on the influence of personality factors on intention to use robo-advisor. *Journal of Engineering and Applied Sciences*, *13*(19), 7795–7802.

Safari, M., Mansori, S., & Sesaiah, S. (2016). Personal financial planning industry in Malaysia: A market survey. *Journal of Wealth Management*, *18*, 29–35.

Singh, N. & Sinha, N. (2020). How perceived trust mediates a merchant's intention to use a mobile wallet technology. *Journal of Retailing and Consumer Services*, *52*, 101894.

Shanmuganathan, M. (2020). Behavioral finance in an era of artificial intelligence: Longitudinal case study of robo-advisors in investment decisions. *Journal of Behavioral and Experimental Finance*, *27*, 100297.

Soodan, V. & Rana, A. (2020). Modeling customers' intention to use E-wallet in a developing nation: Extending UTAUT2 with security, privacy, and savings. *Journal of Electronic Commerce in Organizations*, *18*(1), 89–114.

Statista (2019). Number of Mobile Phone Users Worldwide from 2015 to 2020. Available at: https://www.statista.com/statistics/274774/forecast-of-mobile-phone-users-worldwide/.

Statistica (2022). Robo advisors Vietnam. Available at: https://www.statista.com/topics/7840/fintech-in-vietnam/#editorsPicks.

Stewart, H. & Jürjens, J. (2018). Data security and consumer trust in fintech innovation in Germany. *Information & Computer Security*, *26*, 109–128.

Thoumrungroje, A. (2014). The influence of social media intensity and EWOM on conspicuous consumption. *Procedia-Social and Behavioral Sciences*, *148*, 7–15.

Tran, B. X., Nguyen, H. T., Le, H. T., Latkin, C. A., Pham, H. Q., Vu, L. G., & Ho, R. C. (2020). Impact of COVID-19 on economic well-being and quality of life of the Vietnamese during the national social distancing. *Frontiers in Psychology*, *11*, 565153.

Todd, T. M. & Seay, M. C. (2020). Financial attributes, financial behaviors, financial-advisor-use beliefs, and investing characteristics associated with using a robo-advisor. *Financial Planning Review*, *3*(3), e1104.

Venkatesh, V., Thong, J. Y., & Xu, X. (2012). Consumer acceptance and use of information technology: Extending the unified theory of acceptance and use of technology. *MIS Quarterly*, *36*(1), 157–178.

Venkatesh, V., Morris, M. G., Davis, G. B., & Davis, F. D. (2003). User acceptance of information technology: Toward a unified view. *MIS Quarterly*, *27*(3), 425–478.

Widodo, M., Irawan, M. I., & Sukmono, R. A. (2019). Extending UTAUT2 to explore digital wallet adoption in Indonesia. In *2019 International*

Conference on Information and Communications Technology (ICOIACT) (pp. 878–883).

Yang, A., Xu, J., Weng, J., Zhou, J., & Wong, D. S. (2018). Lightweight and privacy-preserving delegatable proofs of storage with data dynamics in cloud storage. *IEEE Transactions on Cloud Computing*, *9*(1), 212–225.

Yeh, H. C., Yu, M. C., Liu, C. H., & Huang, C. I. (2022). Robo-advisor is based on a unified theory of acceptance and use of technology. *Asia Pacific Journal of Marketing and Logistics* (ahead-of-print).

Zhou, M., Qu, S., Zhao, L., Campy, K. S., Wang, S., & Huang, W. (2019). Understanding psychological determinants to promote the adoption of the general practitioner by the Chinese elderly. *Health Policy and Technology*, *8*, 128–136.

Appendix

Table A.1. Measurement of variables.

Items	Variables	References
Performance expectancy		
PE1	Using robo-advisors would increase my investment efficiency.	Gan *et al.* (2021)
PE2	Using robo-advisors would help me carry out investment activities quickly.	
PE3	I would find robo-advisors to be convenient.	
PE4	I would find the robo-advisors to be helpful in my investments.	
Effort expectancy		
EE1	Using the robo-advisors would be clear and understandable.	Gan *et al.* (2021)
EE2	Learning how to use robo-advisors would be easy for me.	
EE3	Transactions through robo-advisors would be easy.	
EE4	It would be easy for me to become skillful at using robo-advisors.	

(*Continued*)

Table A.1. (*Continued*)

Items	Variables	References
Social influence		
SI1	People who are important to me would think that I should use robo-advisors.	Gan *et al.* (2021)
SI2	People who influence my behavior would think that I should use robo-advisors.	
SI3	People whose opinions I value would prefer that I use robo-advisors.	
SI4	People who use robo-advisors have a high profile.	
Facilitating conditions		
FC1	I have the necessary resources (smartphone/computer) to use robo-advisors.	Gan *et al.* (2021)
FC2	I have the necessary knowledge to use robo-advisors.	
FC3	I have enough experience with the Internet to use robo-advisors.	
FC4	I can get help from others when I have difficulties using robo-advisors.	
Trust		
T1	I would trust the portfolios recommended by robo-advisors.	Gan *et al.* (2021)
T2	I am willing to reveal sensitive personal information to robo-advisors.	
T3	I believe that robo-advisors are trustworthy.	
Security and privacy		
SP1	I would trust in the ability of robo-advisors to protect my privacy.	Hu *et al.* (2019); M.T.H. Le (2021)
SP2	Using robo-advisors would be financially secure.	
SP3	I would not be worried about the security of robo-advisors.	

Table A.1. (*Continued*)

Items	Variables	References
Tendency to rely on robo-advisors		
R1	I would seek advice from robo-advisors concerning my financial services rather than from a human advisor.	Gan *et al.* (2021)
R2	I would rely on robo-advisors for financial planning instead of seeking advice from a human advisor.	
R3	I would rely on robo-advisors for investment management instead of seeking advice from a human advisor.	
R4	I would rely on robo-advisors when making financial decisions instead of seeking advice from a human advisor.	
Financial knowledge		
PFK1	I am well informed about the financial market.	Gan *et al.* (2021)
PFK2	I am familiar with the stocks I trade (e.g., their business and financial status).	
PFK3	I am well informed about the major economic news that impacts the stock market.	
PFK4	I have a high level of financial knowledge.	
The impact of the COVID-19 pandemic		
CV1	I need to use Robo-advisors due to COVID-19.	Fu & Mishra (2020); M.T.H. Le (2021)
CV2	I would use Robo-advisors to improve my financial situation during the COVID-19 crisis.	
CV3	I would use Robo-advisors to keep my distance from others during the COVID-19 pandemic.	
Intention to use robo-advisors		
INT1	I would recommend robo-advisors to others.	Jung và Shin (2019); M.T.H. Le (2021); Venkatesh *et al.* (2003, 2012)
INT2	To protect myself from the COVID-19 pandemic, I would use robo-advisors instead of traditional financial advisors.	
INT3	I intend to use robo-advisors.	

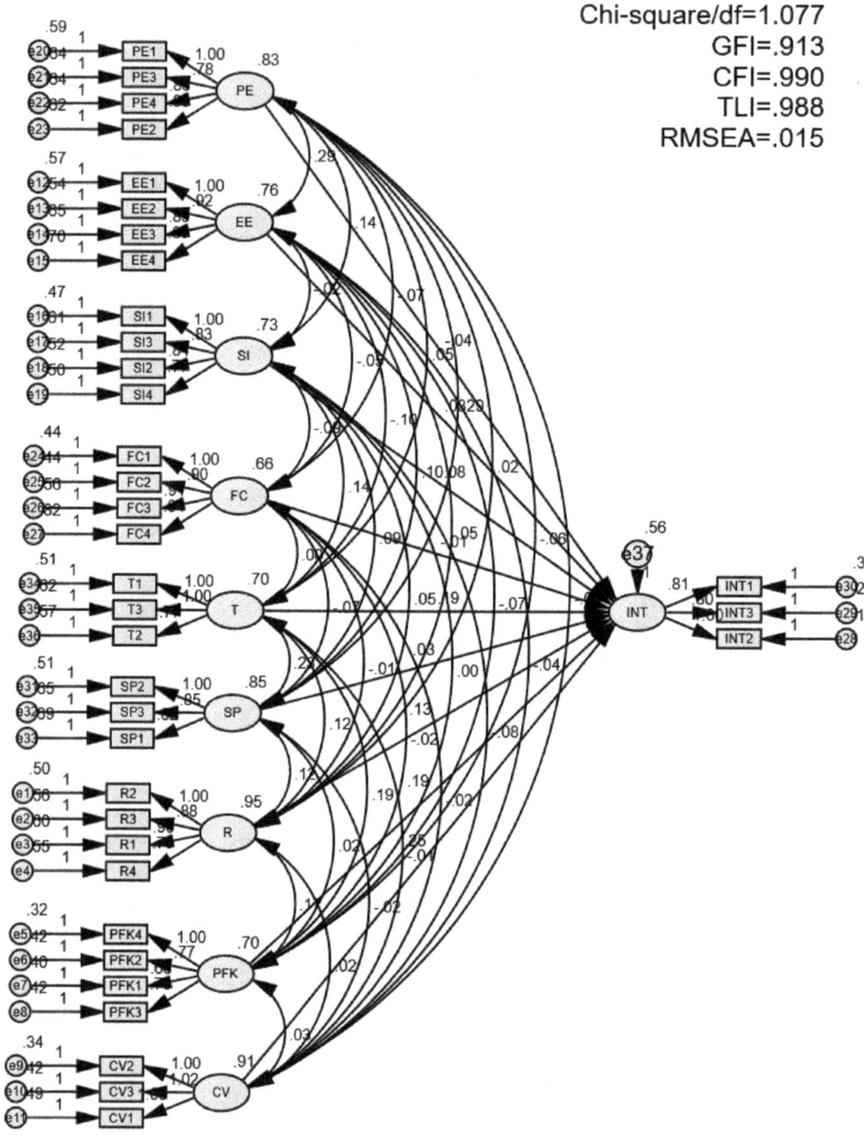

Figure A.1. Analysis of the results of the structural equation modeling (SEM).

https://doi.org/10.1142/9789811286100_0012

Chapter 12

New Managerialism in Vietnamese Higher Education: Internationalization from Vietnamese University Leaders' Perspective

Hoai Trong Nguyen[*,‡] and Ba-Linh Tran[†,§]

[*]*School of Economics - College of Economics, Law and Government, University of Economics Ho Chi Minh City, Vietnam*

[†]*International School of Business, University of Economics Ho Chi Minh City, Vietnam*

[‡]*hoaianh@ueh.edu.vn*

[§]*balinh.tran@isb.edu.vn*

Abstract

The internationalization of higher education has important implications for the development of a nation. The Vietnamese authorities have recognized it and issued various supporting policies, covering national human resources, international cooperation, and foreign language teaching and learning. This chapter presents and discusses the response of 91 Vietnamese university leaders with regard to internationalization at their institutions. Overall, these leaders find internationalization to be a positive change, but it leaves a lot to be desired. A number of recommendations are proposed to accelerate internationalization, with a specific focus on budget allocation, FDI attraction, and university autonomy. In this way, internationalization might also further new managerialism in Vietnamese higher education.

Received on February 14, 2023; accepted on May 8, 2023

Keywords: Higher Education, Internationalization, New Managerialism, Vietnamese Universities.

1. Internationalization in Higher Education

Post-World War II, international education and particularly international higher education drew great attention both from academia and the broader society (Harari, 1972). The concept of internationalization thus emerged as its own research topic, notably in the early 1920s, and has since been developed by many scholars. Arum and van de Water (1992) state that internationalization involves all activities that fall under learning and teaching, exchanges, and technology cooperation. In comparison, Knight (1994) views internationalization not as a collection of discrete component activities, but rather as a process of integrating international, intercultural characteristics into the teaching, research, and functions and services of educational institutions. Her process view is expanded on by Van der Wende (1997), who adds globalization, the economy, and the labor market as the constituents of internationalization. The process view was carried into the following decade, with Soderqvist (2002) defining internationalization as an institutional process of changing from a national to an international outlook, resulting in an international perspective in all aspects of management to improve the quality of teaching, learning, and capacity development of learners.

Conceptual work on internationalization continued well into the 2000s and 2010s (e.g., Teichler, 2004; European Parliament, 2015). Knight (2004a, 2008) herself updates her definition to posit internationalization not only at the institutional level but also national level — i.e., involving inter and super-institutional bodies like university unions and governmental agencies in the process. Meanwhile, De Wit (2013; see also De Wit and Hunter, 2015) cautions that many new labels of internationalization, like *deep internationalization* or *comprehensive internationalization*, are simply tautologies because they only refer to themselves without adding new value to the core concept of internationalization; for instance, proponents of comprehensive internationalization argue that internationalization cannot be without being comprehensive. That being said, other works focus less on defining than elaborating on the various aspects of internationalization, like its economics as an export activity (De Wit, 2002; Maringe,

2010), competition and status (Marginson and Van der Wende, 2007), or the role of English as a lingua franca (Altbach, 2015).

A viewpoint of note is Rudzki's (1995), which postulates that all universities are intrinsically international. This is because the knowledge produced by a university should not be confined to a national context, but should be applicable to the world. Rudzki's argument is furthered by Maringe *et al.* (2013) in that internationalization is not about the integration of international elements (since all universities are international by nature) but rather intensification. Nonetheless, the 'intrinsic' argument will not be adopted in this study because many universities might very well be created to address national issues (Scott, 2000), even with regard to knowledge production; therefore, their teaching and research might bear little relevance and use to the outside world. This emphasizes the need for internationalization as an integration process, so that local knowledge could be bridged or translated with other contexts, and vice versa.

Ultimately, contributions to the internationalization concept differ with regard to the nature of internationalization (discrete activities or a process), its purpose (e.g., response to globalization), and its level (national, sectoral, institutional).

2. Internationalization Policies in Vietnam

To realize the vision of internationalization, the Vietnamese National Assembly and Government have issued a number of legal and policy documents. These documents concretize aspects of internationalization such as: (i) strengthening national human resources, (ii) encouraging and managing international cooperation, and (iii) implementing foreign language teaching and learning.

First, the Government advocates strengthening national human resources via international higher education. Priority is given to building world-class institutions and training experts and qualified human resources in key industries, equaling those from advanced countries. To achieve this, the Government has come up with solutions to attract overseas capital, including foreign direct investment, aid and sponsorship by foreign organizations and individuals, and contributions by the Vietnamese diaspora and expatriates. All these are used to build world-class universities and high-quality vocational institutions. At the same time, the Government has launched multiple cooperative projects in human resource training with other countries, such as developing vocations with Denmark (NLD, 2019). Further, national human resource development is underpinned by an education development strategy, of which the key areas are the training of internationally qualified teachers and administrators, the renovation of teaching and assessment to match advanced programs around the world, and the building of excellent universities with international quality.

Second, the Government encourages international cooperation in education. There are initiatives to facilitate contact and cooperation between Vietnamese and foreign institutions, as well as to support Vietnamese citizens to go abroad for teaching, learning, and research; indeed, there is even a state budget dedicated to sending people abroad for further study and research. Moreover, the Government welcomes foreign institutions to conduct teaching, research, and technology transfer in Vietnam, ranging from joint programs to strategic alliances with local institutions or even a branch campus. Such support for international cooperation has been consistently maintained in legal documents, since the Education Law in 1998, to the revised Education Law in 2005, 2015, and 2018. It is also important to note that the push toward international cooperation is to be accompanied by measures of quality control. All joint teaching programs are subject to appraisal, approval, and assessment by the Government, and institutions operating in Vietnam must comply with the standards, processes, and cycles of quality accreditation issued by the Ministry of Education and Training or by international accrediting organizations approved by the Ministry (Decree 165/2004/ND-CP, Circular 34 /2014/ TT-BGDDT, Decree 73/2012/ND-CP, Decree 86/2018/ND-CP).

Third and finally, the Government promotes the teaching and learning of foreign languages. Foreign language learning is organized in accordance with the professional requirements of the labor market, and it is also strongly believed that foreign languages, especially English, are an optimal tool for internationalization. The most notable policy to support foreign language is the National Project on Foreign Languages (ngoainguquocgiaen.moet.gov.vn), which seeks to revolutionize the whole education system from primary to higher education — even including informal education, in terms of not only language capacity itself but also studying and working in a foreign language. The project was initiated in 2008, and its current plan extends to 2025.

3. Internationalization in Vietnam, a Conceptual Gap?

A comparison between internationalization policies in Vietnam and internationalization as conceptualized in the literature reveals a few important points of departure. For one, internationalization in Vietnam is yet considered a process that permeates all functions of higher education, as it favors specific areas (e.g., teaching) over others (e.g., research). In addition, policies on internationalization seem to be non-specific and leaning inwards when it comes to an overarching goal, as they revolve around a general improvement of national human resources at the national level, with little mention of, for example, specific outcomes for learners in response to globalization or the changing labor market. That said, the integration of international elements is being legislated and conducted step-by-step, including comparative curricula, accreditation, management, and ranking in Higher Education. Policies on internationalization do not seem to be systematic either, in that despite having a strategy, there is yet to exist an action plan, resource allocation, or quantitative indicators to guide the whole process. One potential barrier to internationalization in Vietnam is the dual missions that the country's higher education system has to execute — internationalization and autonomy; as institutions are mandated to transition away from state funding (in most cases, completely), they are faced with increasingly limited budgets, the spending of which has to be first and foremost directed toward operational costs.

A more detailed comparison with Knight's (2012, see Table 1) components of internationalization shows further differences. Internationalization

Table 1. Components of internationalization.

Components			
50 years ago	**30 years ago**	**20 years ago**	**10 years ago**
• Foreign students • Student exchange • Development projects • Cultural agreements • Language study	• International students • Study abroad • Institutional agreements • Partnership projects • Area studies • Bi-national cooperation	• Education providers • Corporate universities • Liberalization of education services • Networks • Virtual universities • Branch campus • Twinning and franchise programs	• Regional education hubs • International competencies • Degree mills • Visa factories • Joint, double, combined degrees • Branding, status-building

in Vietnam appears to contain many components dating back 30 to 50 years in countries surveyed by Knight (*ibid.*), notably development projects, language study, study abroad, and institutional agreements. A more recent component — twinning and franchise programs — is also prominent in Vietnam, but even this dates back to 20 years ago. Most components in the past 10 and 20 years, like corporate universities, regional hubs, or international competencies, have not made a substantial appearance in the country. This suggests that Vietnamese higher education is in an early stage of internationalization, and that there are many venues along which institutions can internationalize.

4. A Study of Internationalization in Vietnam

Although internationalization enjoys much coverage in policies in Vietnam, there is no clarity as yet on how it actually plays out at the institutional level, and thus whether and how the components espoused by the Government are translated into institutional practices. This motivated the present study on the process of internationalization at 91 universities across Vietnam, of which the leaders were surveyed with regard to the motivation, execution, and results of internationalization at their individual organizations. The study is exploratory in nature and seeks to contribute a contextual and empirical basis for further studies into more specific matters. While the findings only shed some preliminary light on the reality(ies) of internationalization in the country, they do provide policy and practical recommendations.

4.1. *Analytical framework*

The framework of this study was developed via expert interviews with scholars, legislators, and policymakers in Vietnam and abroad. The interview questions had previously been built by combining the literature and Vietnam's internationalization policies, focusing on issues frequently found in both spheres like mobility and quality standards. Overall, the goal of the analytical framework was to identify and synthesize various viewpoints and practices in internationalization. This framework (Figure 1) was drawn by the authors based on empirical data from expert interviews.

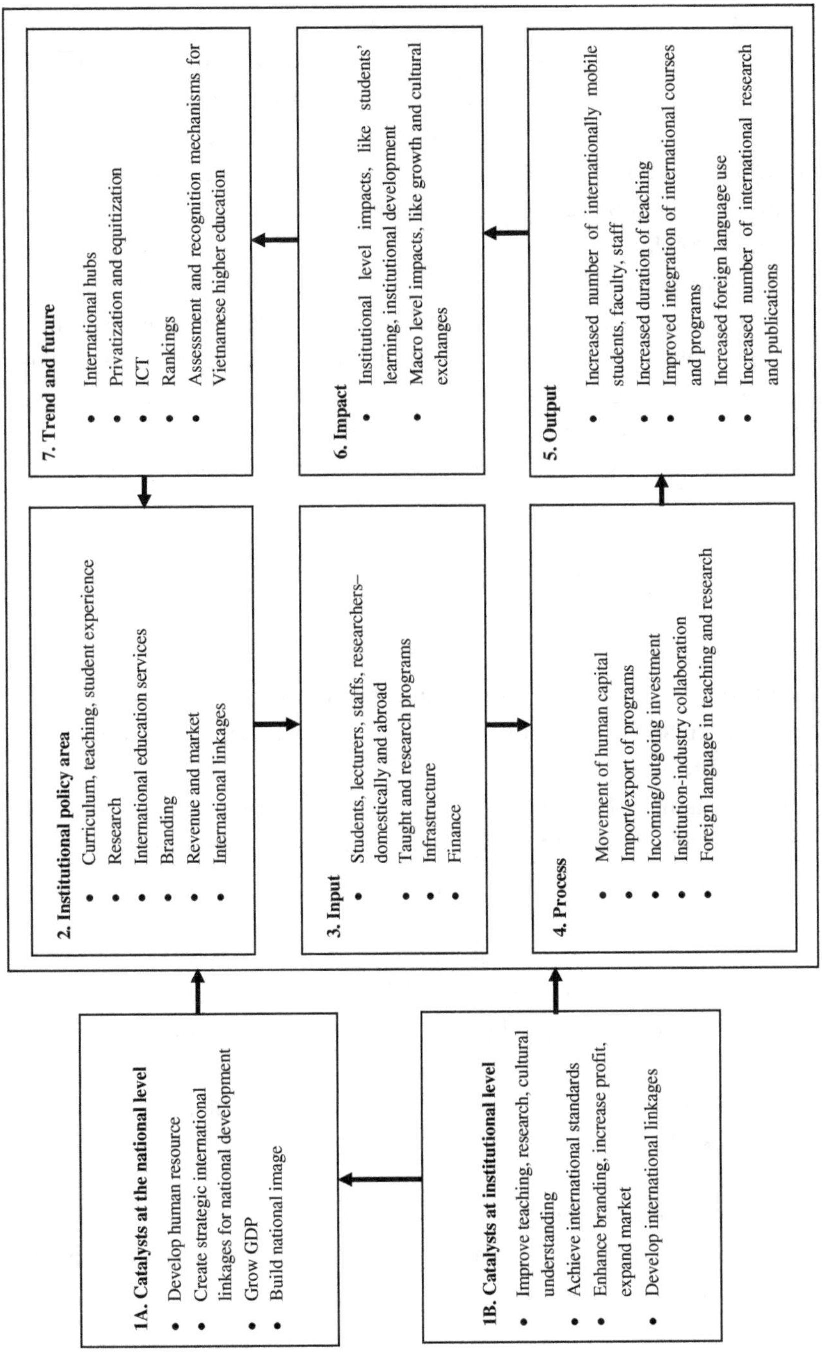

Figure 1. Analytical framework for Vietnamese higher education in the context of internationalization.

Note: Illustrated by the authors.

Based on the expert interviews, internationalization was conceptualized as a process comprising seven steps, namely, motivation, institutional policy (or strategy), input, process, output, impact (or indirect output), and trend (or potential future output and impact). Policy, input, and process together comprise the execution of internationalization, while output, impact, and trend comprise the results. This framework ensures the comprehensiveness of the study as it covers the analysis of the driving force behind internationalization, policies aligned with each institution's conditions, human and capital input, implementing processes of policies, direct outputs (e.g., opening of joint programs), impact (e.g., improved communication skills for students), and finally future development trend for Vietnamese Higher Education (e.g., becoming a regional hub). Each step was further specified into factors to be measured in our survey, based on a combination of the literature and the Government's policies.

4.1.1. *Motivation*

As mentioned, internationalization in Vietnam is envisioned by the Government to be a powerful instrument for improving national human resources with specialized skills, as well as capabilities for science and technology applications and innovation. This requires institutions to not only focus on teaching but also on research, even to the extent of international competitiveness. Specifically, motivations for internationalization might include the following:

- Improve the quality of degree programs (e.g., infrastructure, facilities, and services) (Jiang, 2012; Hudzik, 2011);
- Improve academic research, knowledge, and working skills (Altbach and Knight, 2007);
- Improve international cultural understanding of students, lecturers, and scientists (*ibid.*);
- Achieve international standards (Jiang, 2012);
- Enhance the brand (Altbach and Knight, 2007) and prestige (Hudzik, 2011) to increase the competitiveness of Vietnamese universities in the world;

- Increase profits and expand markets (*ibid.*);
- Develop a network of national and international universities (Hudzik, 2011).

4.1.2. *Institutional policies*

To realize their motivations, it is necessary that Vietnamese universities develop institutional policies and supporting activities/programs/projects with clear short-term and long-term goals. The policies more or less parallel the motivations, covering the following strategic areas:

- Curriculum and teaching quality, and student experience;
- Scientific research;
- International educational services;
- Prestige and brand building, both domestically and abroad;
- Revenue and market development and penetration;
- Networking with countries, universities, and businesses.

4.1.3. *Inputs for internationalization*

The input factor plays an enabling role in the internationalization of Vietnamese universities, as it provides different kinds of resources necessary to organize and sustain international activities. Inputs can be divided into four groups:

- Human resource including students, academics, and administrative staff;
- International taught and research programs of different arrangements (e.g., 2+2, distance), including exchange programs for both international students and academics (Knight, 2004b);
- Infrastructure, including campuses, specialist buildings, laboratories, and libraries (Mohrman *et al.*, 2008);
- Financial sources, including government funding, industry funding, and institutional budget.

4.1.4. *Process of internationalization*

The internationalization process refers to a system of activities organized in accordance with an institution's internationalization strategies. These activities might include:

- Movement of students, faculty, staff, and scientists (Kehm and Teichler, 2007; Knight, 1994; Throsby, 1998; Van Damme, 2001). Movement can be short-term (e.g., exchanges, visits) or longer-term (e.g., research projects, joint degrees);
- Import or export of degree programs (*ibid.*);
- Investment abroad (e.g., branch campus) or attracting foreign investment (Altbach *et al.*, 2009);
- Collaboration between transnational universities and businesses (e.g., experience sharing, resources, technical assistance, technology transfer) (Kehm and Teichler, 2007);
- Use of foreign languages in teaching and research.

4.1.5. *Outputs on internationalization*

The outputs of the internationalization process must reflect an increase in the quantity and quality of international elements in a Vietnamese institution. At the same time, the outputs must meet the objectives initially set out in the internationalization strategies. Internationalization outputs for Vietnamese universities can include the following (Hudzik and Stohl, 2009):

- Increased number of domestic students, lecturers, staff, and researchers who study/work abroad;
- Increased number of international students, lecturers, staff, and researchers who study/work in Vietnam;
- Increased number and duration of international courses and programs;
- Improved integration of international courses and programs into the institution's teaching;
- Increased use of foreign languages in teaching and research;

- Increased number of scientific works published internationally;
- Increased number of international projects and project participants.

4.1.6. *Impacts of internationalization*

Some outputs of internationalization might be indirect, leading to far-reaching impacts on both the institution and the Vietnamese higher education system, and even beyond. Potential impacts at the institutional level can be the changes in terms of the following (Hudzik and Stohl, 2009):

- Students' knowledge, learning attitudes, life skills, and career choices and prospects;
- Institutional income and development;
- Academic prestige.

At the higher education system level and beyond, impacts might include (Jacob and Meek, 2013; Altbach *et al.*, 2009).

- Economic development;
- Cultural exchanges;
- Movement of knowledge and human capital.

4.1.7. *Future development trends*

In addition to impacts, internalization can create new development trends in the future for Vietnamese higher education, such as

- Development of an international education hub (University of Oxford, 2017);
- Privatization (Altbach *et al.*, 2009) and equitization (Lee and Gopinathan, 2008) of universities;
- Application of information and communication technologies in teaching and research (e.g., online degree programs) (Gül *et al.*, 2010);
- Creation of domestic rankings, and participation and competition in global ranking (Mok, 2007);
- Development of assessment and recognition mechanisms for Vietnamese degree programs (Yonezawa *et al.*, 2014).

4.2. *Data collection*

Based on the analytical framework, a questionnaire was designed and sent to 91 leaders of Vietnam universities. The sample included 76 public universities and 15 non-public universities in Vietnam, from the north and the south. The questionnaire focused on all factors of our analytical framework, except policy and trends.

5. Findings from Vietnamese University Leaders

5.1. *Motivation*

Figure 2 shows the frequency distribution of the main channels of international cooperation being adopted by a university. In the past 5 years, 70% of the universities surveyed actively linked up out of their own strategic volition, and 50% opened up cooperation following invitations from partners. These channels overwhelmed others, such as with introductions from government agencies, or opportunistic introductions from third parties. It is worth mentioning that while university autonomy is gradually

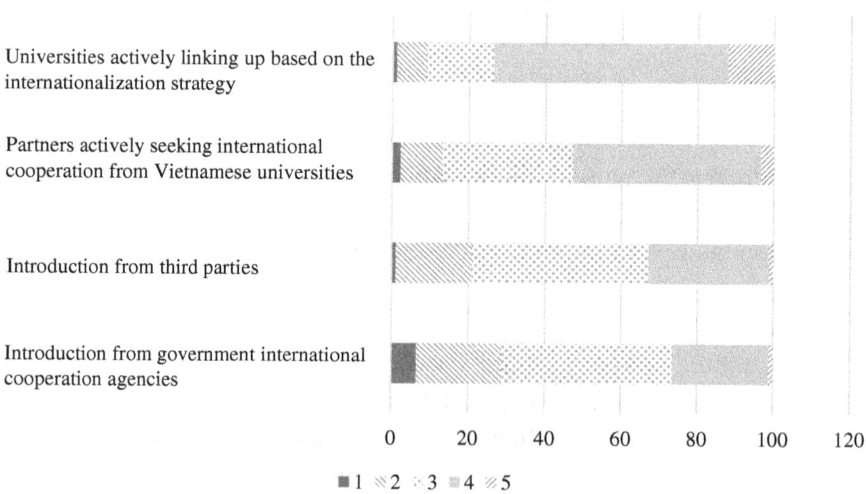

Figure 2. Frequency of main channels of cooperation with international partners of the universities surveyed (1 = very low, 5 = very high).

increasing throughout the Vietnamese higher education system, the role of the Government is still important, at least in an indirect steering or supervisory manner. Thus, the finding that only 25% deemed governmental agencies a main channel of international cooperation should be paid attention to by policy makers.

5.2. *Input*

An important finding of the survey was the types of input currently posing a barrier to internationalization. A significant number of universities ranked foreign language ability of students (32%) and of the faculty (27%), financial resources for facilities (31%), research for international publication (28%), attraction toward international scholars (23%), and constraints on autonomy regarding international activities (21%) high to very high (Figure 3). However, a positive sign was that the unpreparedness of faculty leaders and lecturers was deemed as a minor barrier, as only 18% and 15%, respectively, of the universities surveyed ranked them high or very high. All in all, the findings show that inputs for internationalization in Vietnam are quite limited.

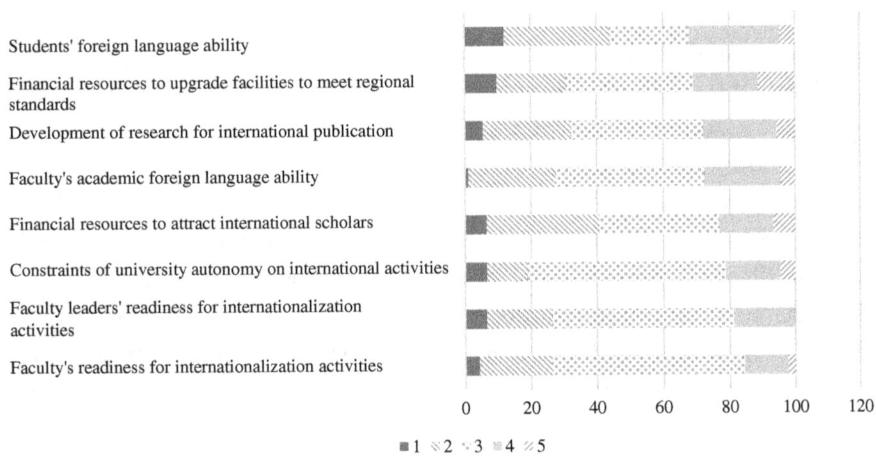

Figure 3. Barriers for the university to conduct internationalization activities (1 = very low, 5 = very high).

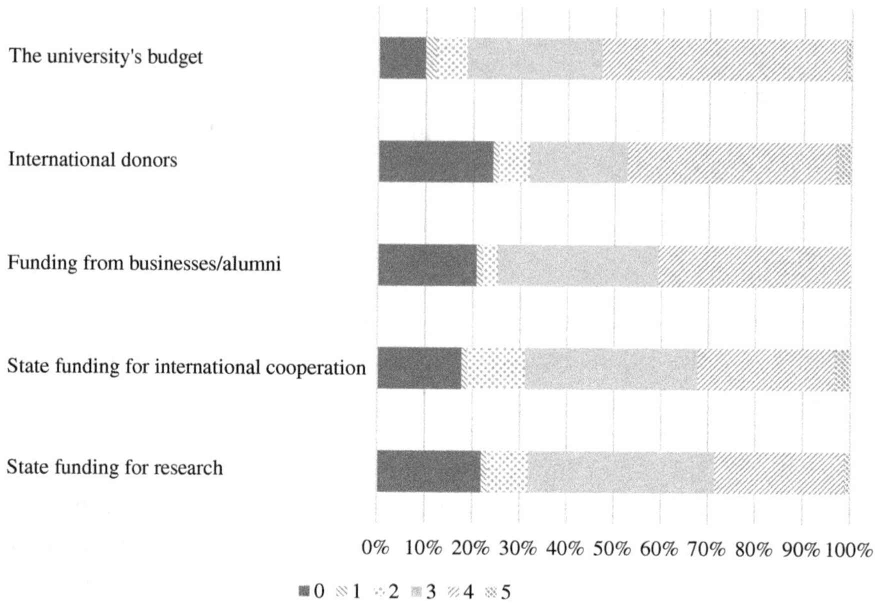

Figure 4. Change in funding sources for internationalization activities during the period 2016–2019 (0 = no comment, 1 = significant decrease, 5 = significant increase).

The input factor of finance was further surveyed separately given its significance and complexity (Figure 4). The findings show an optimistic signal in that the majority of universities rated funding changes to support internationalization as considerable (29%) or as significantly increased (53%). More specifically, increases came from the university's budget (53%), international donor organizations (47%), businesses/alumni (41%), governmental programs/projects (32%), and finally ministerial research budgets (29%). Conversely, some universities — more than 13% surveyed — saw state funding sources (through higher education programs/projects or research) being more reduced than other funding sources. This reflects the fact that a university's own budget increasingly plays a key role in internationalization activities.

5.3. *Implementation process*

An important area of the internationalization process is monitoring, and thus, part of the survey focused on mechanisms to monitor and evaluate internationalization. Most universities surveyed had one or more mechanisms in place, and the extent of their use was extensive — on average, monitoring mechanisms were extensively used by 80% of university leaders surveyed. The monitoring mechanisms ranged from having an annual internationalization plan (ranked by 58% as high or very high in use), having an internationalization annual report (50%), having internationalization as a dedicated part of the overall strategy (49%), having a separate internationalization strategy (33%), and finally having annual key performance indicators (KPIs) for internationalization (28%) (Figure 5). However, it was found that most mechanisms were scattered, and thus despite the many mechanisms in place, university leaders had some difficulty in gaining a holistic picture of internationalization at their institutions.

Figure 5. The extent of mechanisms to monitor the implementation of internationalizing universities (0 = no mechanism, 1 = very low, 5 = very high).

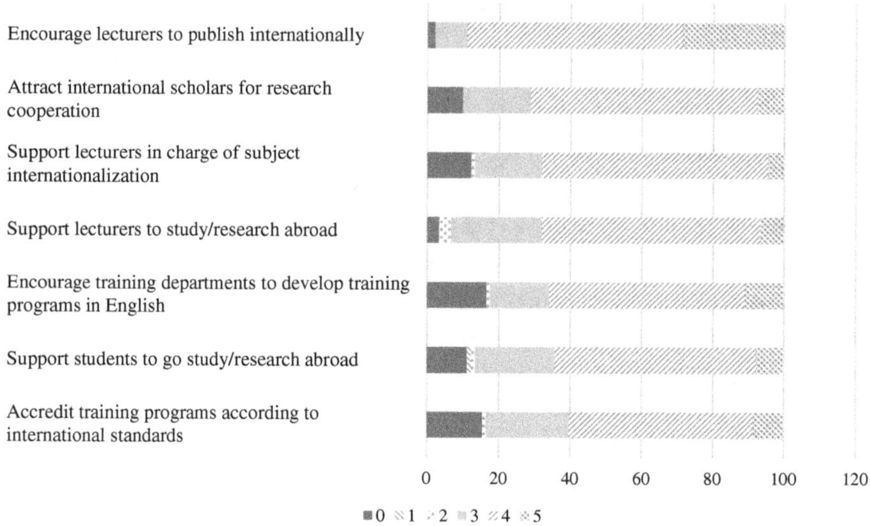

Figure 6. Degree of change in internationalization funding policy 2016–2019 (0 = no comment, 1 = significant decrease, 5 = significant increase).

Another important area for the implementation of the internationalization process was funding for different international activities. In almost all cases, there was an increase (60% universities surveyed) or significant increase (89%) in funding for internationalization (Figure 6). In particular, Vietnamese institutions spent money on encouraging lecturers to publish internationally (89%), attracting international scholars (72%), supporting internationalization in taught programs (68%), and supporting student and faculty mobility (68%). Examples of funding initiatives were the development of English medium programs (including training for faculty to deliver content in English), student exchanges, and accreditation activities. Overall, however, increases in funding were seemingly aimed more at faculty and research rather than students and teaching.

Finally, the survey found uneven priorities across different international activities (Figure 7). Universities having high to very high priority for strengthening cooperation with regional partners accounted for 84% of the sample. Other strong priorities included the internationalization of degree programs (found in 76% of the universities surveyed), international sponsorship program activity (68%), and international affiliate

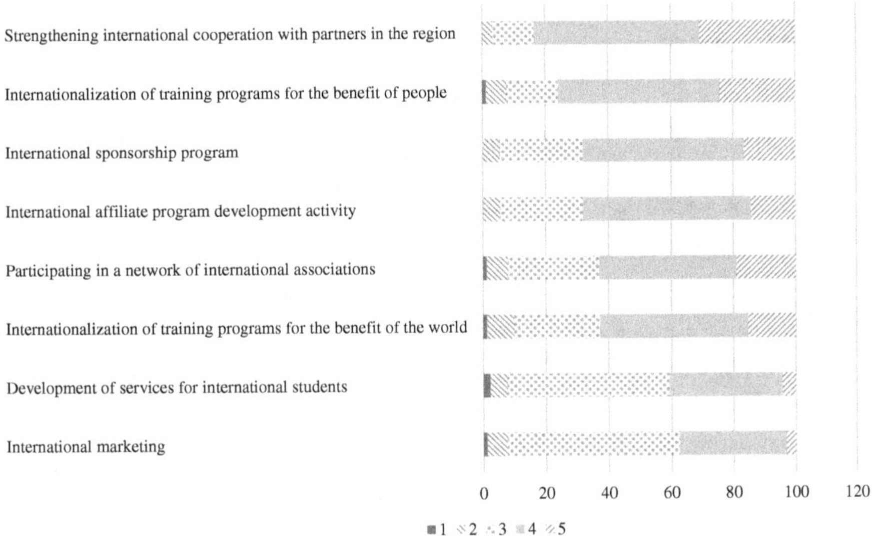

Figure 7. Priority for university internationalization (1 = very low, 5 = very high).

program development activity (68%). By contrast, many activity areas received much less attention, like the development of services for international students (41%) and international marketing (37%).

5.4. *Output*

From 2016 to 2019, between 56% and 93% of universities reported an increase to significant increase in various types of internationalization activities (Figure 8). The highest increases were found in the number of international visits from individuals or institutions and in the number of international publications by faculty, rated at 93% and 88%, respectively. The smallest increases were the number of international projects (63%) and the number of English-taught programs (56%), but even here it can be seen that, at least quantitatively, the output of internationalization was remarkable. Though few and far between, there existed cases where international activities actually saw a decline, like in the number of students opting for exchanges or in the number of international projects.

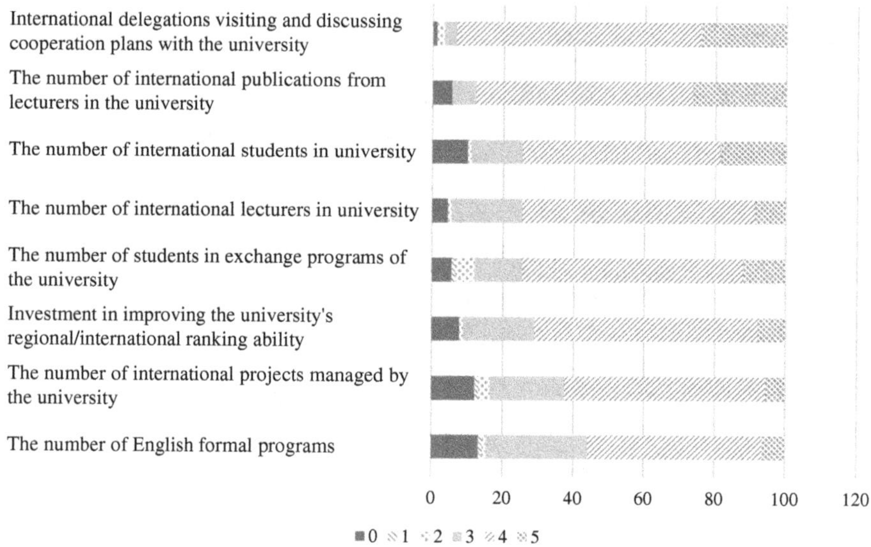

Figure 8. The degree of change of university internationalization activities 2016–2019 (0 = no comment, 1 = significant decrease, 5 = significant increase).

5.5. *Impacts*

The survey found internationalization did have wider effects on other areas of an institution. Between 57% and 88% of university leaders rated the impact of internationalization activities on institutional quality as high and very high (Figure 9). More specifically, five out of 10 quality aspects were assessed to have been improved significantly by internationalization, including training quality (88%), students' capacity for international integration (84%), the university's international reputation (83%), regional integration via international practices (83%), and the number of internationally published research (81%).

6. Policy Implications

Findings from the survey, in combination with an analysis of the Government's policy documents, provide important implications at both the national and institutional levels.

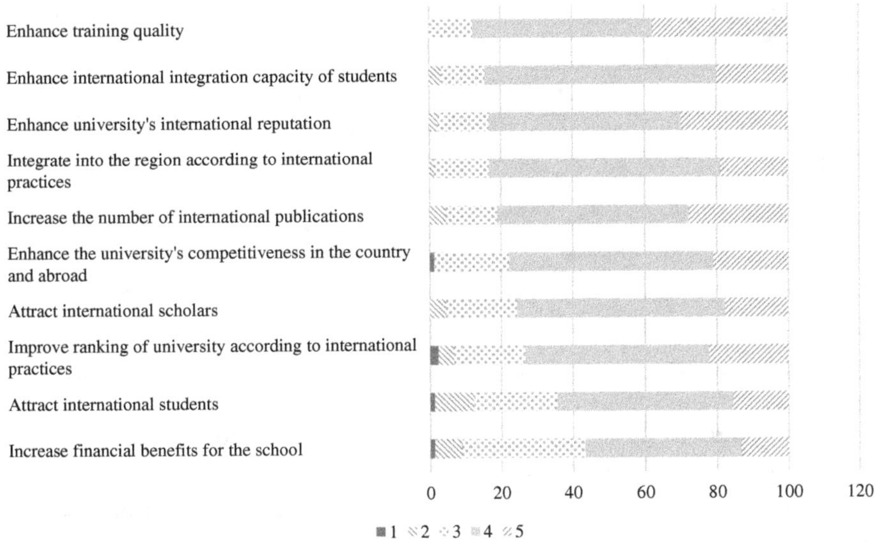

Figure 9. Priority for university internationalization strategies (1 = very low, 5 = very high).

6.1. *Macro implications*

At the national level, the key policy areas that deserve further attention are budget allocation and FDI.

6.1.1. *Budget allocation for the higher education system*

This study has found that the university budget plays an important role in internationalization, but this budget alone is currently not enough without state support. In fact, the proportion of the state budget allocated for all higher education activities is low, placing the burden on individual institutions to build their finances, almost all of which are dependent on tuition fees — the ratio of tuition fees to unit costs (in %) at public universities in Vietnam is higher in comparison with other countries (Table 2).

Given the importance of internationalization and more generally of higher education to economic development, this study recommends a budget mechanism for the Vietnamese higher education system to achieve

Table 2. Budget expenditure and tuition rates of Vietnam and other countries (World Bank, 2019).

		Proportion of budget expenditure as % of GDP		
The ratio of tuition to unit costs (%) of public universities		**Under 0.5%**	**0.5%–1%**	**Over 1%**
	Over 40%	Vietnam, Mongolia	Chile	
	20%–40%		South Korea, Thailand	China, Indonesia, Malaysia
	Under 20%	Peru	Argentina, Brazil, Colombia, Mexico	

a breakthrough in quality and its position in the region and the world. First, budget allocation should be based on an assessment of the university's quality and efficiency. Such assessment might include a number of internationalization output and impact factors like the number of international faculties, students, and international publications, or the number and scale of technology transfers that have socioeconomic impact, or international rankings. Assessment results should then decide state budget allocation on a competitive basis, regardless of whether the recipient university is public or private. Competition will push universities to focus on improving internationalization as well as quality in general, via proposing and implementing meaningful and feasible policies.

Second, budget allocation must accommodate the breakthroughs set out by the Government's vision to establish world-class universities. It should focus on degree programs that are high-cost, especially in fields necessary for Vietnam's accelerated development like healthcare, high-tech agriculture/forestry/fishery, automation, and information technology.

6.1.2. *Attracting FDI in the higher education sector*

In addition to state funding, it can be argued that FDI can also play a role in internationalization in Vietnam. This is because Vietnamese institutions can leverage the significant increase in visits from overseas delegations and in new partnerships of various kinds (e.g., joint degrees, international research projects), not to mention the fact that Vietnam has been one of the destination countries for FDI in the region. Thus, this study proposes a few solutions to attract FDI, especially from foreign institutions. First, the Government's Decree 86 could be changed with regard to investment sources. Instead of just cash, investment capital should be diversified to suit foreign investors who might have many kinds of valuable capital, like qualified academics and internationally accredited curricula. In addition, it is not reasonable to impose the capital requirement of establishing a domestic university, which is currently VND1000bil ($43 million), on foreign institutions that seek to open branches in Vietnam. This figure needs to be adjusted down, as it presents much of a barrier and risk for foreign investors; a smaller figure might also encourage investment into provinces and cities apart from Ho Chi Minh and Hanoi. Another figure that needs adjustment is the percentage of foreign students (in the total student body) required for opening branch campuses in Vietnam; at the moment, this sits at 50%, which is impossible to achieve. In other countries such as Malaysia, China, Korea, and Singapore, the proportion of domestic students is always higher than that of international students, amounting possibly up to 90% (Hou *et al.*, 2018). Therefore, the study recommends increasing the proportion of Vietnamese students in international branches to encourage foreign investment in this field.

Following on capital and student body requirements, the study proposes new or amended laws related to both investment and education in order to separate foreign from domestic investment. All requirements, whether academic or governance/management-related, should not be applied in a blanket manner, but instead be studied and drafted in accordance with international practices. In addition, at present, the governments of other countries have not yet agreed on the method of accrediting programs at international branches since some countries use domestic accreditation centers, and others do not. Given Vietnam's inexperience with international accreditation, the study recommends the Korean experience, i.e., giving more autonomy and responsibility to foreign universities. The Government should only play an oversight role through financial audits and inspection of facilities to ensure that students are provided with an international-standard environment at home without spending a lot of money.

6.2. *Micro implications*

At the institutional level, the implications drawn from this study are comprehensive, covering governance and management with an emphasis on autonomy, capacity building, international human capital, teaching, and research.

6.2.1. *Governance and management*

There should be a delineation between a university's council and its top management. The governance of Vietnamese universities is conducted by a university council, and decisions are then executed by the rector, as specified in Articles 16 to 20 of the Law on Higher Education. The council does not interfere in management and operations but focuses on reviewing and approving the strategy and action plans, and supervising the management of the rector and other senior managers to ensure that the university fulfills its mission. Furthermore, the council is supposed to act on behalf of stakeholders, potentially including international students, faculty, and partners, as well as the broader society, thereby ensuring the university develops in harmony with public interests. As of now, however, the governance responsibilities of the council are not clearly defined or enforced, and in many cases, both the rector and other senior managers simultaneously make and execute decisions. This overlap of governance and management causes confusion and inefficiencies in many functions of a Vietnamese university, the most so when it comes to novel, groundbreaking tasks like internationalization.

6.2.2. *Autonomy*

More autonomy should be given to institutions. Due to the complexity and diversity of internationalization approaches, it would be more feasible to enable individual institutions to decide, for example, the type of foreign institutions to cooperate with and the nature of the cooperation. The Government's role should be more along the lines of oversight and strategic steering-from-a-distance via competitive funding. Current legislation on university autonomy in Vietnam poses many obstacles and difficulties for institutions due to the lack of consensus on how to decentralize governance and management away from the central ministerial agencies. A number of changes therefore need to be made. First, institutions should have the right to build their own governance structures. The university council mechanism, as mentioned above, ensures that decisions are made flexibly and more swiftly than in the case of centralization, so that the institution can more easily take advantage of internationalization opportunities. Second, the range of issues that the council can decide on should be comprehensive, not partial. The functions of an institution form an interdependent network, and this means autonomy in internationalization could only be effective if there is also autonomy in teaching, research, finance, infrastructure, and human resource (including admission). It should be emphasized that institutional autonomy, overseen by the Government, is only feasible in the presence of impartial quality control. This role could be delegated to independent accrediting and evaluation organizations separate from the Government.

6.2.3. *Capacity building*

Internationalization requires more capacity in Vietnamese institutions. This involves both strengthening existing capacities such as infrastructure size and quality and developing new ones such as foreign language teaching and learning. More specifically, there are three new capacity areas that institutions need to invest in. First, foreign languages, especially but not exclusively English, should be integrated into all functions of the institution, not just teaching and research. This necessitates the inclusion of foreign languages into the overall strategy, and professional development programs for lecturers and key administrative staff to go overseas. In parallel, the intercultural skills of students, faculties, and other staff also need improvement. This can be done by organizing cultural festivals of different countries, screenings, exhibitions, and exchanges. Second, there should be arrangements to attract international students and faculties to study and work in Vietnam, even on a short-term basis. These might range from major initiatives (e.g., new laboratories, research funding) to minor ones (e.g., conferences, cultural exchanges). Inbound mobility not only creates learning opportunities for the host institution but also motivates and pressures domestic lecturers and students to improve their language and intercultural and academic skills. Nonetheless, capacity building must be underpinned by incentives and, in the case of faculties and staffs, remuneration and bonus policies at least at a level competitive with countries in the region.

6.2.4. *International students*

When it comes to mobility, students comprise a gap in Vietnamese higher education. Existing exchanges are concentrated in a few universities, and even they only bring in a small number of international students and send abroad a small number of Vietnamese students. Existing barriers to student mobility include lack of information and communication from the institutions, lack of support in academic matters, accommodation, and acclimatization, and (for inbound mobility only) lack of a playground such as international food fairs and student festivals. Thus, this study recommends that student exchanges, inbound and outbound, be one of the goals in an institution's strategy, for which key performance indicators can be set per semester or year. The input and process for student exchange must then follow. In terms of input, information to facilitate mobility must be prepared in at least Vietnamese and English and published on the universities' websites — which must also be at least bi-lingual. Moreover, financial support must be available to support at least part of the living expenses of mobile students; institutions may also boldly build a scholarship regime for inbound students and advertise it on the internet. In terms of process, there should be meticulous academic, pastoral, and legal orientation and counseling for mobile students, and outbound students should be able to convert or add overseas credits into their progress toward a local degree.

Apart from exchange students, Vietnamese universities with spare resources should try to attract full-time international students. Currently, Vietnam does receive full-time students from Laos and Cambodia, but given the rising popularity and quality of English-taught programs, local institutions should develop plans to market to other countries.

6.2.5. *International lecturers*

Faculty mobility, more so on the inbound side, has also been a gap for Vietnam. While Vietnamese lecturers are even willing to compete to further their training abroad, the number of international academics coming to work in Vietnam, both short and long-term, leaves much room for improvement. This study suggests that local institutions exploit bilateral meetings at the national and institutional levels to seek and invite foreign lecturers to teach a semester or at least one subject, or to participate in a research activity or conference. Such opportunistic inbound mobility, however, must be underpinned by support mechanisms that are prepared beforehand, in terms of communication, migration, traveling, accommodation, and remuneration.

At the same time, outbound mobility should be further encouraged. Local lecturers should be trained in language and intercultural skills, and be informed of opportunities abroad. As is the case with inbound academics, support mechanisms must be available to assist local lecturers in finding, migrating, and settling down (temporarily) in another country. Returnees whose performance is improved or who bring contributions and innovations should be recognized and rewarded.

6.2.6. *Teaching*

It can be said that the internationalization of teaching has been the top priority of all Vietnamese universities, judging by the rapidly increasing number and diversity of joint programs and local English-taught programs. Therefore, there are not many recommendations that this study can provide with regard to this area. However, what could be of great benefit to local universities is more proactive in analyzing, learning from, and adapting the design, delivery, and management of joint programs, which provides a shortcut to achieving international standards. This also helps with synchronizing (or mapping) local programs with joint and overseas programs, in turn facilitating future cooperation in teaching.

6.2.7. *Research*

Last but definitely not least, research has been another high-priority target for internationalization at Vietnamese universities. Most internationalization efforts have been aimed at enhancing local academics' abilities to publish internationally, particularly research articles in reputable journals. A few universities have also conducted joint research projects with foreign counterparts. This study recommends that, for internationalization in research to further, institutions should invest in the research knowledge and skills, and language skills of lecturers, since most investment so far has been in the form of incentives for able academics to publish — data has shown incentives do increase Vietnam's publication output, but incentives alone might not be sustainable on a large scale. Moreover, more local institutions should seek or organize joint research projects, especially large-scale ones, which will provide not only publishing opportunities but also learning opportunities for local lecturers. These projects must be drafted at an institutional level to highlight their significance, and supported by clear strategies to attract international funding.

Acknowledgement

This research is funded by the Ministry of Education and Training of Vietnam (project No. KHGD/16-20.DT.018) and University of Economics Ho Chi Minh City, Vietnam.

References

Altbach, P. (2015). Perspectives on internationalizing higher education. Available at: http://ejournals.bc.edu/ojs/index.php/ihe/article/view/6975.

Altbach, P. G. & Knight, J. (2007). The internationalization of higher education: Motivations and realities. *Journal of Studies in International Education*, *11*(3–4), 290–305.

Altbach, P. G., Reisberg, L., & Rumbley, L. (2009). Trends in global higher education: Tracking an academic revolution: A report prepared for the UNESCO 2009 world conference on higher education. Available at: www.unesdoc.unesco.org/images/0018/001832/183219e.pdf.

Arum, S. & Van de Water, J. (1992). The need for a definition of international education in U.S. universities. In C. Klasek (ed.), *Bridges to the Future: Strategies for Internationalizing Higher Education* (pp. 198–206). Carbondale, IL: Association of International Education Administrators.

Becker, R. F. (2009). *International Branch Campuses: Markets and Strategies.* Observatory on Borderless Higher Education.

de Wit, H. (2002). *Internationalisation of Higher Education in the United States of America and Europe: A Historical, Comparative, and Conceptual Analysis.* London, UK: Greenwood.

de Wit, H. (2013). Reconsidering the concept of internationalization. *International Higher Education, 70*, 6–7.

European Parliament. (2015). *Internationalisation of Higher Education.* European Union: Policy Department.

Gül, H., Gül, S. S., Kaya, E., & Alican, A. (2010). Main trends in the world of higher education, internationalization and institutional autonomy. *Procedia-Social and Behavioral Sciences, 9*, 1878–1884.

Harari, M. (1972). *Global Dimensions in U.S. Education: The University.* New York: Center for War/Peace Studies.

Hou, A. Y. C., Hill, C., Chen, K. H. J., & Tsai, S. (2018). A comparative study of international branch campuses in Malaysia, Singapore, China, and South Korea: Regulation, governance, and quality assurance. *Asia Pacific Education Review, 19*(4), 543–555.

Hudzik, J. K. (2011). *Comprehensive Internationalization: From Concept to Action.* NAFSA: Association of International Educators.

Hudzik, J. K. & Stohl, M. (2009). Modelling assessment of the outcomes and impacts of internationalisation. *Measuring success in the Internationalisation of Higher Education, 22*, 9–21.

Jacob, M. & Meek, V. L. (2013). Scientific mobility and international research networks: Trends and policy tools for promoting research excellence and capacity building. *Studies in Higher Education, 38*(3), 331–344.

Kehm, B. M. & Teichler, U. (2007). Research on internationalisation in higher education. *Journal of Studies in International Education, 11*(3–4), 260–273.

Knight, J. (1994). *Internationalization: Elements and Checkpoints.* Canadian Bureau for International Education, Research Paper No. 7. Ottawa: CBIE.

Knight, J. (2004a). Internationalization remodeled: Definition, approaches, and rationales. *Journal of Studies in International Education, 8*(5), 5–31.

Knight, J. (2004b). Updating the definition of internationalization. *International Higher Education, 33*(6), 2–3.

Knight, J. (2008). *Higher Education in Turmoil. The Changing World of Internationalisation.* Rotterdam, The Netherlands: Sense Publishers.

Lee, M. H. & Gopinathan, S. (2008). University restructuring in Singapore: Amazing or a maze? *Policy Futures in Education, 6*(5), 569–588.

Marginson, S. & van der Wende, M. (2007). To rank or to be ranked: The impact of global rankings in higher education. *Journal of Studies in International Education*, *11*, 306–329.

Maringe, F. (2010). The meanings of globalization and internationalization in HE: Findings from a world survey. In Maringe, F., & Foskett, N. (eds.), *Globalization and Internationalization in Higher Education: Theoretical, Strategic and Management Perspectives* (pp. 17–34). London: Continuum.

Maringe, F., Foskett, N., & Woodfield, S. (2013). Emerging internationalisation models in an uneven global terrain: Findings from a global survey. *Compare: A Journal of Comparative and International Education*, *43*(1), 9–36.

Mohrman, K., Ma, W., & Baker, D. (2008). The research university in transition: The emerging global model. *Higher Education Policy*, *21*(1), 5–27.

Mok, K. H. (2007). Questing for internationalization of universities in Asia: Critical reflections. *Journal of Studies in International Education*, *11*(3–4), 433–454.

NLD (2019). Project initiation, developing vocations Vietnam-Denmark. Available at: https://nld.com.vn/cong-doan/khoi-dong-du-an-phat-trien-giao-duc-nghe-nghiep-viet-nam-dan-mach-20191214220707575.htm.

Rudzki, R. E. J. (1995). The application of a strategic management model to the internationalization of higher education institutions. *Higher Education*, *29*, 421–441.

Scott, P. (ed.) (2000). *The Globalisation of Higher Education*. London: The Society for Research into Higher Education and Open University Press.

Soderqvist, M. (2002). *Internationalization and Its Management at Higher-Education Institutions: Applying Conceptual, Content and Discourse Analysis*. Helsinki, Finland: Helsinki School of Economics.

Teichler, U. (2004). The changing debate on internationalisation of higher education. *Higher Education*, *48*, 5–26.

Throsby, D. (1998). Financing and effects of internationalisation in higher education: The economic costs and benefits of international student flows. Available at: http://citeseerx.ist.psu.edu/viewdoc/summary?doi=10.1.1.495.2888.

University of Oxford. (2017). International trends in higher education 2016–17. Available at: www.ox.ac.uk/sites/files/oxford/trends%20in%20globalisation_WEB.pdf.

Van Damme, D. (2001). Quality issues in the internationalisation of higher education. *Higher Education*, *41*(4), 415–441.

Van der Wende, M. (1997). Missing links: The relationship between national policies for internationalization and those for higher education in general. In Kalvermark, T., & Van der Wende, M. (eds.), *National Policies for the Internationalization of Higher Education in Europe* (pp. 10–31). Stockholm, Sweden: Hogskoleverket Studies, National Agency for Higher Education.

Vietnamese Government (2004). Decree No. 165/2004/ND-CP (on implementing the education law on the management of international cooperation). Available at: https://chinhphu.vn/default.aspx?pageid=27160&docid=13475.

Vietnamese Government (2012). Government Decree No. 73/2012/ND-CP (on foreign cooperation and investment in education). Available at: https://vanban.chinhphu.vn/default.aspx?pageid=27160&docid=163907.

Vietnamese Government (2018). Government Decree No. 86/2018/ND-CP (on foreign cooperation and investment in education). Available at: https://vanban.chinhphu.vn/default.aspx?pageid=27160&docid=193897.

Vietnamese Ministry of Education and Training (2014). Circular No. 34/2014/TT-BGDDT (on guidelines for foreign cooperation and investment in education, as stated in Decree No. 73/2012/ND-CP). Available at: https://chinhphu.vn/default.aspx?pageid=27160&docid=177413.

World Bank (2019). Policy options to improve the effectiveness of higher education in Vietnam. Consultation Workshop on Developing Strategy for Vietnam Higher Education Development 2035.

Yonezawa, A., Kitamura, Y., Meerman, A., & Kuroda, K. (2014). The emergence of international dimensions in East Asian higher education: Pursuing regional and global development. In *Emerging International Dimensions in East Asian Higher Education* (pp. 1–13). Dordrecht: Springer.

https://doi.org/10.1142/9789811286100_0013

Chapter 13

Digital Literacy, Financial Literacy, and Financial Management Behavior: Empirical Evidence from Vietnam

Thuy Chung Phan[*,§], Thai Thi Van Anh[†,¶], Hien Thu Phan[*,‖], Lam Van Le[*,**] and Trang Minh Thai Phung[‡,††]

[*]*School of Banking, College of Business, University of Economics Ho Chi Minh City, Vietnam*

[†]*School of Finance, College of Business, University of Economics Ho Chi Minh City, Vietnam*

[‡]*Faculty of Finance — Banking, Hoa Sen University, Vietnam*

[§]*phanthuy@ueh.edu.vn*

[¶]*anhthai.31201022049@st.ueh.edu.vn*

[‖]*phanthuhien@ueh.edu.vn*

[**]*levanlamtcnh@ueh.edu.vn*

[††]*trang.phungthaiminh@hoasen.edu.vn*

Abstract

Many studies have suggested that financial literacy (FL) helps increase individual economic well-being, particularly by enhancing financial inclusion across countries. However, there is no consensus on measuring FL. Moreover, the rapid

Received on December 8, 2022; accepted on March 9, 2023

growth of digital financial services (DFS) due to the COVID-19 pandemic has continuously raised concerns that traditional FL is insufficient for individuals to access and use DFS effectively. In this study, we aim to investigate the impact of FL and digital literacy (DL) on financial management behavior (FMB), including spending, saving, borrowing, and investment. This research uses data from the responses of 377 Vietnamese. The results show that both FL and DL significantly impact FMB. In particular, FL and DL are positively associated with spending, saving, and borrowing — especially on digital platforms. However, the opposite trend is observed regarding individuals' overspending and formal lending by banks. This investigation suggests policymakers should develop educational programs to increase both FL and DL to improve the FMB of the young generation.

Keywords: Financial Literacy, Digital Literacy, Personal Financial Management, Digital Financial Services, Vietnam.

1. Introduction

Recently, the digital transformation of the world economy has become an inevitable trend to follow for the development of any nation. With its pioneering role in digital transformation and the rapid growth of digital financial services (DFS) and financial technology (fintech), the financial industry promises to increase financial inclusion and improve personal financial management. The advent of online banking, mobile banking, and digital payment/transfer services has changed how we manage our financial transactions. The recent application of modern technology to personal financial management has also provided innovative tools to assist many consumers in improving their economic well-being. However, the increasing complexity of financial products and services is causing many difficulties, even for financially savvy people. Therefore, the use of DFS can widen the gap in financial literacy (FL) and digital literacy (DL), especially for the most vulnerable groups, thus putting these groups at risk of being left behind financially and digitally (Lyons and Kass-Hanna, 2020; Sahay *et al.*, 2020).

Many developing countries have rapidly improved their financial industries by "taking a shortcut" away from traditional financial services (such as conventional banks and ATMs) to DFS (Demirgüç-Kunt *et al.*, 2018; Lyons *et al.*, 2022). The widespread use of cell phones has largely facilitated this transformation. Specifically, recent data show that at least

67% of the global population uses mobile phones. Compared to other countries in Asia, Vietnam has one of the highest smartphone penetration rates, with approximately 70% of the people using smartphones (Statistica, 2022a).

Assessing DFS is essential in improving people's livelihoods in the digital age. DFS users can improve financial resilience and achieve long-term financial satisfaction (Demirgüç-Kunt *et al.*, 2018; Kass-Hanna *et al.*, 2022; Lyons *et al.*, 2021, 2022). During the COVID-19 pandemic, many governments have imposed strict social distance regulations, which have caused many people to change their payment behavior. For instance, people have started using e-wallets and QR code payment scanning, besides ordering goods without going directly to stores. The pandemic has also heavily impacted people's financial behavior and significantly changed their consumption. This effect can be explained by the fact that DFS allows every individual flexibility in making daily cashless transactions efficiently and securely (Agur *et al.*, 2020; Pazarbasioglu *et al.*, 2020; Sahay *et al.*, 2020). FL and DL can assist individuals along their financial roadmaps in an increasingly complex financial system.

Fintech is a digital financial system that provides financial services through mobile technology linked to investment or digital payment applications, including smartphones, computers, and the Internet. Fintech offers products and services for payment, saving, borrowing, remittance, investment, business, insurance, and small and medium enterprise systems (Setiawan *et al.*, 2021). In Vietnam, the fintech market is growing fast (Statistica, 2022b). Nevertheless, this emerging market, such as Vietnam, still faces many challenges and barriers, such as weak regulations and unpreparedness for a digital society. The lack of financial and digital knowledge can also affect how individuals make financial decisions, such as spending, saving, and borrowing, and using the digital products and services offered by fintech. By improving FL and DL, individuals can avoid the risks of fraud related to DFS, such as stealing and exposing one's identity and personal information, authentication of malware, and phishing attacks.

Thanks to the rapid growth of DFS and fintech, attention has been given to individuals needing FL and DL to manage their finances. Nonetheless, previous research has been limited to examining the impact of FL on financial management behaviors (FMB) without considering DL. Furthermore, relatively few studies have investigated the combined effect of DL and FL on FMB. To our knowledge, Kass-Hanna *et al.* (2022) are among the first researchers to rigorously measure the impact of multidimensional indicators, including FL and DL, on financial behaviors. However, their study focused on the context of financial health-resilient behaviors, including risk management, insurance, saving, and formal and informal borrowing.

This study aims to measure the effects of FL and DL on FMB, including spending, saving, borrowing, and investing, in an emerging and developing country such as Vietnam. The study uses data from a survey conducted across Vietnam. The results show that DL and FL are important driving factors for FMB. In particular, FL and DL are positively associated with spending, saving, investing, and borrowing, especially on digital platforms. However, the opposite effect is significant in explaining individuals' overspending and bank borrowing. The findings highlight the need to redefine traditional FL by including DL and note that being financially and digitally literate is essential in making financial decisions and improving FMB.

This study contributes to the literature in several ways. First, it provides empirical evidence about the effects of FL and DL on FMB. Second, it is one of the first studies which assesses the level of FL and DL in the context of an emerging and developing country such as Vietnam. Third, this research has important implications when considering DL and FL as a dual approach toward achieving a cashless society and providing economic security for individuals.

The rest of this study is structured as follows: the next section discusses the concept of FMB and its link to FL and DL, followed by hypothesis development. The methodology section, Section 4, describes the questionnaire design, data collection procedure, and measures used in the study. Sections 5 and 6 report descriptive statistics and regression results, respectively. The final section summarizes the main findings and outlines the implications and limitations of the research.

2. Literature Review and Hypothesis Development

2.1. *Financial management behaviors*

Financial behavior is the management of an individual's savings, spending, and budget (Perry and Morris, 2005). Financial behavior pertains to how a person takes action in the decision-making process in financial management in response to information obtained (Marsh, 2006). Garman and Forgue (2014) consider financial behavior to include short-term and long-term investment behavior, savings behavior, credit usage, and expenditure behavior.

FMB is a person's ability to manage money, including planning, budgeting, checking, organizing, controlling, searching for, and storing it daily (Kholilah and Iramani, 2013). Thus, FMB refers to human behavior in financial management from the psychological and personal habits perspective. FMB is a set of multidimensional behavioral indicators used in planning, implementing, and evaluating financial matters such as household income and cash flow, credit, savings and investments, insurance, retirement, and estate planning (Goyal *et al.*, 2021).

2.2. *Financial literacy and financial management behaviors*

FL is a person's ability and confidence to use financial knowledge to make financial decisions (Huston, 2010). FL represents a person's ability, including skills and knowledge, to understand, analyze, manage, and communicate personal financial matters and thus make effective financial decisions (Prasad and Meghwal, 2017). Lusardi *et al.* (2010) stated that FL is how knowledge, skills, and beliefs influence attitudes and behaviors to improve decision-making and financial management.

Chen and Volpe (2002) reported that FL is necessary for financial management when making financial decisions. Atkinson *et al.* (2012) and Susanti *et al.* (2018) said that a person's level of financial knowledge is positively related to his financial responsibility. A person with a high level of financial expertise is capable of effective financial management, including budgeting, saving, controlling spending and investing, and meeting debt obligations on time. In addition, strong financial knowledge and decision-making skills combined with optimal resources create contextual knowledge for managing information and making financial decisions (Arifin, 2017; Fraczec and Klimontowicz, 2015; Henager and Cude, 2016; Widyastuti *et al.*, 2016; Kaiser, 2016; Riitsalu and Murakas, 2019). Widdoson and Hailwood (2007) also found that individuals' level of FL affects how they save, borrow, invest, and manage their finances. Idris *et al.* (2013) showed the importance of people's FL to their FMB because their FL will make a difference in their saving, investing, and borrowing behaviors. These statements demonstrate the importance of FL for FMB.

FMB and FL are closely related. People with a high level of FL and who can make sound financial decisions are often likely to have superior FMB and not have financial problems in the future (Laily, 2013). Many studies found that FL has positive effects on FMB. For example, using a meta-analysis of 201 previous studies, Fernandes *et al.* (2014) found a positive and robust relationship between FL and financial behaviors. Sevim *et al.* (2012) suggested that FL enhancement efforts can be crucial in preventing over-borrowing. In addition, overspending can be minimized if consumers are financially literate. Furthermore, Xiao *et al.* (2014) indicated that subjective and objective financial knowledge reduces risky borrowing behavior.

Many recent studies have also provided evidence of the positive effects of FL on FMB in different settings. Using household data in developed economies such as those of the United States or Europe, many researchers (i.e., Gaudecker, 2015; Lusardi and Mitchell, 2008, 2011, 2014; Lusardi and Tufano, 2015; Stolper and Walter, 2017, Van Rooij *et al.*, 2011) showed that FL positively impacts saving, investment, retirement planning, and borrowing behavior. Using the OECD/INFE theoretical framework for FL in emerging markets, Morgan and Trinh (2019) provided evidence that in low-income regions of Laos, FL increased savings rates and financial inclusion capability. Similar observations were made in Malaysia (Sabri and MacDonald, 2010) and Cambodia (Seng, 2017). Thus, our first hypothesis is as follows:

H1: FL has a positive influence on FMB.

2.3. *Digital literacy and financial management behaviors*

DL is defined as an individual's essential skill or ability to use computers confidently, safely, and effectively, for example, the capacity to use Office software and the capability to use web browsers and Internet search engines (Furber, 2012). DL also refers to a person's ability to "access, manage, understand, integrate, communicate, evaluate and create information safely and appropriately through digital technologies". DL involves computer, information, and communications technology, information, and media literacy (Law *et al.*, 2018).

DL is becoming popular because it is closely related to different sectors of the economy. One of the areas strongly influenced by digitalization is the financial sector. In Industry 4.0, a country's economy is increasingly dependent on technology, and e-banking products and services will gradually replace cash and bank cards (Ionescu and Radulescu, 2019). Therefore, DL can determine how individuals approach modern financial solutions such as e-wallets, payments, money transfers, digital borrowing, and other DFS. For individuals to participate effectively in the digital economy, they need the knowledge and skills to conduct digital financial transactions and operate digital devices such as mobile phones, smartphones, and tablets (Carlin *et al.*, 2019a; Vogels and Anderson, 2019).

Global organizations such as the OECD, UNESCO, and the European Commission are also trying to create conceptual frameworks to define and measure DL across various contexts and on digital devices such as mobile phones, computers, tablets, the Internet, applications, and digital platforms (Lyons and Kass-Hanna, 2020b; Lyons *et al.*, 2019). Several studies have measured the level of DL (Chetty *et al.*, 2018) and provided evidence that it affects individuals' financial attitudes and behaviors (Meyers *et al.*, 2013; Eshet-Alkalai and Chajut, 2009). So far, the studies on the impact of DL and FL on digital financial behaviors have mainly focused on two specific research directions. The former direction investigates the effects of FL on the access and use of DFS and fintech rather than evaluating the impact of DL. In contrast, the latter tests the relationship between access and use of DFS and financial behaviors/decisions.

In the first research direction, studies mainly identify influencing factors and heterogeneity related to FL and the use of DFS. For example, Morgan and Trinh (2019b) examined the relationship between FL and Laotian use of DFS on the Internet or mobile phones. They found that high FL levels were positively associated with an individual's perception of fintech products. However, they did not find a significant relationship between using FL and DFS. While using customer survey data from a German retail bank, Königsheim *et al.* (2017) suggested that FL and risk tolerance are positively related to the need to use DFS. Shen *et al.* (2018) showed that FL and the use of DFS have a positive relationship with financial inclusion. They pointed out that DFS is seen as a direct mediator between FL and financial inclusion and an indirect mediator between Internet use and financial inclusion. Therefore, the researchers argued that FL effectively promotes DFS, financial risk management, and financial inclusion.

In the second research direction, many recent studies have examined the effect of mobile money on financial behaviors, such as spending and saving, in developing countries. Overall, empirical results have shown that accessing and using mobile money services leads to flexible spending, reduced food insecurity, and poverty alleviation when a country faces major financial shocks or disasters (Blumenstock *et al.*, 2016; Jack and Suri, 2014; Lyons *et al.*, 2020; Munyegera and Matsumoto, 2016; Riley, 2018; Suri and Jack, 2016; Wieser *et al.*, 2019). Some studies have also provided evidence that DFS impacts saving behaviors. Specifically, using mobile money increases one's ability to save, increases remittances on digital platforms, and reduces informal savings channels (Apiors and Suzuki, 2018; Bharadwaj *et al.*, 2019; Demombynes and Thegeya, 2012; Lyons *et al.*, 2022; Mbiti and Weil, 2015; Ouma *et al.*, 2017). In contrast, Grootenhuis (2019) and Wieser *et al.* (2019) did not find that mobile money influences the saving ability.

When evaluating the role of FL and DL on individuals' FMB using fintech services, many studies have shown the vital role of FL and DL in spending, saving, and borrowing behaviors. For example, Cobla and Osei-Assibey (2018) indicated that fintech digital payments significantly impact young people's spending behaviors. Agarwal *et al.* (2019) also found that digital payments cause overspending in India. Besides affecting spending, fintech influences saving behaviors (Moenjak *et al.*, 2020). Therefore, the higher the financial and digital literacy level, the more it is expected to improve individuals' saving and spending behaviors. Thus, fintech can change consumer spending behaviors. The Global Findex Database (2017) also shows a significant gap between the proportion of adults saving in financial institutions and those making savings outside financial institutions, including through digital savings. The tendency to hold in financial institutions gradually decreases while increasing in different channels. This tendency could allow digital savings to play a role in the financial system and necessitate policymakers to bring digital savings into the regulated financial sector. Recently, Tony and Desai (2020) found that digitization in the financial industry could increase the ability to save and spend using digital platforms.

However, compared to FL, the role of DL in FMB has not been thoroughly and extensively investigated. Studies examining DL and FL's simultaneous effects on financial behaviors are limited and relatively primitive. Among these studies, the survey by Lyons and Fontes (2021) analyzed the influences of FL and DL on the financial portfolios of US households, including holdings of financial assets (liquidity, investment, and retirement assets), non-financial assets (residential and real estate), and liabilities (mortgage, credit applications, and student loans). Kass-Hanna *et al.* (2021) also examined the impacts of FL and DL on the behaviors that build the financial resilience of households. The researchers used data from seven African countries to construct multidimensional scales for FL and DL through a composite index of digital FL. Finally, the authors estimated the impact of multifaceted indices on financial behaviors. The same authors also studied the effects of the FL and DL composite index by constructing a DFL composite index. The above two studies show that FL and DL are the main drivers of positive financial behavior and long-term financial satisfaction. It is noteworthy that DL substantially impacts financial behaviors more than FL. This difference highlights the need to redefine traditional FL to include more DL, especially in defining and measuring DFL. According to our limited knowledge, this is the first study to consider the multidimensional effects of FL and DL on financial behaviors (such as spending, saving, and borrowing) in the context of developing countries such as Vietnam. Thus, we propose the second hypothesis to be the following:

H2: There is a positive influence of DL on FMB.

3. Questionnaire Design, Data Collection, and Measures

3.1. *Questionnaire design*

The questionnaire consists of 45 questions, which are divided into three parts. The first part deals with the demographic characteristics of each respondent (including gender, age, place of residence, education level, income, current employment/studies in the financial sector, and risk preference). In the rest of the questionnaire, we focus on measuring FL and DL levels and understanding each respondent's FMB. Therefore, the second part has 20 questions that measure FL and DL, whereas the third part includes FMB (such as spending, saving, borrowing, and investing).

3.2. *Data collection*

To collect data for this survey, 500 questionnaires were randomly sent to people who have used DFS and e-commerce in Vietnam. In 2 months, between September and November 2021, we received 377 fully completed and valid responses that satisfied the minimum sample size requirement, following Hair *et al.* (2014). Of the 377 respondents, 56.8% were female, and 43.2% were male. Nearly 39.3% of the respondents had below senior high school and vocational school level education, 57.5% had Bachelor's degrees, and only 3.2% had master's degrees or above. Approximately half of them lived in rural areas. Moreover, 66.3% of the respondents were younger than 25 years, whereas 33.7% were between 26 and 40 years. Almost half of our sample had a monthly income of less than 10 million VND, reflecting the average monthly salary in Vietnam (Statista, 2023). Regarding work experience, 32.1% of the respondents had more than two years of experience working in the finance industry.

3.3. *Measures*

3.3.1. *Financial management behaviors*

All the constructs of FMB were measured by adopting well-established scales (see Table A.1). *Digital spending* was measured using items from Furnham (1999) and Watson (2003). A sample item included, "I prefer shopping using a digital platform (Shopee, Lazada, Tiki, etc.) to a conventional platform (traditional market, supermarket, mall, etc.)". We measured *digital saving* using scale items from Watson (2003) and Garcıa *et al.* (2017). A sample item assessing *digital saving* includes, "I save on digital financial products from a precautionary motive". *Digital borrowing* was measured by drawing on Sevim *et al.* (2012): a sample item reads, "I withdraw money from my credit card account to pay my bills". All the scales used a 5-point Likert scale ranging from 1 = strongly disagree to 5 = strongly agree. Moreover, we also measured how frequently participants spend and save on digital platforms and their monthly average spending. Regarding other FMBs such as overspending, investing and non-digital saving, and borrowing, we used a few questions measuring whether participants saved and borrowed at banks, whether their spending exceeded incomes, and, most importantly, their investment experience in financial assets or real estate.

3.3.2. *Financial literacy and digital literacy*

In this study, FL and DL were measured using multidimensional indices. In particular, for FL, we measured subjective and objective elements. To accurately calculate FL, we asked respondents to answer five FL-related questions developed by OECD (2018). We gave 1 point for a correct answer and then summed up the number of correct responses to these OECD questions covering knowledge of interest, inflation, and risk diversification. To measure the subjective FL, we employed a self-reported question about financial capability using a 5-point Likert scale (1 = strongly disagree and 5 = strongly agree). However, we divided our sample into two groups. In the first group, we scored 1 for the statements "neutral", "agree", or "strongly agree", which indicates that the respondents had the skills and knowledge to manage their finances well. The second group got a 0 if they chose "strongly disagree" or "disagree" for a question. Therefore, the overall score of the FL index (which includes both subjective and objective FL) ranged from 0 to 6.

Regarding the DL index, we based our analysis on three dimensions: mobile technology access, mobile phone proficiency, and mobile payment proficiency, following the study by Kass-Hanna *et al.* (2021). The first dimension contained indicators of whether a respondent owns a smartphone. The second dimension was related to the number of tasks that respondents completed using a smartphone in the past 90 days, including making or receiving calls, exchanging text messages, sharing photos, browsing the Internet, downloading music, videos, or games, conducting financial transactions, and accessing social media sites. The overall scores for assessing mobile phone usage ranged from 0 to 7. Finally, the third dimension was related to the number of tasks respondents can perform using mobile payments without external assistance, including assessing a mobile money menu, locating specific options within the menu, initiating and commencing a transaction, fixing a mistake, and reversing/canceling a transaction. The overall scores for mobile payments proficiency ranged from 0 to 6. Therefore, the DL index was created by summing the scores for all three dimensions, ranging from 0 to 14. For further details, see Table A.2.

Note that the FL and DL indices in the study are multidimensional and have different types of sub-indices in each index (6 items vs. 14 items, respectively). Therefore, we normalized the indices using z-score normalization to make it easy to explain, compare, and interpret in a statistically significant manner. The following equation was used to convert from the base score to the *z* score:

$$\text{Z-score}_{ij} = Z_{ij} = \frac{\text{actual score}_{ij-\mu j}}{\sigma_j}$$

In the equation, Z-score$_{ij}$ represents the *z*-score for the *j*th knowledge index (FL and DL) where $j = \{1, 2, 3\}$ for the *i*th respondent, and $i = \{1, 2, ..., I\}$. μ and σ represent the mean and standard deviation of the *j*th literacy index in the total sample.

3.3.3. *Other control variables*

Our survey also includes a measure of respondents' risk tolerance in the financial sector, using the general risk question of Kass-Hanna *et al.* (2022) on a 10-point scale ranging from 1, which indicates "not willing to take financial risks", to 10, which means "willing to take financial risks". Another set of controlled variables was included in our survey, revealing participants' personal information such as age, gender, rural or urban living area, education level, income, and employment in the finance industry.

4. Methodology

We first estimated probit models to empirically investigate the impact of FL and DL on each FMB. These FMBs are grouped into four categories: (1) spending (digital and overspending) (2) saving (digital and formal) (3) borrowing (digital and formal) (4) investment behavior. Empirically, the relationship for each behavior is represented as follows:

$$\text{PFM}^*_{ij} = \alpha_i \, \text{FL}_{ij} + \beta_i \, \text{DL}_{ijk} + \gamma_i X_{ij} + \varepsilon_{ij}$$

In this equation, for dependent variables indicating digital spending, digital saving, and digital borrowing behaviors, $\text{PFM}_{ij} = 1$ if $\text{PFM}^*_{ij} > 3$ and 0 otherwise, where $i = \{1,\ldots, I\}$ and $j = \{1,\ldots, J\}$. In this case, PFM^*_{ij} is a continuous, latent random variable that represents the actual scores of the *i*th financial behavior of the *j*th respondent. Regarding the remaining dependent variables, including overspending, formal saving, formal borrowing, and investment behavior, $\text{PFM}_{ij} = 1$ if $\text{PFM}^*_{ij} > 0$ and 0 otherwise, where $i = \{1,\ldots, I\}$ and $j = \{1,\ldots, J\}$. The error terms ε_{ij} are assumed to be normally distributed standard with a mean of 0 and a variance equal to 1.

The factors determining PFM^*_{ij} are represented by FL_{ij} and DL_{ij}, two multidimensional indices for measuring FL and DL in the survey. The vector X_{ij} includes the psychometric controls related to respondents' risk tolerance and socio-demographic characteristics. Please find a detailed description of all variables in Table A.2.

5. Empirical Results

5.1. *Descriptive profile of the sample*

Table 1 illustrates the sample's descriptive statistics, including FL, DL, FMB, risk tolerance, and socio-demographic variables. Regarding spending, the great majority of the respondents were familiar with digital expenditures (89%). A similar tendency was observed in digital saving. In particular, the percentage of digital savers was 45%, and only 33% kept their savings in banks. Due to social restrictions during the COVID-19 pandemic, saving and spending on digital platforms seemed the best

Table 1. Descriptive profile of respondents.

Variables	%	*N*
Panel A: FMBs		
Spending behaviors		
Digital spending	89	335
Overspending	19	71
Saving behaviors		
Digital saving	69	171
Formal saving	41	125
Borrowing behaviors		
Digital borrowing	31	260
Formal borrowing	59	155
Investment behavior	29	108
Panel B: FL and DL	**Mean**	**S.D.**
FL index (raw score)	4.21	1.46
Interest rates (FL1)	0.65	0.48
Compound interest 1 (FL2)	0.69	0.46
Compound interest 2 (FL3)	0.52	0.50
Inflation (FL4)	0.70	0.46
Diversification (FL5)	0.77	0.41
Financial capability (FL6)	0.88	0.33
DL index (raw score)	12.74	2.36
Owns a smartphone (DL1)	0.97	0.18
Smartphone proficiency score	6.64	1.05
Sends or receives calls (DL2)	0.96	0.18
Sends or receives text messages (DL3)	0.95	0.21
Sends or receives photos (DL4)	0.96	0.20
Browses or uses the Internet (DL5)	0.96	0.20
Listens to music and downloads music/videos or games	0.92	0.27
(DL6)	0.91	0.28
Makes financial transactions (DL7)	0.96	0.19
Access and usage of social networking sites (DL8)		
Mobile money proficiency score	5.13	1.62
Opens a mobile money menu (DL9)	0.85	0.36
Finds particular menu options (DL10)	0.89	0.31

Table 1. (*Continued*)

Variables	%	*N*
Initiates a transaction (DL11)	0.88	0.32
Completes a transaction (DL12)	0.89	0.31
Corrects an error (DL13)	0.79	0.40
Reverses or cancels a transaction (DL14)	0.81	0.38
Panel C: Psychometrics	%	*N*
Risk tolerance toward financial services	44	166

choice. We also found a lower proportion of bank borrowers than those with digital loans (41% vs. 69%). Similarly, only 29% of the respondents in the sample reported that they had been investing over the past few years. It can therefore be said that digital spenders, savers, and borrowers were dominant during the pandemic.

Regarding DL and FL, the average score of the sample was 4.21 and 12.74, respectively (*Panel B*). A close look at the five indicators of financial knowledge reveals that participants seem to be better at diversification than the rest of the FL questions covering inflation and interest. Moreover, scores for "smartphone proficiency" and "mobile payment proficiency" were 6.64 and 5.13, respectively, indicating that survey participants are more familiar with smartphones than mobile money in their daily lives. Concerning the psychometric variable, we found that nearly half of the participants in our survey sample (44%) were risk-averse.

5.2. *Digital spending and saving behaviors*

Table 2 presents respondents' frequency of spending and average monthly savings and spending on digital platforms and shows that survey participants spend more often than they save digitally. Indeed, the percentage of the respondents who spent digitally less than three times per month were approximately 65.5%, whereas only 24.8% held the same frequency on

Table 2. Digital spending and saving.

Panel A: Digital Spending	%
Monthly spending frequency on digital platforms	
1–2 times	34.5
3–7 times	36.9
8 times or more	28.7
Monthly spending values on digital platforms	
Less than 100,000 VND	19.6
100,001–500,000 VND	29.4
500,001–1,000,000 VND	29.4
1,000,001–3,000,000 VND	14.6
3,000,001–5,000,000 VND	4.0
5,000,001 VND or more	3.0
Panel B: Digital Saving	
Monthly saving frequency on digital platforms	
1–2 times	75.3
3–6 times	19.2
7 times or more	5.6
Monthly saving values on digital platforms	
Less than 100,000 VND	28.3
100,000–500,000 VND	26.8
500,001–1,000,000 VND	16.2
1,000,001–3,000,000 VND	14.7
3,000,001–5,000,000 VND	5.6
5,000,001 VND or more	8.6

digital platforms. Moreover, the table shows that the respondents spent modest sums of money through digital channels. In particular, about half of our respondents (51%) spent more than 500,000 VND per month (equivalent to 6 million VND per year). This figure is comparable to what is contained in the recent report of Vietnam's E-commerce and Digital Economy Agency, which shows that Vietnamese people spent approximately 6 million VND on online shopping.

Table 3 presents the relationship between FMB and FL and DL. Regarding saving, digital savers' FL levels are higher than non-digital

Table 3. Relationships for FL and DL indices according to key FMBs.

	Spending				Saving				Borrowing				Investment	
	Digital spending		Overspending		Digital saving		Formal saving		Digital borrowing		Formal borrowing			
Variables	**Yes (*n* = 335)**	**No (*n* = 42)**	**Yes (*n* = 71)**	**No (*n* = 306)**	**Yes (*n* = 171)**	**No (*n* = 206)**	**Yes (*n* = 125)**	**No (*n* = 251)**	**Yes (*n* = 260)**	**No (*n* = 117)**	**Yes (*n* = 155)**	**No (*n* = 222)**	**Yes (*n* = 108)**	**No (*n* = 269)**
FL index *(raw score)*	4.3	3.3	3.7	4.3	4.3	3.07	4.4	4.1	4.1	3.8	3.5	4.3	4.5	3.9
DL index *(raw score)*	12.9	10.8	11.6	13.1	12.9	11.6	12.5	12.8	12.5	11.3	11.5	12.8	12.8	12.6

savers. Specifically, FL scores were 4.3 for digital savers but only 3.07 for non-digital savers. Similar trends were also observed in spending behavior (4.3 vs. 3.3, respectively) and borrowing (4.1 vs. 3.8). Moreover, DL levels were higher for those saving, spending, and borrowing digitally from banks or mobile money service providers than for those doing the same formally via traditional banks. Interestingly, DL scores were 11.6 for overspending and increased to 13.1 for those not prone to overspending. Similar trends and scores were observed for borrowing formally in banks (11.5 vs. 12.8, respectively). Regarding investment, persons currently investing have high FL and DL levels, with experienced investors reporting slightly higher scores than those without investing experience (12.8 vs. 12.6).

6. Regression Analysis

Probit results for financial behaviors are presented in Table 4. The FL and DL indices' effects on digital spending and saving are positive and significant. Specifically, a one-standard-deviation increase in FL and DL is associated with a 2.8% and 3.7% increase in the likelihood of digital spending. These corresponding figures are an 8.4% and a 0.7% increase in the possibility of digital saving, respectively. Similar trends were observed regarding digital borrowing, but to a lesser extent. Specifically, a one-standard-deviation increase in FL and DL is associated with a 4.5% and 2.1% increase in the likelihood of digital borrowing. Moreover, we also found the marginal effects of FL and DL indices on investing behavior.

When comparing FL and DL, we saw a more significant impact of DL than of FL, particularly on digital spending (2.8 vs. 3.7, respectively). However, the opposite effect was found for digital saving (8.4 vs. 0.7, respectively). Furthermore, increased FL and DL levels were associated with decreased overspending and formal borrowing. Specifically, a one-standard deviation increase in FL and DL was associated with a 4.2% and 3.7% decrease in the likelihood of overspending, respectively. The figures were 0.2% and 0.1% for formal bank borrowing, which indicates that the

Table 4. The marginal effect of FL and DL on FMB in Vietnam.

	Spending		Saving		Borrowing		Investing
Variables	**Digital spending**	**Over-spending**	**Digital saving**	**Formal saving**	**Digital borrowing**	**Formal borrowing**	
FL index (*z*-score)	**0.028*****	**–0.042*****	**0.084*****	**0.012****	**0.045***	**–0.002****	**0.012***
	(0.012)	**(0.014)**	**(0.021)**	**(0.027)**	**(0.150)**	**(0.001)**	**(0.023)**
DL index (*z*-score)	**0.037*****	**–0.037*****	**0.007***	**0.034****	**0.021***	**–0.001****	**0.026***
	(0.012)	**(0.015)**	**(0.015)**	**(0.026)**	**(0.107)**	**(0.001)**	**(0.026)**
Demographics							
Age: 18–25	–0.030*	–0.044	0.006	–0.095	–0.181***	–0.025**	0.205*
	(0.037)	(0.059)	(0.064)	(0.086)	(0.056)	(0.018)	(0.106)
Female	0.062**	0.048	0.013	0.004	–0.051	–0.004*	–0.031
	(0.028)	(0.032)	(0.033)	(0.056)	(0.057)	(0.003)	(0.055)
Rural	0.012	0.050	0.051	–0.018	0.050	0.001	–0.010
	(0.026)	(0.032)	(0.050)	(0.059)	(0.062)	(0.002)	(0.054)
Education:	–0.112	–0.026	–0.121	0.152	0.085	0.817***	–0.003
Senior high school	(0.103)	(0.059)	(0.131)	(0.115)	(0.083)	(0.148)	(0.134)
Education:	–0.317*	0.085	–0.643***	0.138	–0.759***	0.986***	0.266
Vocational school	(0.182)	(0.106)	(0.204)	(0.147)	(0.158)	(0.018)	(0.192)
Education:	0.110**	0.040	0.160**	0.069	–0.023	0.365***	0.213**
Bachelor's degree	(0.054)	(0.063)	(0.064)	(0.106)	(0.129)	(0.079)	(0.106)

(*Continued*)

Table 4. (*Continued*)

	Spending		Saving		Borrowing		Investing
Variables	**Digital spending**	**Over-spending**	**Digital saving**	**Formal saving**	**Digital borrowing**	**Formal borrowing**	
Financial industry	–0.006	0.020	0.030	0.066	0.074*	0.001	0.161***
	(0.028)	(0.039)	(0.036)	(0.065)	(0.054)	(0.002)	(0.060)
Income:	–0.013	0.892***	0.029	–0.340***	–0.938***	0.005	–0.329***
Less than 10 million VND	(0.074)	(0.057)	(0.087)	(0.122)	(0.045)	(0.007)	(0.122)
Income:	0.014	0.951***	0.070	0.362***	0.996***	0.002	–0.372***
10–20 million VND	(0.068)	(0.033)	(0.056)	(0.101)	(0.004)	(0.006)	(0.096)
Income:	0.087	0.957***	0.109***	–0.179*	0.975***	0.004	0.149
20–30 million VND	(0.120)	(0.014)	(0.033)	(0.104)	(0.014)	(0.008)	(0.097)
Psychometrics							
Risk tolerance	0.002	0.018***	0.007	0.004	0.002	–0.000	0.045***
	(0.004)	(0.006)	(0.006)	(0.010)	(0.011)	(0.000)	(0.009)
Observation (N)	377	377	377	377	377	377	377
R^2	0.210	0.140	0.279	0.089	0.243	0.222	0.282

Note: Marginal effects were reported for each model, and robust standard errors were presented in parentheses. Omitted categories include Age: 26–40; Educ: Postgraduate degree. Income: More than 30 million VND. *** $p < 0.01$; ** $p < 0.05$; * $p < 0.17$.

marginal effects for traditional borrowing are considerably smaller than those for overspending behaviors.

Regarding the control variables, risk tolerance is generally positively associated with overspending and investing behavior. Moreover, risk tolerance tends to be more significant for investing than overspending (4.5 vs. 1.2, respectively). Women are more likely than men to spend digitally but are less prone than men to borrow from banks. The marginal effects are significant, with women being 6.2% more likely to be digital spenders and 0.4% less likely to be bank borrowers than men. Interestingly, low-income and non-finance-related employed participants are unlikely to invest in financial assets or real estate. As for the other demographic controls, young people with low education have a significantly low likelihood of borrowing digitally and formally, especially from a bank.

7. Conclusion and Discussion

This study used data from the responses of 377 Vietnamese people experienced with DFS and e-commerce to investigate the relationship between FL and DL and various FMBs, including saving, spending, borrowing, and investing. First, it was found that FL and DL significantly affect saving and spending through digital platforms. However, the effects seem somewhat low regarding borrowing and investing behavior. Interestingly, FL and DL help reduce overspending and formal lending from banks. These results implied that the higher the FL and the DL that people possess, the better they manage their finances and the less likely they excessively spend or need to borrow. Second, the study showed that DL has a more significant effect on digital spending and investing than FL. A possible explanation is that DL helps stimulate shopping through e-commerce, online banking, and other DFS. The results also showed that FL significantly affects overspending, digital saving, and bank borrowing. The results suggested that being financially and digitally literate is essential for making financial decisions and improving FMB. This tendency is consistent with the recent findings of Kass-Hanna *et al.* (2022) concerning building financial resilience through FL and DL.

Unlike many other studies that have focused on evaluating the impact of FL on financial inclusion and financial behaviors and neglected its effect on DFS (i.e., Grohmann, 2018), this study highlighted the role of DL in managing financial issues digitally. Specifically, DL is essential for DFS, such as internet banking and mobile banking. A high level of DL creates autonomy and confidence, thus heightening the uptake of DFS. However, the increased use of DFS does not equate to improved financial decision-making. Users can take full advantage of DFS capacity and make digital payments, transfer money, and access loan services, especially when they consider DFS an effective tool to save money to prepare for and prevent instability in the future.

This study indicated a need for instituting various education programs specialized in FL and DL for vulnerable groups, such as women, older people, and people with low socioeconomic status in Vietnam and other developing countries. Moreover, switching to DFS or fintech does not widen the gap in these people's access to DFS because the DL rate of these groups tends to be low. Therefore, it is necessary to have a plan to disseminate training programs and instructions on accessing and using DFS. The results also showed that the DL rate for digital saving is still limited. Therefore, policymakers should implement training programs to increase people's digital and financial knowledge because such programs can provide people with the proper knowledge and skills to ensure that they can quickly adapt to new financial solutions in the digital landscape.

Despite its significant contributions, we acknowledge the limitations of this study. These limitations can serve as avenues for future research. Due to constraints in time and resources, the study did not consider the heterogeneity of the data: many studies about FL report empirical results as the respondents' mean scores. The researchers assume that their data follow a normal distribution (Lyons and Kass-Hanna, 2022). However, recent studies have shown significant heterogeneity between geographic locations and population differences concerning financial knowledge and behaviors (Grohmann *et al.*, 2018; Lyons and Kass-Hanna, 2022). For instance, studies have found that women, adolescents, and people with low economic backgrounds tend to have lower FL levels than other groups.

Another problem is that data selection bias might exist in our study. Individuals' financial and digital levels highly depend on whether they have access to the Internet, wireless networking technology (Wi-Fi), and mobile devices (cell phones, computers, and tablets). Thus, this study's econometric models and analysis may be subject to selection bias. In addition, this research did not address the potential endogeneity between FL, DL, and financial behavior. Therefore, new studies are required to handle these points to understand the effect of FL and DL as an antecedent of FMB.

Acknowledgment

We thank two anonymous reviewers for their constructive feedback and suggestions. This research was funded by the University of Economics Ho Chi Minh City, Vietnam [Grant ID No. 2023-03-20-1465].

References

Agarwal, S., Ghosh, P., Li, J., & Ruan, T. (2019). Digital payments induce overspending: Evidence from the 2016 demonetization in India. Unpublished manuscript.

Agur, I., Peria, S. M., & Rochon, C. (2020). Digital financial services and the pandemic: Opportunities and risks for emerging and developing economies. *International Monetary Fund Special Series on COVID-19, Transactions*, *1*, 2–1.

Apiors, E. K. & Suzuki, A. (2018). Mobile money, individuals' payments, remittances, and investments: Evidence from the Ashanti Region, Ghana. *Sustainability*, *10*(5), 1409.

Arifin, A. Z. (2017). The influence of financial knowledge, control, and income on individual financial behavior. *European Research Studies Journal*, *20*(3), 635–648.

Atkinson, A. and Messy, F. (2012). Measuring Financial Literacy: Result of the OECD/International Network of Financial Education (INFE) Pilot Study (No. 15).

Bharadwaj, P., Jack, W., & Suri, T. (2019). Fintech and household resilience to shocks: Evidence from digital loans in Kenya. *Working Paper w25604*. Cambridge, MA: National Bureau of Economic Research.

Blumenstock, J. E., Eagle, N., & Fafchamps, M. (2016). Airtime transfers and mobile communications: Evidence in the aftermath of natural disasters. *Journal of Development Economics*, *120*, 157–181.

Chen, H. & Volpe, R. (2002). Gender differences in personal financial literation among college students. *Financial Services Review*, *11*, 289–307.

Chetty, K., Qigui, L., Gcora, N., Josie, J., Wenwei, L., & Fang, C. (2018). Bridging the digital divide: Measuring digital literacy. *Economics*, *12*(1).

Demirgüç-Kunt, A., Klapper, L., Singer, D., Ansar, S., & Hess, J. (2018). *The Global Findex Database 2017: Measuring Financial Inclusion and the Fintech Revolution*. Washington, DC: The World Bank.

Demombynes, G. & Thegeya, A. (2012). *Kenya's Mobile Revolution and the Promise of Mobile Savings*. Washington, DC: The World Bank.

Eshet-Alkalai, Y. & Chajut, E. (2009). Changes over time in digital literacy. *CyberPsychology & Behavior*, *12*(6), 713–715.

Fernandes, D., Lynch, J. G. & Netemeyer, R. G. (2014). Financial literacy, financial education, and downstream financial behaviors. *Management Science*, *60*(8), 1861–1883.

Fraczec, B. & Klimontowicz, M. (2015). financial literacy and its influence on your customers' decision factor. *Journal of Innovation Management*, *3*(1), 62–84.

Furber, S. (2012). *Shut Down or Restart? The Way Forward for Computing in U.K. Schools*. London: The Royal Society.

Furnham, A. (1999). The saving and spending habits of young people. *Journal of Economic Psychology*, *20*(6), 677–697.

G20 Global Partnership for Financial Inclusion (GPFI, 2017). Digital financial inclusion: Emerging policy approaches.

Garcıa, J., Bateman, H., Bonekamp, J., van Soest, A., & Stevens, R. (2017). Saving preferences in retirement: The impact of pension policy design and health status. *CEPAR Working Paper Series No. 2017/19.*

Garman, E. T. & Forgue, R. (2014). *Personal Finance.* Cengage Learning.

Gaudecker, H. M. V. (2015). How does household portfolio diversification vary with financial literacy and financial advice? *Journal of Finance*, *70*(2), 489–507.

Goyal, K., Kumar, S., & Xiao, J. J. (2021). Antecedents and consequences of personal financial management behavior: a systematic literature review and future research agenda. *International Journal of Bank Marketing*, *39*(7), 1166–1207.

Grohmann, A. (2018). Financial literacy and financial behavior: Evidence from the emerging Asian middle class. *Pacific-Basin Finance Journal, 48*, 129–143.

Grohmann, A., Klühs, T., & Menkhoff, L. (2018). Does financial literacy improve financial inclusion? Cross-country evidence. *World Development*, 111, 84–96.

Grootenhuis, A. L. (2019). Mobile money and financial inclusion: A case study on Myanmar. Unpublished master's thesis. School of Economics and Management, Lund University, Lund, Sweden.

Hair, J. F., Black, W. C., Babin, B. J., & Anderson, R. E. (2014). *Multivariate Data Analysis* (7th edn.). Harlow: Person Education Limited.

Henager, R. & Cude, B. J. (2016). Financial literacy and long-and short-term financial behavior in different age groups. *Journal of Financial Counseling and Planning*, *27*(1), 3–19.

Huston, S. J. (2010). Measuring Financial Literacy. *Journal of Consumer Affairs*, *44(2)*, 296–316.

Idris, F., Devi Krishnan, K. S., & Azmi, N. (2013). Relationship between financial literacy and financial distress among youths in Malaysia — An empirical study. *Malaysian Journal of Society and Space*, *4*, 106–117.

Ionescu, R. & Radulescu, I. (2019). Behavioral Finance and the fast-evolving world of Fintech. *Economic Insights–Trends and Challenges*, *VIII*(LXXI), (4).

Jack, W. & Suri, T. (2014). Risk sharing and transactions costs: Evidence from Kenya's mobile money revolution. *American Economic Review*, *104*(1), 183–223.

Kaiser, T. & Menkhoff, L. (2016). Does financial education impact financial behavior, and if so, when? (DIW Berlin Discussion Paper No. 1562). German Institute for Economic Research.

Kass-Hanna, J., Lyons, A. C., & Liu, F. (2022). Building financial resilience through financial and digital literacy in South Asia and Sub-Saharan Africa. *Emerging Markets Review*, *51*(Part A), June 2022, 100846.

Kholilah, N.A dan Irmani, & May, Rr. (2013). Studi financial management behavior Pada Masyarakat Surabaya. *Journal of Business and Banking*, *3*(1), 69–80.

Königsheim, C., Lukas, M., & Nöth, M. (2017). Financial knowledge, risk preferences, and the demand for digital financial services. *Schmalenbach Business Review*, *18*(4), 343–375.

Laily, N. (2013). Pengaruh Literasi Keuangan Terhadap Perilaku Mahasiswa Dalam Mengelola Keuangan. *Journal of Accounting and Business Education, 1*(4) [Jurnal Pendidikan Akuntansi (JPA): Vol. 1, No. 4, September 2013), 2013].

Law, N., Woo, D., & Wong, G. (2018). A Global framework of reference on digital literacy skills for indicator 4.4.2. *Information Paper No. 51* (p. 146). UNESCO.

Lusardi, A. & Mitchell, O. S. (2008). Planning and financial literacy: How do women fare? *American Economic Review, 98*(2), 413–417.

Lusardi, A. & Mitchell, O. S. (2011). Financial literacy and retirement planning in the United States. *Journal of Pension Economics and Finance, 10*(4), 509–525.

Lusardi, A. & Mitchell, O. S. (2014). The economic importance of financial literacy: Theory and evidence. *Journal of Economic Literature, 52*(1), 5–44.

Lusardi, A. & Tufano, P. (2015). Debt literacy, financial experiences, and over indebtedness. *Journal of Pension Economics & Finance, 14*(4), 332–368.

Lusardi, A., Mitchell, O. S., & Curto, V. (2010). Financial literacy among the young. *Journal of Consumer Affairs, 44*(2), 358–380.

Lyons, A., Grable, J., & Zeng, T. (2017). Infrastructure, urbanization, and the financial inclusion of Chinese households.

Lyons, A., Kass-Hanna, J., & Liu, F. (2021). Building financial resilience through financial and digital literacy in South Asia and Sub-Saharan Africa.

Lyons, A. C. & Fontes, A. (2021). Impacts of financial and digital literacy and social media on the financial health of U.S. households.

Lyons, A. C. & Kass-Hanna, J. (2019). Financial inclusion, financial literacy, and economically vulnerable populations in the Middle East and North Africa. *Emerging Markets Finance and Trade*, 1–40.

Lyons, A. C. & Kass-Hanna, J. (2020a). Rebuilding the livelihoods of forcibly displaced populations using digital financial inclusion. *T20 Saudi Arabia Policy Brief.*

Lyons, A. C. & Kass-Hanna, J. (2020b). A human development approach to measuring and improving the digital livelihoods of vulnerable populations. (T20 Saudi Arabia Policy Brief Prepared for 2020 G20 Summit by T20 Saudi Arabia, Task Force 6: Economy, Employment, and Education in the Digital Age). Available at: https://t20saudiarabia.org.sa/en/briefs/Pages/Policy-Brief.aspx?pb=TF6_PB9.

Lyons, A. C. & Kass-Hanna, J. (2021). A methodological overview to defining and measuring "digital" financial literacy. *Financial Planning Review, 4*(2), e1113.

Lyons, A. C., Grable, J. E., & Zeng, T. (2019). Impacts of financial literacy on the loan decisions of financially excluded households in the People's Republic of China. *ADBI Working Paper Series, No. 923.* Tokyo, Japan: Asian Development Bank Institute.

Lyons, A. C., Kass-Hanna, J., & Fava, A. (2022). Fintech development and savings, borrowing, and remittances: A comparative study of emerging economies. *Emerging Markets Review*, *51*, 100842.

Lyons, A. C., Kass-Hanna, J., & Greenlee, A. (2020). Impacts of financial and digital inclusion on poverty in South Asia and Sub-Saharan Africa. *ADBI Working Paper Series*. Tokyo: Asian Development Bank Institute.

Lyons, A. C., Kass-Hanna, J., Zucchetti, A., & Cristobal C. (2019). Leaving no one behind: Measuring the multidimensionality of digital literacy in the age of A.I. and other transformative technologies. T20 Japan Policy Brief. Prepared for 2019 G20 Summit by T20 Japan, Task Force 7: The Future of Work and Education in the Digital Age.

Marsh, B. A. (2006). Examining the personal finance attitudes, behaviors, and knowledge levels of first-year and senior students at Baptist Universities in The State Of Texas. Doctor of Philosophy.

Mbiti, I. & Weil, D. N. (2015). Mobile banking: The impact of M-Pesa in Kenya. In *African Successes*, *Volume* III*: Modernization and Development*. Chicago, IL: University of Chicago Press.

Meyer, B. D. & Sullivan, J. X. (2013). Consumption and income inequality and the great recession. *American Economic Review*, *103*(3), 178–183.

Moenjak, T., Kongprajya, A., & Monchaitrakul, C. (2020). Fintech, financial literacy, and consumer saving and borrowing: The case of Thailand.

Morgan, P. J. & Trinh, L. Q. (2019a). Fintech and Financial Literacy in the Lao PDR. *ADBI Working Paper Series No. 933*. Tokyo: Asian Development Bank Institute.

Morgan, P. J. & Trinh, L. Q. (2019b). Fintech and financial literacy in the Lao PDR.

Munyegera, G. K. & Matsumoto, T. (2016). Mobile money, remittances, and household welfare: Panel evidence from Rural Uganda. *World Development*, *79*, 127–137.

OECD. (2018). G20/OECD INFE policy guidance on digitalization and financial literacy. Paris, France.

Ouma, S. A., Odongo, T. M., & Were, M. (2017). Mobile financial services and financial inclusion: Is it a boon for savings mobilization? *Review of Development Finance*, *7*(1), 29–35.

Pazarbasioglu, C., Mora, A. G., Uttamchandani, M., Natarajan, H., Feyen, E., & Saal, M. (2020). Digital financial services. *World Bank*, 54.

Perry, V. G. & Morris, M. D. (2005). Who is in control? The role of self-perception, knowledge, and income in explaining consumer financial behavior. *Journal of Consumer Affairs*, *39*(2), 299–313.

Prasad, H. & Meghwal, D. (2017). Digital financial literacy: A study of households of Udaipur. *Global Journal of Advanced Research*, *4*(5), 201–209.

Riitsalu, L. & Murakas, R. (2019). Subjective financial knowledge, prudent behavior, and income: The predictors of financial well-being in Estonia. *International Journal of Bank Marketing*, *37*(4), 934–950.

Riley, E. (2018). Mobile Money and risk sharing against village shocks. *Journal of Development Economics*, *135*, 43–58.

Sabri, M. F. & MacDonald, M. (2010). Savings behavior and financial problems among college students: The role of financial literacy in Malaysia. *Cross-cultural Communication*, *6*(33), 103–110.

Sahay, M. R., von Allmen, M. U. E., Lahreche, M. A., Khera, P., Ogawa, M. S., Bazarbash, M., & Beaton, M. K. (2020). The promise of fintech: Financial inclusion in the post-COVID-19 era. *International Monetary Fund.*

Seng, K. (2017). Considering the effects of mobile phones on financial inclusion in Cambodia. *MPRA Paper No. 82225.* Munich, Germany: Munich Personal RePEc Archive.

Setiawan, B., Nugraha, D. P., Irawan, A., Jeyakumar Nathan, R., & Zeman, Z. (2021). User innovativeness and fintech adoption in Indonesia. *Journal of Open Innovation: Technology, Marketing, and Complexity*, *7*, 188.

Sevim, N., Temizel, F., & Sayılır, Z. (2012). The effects of financial literacy on the borrowing behavior of Turkish financial consumers. *International Journal of Consumer Studies*, *36*(5), 573–579.

Shen, Y., Hu, W., & Hueng, C. J. (2018). The effects of financial literacy, digital financial product usage, and internet usage on financial inclusion in China. *MATEC Web of Conferences, 228(05012). EDP Sciences.*

Statistica (2022a). Smartphone market in Vientam. Available at: https://www.statista.com/topics/9168/smartphone-market-in-vietnam/#dossier-chapter2.

Statistica (2022b). Fintech in Vietnam — Statistics & facts. Available at: https://www.statista.com/topics/7840/fintech-in-vietnam/#topicOverview.

Statistica (2023). Average monthly salary for paid workers and employees in Vietnam from 4th quarter 2020 to 4th quarter 2022. Available at: https://www.statista.com/statistics/1070795/vietnam-average-monthly.

Stolper, O. A. & Walter, A. (2017). Financial literacy, financial advice, and financial behavior. *Journal of Business Economics*, *87*(5), 581–643.

Sundarasen, S. D. D., Rahman, M. S., Othman, N. S., & Dnaraj, J. (2016). Impact of financial literacy, financial socialization agents, and parental norms on money management. *Journal of Business Studies Quarterly*, *8*(1), 137–135.

Suri, T. & Jack, W. (2016). The long-run poverty and gender impacts of mobile money. *Science*, *354*(6317), 1288–1292.

Susanti, S., Hasan, M., Ahmad, M. I., & Marhawati, S. (2018). Faktor-Faktor yang Mempengaruhi Minat Mahasiswa Berinvestasi di Galeri Investasi Universitas Negeri Makasar. *Prosiding Seminar Nasional Pendidikan Ekonomi*, 4.

Tony, N. & Desai, K. (2020). Impact of digital financial literacy on digital financial inclusion. *International Journal of Scientific and Technology Research*, *9*(1), 1911–1915.

Van Rooij, M. C., Lusardi, A., & Alessie, R. J. (2011). Financial literacy and retirement planning in the Netherlands. *Journal of Economic Psychology*, *32*(4), 593–608.

Vogels, E. A. & Anderson, M. (2019). Americans and digital knowledge. Pew Research Center. Available at: https://www.pewresearch.org/internet/2019/10/09/americans-and-digital-knowledge.

Vogels, E. A., Rainie, L., & Anderson, J. (2020). Experts predict more digital innovation by 2030 aimed at enhancing democracy. *Pew Research Center*.

Wangmo, P. (2015). Assessing the level and impact of financial literacy on individual saving and spending habits in royal institute of management. *PGDPA Research Report 2018*. Bhutan.

Watson, J. J. (2003). The relationship of materialism to spending tendencies, saving, and debt. *Journal of Economic Psychology*, *24*.

Widdowson, D. & Hailwood, K. (2007). Financial literacy and its role in promoting a sound financial system. *Reserve Bank of New Zealand Bulletin*, *70*(2), 37–47.

Widyastuti, U., Suhud, U., & Sumiati. A. (2016). The impact of financial literacy on student teachers' saving intention and saving behavior. *Mediterranean Journal of Social Sciences*, *7*(6), 41–48.

Wieser, C., Bruhn, M., Kinzinger, J., Ruckteschler, C., & Heitmann, S. (2019). The impact of mobile money on poor rural households: Experimental evidence from Uganda. *Policy Research Working Paper 8913*. Washington, DC: The World Bank.

Xiao, J. J., Chen, C., & Chen, F. (2014). Consumer financial capability and financial satisfaction. *Social Indicators Research*, *118*(1), 415–432.

Appendix

Table A.1. Scale items.

Construct and Item	Source
Digital spending	
I engage in routine shopping using e-commerce (SP1)	Watson (2003); Furnham (1999)
I prefer to choose shopping using a digital platform (Shopee, Lazada, Tiki, etc.) to a conventional one (traditional market, supermarket, mall, etc.) (SP2)	
I have spent more on a digital platform (Shopee, Lazada, Tiki, etc.) than on a conventional one (traditional markets, supermarkets, malls, etc.) (SP3)	
I choose to shop using digital platforms to buy domestic products (SP4)	
I choose to shop using digital platforms to buy personal products (SP5)	
I choose to shop using digital platforms for leisure and enjoyment (SP6)	
I choose to shop using digital platforms because of their convenience (SP7)	
Digital saving	
I save using digital financial products and have a transaction motive (SV1)	Furnham (1999); Watson (2003); Garcıa *et al.* (2017)
I save using digital financial products and have a speculation motive (SV2)	
I save using digital financial products and have a precautionary motive (SV3)	
I save using digital financial products and have a retirement program motive (SV4)	
I save using digital financial products and have a bequest motive (SV5)	
I perform independent financial management and use a digital financial platform for saving (SV6)	
I have a perception that saving using digital financial products is secure (SV7)	
I am satisfied with saving using digital financial products (SV8)	
I make regular savings using digital financial platforms (SV9)	
Digital borrowing	
I withdraw money from my credit card account to pay my credit card bills (BR1)	Sevim *et al.* (2012)

Table A.1. (*Continued*)

Construct and Item	Source
I will use credit if it has attractive features, even if I do not need it (BR2)	
I use consumer credit for my holiday expenses (BR3)	
I have difficulties managing my debt because I use a large number of credit cards (BR4)	
I finance the gap in my budget through consumer credit (BR5)	
I would instead use consumer credit than pay cash when I buy a durable good (BR6)	

Table A.2. Variable definition.

Variable	Definition
Panel A: FMBs	
Spending	
Digital spending	= 1 if respondents have a score in digital expenditures higher than 3
Over-spending	= 1 if respondents reported that they sometimes pay using their credit card balance and hardly pay off their credit card balance
Saving	
Digital saving	= 1 if respondents had a score of digital saving higher than 3
Formal saving	= 1 if respondents reported saving using a traditional banking institution
Borrowing	
Digital borrowing	= 1 if respondents had a score of digital borrowing higher than 3
Formal borrowing	= 1 if respondents reported that they currently had a loan with a bank
Investment	= 1 if respondents reported that they had been investing in financial assets or real estate
Panel B: Financial and digital literacy	
FL index	= objective FL index plus subjective FL index
Objective FL	Objective FL index was calculated by summing the correct answers from 5 questions and assessing knowledge about interest rates (1 question), compound interest (2 questions), inflation (1 question), and diversification (1 question)

(*Continued*)

Table A.2. (*Continued*)

Variable	Definition
Interest rates (FL1)	**Question**: "Suppose you need to borrow 1,000,000 VND. Which is the lower amount to pay back: 1,050,000 VND; 1,000,000 VND plus 3%; I don't know" = 1 if the respondent selected "1,000,000 VND plus 3%"
Compound interest 1 (FL2)	**Question**: "Suppose you put money in the bank for 2 years, and the bank agrees to add 15% per year to your account. Will the bank add more money to your account the 2nd year than it did the 1st year, or will it add the same amount both years?" "More in the 2nd year; More in the 1st year; The same in 2 years; I don't know" = 1 if the respondent selected "More in the 2nd year"
Compound interest 2 (FL3)	**Question**: "Suppose you had 1,000,000 VND in a savings account and the bank adds 10% per year to the account. How much money would you have in the account after 5 years if you did not withdraw any money from the account? Less than 1,500,000 VND; Exactly 1,500,000 VND; More than 1,500,000 VND; I don't know" = 1 if the respondent selected "More than 1,500,000 VND"
Inflation (FL4)	**Question**: "Suppose over the next 10 years the prices of the things you buy double. If your income also doubles, will you be able to buy less than you can buy today, the same as you can buy today, or more than you can buy today? Less; The same; More; I don't know" = 1 if the respondent selected "The same"
Diversification (FL5)	**Question**: "Suppose you have some money. Is it safer to put your money into one business or investment or to put it into multiple businesses or investments? One business or investment; Multiple businesses or investments; I don't know" = 1 if the respondent selected "Multiple businesses or investments"
Subjective FL	
Financial capability (FL6)	= 1 if a respondent reported that they are "neutral", "agreed", or "strongly agreed" that they had the skills and knowledge to manage their finances well

Table A.2. (*Continued*)

Variable	Definition
DL index	The DL index was constructed by summing scores across three aspects: smartphone ownership, mobile phone proficiency, and mobile money proficiency. Scores ranged from 0 to 14
Owns a smartphone (DL1)	= 1 if a respondent owned a smartphone
Mobile phone proficiency score	An index equal to the sum of tasks the respondent undertook using a mobile phone in the past 90 days; scores ranged from 0 to 7
Sends or receives calls (DL2)	= 1 if a respondent used a smartphone in the past 90 days to make or receive calls
Sends or receives text messages (DL3)	= 1 if a respondent used a smartphone in the past 90 days to send or receive text messages
Sends or receives photos (DL4)	= 1 if a respondent used a smartphone in the past 90 days to send or receive photos
Browses or uses the Internet (DL5)	= 1 if a respondent used a smartphone in the past 90 days to browse or use the Internet
Downloads music, videos, or games (DL6)	= 1 if a respondent used a smartphone in the past 90 days to download music, videos, or games
Makes financial transactions (DL7)	= 1 if the respondent used a smartphone in the past 90 days to make financial transactions such as send/receive money or make a payment or a banking transaction
Uses social networking sites (DL8)	= 1 if a respondent used a smartphone in the past 90 days to use Facebook, WhatsApp, Twitter, Instagram, or another social networking site
Mobile money proficiency score	An index equal to the sum of actions the respondent reported being able to perform without assistance from anyone when using mobile money; scores ranged from 0 to 6
Opens a mobile money menu (DL9)	= 1 if a respondent reported finding it "very easy" or "easy" or "neither difficult nor easy" for them to open a mobile money menu without assistance from anyone
Finds particular menu options (DL10)	= 1 if a respondent reported finding it "very easy" or "easy" or "neither difficult nor easy" for them to find particular menu options without assistance from anyone
Initiates transaction (DL11)	= 1 if a respondent reported finding it "very easy" or "easy" or "neither difficult nor easy" for them to initiate a transaction without assistance from anyone

(*Continued*)

Table A.2. (*Continued*)

Variable	**Definition**
Completes transaction (DL12)	= 1 if a respondent reported finding it "very easy" or "easy" or "neither difficult nor easy" for them to complete a transaction without assistance from anyone
Corrects an error (DL13)	= 1 if respondents reported finding it "very easy" or "easy" or "neither difficult nor easy" for them to correct an error in the amount or phone number for a transaction recipient without assistance from anyone
Reverses or cancels a transaction (DL14)	= 1 if respondents reported finding it "very easy", "easy", or "neither difficult nor easy" for them to reverse or cancel a transaction without assistance from anyone
Panel C: Control variables	
Age 18–25	= 1 if a respondent was between the ages of 18 and 25
Age 26–40	= 1 if a respondent was between the ages of 26 and 40
Male	= 1 if a respondent was male
Female	= 1 if a respondent was female
Rural	= 1 if a respondent lived in rural areas
Urban	= 1 if a respondent lived in urban areas
Education Below senior high school	= 1 if respondents reported that they had not attained senior high school-level education
Senior high school	= 1 if respondents reported that they had senior high school education
Vocational school	= 1 if respondents reported that they had vocational school education
Bachelor's degree	= 1 if respondents reported that they had a bachelor's degree
Master's degree or above	= 1 if respondents reported that they had a master's degree or above
Work in the financial industry	= 1 if respondents work in the financial industry
Income Less than 10 million VND	= 1 if a respondent had a monthly income of less than 10 million VND
10 million–20 million VND	= 1 if a respondent had a monthly income of 10 million to 20 million VND
20 million–30 million VND	= 1 if a respondent had a monthly income of 20 million to 30 million VND
More than 30 million VND	= 1 if a respondent had a monthly income of more than 30 million VND
Risk tolerance	= 1 if a respondent chose greater than 5 for their willingness to take financial risks

https://doi.org/10.1142/9789811286100_bmatter

Index

A
accelerate, 369
acceptance of robo-advisors, 357
acceptance of robo-advisory services, 357
adaptive school, 21
added value, 321
adopting robo-advisors, 346, 359
adoption of robo-advisors, 336, 357
adventure-based attitude, 254
advertising, 221
agency theory, 5
AI-based financial services, 336
ambiguity tolerance, 252
analytical and innovative, 256
AR applications, 204
AR-based social network, 209
archaeology, classics, and community arts, 255
AR or VR interface, 222
AR technology, 209
AR, VR, and MR, 217, 225
AR/VR/MR technology, 220
attention and self-regulation, 254
audit committees, 119
Audit of Financial Reports, 123
auditor's tenures, 124
augmented and virtual shopping stage, 196
augmented reality (AR), 193–195, 198–199, 201, 208–209, 216, 222
Augmented virtuality (AV), 199
automated financial planning, 357
automation and industrial production, 242
avoidance, 27

B
behavioral cultural intelligence, 91
behavioral intentions, 359
big data, 44
boosting business growth through entrepreneurship, 169
brand mindfulness, 58
business capital, 320

C
capital demand, 296–297, 300, 302
change-oriented behaviors, 255
changing circumstances, 268
characteristics of mobile devices, 50
China, 285, 291–292, 296, 305

choice uncertainty, 245
co-creation, 49, 142
cognitive cultural intelligence, 91
cognitive diversity, 268
cointegration, 295, 298, 300
collaborative consumption, 141
collective enterprises, 287–289, 291
collective enterprises, 288
comparability, 116
competitiveness, 376
complexity of the task, 246
computer-generated simulated environment, 195
conservation of resources (COR), 94
consumer socialization, 146
control, 27
cooperation, 27
cooperative efforts, 139
corporate culture, 106
corporate environment, 105
corporate governance, 119
cost-effective robo-advisors, 346
COVID-19, 411
COVID-19 pandemic, 335–336
creative performance, 266
creativity, 255
critically determined goals, 256
critical thinking, 256
cross-fertilization benefit business innovation, 268
cultural intelligence (CQ), 87–88, 90
culturally diverse environment, 89
cultural perspective, 244
culture of the region they come, 105
curiosity, 243
curious individuals, 243
customer engagement, 140
customer satisfaction, 140
Customer Satisfaction Index, 65
customer's experience in cyberspace, 48
customers' perceptions and attitudes, 358
customization, 144

D

3D, 222
data security, 345
data security and privacy, 345
decision-making processes, 195
de-marketization, 144
desire for financial incentives, 140
desire for socialization, 137
determinants of financial information, 126
different industries, 316
different regions and countries, 88
different sectors, 317
digital borrowing, 428
digital branding, 138
digital financial services (DFS), 400–401, 406, 419
digitalization of tourism, 179
digital literacy and financial management behaviors, 404
digital literacy (DL), 400–402, 407, 409, 419
digital platforms, 61
digital saving, 414
digital service brands, 140
digital services, 54
digital Spending, 414
discoveries, 252
diverse abilities and talents, 254
diverse advanced skills, 255
DL index, 410, 412, 417
do-it-yourself, 144

domestic and international tourists, 171
dramatic changes, 254, 266
dynamic capability view, 6
dynamic settings, 268
dynamic technology, 268

E

earnings quality, 127
East Asians, 245
Eastern Europe, 285, 292
Eastern European, 291
economic development, 176
economic growth, 283, 285, 288, 290–291, 293–294, 296, 300–303
economic sectors, 317
effective asset management, 339
efficiency of production activities, 89
effort expectancy, 341–343, 349, 358
emerging market, 359, 401
e-mobility, 63
emotionally, 246
empathy, 256
employee performance, 87
employees' job performance, 89
employee work results, 89
empowered employees, 255
English programs, 384
enterprises, 316
enthusiastic and curious leaders, 254
entrepreneurship, 254
environmental view, 4
epistemic curiosity, 266
establishing policies for tourism funding, budgets, and investments, 168
exchanges, 370
explanatory variable, 322
exploratory abilities, 267
export processing zones, 88
extrinsic motivations, 140

F

facilitating conditions, 343, 349
fair value, 59
faithful representation, 115
financial assistance, 170
financial capability, 430
financial consulting services, 347
financial development index, 296, 297
financial information quality, 114
financial issues, 357
financial knowledge, 335, 337, 342, 346, 349, 354, 358
financial literacy, 346
financial literacy and financial management behaviors, 403
financial literacy (FL), 400–402, 404, 406–407, 419
financial management behaviors (FMB), 401–404, 406–407, 419
financial planning, 346
financial reporting process, 121
financial robo-advisors, 335, 338
fintech, 339, 345
flexibility and openness, 268
FL index, 409, 412, 417
foreign direct investment (FDI) enterprises, 87, 369
foreign language, 105, 371
foreign managers, 105
formal reasoning, 244
fresh ideas and solutions, 266

G

generalized method of moments (GMM), 322

global development, 256
globalization, 370
governance and policy factors, 163
government, 371

H

head-mounted display (HMD), 200–201, 203
Hepza, 88
high-complexity jobs, 255
higher education, 369
high tolerance for uncertainty, 252
HMD system, 201
human capital, 376
human motivations, 141
human resource, 377
hypothesis development, 402

I

ICST, 320
IFRS application, 122
immersion, 198
immersive experiences, 217
immersive technologies, 193–198, 200–201, 203–204, 213, 217, 220–221, 223, 225
immersive technology, 197, 200–201, 217
impact of COVID-19, 342, 357
impact of the COVID-19 pandemic, 347
impact of the pandemic, 337
impulse response, 295, 299–300, 302
increasing productivity and innovation, 168
independence of auditors, 124
individual investment advice, 340
individualization, 144
industrial zone, 88
Industrial Zones of Ho Chi Minh (IZHCM) City, 87
industry and construction, 317
industry view, 4
information and communication, 315
information-gathering approach, 27
innovation, 246
innovative skills, 267
institutional environment, 291
in-store applications, 221
intentions to use automated financial advisors, 335
intentions to use robo-advisors, 337, 342–343, 346, 357–358
interactions with consumers, 138
interactive decision-support tools, 51
intercultural, 370
internal diversity, 255
international accreditation, 373
international cooperation, 371
internationalization, 369
Internet of Everything, 72
Internet of Things, 70, 242
intrinsic task motivation, 266
intuitive, 244, 246
intuitive approach, 244
intuitive vs analytical thinking, 244
investment experience, 349

J

job variety, 254

K

key performance indicators, 106

L

labor, 317
Labor Department, 95
labor productivity, 316

lack of financial and digital knowledge, 401
leadership approaches, 243
local government, 286–290, 292
low cost, 357
low-cost financial advice, 343
lower-level technical personnel, 246
low uncertainty avoidance culture, 251

M

managers' intuition, 242
market forces, 283, 287–288
marketing landscape, 46
marketing strategy, 221
market orientation, 283–286, 294, 296, 301, 308
Market Orientation of Public Organizations, 290
measurement of financial information, 125
mechanistic structures, 255
megacognitive cultural intelligence, 91
mentally challenging, 255
middle-level management, 246
mixed reality (MR), 193–194, 199, 210
mobile money proficiency score, 431
model of tourism management, 183
modern retailers, 220
modern retailers, 193, 225
motivational cultural intelligence, 91
MR technology, 199
multichannel marketing boom, 67
multiple platforms, 48

N

networking, 27
new ideas, 255
new managerialism, 369
non-human-based advisors, 346
nontraditional problems, 255
novel solutions, 256
novel solutions and methodologies, 255

O

OECD, 405, 409
online customer interaction, 52
organic structures, 255
output value, 322

P

panel data, 322
perceived financial knowledge, 357
perceptions and adoption behaviors toward robo-advisors, 356
Performance, 88
performance expectancy, 342, 349, 358
personal information, 51
personalization, 144
PFM, 411
physical mobility, 63
planning school, 20
PLS-SEM, 98
policies, 369
positive effects, 252
positive outcomes, 252
post-purchase stage, 196, 225
pre-purchase evaluations, 221
pre-purchase, purchase, and post-purchase stages, 196
pre-purchase stage, 195
prestige, 377
principles versus rules, 122

privacy concerns, 45
private enterprises, 286, 288, 291
privatization, 284, 294, 296, 300
proactive collaboration and cooperation, 27
productivity growth, 316
profit before tax, 317
prosumer behaviors, 137
prosumer concept, 138
prosumption, 137
publication, 381
public organizations, 283
purchase stage, 195, 223

Q

QR code, 222
qualitative characteristics, 117
quality determinants, 114
quality measurement, 114
quality of financial information, 114
questionnaire design, 407

R

rational, 244
rationality or politically based decisions, 256
R&D, 316
reactive collaboration, 27
reality–virtuality continuum, 198, 199
real-world components, 210
recruitment process, 105
relationship, 246
relevance, 115
remote provinces, 105
resource-based view, 4
retail consumers, 221
retail customer experience, 225
retailing, 194
retailing industry, 213
retail investors, 347, 357
retail model, 50
retail sector, 204
retail setting, 220
robo-advisors, 336–337, 339–342, 346, 355–356
robo-advisory, 337
robo-advisory platforms, 346
robo-advisory service providers, 358
robo-advisory services, 340, 342
robustness, 324

S

scanning electron microscope (SEM), 354
scenario planning, 25
science and technology, 316
scientific research capacity, 375
security and privacy, 342
seek financial advice, 357
self-determination theory, 137
sense of belonging, 137
service, 317
service sector, 317
sharing economy, 145
shopping process, 204
skill development and employment opportunities, 173
social and corporate interests, 48
social influence, 341, 343, 349, 358
social investment, 317
socialist market economy, 293–294
social media marketing, 67
social sciences, arts, and humanities, 255
Soviet Union, 285, 290, 292
SOX compliance, 127

state control mechanism, 284, 296
state funding, 376
state-owned enterprises, 284
strategic challenges, 24
strategic flexibility, 18
strategic foresight, 18
strategic formulation, 10
strategic implementation, 11
strategic planning, 9
strategic process, 8
strategy response, 24
structure–conduct–performance (S–C–P) paradigm, 5
substantial synergies, 256
sustainability and nature-related factors, 163
sustainability in tourism, 176
sustainable tourism destination management, 187
SWOT analysis, 23
systematic literature review, 3

T

tactic plans, 256
technical and demand uncertainty, 246
technical decisions, 245
technical interoperability barriers, 248
technocratic style, 244
technologies, 216
technology adoption behaviors, 358
technology and communications (ITC), 316
teleshopping, 62
tendency of retail investors to rely on robo-advisors, 337
tendency to rely on robo-advisors, 335, 342, 346
the adoption behavior, 358
The board of directors, 106
The Human Resources Department, 105
the impact of the COVID-19 pandemic, 349, 354
the intention to adopt robo-advisors, 357
theory, 94
the perception of financial knowledge, 346
the post-purchase stage, 225
the tendency to rely on robo-advisors, 349, 354, 358
Tier-2 industries, 320
Timeliness, 116
total factor productivity (TFP), 316
Tourism Destination Management, 161
tourism management policies and structures, 166
Tourism resources and infrastructure factors, 163
Trade Union, 106
transaction costs, 286–287, 293
transaction costs economics, 5
transformational approach, 21
Transitional economy, 283
transport connectivity, 174
trust, 335, 337, 341–342, 344–345, 349, 354, 356, 358
tuition fee, 387
twinning and franchise programs, 374

U

understandability, 116
UNESCO, 405
unit root test, 297

university autonomy, 369
usefulness of financial statements, 125
user confidence, 344
UTAUT framework, 342
UTAUT models, 357

V

value, 221
value added, 328
value relevance, 122
variance decomposition, 295, 299, 302
various activities, 254
various financial institutions, 348
various innovative approaches, 268
VECM model, 295, 298–300, 302
Verifiability, 116
Vietnam, 285, 294–296, 300–303, 305, 307–308, 317, 337, 339, 342–343, 371
Vietnamese culture, 251
Vietnamese retail investors, 337, 357
Vietnamese stock market, 347
Vietnamese university, 369
virtual reality (VR), 193–195, 199, 201, 204
visionary approach, 21
VND, 418
VR, AR, and MR technologies, 204
VR HMD, 201
VR industry, 201
VR sports broadcasts, 222
VR technology, 195

W

wealth management, 339
Web of Science databases, 28
Westerners, 245
willingness to adopt robo-advisors, 357
word of mouth, 45
work engagement, 87–88
workers, 105

www.ingramcontent.com/pod-product-compliance
Lightning Source LLC
LaVergne TN
LVHW011658200926
848484LV00004B/982